"A thrilling, better-than-fiction history of the covert mission to rescue American sailors taken into slavery in Tripoli in 1803. Plenty of swords and swashbuckling."
—*People*

"*The Pirate Coast* unearths the extraordinary tale of America's first overseas covert operation."
—*New York Magazine*

"Grab a copy of Richard Zacks's rollicking account of the event that put 'the shores of Tripoli' in the Marine Hymn. [A] truly cinematic story . . ."
—*National Review*

"Meticulously researched, gripping account of adventure on the high seas."
—*Men's Health*

"Zacks has researched thoroughly, writes entertainingly and shows a knack for sea stories and characterizations. This is the book that Capt. Eaton has long deserved."
—*Publishers Weekly*

"To understand America's involvement in the Arab world, you need to know the amazing tale—filled with lessons for today—of how it began 200 years ago."
—Walter Isaacson, author of *Benjamin Franklin: An American Life*

The Pirate Coast

Also by Richard Zacks

The Pirate Hunter:
The True Story of Captain Kidd

An Underground Education

History Laid Bare

The Pirate Coast

THOMAS JEFFERSON, THE FIRST MARINES,
AND THE SECRET MISSION OF 1805

RICHARD ZACKS

HYPERION
NEW YORK

Library of Congress Cataloging-in-Publication Data

Zacks, Richard.
    The pirate coast : Thomas Jefferson, the first marines, and the
secret mission of 1805 / Richard Zacks.
      p. cm.
    Includes bibliographical references.
    ISBN 1-4013-0003-0
    1. United States—History—Tripolitan War, 1801–1805.
2. Jefferson, Thomas, 1743–1826. 3. United States—History—
Tripolitan War, 1801–1805—Underground movements. 4. United
States—History—Tripolitan War, 1801–1805—Naval operations.
5. Pirates—Africa, North—History—19th century. I. Title.

E335.Z33 2005
973.4'7—dc22

                        2004060635

Paperback ISBN 1-4013-0849-X

Hyperion books are available for special promotions and premiums.
For details contact Michael Rentas, Assistant Director, Inventory
Operations, Hyperion, 77 West 66th Street, 12th floor, New York,
New York 10023, or call 212-456-0133.

FIRST PAPERBACK EDITION

10 9 8 7 6 5 4 3 2 1

To Mr. Robert Berman, mentor and tormentor

Contents

Cast of Characters (circa 1805)

WILLIAM EATON, ex-captain, U.S. Army; ex-consul to Tunis; secret agent

WASHINGTON
THOMAS JEFFERSON, President
JAMES MADISON, Secretary of State
ROBERT SMITH, Secretary of the Navy
TIMOTHY PICKERING, former Secretary of State, Senator (Federalist, Massachusetts)
STEPHEN BRADLEY, Senator (Federalist, Vermont)
JOHN COTTON SMITH, Representative (Federalist, Connecticut)
JOHN QUINCY ADAMS, Senator (Federalist, Massachusetts)
AARON BURR, Vice President (1801–1804), conspirator plotting to invade Spanish territory

DIPLOMATS
TOBIAS LEAR, U.S. consul general to Barbary Regencies
RICHARD O'BRIEN, former U.S. consul in Algiers
JAMES LEANDER CATHCART, former U.S. consul in Tripoli
NICHOLAS NISSEN, Danish consul in Tripoli
BERNARDINO DROVETTI, French consul in Alexandria, Egypt
ANTOINE ZUCHET, consul in Tripoli for Republique Batave (Holland under Napoleon)

C. BEAUSSIER, French consul in Tripoli

SAMUEL BRIGGS, British consul in Alexandria

MAJOR E. MISSETT, British resident agent at Cairo

U.S. NAVY

RICHARD V. MORRIS, Commodore of second U.S. Mediterranean
   Squadron (1802–1803)

EDWARD PREBLE, Commodore of third U.S. Mediterranean Squadron
   (1803–1804)

SAMUEL BARRON, Commodore of fourth U.S. Mediterranean
   Squadron (1804–1805)

JOHN RODGERS, Commodore of fifth U.S. Mediterranean Squadron
   (1805–1806)

JONATHAN COWDERY, assistant surgeon, USS *Philadelphia*

GEORGE WASHINGTON MANN, midshipman, USS *Argus*

ELI E. DANIELSON, midshipman, USS *Argus*

FOR OTHER NAVAL OFFICERS, see SHIPS on following page

U.S. MARINES

PRESLEY O'BANNON, lieutenant

WILLIAM RAY, private and memoirist

BARBARY AND EGYPTIAN OFFICIALS

YUSSEF KARAMANLI, Bashaw of Tripoli

HAMET KARAMANLI, deposed ruler of Tripoli

MOHAMMED DGHIES, foreign minister of Tripoli

MURAD RAIS (PETER LYLE), admiral of Tripoli

HAMOUDA, Bey of Tunis

AHMET PACHA, Ottoman Viceroy of Egypt

KOURCHIEF, regional Ottoman commander of Demanhour, Egypt

MUHAMMAD ALI, Albanian general commanding Cairo region for
   Ottoman Empire

TAYYIB, sheik, warrior, and camel driver

MISCELLANEOUS

SAMUEL TAYLOR COLERIDGE, poet

ANNA PORCILE, twelve-year-old Sardinian hostage

ANTONIO PORCILE, count of Sant-Antioco, father of hostage

LORD HORATIO NELSON, British admiral

NAPOLEON BONAPARTE, crowned himself Emperor on
    December 2, 1804

ALEXANDER BALL, British Governor of Malta

RICHARD FARQUHAR, Scottish entrepreneur based in
    the Mediterranean

ELIZA DANIELSON EATON, William's wife

SHIPS

USS *PHILADELPHIA*, 36-gun frigate, Captain William Bainbridge

USS *CONSTITUTION*, 44-gun frigate, Commodore Edward Preble,
    then Commodore John Rodgers

USS *PRESIDENT*, 44-gun frigate, Commodore Samuel Barron,
    then Captain James Barron

USS *CONGRESS*, 36-gun frigate, Captain John Rodgers,
    then Captain Stephen Decatur Jr.

USS *ESSEX*, 32-gun frigate, Captain James Barron,
    then Lieutenant George Cox

USS *CONSTELLATION*, 36-gun frigate, Captain Hugh Campbell

USS *INTREPID*, 4-gun captured *Mastico* ketch,
    Lieutenant Stephen Decatur Jr.

USS *ARGUS*, 18-gun brig, Lieutenant Isaac Hull

USS *VIXEN*, 12-gun brig, Lieutenant John Smith

USS *SIREN*, 16-gun brig, Lieutenant Charles Stewart

USS *NAUTILUS*, 12-gun schooner, Lieutenant John Dent

USS *HORNET*, 10-gun sloop, Lieutenant Samuel Evans

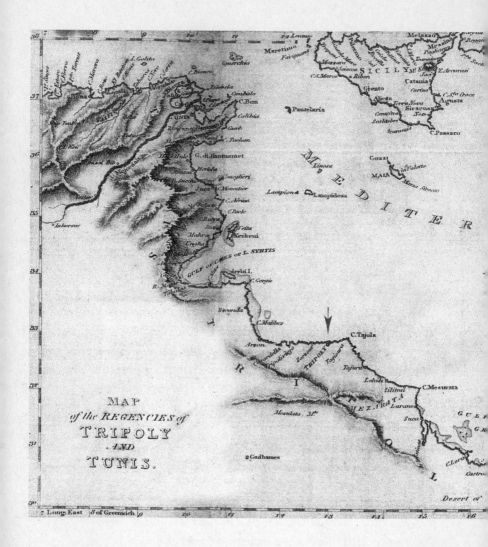

MAP
of the REGENCIES of
TRIPOLY
AND
TUNIS.

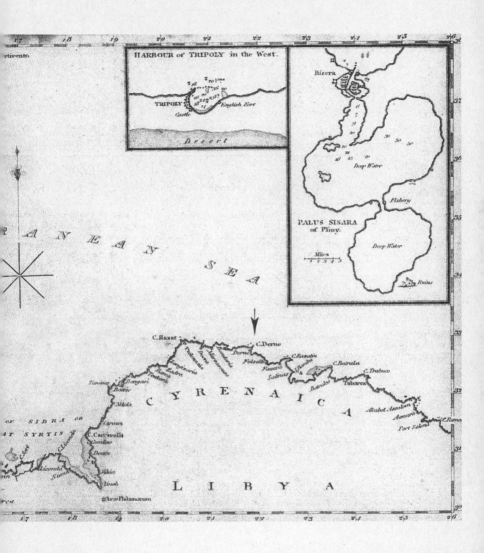

HARBOUR of TRIPOLY in the West.

TRIPOLY

Castle   English Fort

Desert

Bizera

PALUS SISARA
of Pliny.

Deep Water

Fishery

Miles

Deep Water

Ruins

MEDITERRANEAN SEA

C. Razat   C. Derne
                  Derne
                  Folsella   C. Razolin
                  Finaris   Chouba
                  Salinus   C. Batraka
Teronea   Batrilos   C. Trabuco
Bongazi   Teuhera   Tabarca
Bonia   Ababet Asrolom
Mhsla   Asmara   C. Rama
                                        Port Sahani
or SIDRA or Aroan
T SYRTIS C. Carswella
           Cunlao
           Douez

CYRENAICA

Liconda
Suma   Abia
              Ituel
Arx Philaenorum

LIBYA

The Pirate Coast

Prologue

AN HOUR BEFORE DAWN on September 3, 1798, the waves of the Mediterranean tugged at the coast of the island of San Pietro near Sardinia, lullabying the thousand or so sleeping residents. So peaceful was it, so rhythmic and hypnotic the sound—or perhaps it was due to a bottle of local *vino bianco*—that even the two municipal watchmen in the church tower had fallen asleep. So there was no one to puzzle out the faint white flecks of sails growing larger on the pinkish gray horizon, and no one to ring the massive church bells to sound the alarm that a fleet of seven ships was approaching.

Standing silently at the rail of these lateen-sailed ships, visible in faint silhouette, were bearded men in loose billowy pants and turbans, carrying scimitars and pistols. The vessels, packed with one thousand Barbary pirates from Tunis in North Africa, glided to anchor inside the harbor. The crews quietly lowered small landing boats and began to ferry men ashore. The first group, barefoot and heavily armed, raced to seal off the two roads leading out of town.

Surprisingly, the leader of this attacking Moslem fleet, the pirate commodore, as it were, was an Italian who had converted to Islam. The ritual had involved losing his foreskin and gaining a new name. He was now Muhammed Rumelli, and in the Lingua Franca slang of the Mediterranean, he was dubbed a *rinigado*, a renegade. Over the centuries, the rulers of the Barbary countries of Algiers, Tunis, and Tripoli had learned that Christian captains could navigate better than their homegrown Moslem talent.

Another Italian, acting as harbor pilot, had guided the fleet to the perfect anchorage. This fellow from Capri (never identified by name) carried a deeply personal motive for joining the attack. He had married a woman from San Pietro, but she had abandoned him; he was now convinced that she was cuckolding him here on the island. He had turned Turk expressly to seek his revenge.

As the first ray of dawn caught the sails, Muhammed Rumelli gave the signal to "wake up" the townspeople. The pirates unleashed a sudden unholy thunder. The ships' cannons bellowed out broadsides. The sailors onshore added a lunatic's drumroll of small arms fire. The cacophony climaxed as close to a thousand mouths let loose impassioned Arabic war cries and the men rushed into the town. *Allahu akhbar* speeded their pursuit of profit.

The corsairs engulfed the tiny town; they battered down the doors, burst into homes, brandishing torches and scimitars, rousting the stunned citizens from bed and kicking them into the streets. They cursed their victims as *Romo kelb* ("Christian dogs"). The women cowered in corners, trying to avoid what one observer described as "shame and villainies."

A French naval officer, arriving the next day, found that five women had died in their beds of knife wounds, their bodies entwined in sheets caked with blood. The first female victim, according to local accounts, was the unfaithful wife of that pilot from Capri. A Sardinian historian later called her a "fishwife Helen" who had no idea that her husband's jealous rage had drawn the enemy to her homeland.

The attackers spent the entire day hauling money, jewels, church silver, silks to the harbor, but by far the most valuable commodity to be stolen walked on two legs: human slaves. Sura 47 of the Koran allowed these Moslem attackers to enslave and ransom any of these captives. Young Italian women would fetch more than the men in the flesh markets of Tunis and Algiers.

The crews dragged the townspeople aboard various ships, tossing them like ballast willy-nilly belowdeck into the holds for the 160-mile voyage. The prisoners wore only what they had slipped into at bedtime on that seemingly unimportant September night, which would turn out to be their last night of freedom for half a decade.

This was life on a Mediterranean island, circa 1798, in the age of Napoleon and Nelson and the waning days of the Barbary corsairs.

The Bey of Tunis, the country's ruler, had commissioned these seven ships and a thousand men to attack San Pietro. To the Bey, they were his privateers, fighting a legitimate war against Sardinia, which had refused to pay tribute to him for the right to navigate the Mediterranean; to the rest of the world, these seven ships were Barbary pirates, part of a centuries-old extortion scheme.

Fall weather on the Mediterranean can run skittish, and storm winds kicked up. The San Pietro prisoners spent the next four days seesawing in the windowless, foul-smelling dark, appalled at their fate, vomiting, weeping, with no sanitation, and almost no food or water.

That is, all except six young women. "*Six jeunes filles,*" ran a later report in French from a Dutch consul, Antoine Nyssen, in Tunis. "Six young girls, alas, that they were still so, were selected by the Rais [captains] to serve their filthy desires, and the most disgusting forms of volupté were their pastimes during the voyage."

The ships, nearing Tunis, passed the site of ancient Carthage, and the captains fired off celebratory cannon shots to signal their victory. The city of Tunis lies six miles inland from the harbor, connected by a stagnant reddish-colored lake. The pirates rushed the prisoners aboard small barges; boatmen, pushing poles, then strained to follow a winding route indicated by pillars rising a foot or two above the surface. "On these pillars, standing silent, sad, wings furled, seeming like those birds sculpted on tombs, are cormorants," wrote French novelist Alexandre Dumas, who fifty years later took this same route. Dumas said the birds of prey would suddenly swoop down on some fish swimming near the surface, then calmly return to reassume their cryptlike pose. It's doubtful that many of the Italian captives noticed the wildlife.

The city soon announced itself by smell as much as by sight. The prisoners later learned that fecal ditches ran along the northern and eastern walls to receive the human waste from 300,000 inhabitants of various races: Moors, Arabs, Turks, Jews, European merchants and diplomats, African and Christian slaves. Runoff from the ditches fed into the stagnant shallow lake, making the fish poisonous to humans but edible by the likes of cormorants, flamingos, and seagulls.

The corsairs, swinging leather straps, herded the filthy, exhausted prisoners through the narrow byways of the whitewashed city on the unusually hot day of September 8, 1798. "I saw them harassed by blows, by fatigue, covered in dust and dying of thirst, dragging themselves along a burning street, barefoot, hatless," wrote the Dutch consul. "There was a huge crowd drunk with joy to see so many Christian victims of the *bravery* of their soldiers."

These unfortunate captives staggered forward two hours to the palace where the Bey of Tunis, Hamouda, in his jeweled turban and diamond-encrusted silk vest, inspected them. For him it was like counting money. Each of the prisoners was now a slave to be sold at his whim. The Bey's corsairs had captured an astounding 950 people, including 702 women and children.

On the northern coast of Africa circa 1800, blacks *and* whites could still be sold into slavery. Men were usually peddled near naked, or in dangly shirts, in an outdoor auction; women could be inspected privately in stalls nearby. Unlike slave auctions in the southern United States, male buyers here openly acknowledged lustful desires for their human purchases; matrons inspected the women, and virgins were sold at a steep premium, often with a written guarantee.

Of all the fears of people living in the 1780s and 1790s, a fear perhaps exceeding death itself was the terror of being made a slave on the Barbary Coast; in sermon after sermon, it was portrayed as hell in life. (Twenty-one freeborn Americans had spent eleven years in slavery in Algiers from 1785 to 1796, bringing their stories home to the nation.)

Foreign consuls begged the Bey not to break up the San Pietro families, not to sell anyone off to Algerian slave traders. The ruler of Tunis set his opening asking price for the women at 600 Venetian sequins each, about $1,371 at a time when a U.S. sailor earned $144 a year. He would charge half that amount for the men. The Bey, to save on the costs of feeding and dressing, then farmed many of the captives out to the leading citizens of Tunis, including the representatives of foreign countries, who accepted the slaves on humanitarian grounds. (Six years later, Tobias Lear, United States consul general to Algiers, would accept two female Italian slaves to work as housekeepers in the consulate. He would expense-account their $75-a-year upkeep.)

Among the San Pietro prisoners, one young girl stood out. Strikingly beautiful and of aristocratic birth, Anna Maria Porcile was twelve years old, a ripe age on the Barbary Coast, a marriageable age. She was the granddaughter of the Count of Sant-Antioco, the admiral of the Navy of Sardinia. Brought up in a strict Catholic household, Anna had led a sheltered life; private tutors taught music, literature, and dance to this naturally vivacious girl.

The Bey, to keep loyalty high among his officers, decided to allow his six corsair captains to select one female each as his own personal slave. The admiral of the fleet, Rais Muhammed Rumelli, chose Anna.

Rumelli was quoted as saying he "had fixed his desire on her"; he intended her as his concubine unless someone would immediately buy her from him for the record asking price of 16,000 piasters, or almost $5,000 (the price of a mansion in Manhattan).

Anna's entire family had been captured in the raid, including her mother, Barbara; her father, Antonio; and her two sisters. While the negotiations for the rest of the slaves could drag on over months via shipboard messages to and from Sardinia, Anna's fate must be decided quickly. Rumelli demanded an answer. Anna's father desperately tried to find financing. He naturally turned to fellow Italians who happened to be in Tunis, and he fortunately found a Tuscan merchant, one Felipe Borzoni, who would loan him the entire sum. The man paid Rais Rumelli and Anna was suddenly free . . . almost.

She was the human collateral for her father's loan . . . the Bey would not grant a *tiskara*, or passport, to her until the loan was repaid. With Anna as hostage for her father's return, Don Antonio Porcile was allowed to travel to Europe to raise the money, but in the chaos of the Napoleonic Wars, he failed. So the Tuscan merchant sold the debt to the aged prime minister Mustapha Coggia, a man known for his wisdom, courtliness, and complete lack of teeth.

The months of 1799 slipped by, and these white-skinned slaves joined the 2,000 or so slaves of various hues laboring in Tunis. Negotiations dragged on . . . the price for the women dropped in half to 300 Venetian sequins . . . the exasperated Bey, to encourage a speedier payment, sold eleven to slave traders of Algiers; nonetheless, the king of Sardinia, harassed by Napoleon, was unable to redeem his countrymen. Italian slave mothers gave birth to dozens of new slaves in Tunis.

On October 10, 1800, eighty-seven-year-old Mustapha Coggia—who held the Porcile debt—died, and all the prime minister's possessions passed to the Bey of Tunis. The very next day, the Bey demanded that the Porcile family pay off the debt immediately or else the Bey said he would reclaim lovely Anna and add her to his seraglio. Or, more ominously, he said he might instead auction her off in the slave markets of Istanbul. (Since the Bey made little secret of his preference for men over women—his foreign minister Yussef Sapatapa, a thirty-three-year-old former slave, was his lover—selling Anna was the likelier scenario.)

That afternoon, Anna and her mother and her sisters tried desperately to figure out a way to raise the money. Her grandfather, the admiral, had died, and her father, the new count, was at that moment in Sardinia, still trying to amass the huge sum with absolutely no success. The pirates had stolen everything. His credit was suspect. European banking was a mess. The mother and her daughters were running out of options and time. They considered the various consulates, such as British, French, Danish, and the Catholic Redemptionist charities, Jewish moneylenders, European merchants.

On that afternoon of October 11, 1800, frantic, they presented themselves at the door of the consulate of the United States of America, a fledgling nation that trumpeted itself as a bastion of freedom; they sought refuge under the red-white-and-blue flag, which then had fifteen stars and fifteen stripes and was represented in Tunis by one of the most unlikely diplomats ever to be forgotten by history: William Eaton.

A former army captain, Eaton had recently been court-martialed and convicted. He was impetuous, hardheaded, argumentative. His loud voice cut through conversations; his ramrod-straight stance inspired respect;

his Dartmouth education added polysyllables to his vocabulary. Diplomacy, he had very little; he was blunt-spoken, exceedingly direct. He once wrote of the feeble efforts of the U.S. Navy that "a fleet of Quaker meeting houses would have done just as well." This bulldog of a man, age thirty-five, stood 5'8", with deep-set large blue eyes. A friend described his eyes as "expressive of energy, penetration and authority" but also of "impatience and disquietude."

Eaton had arrived in Tunis the previous year on the little merchant brig *Sophia* and was immediately appalled. "Here I am . . . under the mad rays of a vertical sun reflected and refracted from wall and terraces of white-washed houses, hotter than tobacco & rum, with plague and scorpions suspended over my head, menacing death, surrounded by brutal Turks, swindlers, jews, perfidious Italians, miserable slaves, lazy camels, churlish mules, and savage arabs—without society and without amusement. Is not this enough to constitute a hell?"

His irritation only grew as he observed slavery close-up. "For my part, it grates me mortally when I see a lazy Turk [a Moslem] reclining at his ease upon an embroidered sofa, with one Christian slave to fan away the flies, another to hand him his coffee and a third to hold his pipe. . . . It is still more grating to perceive that the Turk believes he has a right to demand this contribution and that we, like Italians, have not the fortitude to resist it." (The U.S. government, with a huge debt from the Revolutionary War, found it cheaper to pay off Tunis—and keep the pirates away—than to fight against them.)

Eaton, a New England patriot, was appalled that the United States would pay bribes to pirates and was deeply annoyed at having personally to hand out diamond-encrusted watches, gold watches, pairs of gold-mounted pistols, gold tobacco boxes, silks, and many other items to sixty different government officials in Tunis from the Bey and admiral down to the infamously ugly eunuch who guarded the Bey's harem, the dark-skinned giant with the raspy mewling infant's voice.

The Porcile women stood crying before William Eaton. Anna's honor hung in the balance. "Imagination better than language can paint their distress," Eaton later wrote. From a conviction about freedom that literally had its roots near Plymouth Rock with Eaton's great-great-grandfather, he could not abide this form of persecution.

Against all common sense, Eaton agreed to guarantee a six-month loan for Anna's father, allowing himself to stand as surety for the repayment of $5,000. "I ransomed your daughter," Eaton later wrote to the count, "because being in my house, both the honor of my flag and my own sensibility dictated it." If at the end of six months Count Porcile couldn't pay, then Eaton was obligated to do so.

What is striking is that Eaton at that moment had absolutely no money. At least, none of his own, and yet he was committing to pay a small fortune to rescue an Italian slave girl. Impetuously. For Honor. William Eaton, throughout his life, would be drawn to commit deeds that he considered righteous and others would consider reckless.

His flurry of letters to Count Porcile received eloquent replies but no money.

And in June of 1801, the homosexual lover of the Bey, Yussef Sapatapa, told Eaton that he must repay the $5,000. Eaton, after failing to raise money through trading ventures, was now forced to borrow the large sum from a Tunisian merchant named Unis ben Unis.

In February of 1803, to show some force and fend off any threat of war, the United States sent armed ships to Tunis. An old Barbary maxim states: "Whoever acts like a sheep, the wolf will eat." So the young United States did not want to be mistaken for a sheep. Commodore Richard Morris, with Captain John Rodgers, arrived with three heavily armed frigates. The mission seemed successful; the odd new nation across the Atlantic did indeed have a navy. But as Commodore Morris, in a blue uniform with gold epaulets, was about to embark to cross that stagnant lake to go to the harbor, he was suddenly arrested . . . because of the thousands of dollars of debt of William Eaton. The highest ranking U.S. Navy officer found himself surrounded by Tunisians wielding scimitars, and he was forced to return to the city. "It was impossible to apprehend that the respect attached to the person of the Commodore would be violated," Eaton wrote. "It is unprecedented, even in the history of Barbary outrage."

Commodore Richard Morris—a scion of the wealthy Morris family of Vermont, whose brother had cast the deciding ballot to elect Jefferson over Burr—was furious with Eaton. He assumed that the man's debts were mostly personal. Eaton, Morris, and Unis ben Unis walked to the palace where Bey Hamouda, wearing a jeweled silk cloak, greeted them on his luxurious sofa. Eaton vehemently denied that he had ever promised to repay Unis ben Unis whenever the American squadron arrived. Unis demanded payment of $22,000 . . . of that, $5,000 came from Eaton's ransom of Anna and $10,000 came from Sapatapa claiming that Eaton had promised him a large bribe, and the remaining $7,000 from a commercial dispute. Eaton snapped. He called the Bey's lover, the foreign minister, a "thief" to his face and said all he had experienced in Tunis was "violence and indignity." The Bey, unaccustomed to contretemps, shouted over and over that Eaton was mad. Eyewitnesses said that the Bey's lip trembled, and he oddly clutched his mustache as he yelled: "I will turn you out of my kingdom." When the Bey had calmed down, he told the commodore: "The Consul is a man of a good heart but a bad head. He is too obstinate and too violent for me. I must have a consul with a disposition more congenial to the Barbary interests."

Commodore Morris had no appetite for remaining in Tunis, for fighting for the loudmouthed consul. He agreed to replace Eaton and to pay off the $22,000. He later wrote: "As security for the money paid by me, I insisted on Mr. Eaton assigning all his real and personal estate to the government."

On March 10, 1803, Eaton boarded the USS *Chesapeake*. Disgraced as a diplomat, he was on the verge of ruin. He was returning home to his wife, financially devastated. This last twist was ironic, since Eaton had accepted the post of consul to Tunis in the hopes that he might make enough money to re-enter his marriage as the financial equal of Eliza, a widow of a wealthy Revolutionary War general. "[I hope] the hour is not far distant," he had written to her before the disaster, "when I may demonstrate to the world that it was not Mrs. Danielson's fortune but her person that <u>Captain Eaton</u> married."

In his official report, Morris stated that "[Eaton] appeared to be a man of lively imagination, rash, credulous. And by no means possessed of sound judgement."

***

Within two years, this disgraced diplomat would lead a band of eight marines, *eight*, and several hundred foreign mercenaries, the dregs of Alexandria, on a mad hopeless mission to march across the hell of the Libyan desert. He would try to finance the mission with the funds owed to him for ransoming Anna, the Italian slave girl. Thomas Jefferson would send Eaton on America's first covert military op overseas, to try to overthrow the government of Tripoli in order to free the *three hundred* American sailors enslaved there. This man on the verge of personal ruin, joined by his handful of marines, including violin-playing Presley O'Bannon, would surprise-attack Tripoli's second-largest city, and they would achieve a near miraculous victory. He would help stamp the then second-class service, the United States Marines, with a new reputation for courage. His exploits would lead future generations of Americans to sing proudly: "From the Halls of Montezuma to the shores of Tripoli, we will fight our country's battles on the land and on the sea."

In 1805, in the first decades of our North American experiment in democracy, when the nation's future prosperity was very much in doubt, William Eaton made one of the loudest statements to the world that the United States was not a country to be mocked or bullied. While politicians and military officers mouthed the same patriotic phrases, Eaton risked his life to back up his statements. He helped set a national tone of defiance and daring.

But in William Eaton's flinty outspokenness and fearlessness, there lurked the seeds of his own destruction. Thomas Jefferson could not abide the man's relentless belligerence. The aftermath of victory in Tripoli for Eaton would be less than sweet. After taking on Tripoli and the Barbary pirates, he would challenge and defy Thomas Jefferson. It would be a battle between unequals, and no good can come of that.

Would to God that the officers and crew of the Philadelphia *had
one and all determined to prefer death to slavery; it is possible such a
determination might save them from either.*

—COMMODORE EDWARD PREBLE TO SECRETARY
OF THE NAVY ROBERT SMITH

THE CARPENTERS WHO BUILT the USS *Philadelphia*, in addition
to their craft skills, demonstrated an extraordinary capacity for al-
cohol. The project overseer, a Thomas FitzSimons, noted in his
expense accounts that he had purchased 110 gallons of rum a month for
thirty carpenters. Sober math reveals that each man working six days a
week consumed about a pint of rum a day.

The stout frigate showed no ungainly lines. The carpenters, sharpening their adzes hourly, had hewed the live oak floated north from Georgia into a 147-foot keel; they had pocked each side of the ship with
fourteen gunports and sheathed the bottom with copper to defeat sea
worms and barnacles. As befitting a ship built in the nation's capital,
famed sculptor William Rush had carved an enormous figurehead: a
Hercules. No ship of the United States would sport a Virgin Mary (religion) or a King Louis (monarchy), but a muscular classical hero had
proven acceptable.

The *Philadelphia*, launched in 1799, added key firepower to the U.S.
Navy, since the entire American fleet in 1803 consisted of six ships. By

contrast, England—then fending off Napoleon's attacks—floated close to six hundred vessels in its Royal Navy. While Admiral Nelson stymied the French with thunderous broadsides, the Americans with a bit of pop-pop from their Lilliputian fleet hoped to overawe the least of the Barbary powers, Tripoli.

Now, in October of 1803, the USS *Philadelphia*, a 36-gun frigate, was prowling the waters off the coast of Tripoli, trying all by itself to enforce a blockade. Very few nations would have even bothered with something as forlorn as a one-ship blockade, but the United States—only a couple of decades old—wasn't exactly brimming with military options.

In 1801, just after the inauguration of Thomas Jefferson, Tripoli (modern-day Libya) had become the first country ever to declare war on the United States. The ruler, Yussef Karamanli, had ordered his Janissaries to chop down the flagpole at the U.S. consulate to signal his grave displeasure with the slow trickle of gifts from America. Jefferson, when he learned the news, had responded by sending a small fleet to confront Tripoli and try to overawe it into a peace treaty.

For more than two centuries, the Barbary countries of Morocco, Tunis, Algiers, and Tripoli had been harassing Christian ships, seizing cargo and capturing citizens. Algiers once boasted more than 30,000 Christian slaves, including one Miguel Cervantes, *before* he wrote *Don Quixote*. European powers in the 1500s and 1600s fought ferocious battles against Moslem pirates like Barbarosa. However, over time, a cynical system of appeasement had developed. The nations of Europe paid tribute—in money, jewels, and naval supplies—to remain at peace. England and France—in endless wars—found it cheaper to bribe the Barbary pirates than to devote a squadron to perpetually trawling the sea off Africa. At its core, expediency outweighed national honor.

When the thirteen American colonies split off from mother England, they lost British protection. The United States found itself lumped in the pile of potential Barbary victims, alongside the likes of Sardinia and Sicily. (From 1785 to 1815, more than six hundred American citizens would be captured and enslaved. This nuisance would prove to be no mere foreign trade issue but rather a near-constant hostage crisis.)

Jefferson wanted to send a message that the United States, with its fresh ideas, refused to pay tribute, but the war with Tripoli was dragging on. Jefferson's first two U.S. fleets had failed to inflict more than scratches on the enemy, and the president expected results from this latest armed squadron.

The USS *Philadelphia* cruised off the coast of North Africa on the lookout for enemy vessels. The youngest captain in the U.S. Navy, William Bainbridge, had drawn the plum assignment. While the U.S. Navy was still evolving its style of command, twenty-nine-year-old Bainbridge, from a wealthy New Jersey family, clearly valued discipline. "I believe there never was so depraved a set of mortals as Sailors," he once wrote. "Under discipline, they are peaceable and serviceable—divest them of that and they constitute a perfect rabble." During one nine-month stretch on an earlier voyage, he had placed 50 men of a 100-man crew in irons and flogged 40 of them at the gangway. Charming to fellow officers, he didn't allow common seamen ever to address him, no matter how politely. One sailor, back home later, standing on what he described as the "maindeck of America," said he expected he would have an easier time speaking to President Jefferson than Captain Bainbridge. This same disgruntled tar said that the captain often addressed crewmen as "You damn'd rascal" and that Bainbridge also cheered on the boatswain's mates, administering cat-o'-nine-tails to a sailor's back, with words such as "Give it to him! Clear that cat! Damn your eyes or I'll give it to him."

In spring of 1803 when the *Philadelphia* had needed a crew, most potential recruits knew nothing about Bainbridge's reputation as a rough commander. They also didn't know Bainbridge's service record included two of the blackest incidents in the history of the young navy.

William Ray, native of Salisbury, Connecticut, certainly didn't. It's unusual in this era for an articulate "grunt," a private, to record his impressions in a memoir, but Ray did just that. (His *Horrors of Slavery*, an extremely rare book, provides a counterpoint to the usual self-aggrandizing officers' letters and memoirs.)

William Ray, 5'4½", thirty-four years old, had failed at many professions. His general store . . . long shuttered; his schoolroom . . . now vacant, and in the latest mishap, he had fallen sick en route from New

England and had lost a newspaper editing job in Philadelphia. So Ray, penniless, exasperated, discouraged, and inebriated, headed down to the Delaware River to call it a day and a life and to drown himself.

There, through the haze, he saw flying from a ship in the river the massive flag of the United States, fifteen stars and fifteen stripes. A drummer was beating the skin trying to encourage enlistment. Ray weighed his options: death or the marines. He weighed them again. At the birth of the Republic, the marines ranked as the lowliest military service, paying $6 a month, one-third of the wages of an experienced sailor. The entire marine corps totaled fewer than 500 men, and though it's true marines wore fancy uniforms and carried arms, they basically came onboard ship to police the sailors and prevent mutiny or desertion. The major glory the U.S. Marines could then claim was its Washington City marching band, which the local citizens of that swampy outpost loved and President Thomas Jefferson despised.

Ray enlisted. Rarely was a man less suited for the marines than diminutive William Ray. As a former colonist who had lived through the War of Independence, he detested tyranny, whether it be that of King George III or his new captain, William Bainbridge. Onshore he saw "liberty, equality, peace and plenty" and on board ship, he said he found "oppression, arrogance, clamour and indigence."

Ray, still smarting that he couldn't find a job onshore in "prosperous" America, was appalled to discover his new maritime career required addressing thirteen-year-olds as "Sir" and treating them like "gentlemen." The Philadelphia's officer list included eleven midshipmen, all in their teens. "How preposterous does it appear, to have brats of boys, twelve or fifteen years old, who six months before, had not even seen salt water, strutting in livery, about a ship's decks, damning and flashing old experienced sailors," complained one veteran sailor, who called the job of midshipmen a "happy asylum" for the offspring of the wealthy too vicious, lazy, or ignorant to support themselves.

Ray once saw a midshipman toss a bucket of water on a sleeping sailor who, as he woke, spluttered some curses. When the sailor recognized it was a midshipman, he tried to apologize, saying he didn't expect "one of the gentlemen" to be tossing water. Captain Bainbridge had the sailor thrown in irons and flogged. "You tell an officer he is no gentleman?" shouted Bainbridge at the man's punishment. "I'll cut you in ounce pieces, you scoundrel."

In that era of sail, navy ships were so crowded that sailors slept in shifts: Half the crew rocked in the foul-smelling dark while the other half performed the watch. Some captains allowed the men six consecutive hours of sleep; Bainbridge allowed four.

A marine comrade of Ray's, David Burling, fell asleep on watch . . . twice. The second time, he was chained in the coal hold until three captains could be gathered for a court-martial. "It will give me infinite pleasure to see him hanging at the yardarm," Bainbridge was overheard saying.

Despite Ray's shock at seaboard life under Bainbridge, the *Philadelphia* for its few months at sea had performed well enough. Then Commodore Edward Preble in mid-September had sent the vessel, along with the schooner *Vixen*, on the important mission to blockade Tripoli. Preble represented the third commodore (i.e., ranking squadron captain) in three years to command the small U.S. fleet in the region; the last two men—Commodore Richard Dale and Commodore Richard Morris— were both accused of spending more time showing their epaulets at dances and balls at various European ports than in the choppy waters off Tripoli. Preble, a no-nonsense New Englander, was eager to blockade and to capture hostile ships even in the stormy fall weather. He hoped to choke the enemy's economy.

Now, on October 31, 1803, in the half light of dawn around 6 A.M., the lookout on the *Philadelphia*, hovering high above the deck, spotted a sail far off on the port bow. Standing orders required alerting the captain. A distant ship, a mere swatch of white at first, usually remains a complete unknown for quite a while. Thanks to elaborate rules of warfare in the early nineteenth century, deception was viewed as an acceptable strategy in the early stages of encountering another ship. (For instance, the *Philadelphia* carried half a dozen foreign flags, including the Union Jack, a Portuguese pennant, a Danish ensign; Bainbridge a month earlier had used the British colors to trick a Moroccan ship into furling canvas and laying by.)

Though a captain might trick another vessel to sidle close, the etiquette of battle demanded that he fly his true colors before opening fire.

The USS *Philadelphia*, at that moment about thirty miles east of Tripoli, was already flying the American flag to announce the blockade. As Captain Bainbridge peered through the spyglass, he watched the other ship suddenly raise the yellow-and-red-striped flag of Tripoli. This amounted to a dare, a taunt. Any other colors, especially British or French, would have made the U.S. ship less eager to pursue.

Bainbridge ordered all possible sail to speed the chase of this 12-gun enemy corsair. Pigtailed men scurried to set the sails. A strong breeze coming from the east and southeast allowed both ships to ignore the danger of drifting too close to the shore to the south. The Tripoli vessel sprinted due west while the *Philadelphia*, farther off the coast, had to zigzag landward to try to catch up.

Officers barked, and the men smartly obeyed. Beyond patriotic zeal, another incentive spurred the crew: prize money. In the early navy, officers and men received shares of legally captured vessels. The roping of a gold-laden ship could change an officer's life and dole out more than rum money to a common sailor.

The chase was on. The men eagerly scampered up the ratlines to unfurl yet more sail, the topgallants. Standing 190 feet above the deck on a rope strung along a topgallant yardarm, as the frigate rolled in the waves, the men were tilted over the sea from starboard, then over the sea to port, over and over again.

The *Philadelphia* proved slightly faster than its quarry, and within three hours of traveling at about eight knots (nine-plus miles per hour), it reached within cannon shot for its bow chasers. The Tripoli ship, much smaller, smartly hugged the shore to tempt the *Philadelphia* to follow landward and accidentally beach itself. Bainbridge kept the *Philadelphia* at least one mile offshore. The port of Tripoli began to loom in the distance . . . at first a minaret then a castle.

"Every sail was set, and every exertion made to overhaul the ship and cut her off from the town," Ray wrote. "The wind was not very favourable to our purpose, and we had frequently to wear ship. A constant fire was kept up from our ship, but to no effect. We were now within about three miles of the town, and Captain Bainbridge not being acquainted with the harbour, having no pilot nor any correct chart, trusted implicitly to the directions of Lieutenant Porter, who had been here several times and who professed himself well acquainted with the situation of the harbour. We however went so close in that the captain began to be fearful of venturing any farther, and was heard by a number of our men, to express to Lt. Porter the danger he apprehended in pursuing any farther in that direction and advising him to put about ship."

David Porter, then a twenty-three-year-old lieutenant, and a six-foot bull of a man, would go on to achieve a remarkable and controversial career. He would almost singlehandedly wipe out the British whaling fleet in the Pacific during the War of 1812. He would help root out the pirate Jean Lafitte from New Orleans, but his reluctance to follow orders would ultimately lead to court-martial. He was, indeed, a bit of a wild man.

A year earlier, he had killed a fellow in a Baltimore saloon during a brawl while trying to land new recruits. Six months after that, his aggressiveness had surfaced again, this time against the enemy. The U.S. squadron—under Commodore Morris—had trapped in a cove eleven small Tripoli merchant ships carrying wheat; Porter took four men in an open boat at night to sneak in and scout the enemy ships. He discovered that the Moslem merchants had tucked all the vessels by the shore, unloaded their bales of wheat into breastworks, and were now backed on land by a thousand militiamen. Porter begged permission, and received it, for the foolhardy mission to attack in open boats to try to set fire to the wheat. Within a stone's throw of the shore, he was shot through his left thigh, and another ball grazed his right thigh. His men managed to set fire to the wheat, but the Moslems eventually succeeded in extinguishing the blaze. Porter—though bleeding profusely—begged permission to attack again, but Morris refused.

Now as the *Philadelphia* skirted the shore, Porter encouraged Bainbridge to go deeper into the harbor; he also gave orders that three leadlines be cast and recast to look for any perilous change in the depth of the water. Two lieutenants and one midshipman oversaw sailors who slung forward a lead weight, itself weighing as much as twenty-eight pounds. If the toss was timed right, the lead weight would strike bottom as the ship passed, giving a true vertical depth by a reading of colored markings tied to the rope. The men sang out lead-line readings of at least eight fathoms (or forty-eight feet of water), plenty for a ship that needed a little over twenty feet in depth.

The city of Tripoli stood about three miles away. The enemy ship looked too far ahead to catch. Captain Bainbridge granted Lieutenant Porter permission to fire a few more rounds before heading out to sea. Porter, not shy, unleashed quite a few. A diplomat in town hearing the last burst of cannon fire called it a "fanfaronade," that is, a braggadocio, or a mad fanfare of farewell.

Porter then relayed the captain's order to haul the ship about and head out to sea. The topgallant sails used in the chase were furled, ropes were tied to change the angle of the sails. Bainbridge sent Porter up the mizzen topmast, the sternmost of the three masts, so he could use the spyglass to assess the vessels in Tripoli harbor as the *Philadelphia* headed back out to sea.

Lieutenant Porter, in his blue uniform with a single gold epaulet, was halfway up the mizzen rigging, about seventy-five feet above the deck, when he felt himself flung forward hard. Porter gripped the ropes as they flung him backward now.

The *Philadelphia* had beached itself on an uncharted reef; the bow rode up on this shelf of sand and rested several feet above its normal water level. Bainbridge later said he couldn't have been more surprised than if this had occurred in the middle of the ocean.

In the first moment of shock, Captain Bainbridge coolly gave the next order: full sail ahead to try to surmount and pass the reef.

Bainbridge hadn't ordered any soundings to determine the height of the reef fore or aft, or to ascertain where the deep water lay. The ship, with wind in its sails, rose up and beached itself higher on the reef. Lieutenant Porter would later confirm Bainbridge's command at a Court of Inquiry. "All sails were instantly set to force her over the bank," testified Lieutenant Porter, who added a touch cattily: "*After* this did not succeed, Captain Bainbridge asked the witness's opinion."

At that moment, the Tripoli blockade runner, which had been darting away, now hove to and rolled out its guns for the first time. A couple miles beyond that vessel, more than a dozen ships bobbed inside Tripoli harbor. (The U.S. schooner *Vixen* would have come in handy now, but Bainbridge had sent it away toward Tunis two weeks earlier to scout for other ships.)

Philadelphia was stuck in Tripoli. Anyone on duty in the Mediterranean knew the consequences of being captured: Barbary slavery. For many of the 307 men aboard, it evoked a greater fear than shipwreck, which brought quick death, because Barbary slavery was portrayed as long, humiliating death-in-life.

In colonial days, preacher Cotton Mather had described Barbary slaves as living for years in dug-out pits with a crosshatch of bars above, and their taskmasters were "barbarous negroes." Galley slaves also lived to tell of being chained naked to an oar, forced to row ten hours at a stretch. Slaves, facing forward, pushed the forty-foot-long oars by rocking back to near horizontal, as though in a grotesque limbo contest, and then lurching with full strength, again and again. During hard chases, they were sustained by a wine-soaked rag shoved in their mouths.

Accounts of North African slave auctions showed white Americans treated like black slaves. Rituals varied, but in one account an American stated that after being purchased: "[I] was forced to lie down in the street and take the foot of my new master and place it upon my neck." Another described being forced to lick the dust along a thirty-foot path to the throne of the Dey of Algiers.

John Foss survived captivity in Algiers, and his popular account ran in several American newspapers in the late 1790s, fleshing out the nightmare. He wrote of prisoners routinely shackled with forty-pound chains, forced to perform sunrise-to-sunset labor ranging from digging out sewers to hauling enormous rocks for a harbor jetty. He matter-of-factly described the most common Barbary punishment for *light* infractions: bastinado of 150 strokes. "The person is laid upon his face, with his hands in irons behind him and his legs lashed together with a rope. One taskmaster holds down his head and another his legs, while two others inflict the punishment upon his breech [his buttocks] with sticks, some what larger than an ox goad. After he has received one half in this manner, they lash his ankles to a pole, and two Turks [Moslems] lift the pole

American and European accounts depicted a slave's life in Barbary as an unending hell of tortures, including the bastinado (*left*) and forced circumcision (*right*).

up, and hold it in such a manner, as brings the soles of his feet upward, and the remainder of his punishment, he receives upon the soles of his feet."

With cheery thoughts such as these running through their heads, the crew and officers of *Philadelphia* worked desperately to free the 150-foot-long vessel off Kaliusa Reef.

Porter advised Bainbridge to consult all the officers. They quickly suggested lowering a boat to sound the depth all around the ship. The bow lead drew only twelve feet as far back along the ship as the foremast—at least six feet less depth than required—but the stern still floated free with plenty of deep water there. Clearly, the ship needed to back up. The *Philadelphia* was pointing to the northeast; the winds flowed briskly to the northwest directly across the beam of the ship, a decidedly unhelpful direction. The officers recommended putting the sails aback, that is, facing them into the wind by tying off the yardarms to move the ship backward. That amounted to the exact opposite tack from Bainbridge's original command.

The American sailors noticed a flurry of activity taking place on the ships in harbor; the men of Tripoli were racing to ready their vessels; speed was vital for both sides. "I could not but notice the striking alteration in our officers," wrote Private Ray. "It was no time to act the haughty tyrant—no time to punish men for snoring—no time to tell men they had 'no right to think' . . . It was not 'go you dam'd rascal' but 'come, my good fellow, my brave lads.'"

The men tied the sails, prepared the canvas. The blustery winds pushed against backed sails, but instead of inching the *Philadelphia* backward, the strong breezes tipped the ship far over onto its left side till the gunports hovered just above the waterline. A few more inches of tip and water would rush in. This unexpected result caused the deck not only to slope downhill (from the elevated reef) but also to lean left. Carved Hercules looked drunk and falling sideways at the masthead. Worse, this careening caused one bank of eighteen cannons to point into the water, and the cannons on the other side to aim high into the sky.

The one enemy gunboat—downwind—kept up a fitful fire from a respectful distance, but so far almost all balls splashed harmlessly in the water.

The American officers, to lighten the bow quickly, ordered the men to cut the ship's three heavy bow anchors; no one wanted to part with valuable equipment, but this was an emergency; the sailors chopped with axes at the fat cables. The ship still stuck firm. Then the officers ordered the crew to shift the heavy cannons to the stern. The gun carriages must be unchained and the men must lash ropes to the cannon barrels and wooden gun carriages to ease them down the tilted gun deck. The men, who could barely outstretch their arms in the cramped areas belowdeck, now tried to haul 2,000-pound cast-iron long-barreled cannons in a hurry.

The gun crews—trained to load, fire, swab, reload in battle rush—strained to pile the humongous weapons in the stern. That hard maneuver failed to free the bow, so the officers told the men to hoist and toss many of the 2,000-pound cannons overboard. They jettisoned most of the twenty-eight beautiful long guns capable of shooting eighteen-pound balls and the sixteen stubby carronades that plunked thirty-two-pound balls . . . except for a handful on the quarterdeck and in the stern cabin. Sailors shot-put cannonballs into the harbor water. The men sought out heavy articles everywhere—from barrels to ballast—and cast them overboard. Even David Burling, the marine imprisoned for sleeping, was freed from the coal hold to lend a hand.

With massive effort, the crew lightened the vessel by sixty tons, but the *Philadelphia* still stuck fast. Meanwhile, the blockade runner continued to line up a broadside of its guns and to fire. The balls, surprisingly, either whizzed through the rigging or fell harmlessly in the water. Not a single shot caused a direct hit. No splinters flew. The *Philadelphia*, with most of its remaining guns underwater or aimed askew, couldn't fire back. Bainbridge later compared himself to a chained helpless animal.

While the crew worked hard over the ensuing hours, several more gunboats, finally readied, stirred out of Tripoli harbor. (A gunboat might carry 50 to 75 men and sport a half dozen or so cannons.) The number of enemy gunboats sailing to attack the *Philadelphia* is up for debate. According to Private Ray, only one gunboat risked passing by the *Philadelphia*'s stern to get upwind while two others remained almost out of gunshot downwind. Captain Bainbridge, however, pegged the ultimate number at nine.

As an occasional cannonball whizzed overhead, the men labored and the officers remained calm. The Americans were sitting ducks in an arcade where the customers couldn't hit the side of a barn. The carpenter and his men tried to chop away enough of a cabin wall to allow at least one cannon to bear on the Tripoli gunboat upwind. The gun crew fired several shots, but the cannon failed to roll out far enough, and the blast caused a small fire. The men doused the flames quickly and abandoned using the cannon.

George Hodge, the boatswain, a non-commissioned officer, suggested using the ship's boats to try to float out the huge stern anchor a distance behind the ship, drop it, and then try to haul or warp the ship backwards. Ideally, the anchor's giant triangular flukes would bury themselves in the sandy bottom; the men would turn the capstan to pull on the anchor cable. Bainbridge rejected his idea and later stated enemy gunboats "commanded the ground" where the anchor would have had to have been dropped. Hodge and many sailors privately grumbled that the effort was well worth the risk.

Now deeper into the afternoon, the officers regarded the situation as desperate. They suggested a radical move, and Bainbridge concurred: chop down the foremast. With topmast and topgallant perched above, this stout pole towered 176 feet. Bainbridge hoped it would fall to the right, and this would cure the ship's tilt left or, even better, without the weight, the ship would float free. The carpenters wielded axe blows on the right side of the base; oak chips flew. They chopped it down, but the men hadn't planned their tree-cutting well enough. The foremast fell to the left and, even worse, yanked the main topgallant mast with it. The decks tilted more. The bow was a mess of tangled ropes and shattered masts.

Around 3 P.M. Bainbridge yet again called all his officers together to consult on the situation. (At this time, Ray observed three more gunboats just leaving the harbor, which would have brought his total to six potential attacking vessels.) Bainbridge saw the decision in stark terms: surrender or fight against overwhelming odds, with scant means of self-defense. (While the Tripoli ships might eventually prove overwhelming, up to that moment, not one cannonball had hit the deck of the *Philadelphia*, nor were any sailors killed or wounded.)

What many men aboard didn't realize was that William Bainbridge had *already* surrendered a U.S. Navy ship; he had *already* gained the unwelcomed distinction of becoming the first officer in the history of the United States Navy (after the end of the War of Independence) to surrender.

A half decade earlier, back in 1798, the United States was fighting an undeclared war against France over commerce, mainly against Caribbean privateers. Bainbridge, then a twenty-four-year-old lieutenant, was given command of the *Retaliation*, eighteen guns, and 140 men, joining a small squadron of three American ships off Guadeloupe. Commodore Alexander Murray was chasing a French privateer when on the morning of November 20, 1798, he reconnoitered with Bainbridge. They spotted two large sails in the distance. Murray consulted Bainbridge, who informed him that he had spoken earlier with a British warship, and he was convinced these two arriving ships were also British, then our ally.

Murray in the *Montezuma* sailed off after a French privateer, leaving Bainbridge in the *Retaliation*, who headed in the direction of the arriving sails. He gave the flag signal agreed upon for encountering British ships. No answer. He drifted closer. He gave the signal for American ships and received a muddled answer.

By now, the large frigates were bearing down upon him. The first ship, 36 guns, fired across his bow and hoisted the tricolor of Revolutionary France. The second ship, a 44-gun leviathan, arrived, and Commodore St. Laurent of the *Voluntaire* demanded that Bainbridge surrender. Without firing a shot, after having carelessly sidled up to unknown ships, William Bainbridge ordered the Stars and Stripes to be lowered, and he surrendered.

The men aboard the *Philadelphia* also might not have been aware of another stain on Bainbridge's navy record. After being released from prison in Guadeloupe, Bainbridge had somehow avoided censure and was made a captain and sent on a mission commanding the *George Washington* to deliver naval supplies and other tributary gifts to Algiers in 1800. Bainbridge navigated across the Atlantic without incident, but once in Algiers he allowed the harbor pilot to guide him to a berth directly under the massive guns of the fortress. The Dey of Algiers then arrogantly demanded that Bainbridge run an errand for him, carrying presents to the Sultan of the Ottoman Empire in Istanbul. Bainbridge objected, as did the American consul, Richard O'Brien, who pointed out the Algiers–United States treaty called for American *merchant* vessels to run emergency errands but certainly not U.S. Navy ships. The Dey threatened war.

With *George Washington* tucked under the massive guns of Dey Bobba Mustapha, Bainbridge felt himself constrained to agree to run the Dey's errand. To add insult to injury, the Dey demanded *George Washington* sail under the Algerian flag. Bainbridge agreed to this as well, and the 100-foot-long American pennant was struck. As a midshipman noted in the ship's log: "The Algerian Flag hoisted on the Main top Gallant royal mast head [the ship's highest point] . . . some tears fell at this Instance of national Humility."

Bainbridge delivered to Istanbul: 4 horses, 150 sheep, 25 horned cattle, 4 lions, 4 tigers, 4 antelopes, 12 parrots, as well as 100 African slaves, many of them females bound for the harems.

When William Eaton, then consul in Tunis, heard of Bainbridge's mission, he was appalled. "History shall tell that the United States first volunteered a ship of war, equipt, a carrier for a pirate. It is written. Nothing but blood can blot the impression out. I frankly own, I would have lost the peace, and been myself impaled rather than yielded this concession. Will nothing rouse my country?"

Aboard the *Philadelphia* in Tripoli harbor, at 3 P.M., Captain Bainbridge consulted with his officers, asking their opinion on surrender. "We all answer'd that all was done," wrote William Knight, sailing master. "Nothing remain'd but to give the ship up."

Although not a single cannonball had hit the ship, causing any leaks, Bainbridge apparently perceived a danger of being sunk; he regarded further defense as fruitless and further delay as a possible death sentence for everyone aboard.

Bainbridge now faced a rather unusual problem . . . one that most captains rarely face in the course of a long career. Obviously he didn't want to hand the Bashaw of Tripoli an immaculate 1,200-ton frigate. He needed to scuttle and sink his own ship but do so at a stage-managed pace that would allow all his crew to exit safely. Timing would be crucial. (Many sailors couldn't swim, including Bainbridge.)

Bainbridge ordered the gunner to drown the gunpowder magazine. In case of fire, a supply of water stood at the ready to soak the explosives. The gunner, Richard Stephenson, used a key to gain access to a stopcock, which he turned to send water into the magazine. Bainbridge also ordered the carpenter to bore holes in the ship's oak-and-copper-sheathed bottom. Carpenter William Godby and his two assistants, turning T-shaped augers and pounding sharpened chisels, pierced an unspecified number of holes in the bow below the waterline. Seawater sprayed in. First it spritzed onto puddles in the hold, then it began to rise. More water. Within an hour, one eyewitness said it reached four feet in the hold. Bainbridge decided it was time for him to surrender once again.

The USS *Philadelphia* carried four American flags: The largest was twenty-two feet by thirty-eight feet; the Stars and Stripes announced the ship's nationality at a great distance; they proclaimed that nationality to the men serving on board.

"About four o'clock, the Eagle of America, fell a prey to the vultures of Barbary—the flag was struck!!" wrote Ray.

"Many of our seamen were much surprised at seeing the colours down, before we had received any injury from the fire of our enemy, and begged of the captain and officers to raise it again, preferring even death to slavery. The man who was at the ensign halyards positively refused to obey the captain's orders . . . to lower the flag. He was threatened to be run through and a midshipman seized the halyards and executed the command, amidst the general murmuring of the crew."

The captain tore up the signal books; a midshipman tossed them overboard; the men rushed to destroy and fling seaward: battle-axes, pikes, cutlasses, pistols, muskets, anything that might be useful to the enemy. They took axes to the captain's furniture and generally rampaged throughout the ship.

The rules of war are complicated; many are observed more in the breach than the observance. The Congress of the United States had clearly stated in the Navy Act of 1800 (Article IX) that when capturing another ship as a prize, the American sailors should not "strip of their clothes, or pillage or in any manner maltreat" the enemy on board the prize vessel.

Somehow, word spread among the hundreds of crewmen of the *Philadelphia* that the enemy sailors of Tripoli might honor more humane rules of surrender, and that they would not be stripped or harassed. William Ray observed that the crewmen, from the marines to foretopmen, started to put on layer upon layer of clothing. The most common outfit was for each man to put on four pairs of blue trousers, and four white shirts and four black neckerchiefs. In their pockets they stuffed their prized possessions: money, knives, jewelry, food, keepsakes. Former schoolteacher William Ray said the overstuffed men resembled Falstaff in Shakespeare's *Henry IV*.

The captain ordered the entire crew to assemble on the sloping deck. And they did, in their ballooning outfits. As they stood there, Captain Bainbridge solemnly read the articles of war and informed them that their wages would continue in captivity, that they should hope and pray for ransom, and told them "to behave with circumspection and propriety among our barbarous captors."

The puffed men swayed on the deck as Bainbridge talked. Ray said that a dying saint would have had trouble not laughing.

In the ensuing minutes, men rummaged for more food and valuables to stuff into their pockets; officers filled satchels; marines guarded the liquor. But mostly, the crew and officers awaited the boarding by the enemy, and waited, as the water rose in the hold. And they waited. The enemy did nothing but lob the occasional cannonball over the rigging.

Captain Bainbridge eventually realized that the enemy—even though it had seen Ol' Glory drop—didn't believe the *Philadelphia* was surrendering.

In hard-fought battles, ships of certain nations had been known to raise the flag of surrender in order to lure a boarding party and then blow them up.

If the enemy did not board the *Philadelphia* soon, the crippled ship, with waters rising in the hold, might sink, and then many of the officers and crew would drown. Embittered William Ray might have his death by drowning after all.

Lieutenant Porter volunteered to take a boat under a white flag over to the enemy. As Ray caustically put it: "We sent a boat and persuaded them that it was no farce, no illusion, assuring them that our frigate had in reality struck to one gunboat, and entreated them to come and take possession of their lawful booty!!"

Finally, around sunset, the first boarding boats of the enemy arrived. The prospect of Barbary slavery grew all too real. As the orange disc descended into the western Mediterranean, a parade of Moslem officers and men climbed aboard, a fierce costume pageant of baggy pants, turbans, bright-colored vests, made all too real by the glint of scimitars and drawn daggers.

The officers intermixed Arabic commands to their men with Lingua Franca attempts to communicate with the Americans. The valuables aboard this prize frigate and on the persons of the captives incited a frenzy among the attackers. As boatloads of boarders arrived, fights broke out among the attackers over whom to rob. While Americans had drawn no blood, the men of Tripoli drew blood among themselves over plunder. The American Falstaffs slimmed down quickly. The frenzy wasn't surprising, to veteran observers. While perhaps a Barbary captain might share in the profits from ransoming slaves or selling cargo, "most Barbary crewmen have no other means of drawing profit than stripping prisoners completely," wrote an Italian, a Barnabas monk, who had been captured in nearby Tunis, around this time.

The words *Romo kelb* ("Christian dog") and *Senza Fede* ("Infidel") echoed along the chaotic decks. The Moslem officers separated out the thirty-plus American officers to go in the first three boats ashore; it was more than a three-mile pull ashore, with twenty men or more to a long-boat. As the American officers climbed over the rail, the pillaging began anew. Someone tore Captain Bainbridge's gold epaulets off his shoulders; that same man claimed Lieutenant Porter's sword. The surgeon's mate, Dr. Jon Cowdery, had his pocket picked of a $10 gold coin, then lost his surtout, a winter cloak. Dr. Harwood, an ill man, and Carpenter William Godby were wrestled to the bottom of one boat, then robbed. The captors forced the Americans to row. Near shore, someone smacked Cowdery hard on the side of his head. He then lost his surgeon's instruments, his silver pencil, and a silk handkerchief from around his neck.

By the time the boat reached shore, swarthy hands had lightened the American officers of all watches, cravats, and money and had left them with only their trousers, shirts, and jackets. As they debarked at the stone steps of the castle in the harbor, the Americans expected the worst, having long been filled with Barbary pirate horror stories. Instead they were ushered into a room in the palace, where a long table had been set European style. Italian slaves served the surprised American officers a decent supper. "We are treated much better than I expected," later wrote sailing master William Knight.

The 270 crewmen, however, ferried ashore in relays over several hours, found a harsher fate. In the boats, the enemy raised sabers over their heads while enemy crewmen stripped them down, in a tug-of-war where no American sailor dare put up any resistance. About fifty feet from shore, most of the Americans were yanked overboard to scramble through the October surf.

"At the beach stood a row of armed men on each side of us, who passed us along to the castle gate," wrote William Ray. "It opened and we ascended a winding, narrow, dismal passage, which led to a paved avenue, lined with terrific janizaries, armed with glittering sabres, muskets, pistols, and tomahawks. Several of them spit on us as we passed. We were hurried forward through various turnings and flights of stairs, until we found ourselves in the dreadful presence of his exalted majesty, the puissant Bashaw of Tripoli."

The Bashaw—Yussef Karamanli—enjoyed the notoriety of being the first foreign ruler ever to declare war on the United States. (Arabic lacks a "P" so the Turkish word *pasha* was pronounced *bashaw* on the north coast of Africa.)

Ray, who had wanted to be a newspaperman, captured the scene.

His throne on which he was seated, was raised about four feet from the surface, inlaid with mosaic, covered with a cushion of the richest velvet, fringed with cloth of gold, bespangled with brilliants [jewels]. The floor of the hall was variegated marble, spread with carpets of the most beautiful kind. The walls were of porcelain, fantastically enameled but too finical to be called elegant. The bashaw made a very splendid and tawdry appearance. His vesture was a long robe of cerulean silk, embroidered with gold and glittering tinsel. His broad belt was ornamented with diamonds, and held two gold-mounted pistols, and a sabre with a golden hilt, chain and scabbard. On his head, he wore a large white turban decorated with ribbons. His dark beard swept his breast. He is about five feet ten inches in height, rather corpulent, and of a manly majestic deportment. When he had satiated his pride and curiosity by gazing on us with complacent triumph, we were ordered to follow a guard.

Bashaw Yussef was ecstatic at the victory granted him by Allah. He told diplomats that he felt deeply indebted to his local marabout, or

Moslem holyman, for he believed that the man's prayers had delivered, like a present, almost gift-wrapped, an armed American frigate.

Guards crammed the soaking wet American crewmen into a chamber that barely had room enough for them to stand. Slaves, most from Naples or Malta, came with bundles of tattered but dry clothes to exchange for the Americans' wet garments. The prisoners naïvely expected their own clothes to be returned; instead, they were sold to Jewish merchants, who would later offer to *sell* them back to the American prisoners at a steep premium.

Near midnight, soldiers herded the American sailors to a covered piazza, walled on three sides but open on the fourth to the sea winds. Their just-received "new" clothes did little to keep them warm. The prisoners, such as seventeen-year-old Thomas Prince from Rhode Island, curled up shivering and tried to sleep on the frigid tile floors.

The loss of the *Philadelphia* and its 307 crewmen and officers on Kaliusa Reef in Tripoli harbor marked a national disaster for the young United States. The Bashaw, a wily and worthy adversary, would set his first ransom demand for the American slaves at $1,690,000, more than the entire military budget of the United States.

Navy officers like the fierce Captain John Rodgers would beg for the chance to attack Tripoli to avenge and free his comrades; diplomats such as Tobias Lear, a Harvard graduate, yearned for the glory of negotiating their release. But the man who would one day speed their freedom more than all others was a stubby disgraced former army officer on his way to the nation's new capital, Washington City.

CHAPTER 2 *Washington City*

If the Congress do not consent that the government shall send a
force into the Mediterranean to check the insolence of these
scoundrels and to render the United States respectable, I hope they
will resolve at their next session to wrest the quiver of arrows from
the left talon of the [American] Eagle . . . and substitute a fiddle
bow or a cigar in lieu.

—WILLIAM EATON

VISITORS WHO HAD SEEN grandiose maps of the nation's new capital were flummoxed on arrival, some even asking where Washington City was, while standing in the middle of it. Pennsylvania Avenue was a triumphant three miles long but contained only a handful of unfinished and gargantuan neoclassical buildings. These stood out like bizarre experiments in the swampy greenery, like wishful thinking for a toddler nation. That "Goose Creek" had been renamed the "Tiber" said it all.

No bridge crossed the Potomac, and fewer than 5,000 people lived in the humid district that ex-surveyor George Washington had personally selected because of the site's commercial potential as a river-and-sea port. (While General George lived, the place was called "Federal City"; the river traffic bonanza never materialized thanks to waterfalls, mudbanks, and dangerous currents at Greenleaf's Point.) With building going so slowly, land values had crashed, and empty shacks tilted against unfinished brick edifices. "It looks like a deserted city," wrote one senator. Hunters shot quail near the president's house. Running water connected to indoor plumbing remained a dream, as did the hope for rows of retail shops. Many of the thirty-four senators stayed at the same overpriced boardinghouses, and often, more politics happened there over ham and peas than at the half-built, wing-less Capitol; entertainment consisted of the Marine Band and itinerant jugglers and actors visiting the Washington Theater; there was little to do there but drink, drink more, talk, or wait for the next government meeting. Congressmen were so exasperated with the discomfort and dullness of the place that they soon introduced a bill to move the nation's capital to that nearby metropolis, Baltimore.

William Eaton arrived in Washington City on January 10, 1804, a cold Tuesday morning, to plead his case on his expense account and his diplomatic career. He considered himself on a crusade, and he knew that

The unfinished Capitol building in bucolic Washington City, 1800.
Watercolor by William R. Birch.

one man—with the nod of his head or the scratch of his pen—could wipe his slate clean: Thomas Jefferson.

Eaton's journey from Brimfield, Massachusetts, had taken him ten arduous days on horseback, sailboat, and stagecoach. Just as travel along the eastern seaboard remained slow and difficult in the early 1800s, even slower and more fitful was the delivery of news from across the Atlantic.

Word of the *Philadelphia* disaster, though it had occurred ten weeks earlier, still hadn't reached America. Winter storms and steady eastward trade winds kept nautical traffic to a crawl. Official Washington remained blissfully unaware that Bashaw Yussef Karamanli of Tripoli now owned 307 American sailor slaves.

It is difficult for a modern reader to conceive just how small and accessible the entire federal government of the United States was under President Thomas Jefferson. The Department of State—today 28,000 employees—then consisted of Secretary of State James Madison and a handful of assistants. Visitors willing to ride to this odd outpost of governance sometimes presented themselves at the door of the president's house and were rewarded, especially in the mornings, with an immediate audience with Jefferson.

Sometime during the week of January 16, William Eaton walked from his boardinghouse over to the Treasury Department, where he met with Richard Harrison, an auditor. With copious notes and vouchers, Eaton presented his case. In the broad scope of history, the expense account of the consul to Tunis might seem trivial or unimportant, but it certainly wasn't to William Eaton. His future was on the line here, and his past.

He owed at minimum $22,000, and possibly quite a bit more. The debt would ruin him and his family. The shame of it, coming after his army court-martial and his dismissal from Tunis, would almost certainly crush his career.

The auditor sent a note to Secretary of State James Madison asking him to review material submitted by Eaton. Sometime during the week of February 5, Madison walked over to the president's house and discussed the matter with Thomas Jefferson. Eaton also paid him a quick visit. In sparse Washington City, all roads eventually led to Thomas Jef-

ferson. The Virginia architect-statesman-farmer had a hand in an uncanny array of decisions from nation-building land purchases to niggling
line items on diplomats' expense accounts.

When Jefferson talked to either Eaton or Madison, he towered over
the other man. Jefferson stood a lanky 6'2", and at age sixty, his often un-
kempt hair had frizzled from reddish to gray and framed a pale, freckled,
sun-damaged face and often parched lips. Thomas Jefferson, though
raised as landed gentry, was now notorious for his slovenly dress, for his
common-man refusal to don ceremonial garb. Instead, visitors such as
Senator William Plumer (Federalist, New Hampshire) observed that the
president often opted to greet guests in down-at-heel slippers, an untidy
red undervest, and corduroy long pants, and that his white shirts were often stained. He rarely tied back, groomed, or powdered his unruly hair. A
British diplomat that year compared Jefferson's appearance to that of a
"tall, large-boned farmer" but added that Jefferson was "good natured,
frank and rather friendly." In one-on-one conversation, the widower favored a stream-of-consciousness delivery that one senator described as
"loose and rambling" but full of "information" and "even brilliant sentiments." A prodigious scholar, his 6,487-volume personal library would
one day form the basis of the Library of Congress.

Jefferson, at that moment in 1804 at the end of his first term, was
riding extremely high, thanks to the just finalized Louisiana Purchase
from France. In effect Jefferson, the negotiator, had acquired far more
territory than Napoleon, the conqueror. Whiskey toasts at Stelle's Hotel
on Capitol Square echoed far into the night.

William Eaton had picked an especially bad time to come to Jefferson, cap in hand, to ask to be released from his debts. The president had
consistently preached "economy" (then a buzzword for "fiscal responsibility") so as to pay off the $75 million in Revolutionary War debts, to which
would now be added $15 million for his huge western land purchase.

At first glance, Eaton and Jefferson made a very odd couple. Jefferson
was a tall thin Virginian; Eaton a fairly short muscular New Englander.
Jefferson, as governor of Virginia, was forced to flee the British and held
a lifelong distrust of large standing armies and navies. Eaton, a career

army officer before his diplomatic appointment, deeply resented the dearth of captaincies in the U.S. Army. Jefferson spoke softly, thoughtfully. Eaton often ranted. Jefferson's letters reveal a serene intelligence, filled with articulate lawyerly arguments. Eaton's letters pack passion, bombast, sarcasm. Eaton was a friend of the Federalists and had been appointed consul by the Federalist administration of John Adams; Jefferson was a Republican, deeply wounded by recent Federalist gutter attacks in the press.

However, the two men shared a few traits: an enormous love of country and a sense of disgust at the actions of the Barbary powers of North Africa. "I am an enemy to all these douceurs, tributes and humiliations," Jefferson had once written to Madison. "I know nothing will stop the eternal increase from these pirates but the presence of an armed force." But Jefferson's "economy" at times prevented him from ample military spending. An internal tug-of-war, not his first, slowed Jefferson, the would-be warrior.

On Wednesday, February 8, 1804, the Virginian reviewed Eaton's expense accounts and drafted a long unflattering letter to him. Jefferson devoted two handwritten pages to analyzing Eaton's two biggest expense items. The president's training decades earlier in the law served him well. Jefferson eviscerated the idea that Eaton as a consul—for no matter how patriotic a cause—could commission and hire his own armed merchant ship, *Gloria,* to act as part of the U.S. Navy. "Only the Legislature [Congress] can add to or diminish our naval force," wrote Jefferson, who added that the Executive Branch would "carry its indulgence to the utmost" and allow Eaton's expenses for the *Gloria* when delivering important government messages.

Jefferson was even more dismissive of the $10,000 that Eaton was tricked into giving to the prime minister of Tunis. Eaton had promised the man a bribe if he would help overthrow the ruler of Tripoli, a bribe that would be paid only if the United States's ally, Hamet, mounted the throne. Since Hamet never gained power, Eaton argued, the minister had no right to claim an extra $10,000 during a business transaction. Jefferson regarded the matter as a private business dispute and offered—very cold comfort indeed—that Eaton's successor as consul to Tunis would "lend [his] aid in recovering the money . . . but this is the utmost to which [the United States] are bound."

Jefferson finished the letter, tamped it dry, then abruptly changed his mind and decided not to send it. He apparently didn't relish a head-to-head confrontation with Eaton, since he had other means available. Three days later, Secretary of State Madison delivered an almost identical message to the Treasury auditor, who in turn relayed it to Eaton, who became furious.

To make matters worse, the auditor also tallied a tentative total for Eaton's accounts, based on Jefferson's decision. He informed Eaton that he would owe the staggering sum of $40,803. That was twenty years' salary for a navy captain. If the judgment stood, not only Eaton but his wife, his three stepchildren, his three daughters, would all be ruined.

The bad financial news mirrored even worse personal news. From every scrap of correspondence, it's clear that Eaton regarded his expense-account ruling as a kind of tribunal for his handling of Barbary Coast affairs. His *honor* and *reputation* were on the line. If his expenses were justified, so was his conduct in pulling out all stops to try to launch civil war and overthrow the enemy government in nearby Tripoli and defy these Barbary pirates.

Eaton wasted no time in taking his case directly to Congress. The stroll to the rickety underheated Capitol building took but a minute. Access was almost that easy. At the Eighth Congress, First Session, on February 16, 1804, Eaton addressed a long passionate plea to the Honorable Speaker. He shaped it as a vindication of his diplomatic career; and he could not resist mapping out the course he desperately hoped his country would follow against the Barbary pirates of North Africa.

In the speech, he repeated one name over and over again, like a mantra: "Hamet, Hamet, Hamet." William Eaton contended that he had incurred the bulk of his expenses while pursuing a secret plot—approved by Secretary of State Madison—to overthrow the anti-American ruler of Tripoli, Bashaw Yussef, and replace him with his older brother, the rightful heir, Hamet. (The man's correct Arabic name was Ahmet, but Eaton and all Americans called him Hamet.)

Eaton told Congress that he had first met Hamet, then in exile in

Tunis, shortly after Tripoli declared war on the United States in May 1801. On the advice of the U.S. consul to Tripoli, James Leander Cathcart, Eaton had explored the idea of plotting with Hamet to restore him to his rightful throne to achieve a long-term payment-free friendship between the two nations. The American motivation was clear: Hamet would swear *never to enslave Americans or to demand tribute money*; the United States would then have a Moslem ally on the dangerous Barbary Coast. (Hamet had ruled Tripoli briefly in 1795 but had been locked out of his own palace; Yussef, almost a decade later, still held Hamet's wife and children as hostages in Tripoli.)

Plans for an American-backed civil war remained on a slow simmer. Then early in 1802 while Eaton recuperated from an illness in Leghorn, Italy, he learned that Yussef was plotting Hamet's death. Yussef intended to lure his brother with the promise of letting him rule two rich provinces, Derne and Bengazi, and then he would kill him. Eaton desperately wanted to rush from Leghorn back to Tunis to warn Hamet, but no ships were heading in that direction. Here is where Eaton's expenses started to mount. Eaton commissioned his own merchant ship, the *Gloria*, to take him on the voyage from Leghorn to Tunis, which with contrary winds, took two expensive weeks. He reached Tunis on March 12, 1802, just in time to warn Hamet of the danger of leaving with the forty armed Turkish bodyguards sent by his brother. With Hamet now under his wing, Eaton commissioned his own *Gloria* to go to Gibraltar to seek the U.S. Navy squadron to inform them of the critical need to aid Hamet immediately.

Eaton was quite optimistic that their Tripoli coup would fly with American navy cannons supporting Hamet's ground efforts.

Eaton's Captain Joseph Bounds of the *Gloria* found Captain Alexander Murray of the U.S. Navy frigate *Constellation,* freshly arrived from America. Almost without any hesitation for thought, Murray dismissed Eaton's plan with Hamet as a waste of money. He informed the captain of the *Gloria* to proceed wherever he liked but not on the business of the United States of America. Eaton, when notified soon after, was both mortified and irate. He felt betrayed by his own government. Murray in his report home called Eaton's actions "needless expenses" and "extravagances."

Soon after, Commodore Morris, a cautious man, arrived in Tunis and met with Eaton and with Hamet's agents. Morris, despite all entreaties, said the American squadron wasn't ready to attack Tripoli. Eaton said Hamet's agents wept with disappointment at the delay.

It was then—when the Hamet plot was still alive—that Eaton was banished from Tunis over his debts and that Commodore Morris decided Eaton was a lunatic.

Eaton, not surprisingly, was furious over what he perceived as the U.S. Navy's lackadaisical approach to the Tripoli war and Commodore Morris's and Captain Murray's disdain for his Hamet scheme. As he now pointed out in his speech to the House, "It may be asserted, without vanity or exaggeration, that my arrangements with the rival Bashaw did more to harass the enemy in 1802 than the entire operation of our squadron."

Eaton, never one to flick at an enemy when he could pound one, added that during Morris's seventeen months as commodore, Morris spent "only 19 days before the enemy's port!" (Thomas Hooper, a marine lieutenant, had secretly supplied Eaton with that information.) "The very commander who recoils at the prodigality of seeing a single ship employed in the prosecution of a measure which might have decided the fate of the enemy . . . seems wholly unconcerned at having employed the whole operative naval force of the United States an entire year in the Mediterranean, attending the travels of a woman!"

Mrs. Morris—who accompanied her husband along with their young son Gerard and his nursemaid Sal—was nicknamed throughout the fleet as the "Commodoress." A catty midshipman noted in his diary that the book-loving lady "looks very well in a veil." Eaton once groused in an official report to Secretary of State Madison: "Who, except an American, would ever propose to himself to bring a wife to war against the ferocious savages of Barbary?" He added caustically that next time: "I would recommend to the Govt of the US to station a comp.y of comedians and a seraglio before the enemy's port."

(Within six weeks of Eaton's speech, Commodore Morris would be brought up before a Court of Inquiry.)

Eaton contended that he had incurred all these major expenses for his country, in an attempt to bring Hamet to the throne. He couldn't resist adding, "The project with Hamet is still feasible."

Now Eaton worked up a good lather.

> Let my fellow-citizens be persuaded that there is no borne
> [limit] to the avarice of the Barbary princes; like the insatiable
> grave, they can never have enough. Consign them the revenues of
> the United States as the price of peace, they would still tax our
> labors for more veritable expressions of friendship. But it is a humil-
> iating consideration to the industrious citizen, the sweat of whose
> brow supports him with bread, that a tithe from his hard earnings
> must go to purchase oil of roses to perfume a pirate's beard!
>
> It is true that Denmark and Sweden (and even the United States,
> following their example) gratuitously furnish almost all their mate-
> rials for ship-building and munitions of war; besides the valuable
> jewels and large sums of money we are continually paying into their
> hands for their forebearance, and for the occasional ransom of cap-
> tives. . . . Without these resources they would soon sink under their
> own ignorance and want of means to become mischievous. Why
> this humiliation? Why furnish them the means to cut our own
> throats?

A seventeenth-century Barbary war galley with slaves manning the oars.

Eaton concluded: "If the expenses of the measures I have conducted, for which I thought myself authorized to apply public funds, should be admitted to my credit, there may be a small balance due to me from the United States. If not, I am at once a bankrupt and a beggar—net product of the earnings of almost five years' exile!"

The House of Representatives relayed Eaton's speech and supporting documents to the Committee of Claims. Two weeks later, on February 29, John Cotton Smith (Federalist, Connecticut), a descendant of Cotton Mather, delivered an assessment to the House. He praised Eaton for making a "well-founded claim for his sacrifices and expenditures in the public service," but Smith said that the committee believed that the Executive Branch "is both enabled and disposed to render him complete justice." The Committee of Claims's Smith concluded that Eaton's petition was "premature" and that "legislative interference" should be withheld.

They had kicked Eaton back to Treasury and back to James Madison and Thomas Jefferson, who had already nixed the key expense items. Eaton was between a rock and a pair of tight-fisted Republicans. This impatient man faced more lobbying and more delays. It was hard to imagine what could save William Eaton at this point.

Then news arrived that Tripoli had captured the USS *Philadelphia*, and 307 Americans were now slaves on the coast of Barbary.

The news had traveled fitfully indeed. The Boston *Columbian Centinel* broke the story on March 10, having received it from an American merchant ship that had departed February 3 from Cadiz, Spain, carrying a weeks-old London newspaper that had run an item from Italy datelined December 25. Now the shocking report spread down the eastern seaboard of the United States. The New York *Evening Post* picked it up on March 14, quoting from a letter carried aboard that merchant ship. "The officers [of the *Philadelphia*] are said to be treated with humanity but it is said the crew were stript immediately on their landing, even to a single shirt, and that they are on short allowance."

Americans were appalled. This military fiasco and sudden hostage crisis brought the war home; the event clearly ranked among the nation's worst disasters since the founding of the country.

Wasting no time, President Jefferson on Tuesday, March 20, addressed Congress with a call to arms, asking them to "increase our force and enlarge our expenses in the Mediterranean." The *National Intelligencer*, which everyone knew acted as the house organ for Jefferson, ran a prominent item, headlined "Millions for Defense, but not a Cent for Tribute." The piece countered the criticism of the Federalists that Jefferson and his Republicans were weak-kneed on military matters and boasted: "It is thus the present administration evinces its patriotism, and its energy; not by vain vaunting of prowess; but by actions, which will show the world that while the wish of the American nation is peace, she will not hesitate for a moment to make that power feel the vengeance of her arms, that dares, in violation of justice, to invade her rights."

On Monday, March 26, the Senate hopped aboard the war effort, voting to increase import duties by 2.5 percent to raise $900,000 to send another squadron to the Mediterranean.

Navy ships would come out of drydock. Captains, lingering bored on half pay, would dust off uniforms. Stockyards would start salting beef for the long voyages. Preachers would sermonize about ransoming the prisoners.

On this same Monday, William Eaton sought out Thomas Jefferson at one of the most unusual populist rallies ever held in this country, a huge open-to-the-public party in a Senate meeting room.

Festivities began when servants carried in a "Mammoth Loaf" of bread, baked from an entire barrel of flour, and delivered it along with a large sirloin of roast beef and beer, wine, and hard cider.

(The significance of the "Mammoth Loaf" was that two years earlier, the women of a small town in Massachusetts had sent the president a *1,200-pound cheese* to celebrate his tolerance of religious choice. The Federalists had tried to spoof Jefferson, dubbing the gift "Mammoth Cheese" since a Jefferson-funded archaeologist had recently unearthed the bones of a woolly mammoth in New York City. The joke backfired when Americans everywhere embraced the cheese as a fitting symbol of American hard work and political ideas.)

Now, the navy baker had made a Mammoth Loaf to help finish the Mammoth Cheese, of which large chunks still remained. At the stroke of noon, "people of all classes & colors from the President of the United States to the meanest vilest Virginia slave," as one New England senator put it, crowded into the Capitol for dinner. Jefferson, in scruffy common-man clothes, pulled out a jackknife from his pocket and cut off a hunk of roast beef and some bread to eat and even had a drink of liquor. Apparently more than one drink; he was overheard comparing "the drunken frolic to the sacrament of the Lord's supper." The party continued after the dinner hour, and some senators sent the sergeant at arms to demand silence. One humorless senator, a former military officer, yelled at the mob, "If ever you are again guilty of the like, you shall be punished—I will inflict it—The Navy shall be brought up & kill you outright."

Eaton during that chaotic afternoon was able to corner Jefferson just long enough to set up a meeting for four days later at the president's house. On Friday, March 30, with war fever still lingering in the air like cannon smoke, Eaton finally got a chance for redemption. The president and his Cabinet, having waited for meddlesome Congress to leave town, authorized Eaton to go on a secret "enterprise" to the Barbary Coast, to aid the legitimate sovereign Hamet in attacking Tripoli by land. Eaton's ultimate goal would be to free the American captives, impose terms of peace, and secure an ally in that dangerous region. "The President and his Cabinet Council . . . formed sanguine hopes of its success," assessed Eaton later. This mission represented a dream assignment for Eaton, a chance to prove to the doubting politicians and navy men that backing Hamet would not only solve the Tripoli problem but also send a loud message of defiance along the entire Barbary Coast. According to Eaton, the president agreed to send to Hamet "on the score of a loan," some field artillery, one thousand pistols and muskets, and $40,000. The loan angle was very Jeffersonian in its *economy*; if Hamet succeeded, he would be expected to repay the debt.

Sending an American operative to abet civil war in a foreign country is not something thoughtful men such as Jefferson or Madison would do lightly. Madison in an earlier letter to Eaton, then consul in Tunis, had revealed some of the administration's logic. "Although it does not accord with the general sentiments or views of the United States to intermeddle in the domestic contests of other countries, it cannot be unfair, in the prosecution of a just war, or the accomplishment of a reasonable peace, to turn to their advantage, the enmity and pretension of others against a common foe." (August 22, 1802)

Dispatching Eaton marked the first time that the U.S. government ever sent an "agent" or a "covert force" to try to help overthrow a foreign government. It would not be the last: President Madison would finance a team on a secret mission to Spanish Florida; other presidents would tinker covertly to acquire Texas and California. But it was only after World War II, with the birth of the CIA, that the United States began to launch numerous covert operations in countries all around the world: the Philippines, Iran, Guatemala, Vietnam, Cuba, Laos, Afghanistan, to name a few. These murky events—often denied for decades—generally become best known when they fail, such as John F. Kennedy's aborted effort in 1961 at the Bay of Pigs to dislodge Castro. Rarely do covert ops go as smoothly as when the CIA and British intelligence teamed up to reinstall the Shah in Iran in 1953 so as to keep the oil fields open to foreign companies and prevent—or rather postpone—an Islamic fundamentalist regime.

The people of the United States almost seem in denial about the existence of these operations. Secrecy and duplicity are regarded—perhaps wishfully—as un-American.

Eaton's mission marked the first tentative steps by a deeply idealistic government trying to wrestle with ugly problems overseas. When is secrecy justified? What about assassination? What about government deniability? Later generations of politicians and spymasters would grow far more cynical about pursuing American interests abroad.

Jefferson and Madison decided that they should show compassion for the foreign leader who would become embroiled in American plans. They knew that covert operations often fail.

Madison added to Eaton: "Should this aid be found inapplicable or thy own personal object unattainable, it will be due to the honor of the United States and to the expectations he [Hamet] will have naturally formed to treat his disappointment with much tenderness and to restore him as nearly as may be to the situation from which he was drawn." Madison concluded that in the event of a treaty with the current Bashaw

Yussef of Tripoli "perhaps it may be possible to make some stipulation formal or informal in favor of the brother."

Eaton received one key added incentive by taking this assignment. Secretary of State Madison and the auditor at Treasury apparently agreed to hold off from finalizing Eaton's disastrous accounts from Tunis; for Eaton, victory by Hamet and a regime change in Tripoli might open their eyes to his arguments.

Eaton, revived, a man with a mission, hurried to Baltimore to learn details about his new job from Secretary of the Navy Robert Smith, a forty-six-year-old civic-minded lawyer. Eaton would soon become personal friends with Smith, and later describe him "as much of a gentleman and soldier as his relation with the administration will suffer."

Eaton was told he would receive the vague title of "Navy Agent of the United States for the Several Barbary Regencies." Since the new squadron would need at least a month for outfitting and supplies, Eaton had time to squeeze in a *quick* celebratory visit home before returning to North Africa.

At least twice during their marriage, Eaton had come home in disgrace, the first time after his court-martial, and more recently after being exiled from Tunis and accused of squandering government money. Now this headstrong man was a secret agent, animated by his patriotic mission to rescue 307 American men and boys held hostage in Barbary.

CHAPTER 3 _American Slaves in Tripoli City_

I know not what will become of the crew; I suspect very few will ever see home again.

—COMMODORE EDWARD PREBLE

UNLIKE THE OFFICERS, THE crewmen of the _Philadelphia_ on the evening of Bainbridge's surrender were given nothing to eat. They spent a miserable restless night in an outdoor courtyard. William Ray wrote that every clank, every creak set fear that the guards would come to take some of them away to be auctioned. Sleeping aboard ship was cramped and warm in swaying hammocks; that night, hungry, scared men in damp clothes slept on cold hard tile.

At 8 A.M., an effeminate, wrinkled, hunched old man suddenly entered the courtyard, banged his staff three times on the ground, and ululated in victory ("bu-bu-bu-bu" it sounded to Private Ray). It was the holy marabout. Since Bashaw Yussef was convinced the marabout had cast spells to beach the _Philadelphia_, he rewarded him with a very early glimpse of the new slaves. (Yussef's faith in the man's advice ran so deep that he once borrowed pig shit from the American consulate to mix into the royal horses' feed to try to stop a fatal distemper.)

The marabout hobbled up to inspect the Americans; his face showed utter disdain for these Christian prisoners. Were some men being selected to die? To depart Tripoli? After long hesitation, the holy man picked the only black sailor of the crew and ordered him to follow. (Days later, he turned up as a royal cook.)

The rest of the prisoners were then surprised to discover that they were allowed to wander around inside the castle. After twenty-plus hours without food, they approached the Neapolitan slaves and tried to bargain for anything to eat but were told that all that was available was "Aquadiente," a very strong date palm liquor. Some of the desperate men—despite the chilly weather—traded their jackets or shirts for a bottle. Others, who had succeeded in hiding a few coins, were conned into paying four times the going rate.

The guards reherded the men into another courtyard. As the harbor guns blasted out a chest-beating huzzah of victory, Bashaw Yussef and his admiral, Murad Rais, arrived to interrogate the prisoners. The Americans observed that both men had full beards, wore turbans and billowy pants, and carried curved daggers. They soon heard Yussef speaking Arabic and Italian, but they were stunned when Murad addressed them in English with a fine Scottish brogue. Forty-two-year-old Murad Rais was born Peter Lyle in Perth, Scotland; he had a decade earlier been chief mate of an English ship, *Hampden*, but after being twice accused of embezzling, he had jumped ship in Tripoli harbor. To gain the protection of the Bashaw, he had converted to Islam the same day and had been immediately circumcised in a rushed ceremony and clothed in Barbary finery. He had taken the Moslem name of a great sixteenth-century corsair, one who had hounded the Pope's own flagship and terrorized even the Atlantic. Murad was a *rinigado*, and he eventually became admiral of Tripoli and married the Bashaw's daughter. (British records indicate that Lyle had apparently left behind a Christian wife and five children in Wapping Old Stairs in London.) He was described as a "slight" man, of "indifferent morals," with a blondish beard, a foul temper, and an above-average thirst for hard liquor. Reports of his drunken, violent behavior—such as beating servants or cursing strangers—often bobbed up in consular reports. "Hang the d-mned villain if you catch him!" William Eaton once wrote. "Give him a drumhead court martial, and just about enough time to pray God's mercy on his soul!"

Murad Rais, the former Scot and elfin Moor, conducted the interrogation. He began abruptly: "Do you think your captain is a coward or traitor?" The men in gruff unison responded, "Neither." Murad/Lyle pressed it: "Who with a frigate of forty-four guns, and three hundred men, would strike his colours to one solitary gun-boat?" According to Private Ray, some of the crewmen explained that after throwing the guns overboard, the officers decided the *Philadelphia* could not defend itself and would be surrounded and cut to pieces. Murad laughed and said there was no need to throw the guns over because the Americans had only to wait till nightfall when high tide would float the ship free.

Murad the Scot—who seemed to have already had a rum or two—ranted on about the cowardice and stupidity of Bainbridge. The admiral of Tripoli ended with the infuriating claim that the *Philadelphia* had already floated free in the harbor.

The crewmen looked at each other in disbelief. That meant if they had fought a few more hours till darkness, they almost certainly would have escaped. This was stunning news, if true.

Captain Bainbridge, who was allowed to walk on the terrace of the diplomatic house, would contend in numerous letters that the *Philadelphia* did not float free *until forty hours* after beaching. Private Ray, who talked to local sailors, disagreed.

Until now, no independent account has been available. During the early 1800s, Holland was under the dominion of Napoleon and was called République Batave. The National Archives in Amsterdam have recently yielded a long overlooked series of letters by Antoine Zuchet, consul in Tripoli for République Batave, delivering a fresh diary of events. "The sea wasn't choppy and the bottom was sandy . . . not a single cannonball of the corsairs reached [the *Philadelphia*] and no one dared approach it. What further verifies the misconduct of the Americans is that the frigate *during that same night* floated free without any rescue efforts. Panic must have blinded these people."

Zuchet, a generally fair-minded observer, concluded: "What can possibly justify not waiting till the last possible moment to surrender and not negotiating terms of surrender?"

Zuchet was surprised that Captain Bainbridge and the American officers simply didn't understand the unusual nature of Barbary warfare. In a pitched battle between the English ships of Lord Nelson and the French ships of Napoleon, sinking the other's vessels signals a great victory. But on the Barbary Coast, nationalistic rah-rah fell on deaf ears. The attackers clearly chose *not* to try to sink the *Philadelphia*. They much preferred to keep alive the hope of capturing the warship intact, along with the men and valuables aboard.

In the courtyard, Murad and Yussef now told the American prisoners they expected to convert the potent *Philadelphia* to Islam, as it were, and have it lead the Tripoli fleet. Murad immediately claimed command; Yussef, listening to the marabout's advice, planned to rename it: *Gift of Allah*.

Yussef directed questions in Italian about America's military to Murad, who in turn translated them to the crewmen. The American sailors shamelessly exaggerated. Yussef, tired of the hyperbole, asked if there were any skilled men, such as blacksmiths and carpenters, among the crew. Several men raised their hands, and Yussef informed them that if they were willing, they would be paid to work for him. The prisoners were now even more baffled as to what Barbary slavery would be like.

Murad and Yussef departed, and soon after, the 270 crewmen were marched through byways so narrow two loaded camels could barely pass abreast to the castle's main gate. They exited into the old city and were herded to a run-down warehouse, full of sacks of grain, lumber, and assorted rubbish. The overseers ordered them to haul everything outside. Just like the boatswain's mates on the ship, the overseers beat the slaggards.

Ray estimated the dimensions of their new prison to be fifty feet by twenty feet, with a twenty-five-foot-high roof. Three shafts of daylight illuminated the gloomy place, one from a small skylight and the other two from barred windows. The men soon discovered that, just like aboard ship, there wasn't enough space for all of them to lie down at once. Quick calculations reveal that of the one thousand square feet, each of the 270 prisoners would have less than four square feet in which to stand or curl up.

Finally, after twenty-six hours without food, the men were each fed one small white loaf of bread. They were then ordered to march single file into the prison so they could be counted; upon re-entering, they were instructed to doff their hats to the head jailor, Abdallah, a bushy-bearded Moor, whom the men quickly dubbed "Captain Blackbeard." Some prisoners preferred braying to hat-doffing.

The following morning and every morning afterward, the American sailors learned the new rhythm of their lives as slaves on the coast of Barbary. The overseers—from a crooked-legged kindly old Greek nicknamed Bandy to a fierce rod-swinging Tripoli native, Red-Jacket—woke the men just before dawn and quickly parceled them out for various tasks, from hauling pig iron ballast out of the stinking hold of the *Philadelphia* to the far more pleasant job of carrying a cauldron to a harem. (Ray marveled: While the women in the streets were "muffled up in blankets, which conceal their faces and shapes except one eye," the women of the harem "were fantastically wrapped in loose robes of striped silk; their arms, necks and bosoms bare, their eyelids stained round the edges with black, their hair braided, turned up . . . with a broad tinsel fillet. They had three or four rings in each ear as large in circumference as a dollar.")

Despite all the harsh tales they had heard about slavery in Barbary, they were surprised to discover that when the overseers that day couldn't find enough tasks for 270 men, the unassigned were allowed to wander around the city, so long as they returned to the prison at sundown. Christians and Jews ran taprooms, and anyone who had a coin or something of value could buy date palm liquor or some other alcoholic drink.

The second evening of slave life, a handful of sailors returned drunk to the barracks. Captain Blackbeard ordered the bastinado, that preferred North African punishment. The men's feet were twirled in the rope, their bare soles lifted and exposed, as the overseer whacked them with a date palm tree limb, about three feet long like a "walking stick . . . hard and very heavy." The next morning the punished men, who could hardly walk, were forced to do their labors while dragging twenty-pound chains at each ankle.

Hunger also remained a constant nagging annoyance. They were fed once a day, at noon. Each man, working often from sunup to sundown, received two twelve-ounce loaves of black sour bread, made of poorly ground flour chocked with unchewable stalks and chaff. And each night at lockup, the men fought in a mad scramble for floor space to sleep and often wound up sprawled all over one another. Fastidious Private Ray preferred to doze sitting up.

Over the next week, the men—running errands, doing tasks—also began to gather a sense of Tripoli. The city itself, Ray observed, rose up from a lush coastal plain of gardens and endless rows of date palms. The stone houses were cobbled together, built and rebuilt, on the ruins of preceding civilizations such as Greek and Roman; a vegetable market of squatting sellers now occupied the Triumphal Arch of Marcus Aurelius. Thick high medieval walls ringed the entire land side of the city; three heavily guarded gates opened at sunrise and closed at sunset. The bulbous domes of a handful of mosques defied the monotony of white flat-roofed terraced houses, while the minarets, where strong-voiced muezzins called the faithful to prayer, stood like exclamation points of faith. Perched at the highest point of the city overlooking the harbor, the Bashaw's walled castle enclosed a maze of salons and rooms; from the outside, the castle was a nondescript mishmash, but inside, it was ornate, with colorful tiles setting off pious calligraphy, and elaborate carpets quieting footfall.

To Western eyes, such as Ray's, Tripoli appeared like a page out of the *Arabian Nights*. Camels turned the city's flour mill. Wealthy turbaned men congregated daily at the centre-ville coffee house to smoke six-foot-long pipes and drink coffee while slaves fanned away flies. The Bashaw's dinner table was nine inches high, and he ate there sitting cross-legged. Moslem women glided like Cyclopian ghosts through the streets while (comparatively) brazen Jewish women showed both eyes and even their entire faces. Jewish men, constrained by law to wear black, were forced to walk barefoot whenever they passed the street *outside* a mosque. The slave market sold whites as well as blacks. The sounds of Arabic, Turkish, Greek, Italian, and Lingua Franca collided in the streets.

During his second week there, Ray, returning from drawing water,

passed through the main city gate when he saw a hand and a foot hanging from a wall "fresh bleeding." Ray noticed a crowd gathering and
walked over. "The object of their curiosity was a wretch with his left
hand and right foot recently amputated, faint and almost expiring . . .
the stumps had been dipped in boiling pitch." Ray failed to learn the
man's crime, but he discovered this extreme punishment was not rare.
"You will see a great number of men in Tripoli hobbling about the street
thus mutilated."

How a man reacts to his enslavement reveals much about his character. Some prisoners were meek and obsequious to the guards; others refused even to doff their caps and took a beating for it. Ray, a somewhat
despondent bookish man, was amazed by the upbeat behavior of most of
the crew. The ones forced to work repairing *Philadelphia* smuggled salt
pork back to their friends. (The meat was gnawed raw then swallowed,
and hunger made it taste "delicious.") And Ray observed that the American sailors, now slaves, "would caper, sing, jest, and look as cheerful,
many of them, as if they had been at a feast or wedding."

But when Ray soon learned details of the officers' lives in captivity,
he was infuriated. (In truth, it didn't take much to infuriate Ray.) The officers, staying at the spacious former American consulate, had an ample
diet of meat and fruits. They did not have to work. Bainbridge quickly
arranged a line of credit through the kindly Danish consul, Nicholas
Nissen, who also supplied the officers with blankets, provisions, books,
paper, ink, quills. (Few, if any, of the navy men realized that it was
William Eaton's generosity in brokering the return *at face value* of six
Danish ships captured by Tunis in 1801 that had first kindled the friendship of Denmark.)

While the officers had plenty of food and leisure time, they were
hampered in one regard. They lacked clothes, since most of their uniforms had been stolen. The foreign minister of Tripoli, in an apparent
show of sympathy, offered to find their uniforms and return them. Mohammed Dghies did in fact locate twelve trunks and he offered to deliver
them for . . . $1,500, payable over time. The officers declined. And Jew-
ish merchants also tracked down jackets and trousers and shirts, but their

prices were so "enormous," in the words of one officer, that few bothered to buy their own clothes back.

Physical comforts, helpful Danes, bottles of Madeira, however, could not wash away their frustration and disappointment over what had happened to their frigate. From the first moment of captivity, Captain William Bainbridge was tormented by his surrender. From the roof, he could see *Philadelphia*. On the very first day, he wrote an extraordinary letter to his wife in Perth Amboy, New Jersey, one that would not arrive for almost six months. While his navigational and leadership skills might be questioned, William Bainbridge here shows himself as an articulate, at times eloquent, letter writer, and a master at shaping a tale.

My Dear Susan,

> *With feelings of distress which I cannot describe, I have to inform you, that I have lost the beautiful frigate which was placed under my command, by running her a-foul of rocks, a few miles to the east of this harbour, which are not marked on any charts. After defending her as long as a ray of hope remained, I was obliged to surrender, and am now with officers and crew confined in a prison in this place.*

> *My anxiety and affliction does not arise from my confinement and deprivations in prison—these, indeed, I could bear if ten times more severe; but is caused by my absence, which may be a protracted one, from my dearly beloved Susan; and an apprehension which constantly haunts me, that I may be censured by my countrymen. These impressions, which are seldom absent from my mind, act as a corroding canker at my heart. So maddened am I sometimes by the workings of my imagination, that I cannot refrain from exclaiming that it would have been a merciful dispensation of Providence if my head had been shot off by the enemy, while our vessel lay rolling on the rocks.*

> *You now see, my beloved wife, the cause of my distress—my situation in prison is entirely supportable—I have found here kind and generous friends, such as I hope the virtuous will meet in all situations; but if my professional character be blotched—if an attempt be made to taint my honour—if I am censured, if it does not kill me, it*

would at least deprive me of the power of looking any of my race in the face, always excepting, however, my young, kind and sympathizing wife. If the world desert me, I am sure to find a welcome in her arms—in her affection, to receive the support and condolence which none others can give.

I cannot tell why I am so oppressed with apprehension—I am sure I acted according to my best judgement—my officers tell me, that my conduct was faultless—that no one indeed could have done better but this I attribute, (perhaps in my weakness) to a generous wish on their part to sustain me in my affliction.

I hope soon to hear that your health is good, and although grieved at my misfortune, are yet surrounded by dear and condoling friends, who will in some measure assuage your affliction. Perhaps, too, you will be able to tell me, that I have done injustice to my countrymen— that so far from censuring, they sympathize, and some even applaud me. God grant that this may be the case—and why should it not? The Americans are generous as they are brave. I must stop, my dear wife, for I see I am disclosing my weakness—these are the mere reveries which daily pass through my heated brain.

I beg that you will not suppose our imprisonment is attended with suffering—on the contrary, it is, as I have already assured you, quite a supportable state.

Your ever faithful and affectionate husband,

William Bainbridge

While Bainbridge tried to ward off the dark thoughts, one of the crewmen found his own situation unbearable and tried to commit suicide. Charles Rhilander, a merchant seaman from Boston, had survived shipwreck off Portugal only to be duped into boarding the *Philadelphia* with the promise of a free trip home. He had refused to enlist and swore to abandon ship at the next port; now instead he was a slave. He tried to slash his own throat but was so drunk, according to William Ray, that he inflicted "a mere scratch."

The crewmen continued their routine of hard work (building walls),

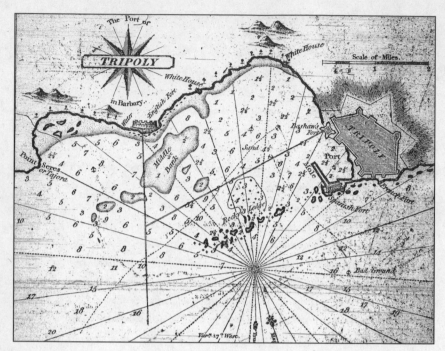

Map (circa 1802) of Tripoli harbor. No reef is marked in the lower left corner near the numeral 20 (fathoms deep) where the *Philadelphia* beached.

little food (black bread and oil), and sleeping on the floor. Everyone knew that ransom might take months or years, but they also knew that there existed a simple way for the men to become free immediately, and that was to convert to Islam. Less than three weeks into captivity, John Wilson, a quartermaster born in Sweden, decided to turn Turk, as did Thomas Prince, a seventeen-year-old from Rhode Island. Three more Americans would soon follow them.

The officials of Tripoli, who encouraged and allowed the religious conversion, took the matter seriously. Since the Koran forbids Moslems from enslaving Moslems, a conversion meant freedom from slavery. As Ray put it, "Thomas Prince was metamorphosed from a Christian to a Turk." His choice of the word *metamorphosed* was quite apt. Not only did the ritual involve words of faith and promises to perform new rituals, but also a change of clothes *and* that inevitable loss of foreskin. While circumcision is not mentioned in the Koran (as it is in the Old Testament, Genesis 17:11), the rite became sanctified by Moslem theologians as far back as the seventh and eighth centuries.

A traveler to Morocco around this time was allowed to watch a public circumcision, and his account reveals some aspects of what the five "turn-Turk" sailors must have experienced. Wrote Ali Bey,

> The boy was then brought forward, and immediately seized by the strong-armed man who . . . lifted up the gown of the child, and presented him to the operator. At this moment the music (flutes and drums) began to sound with its loudest noise; and the children, who were seated behind the ministers, started suddenly up and shouted with great vociferation to attract the attention of the victim, and by the motions of their fingers, directed his eyes to the roof of the chapel. Stunned with all the noise, the child lifted up its head; and that very moment the officiating priest laid hold of the prepuce, and pulling it with force, clipped it off with one motion of his scissors. Another immediately threw a little astringent powder on the wound, and a third covered it with lint, which he tied on by a bandage; and the child was carried away.

In the nineteenth century, a French anthropologist noted that Moslem circumcision in North Africa usually involved the removal of far more outer skin than among the Jews. (The Bedouin performed the circumcision rite at puberty and called it *es-selkh*, or "the flaying.")

No accounts reveal anything specific about the clipping of the five U.S. Navy sailors. Although the five men were nominally free and didn't bunk with the prisoners, they were not allowed to leave Tripoli. They took paying jobs in town. John Wilson, in Moslem garb, would become one of the harshest overseers of the prisoners. His former shipmates despised him. "He . . . acted as a spy carrying to the Bashaw every frivolous and a thousand false tales," wrote Ray. The first lie he told was that Captain Bainbridge was planning an escape; his next was that Bainbridge had dropped nineteen boxes of dollars and a huge sack of gold overboard just before surrendering. Bainbridge very much wanted Wilson hanged as a deserter.

Week by week the men, as they settled into their new lives as slaves, caught glimpses of Bashaw Yussef, and he was always seen in a regal pose. Pomp was de rigueur on the Barbary Coast. "His majesty was mounted on a milk white mare, sumptuously caparisoned and glittering with golden trappings," wrote Ray about November 8 when Yussef came to the prison. "At his right hand rode a huge negro . . . he was followed and attended by his Mamelukes." Slaves held colorful umbrellas over the heads of his children.

But behind the glittering facade, life was not quite as elegant and easy as the impressive-looking Bashaw tried to make it seem. Although Allah had dropped the *Philadelphia* into his lap, his treasury was almost empty, and he was threatened from within by a bloody rebellion in the southern province of Gharian and by another one led by his rival brother, Hamet, in the rich eastern provinces of Derne and Bengazi. His behavior was becoming more erratic under these strains.

The following incident, which occurred that month—recorded by Dutch consul Zuchet—reveals both the ruthlessness and the superstitiousness of the trans-Atlantic foe of Thomas Jefferson. Yussef had convinced the nation's holiest marabout to negotiate a truce in Gharian, an inland city.

> With the sacred promise of the divine marabout, the chief of the rebels was conducted before Yussef, garotted, tied at the neck by a piece of rope, a sign of his desire to repent. The Bashaw granted him immunity . . . but overwhelmed more by a desire for vengeance than respect for his own *parole*, he secretly ordered three loyal citizens of Gharian to murder the rebel chief. The marabout negotiator, informed of this assassination, knew immediately that no one other than the Bashaw would have dared attack a person whom the dervish had protected.
>
> The dervish rushed to the Bashaw and predicted all kinds of calamities and he uttered the most extreme threats and swore never again to see him. . . . The next day, the three loyal citizens arrived to

receive their reward for their mission. The Bashaw, always afraid of the holy man's threats, thought that their deaths would somehow appease him and decided these three loyal followers should be hanged; his orders were immediately executed.

The Bashaw learned he had not at all assuaged the dervish; he grew convinced that he would lose his throne. Along with his family and his entourage, he traveled a half day's march into the desert to find the dervish. Many black sheep were sacrificed to expiate his crimes. Two long hours elapsed before the Bashaw was allowed into the presence of the holy man. Finally he was permitted to see him in a room; the holy man was completely naked, his hair like snakes, making the leaps and gestures of a maniac. He delivered to him the following rude speech: "The Bashaw must respect promises made to an apostle of their Prophet, who alone is able to dethrone him and if he allows him to rule, it is because for the time he knows of no other person more fit to rule." The Bashaw kissed the hand of the dervish and returned a bit more tranquil

To prove his remorse, he said he wanted no more to do with the province of Gharian, and he abandoned all rights and revenues to the Dervish who from now on could dispose of it as he liked.

Thus, Yussef had on a whim executed four people. The giving away of the rebellious region was actually shrewd: The costs in blood and money exceeded the tax revenues. The Dutch diplomat concluded his report with another tidbit of information. The Bashaw now planned to focus on getting rid of his brother, Hamet, who had come to Derne and Bengazi to raise a civil war.

Yussef, with an army assembled and superior weapons, had every reason to believe that he would soon succeed in ousting Hamet. The one factor Yussef didn't count on was the enthusiastic support that Hamet would receive from a defiant American from Brimfield, Massachusetts.

CHAPTER 4 *Home:*

New England Roots

[I hope] the hour is not far distant when we may lie happy in the enjoyment of the fruits of our enterprises.

—WILLIAM EATON TO HIS WIFE, ELIZA

EATON RUSHED HOME from Baltimore to Brimfield, Massachusetts, to deliver news of his mission to his wife and family, and to gather up his swords, knives, pistols, rifles, ammunition, guidebooks, and anything else he might need to help Hamet overthrow Yussef's government.

Rushing home meant enduring nine days of mishaps and discomforts. Heavy winds almost capsized his sail ferryboat in New York harbor; a snowstorm slogged the stagecoach into traveling three miles per hour instead of the usual breakneck pace of six. Horse-drawn carriages, bumping over rutted roads, jolted their cramped passengers so badly that many travelers complained of a kind of seasickness. Sailboats plying the coast might move a touch faster in the event that wind and current cooperated, which they rarely did.

Forty-year-old William Eaton arrived in Brimfield and delivered his good news to his thirty-seven-year-old wife, apparently with a flourish. (A son, their first after three daughters, would be born nine months later.)

Brimfield was (and still is) a small country hill town, not far from the Connecticut border. (Today it's known for an enormous outdoor antiques fair.) It was Eaton's wife and her first husband who had caused all of them to wind up there. Fifty-one-year-old war hero General Timothy Danielson, a wealthy widower from the leading family in town, had chosen for his second wife a local beauty, eighteen-year-old Elizabeth Sykes, known as Eliza. In their six years of marriage, the May-December couple had three children: Timothy, now seventeen; Eli, fifteen; and Sarah, fourteen. The general died, leaving a wealthy widow who one year later in 1792 married Captain William Eaton in nearby Union, Connecticut.

Over the previous decade when Eaton had been consul to Tunis, he had written her passionate letters—"It is this invincible pride which has forced me from the bosom of a companion whose bosom is heaven." "I love you and long to see you." William and Eliza had three daughters: Eliza, Charlotte, and Almira. He once lovingly referred to their children as "the little pledges of our mutual pleasures." He also drew close to his stepchildren, asking them to call him "Pa" and to take the middle initial E as a token of their family bond.

William's frequent absences for career, however, were taking a toll on their marriage. Of their first dozen married years together, Eaton spent no more than a year's worth of days, snatched here or there, in the family home and conjugal bed. Almost every visit resulted in a pregnancy. Eliza, pregnant, running a household, raising little ones, rarely wrote any letters, which infuriated William. Without letters, he started to worry about his wife's fidelity. He once sent her a carnelian gemstone ring of a vestal virgin found in the ruins of Carthage. "It has undoubtedly been worn as a seal by some Roman or Carthaginian Lady many hundred years ago," he wrote. "I beg you to accept it and use it as your seal for the sake of a man who adores you—it is the emblem of <u>Chastity</u>."

Eaton, now on the first day of this visit home, informed Eliza that he had landed a midshipman's berth for her son Eli and that the fifteen- year-old would accompany him to the Mediterranean. The boy would travel the world, join the navy as an officer. Eliza was never happy to see any of her children or her husband leave home. His tone didn't allow for any discussion. He also told her that her son Tim would return to college, and he berated her for wanting to keep their young daughters home instead of sending them off to boarding school.

Eaton—with his hard opinions and passion—had trouble blending gracefully into anything: a family, an army platoon, or someone else's small town. At many times in his life, he was downright combustible. The shock waves from his explosions could rock anyone back on their heels, whether it be a preacher, a wife, a bashaw, or a president.

William Eaton was born in Woodstock, Connecticut, on February 23, 1764, into the sprawling Eaton clan of New England. Their Puritan roots stopped just shy of the *Mayflower*. William's great-great-great-grandfather John had sailed over on the *Elizabeth and Ann* in 1630, had signed the Dedham Covenant to strictly follow the Bible, and in more mundane matters, he had helped build the first footbridge across the Charles River in Boston. William was the second son in the "be-fruitful-and-multiply" family of thirteen children of Sarah and Nathaniel Eaton. Nathaniel eked out a living by farming the craggy soil and teaching school in their home during the winter months.

A neighbor said William early on showed "intellectual vigor" as well as "eccentricity." The boy hated farm work, and his father caught him time and again sneaking off to the woods, carrying a hunting rifle and a book. The family moved to Mansfield, Connecticut, when he was ten, and he quickly gained the reputation as the town daredevil. Some family members didn't expect him to outlive his childhood. After worship one Sunday, he climbed to the top of a cherry tree to halloo the passersby, fell, and was knocked out for three days before waking up with a dislocated shoulder.

One event dominated his coming-of-age years—as it did the lives of everyone else in that region during that era: the American Revolution. Eaton watched and listened as the rebellion grew from whispered indignation to loud protest, from boys throwing stones at Redcoats to men drilling militias on the commons. At that impressionable age, he soaked in the rising passions of defiance. William saw a messenger galloping to inform Mansfield about the Boston Tea Party. In the family kitchen, his father explained to him how Parliament had passed the "Coercive Acts," which closed Boston harbor and revoked the Massachusetts Bay Colony's charter until Boston repaid the English East India Company for the tea thrown overboard. The British Crown hoped to isolate the troublemakers in Boston; instead, in a parade of defiance, town after small New England town rallied to Boston's side.

In many of the colonies, such as New York, neighbors stood divided, as tens of thousands of Tory Loyalists supported England (Bainbridge's family in New Jersey, for one, was Tory), but in Eaton's Mansfield, the town was fiercely rebellious, with its local Sons of Liberty ready to pound renunciations out of any Loyalists foolhardy enough to express their opinions.

On October 10, 1774, at a town meeting, the residents of Mansfield voted to issue a forceful resolution, complaining about the "un*Constitutional* and oppressive measures which have justly alarmed British America." They then vowed, in words that still have a certain ring: "We should, as Men, as Englishmen and as Christians to the utmost of our ability, maintain and hand down to our Posterity—FREEDOM—that sacred Plant of Paradise—that Growth of Heaven—that Freedom which is the grand Constitution of intellectual Happiness, and for the enjoyment of which our Fathers exchanged their seats of Pleasure and of Plenty to encounter the numerous Savages, perils and difficulties of an inhospitable Wilderness."

To William, this wasn't rhetoric, this was their communal taunt aimed at the oppressive lords of England.

Then, the following year, the "shots heard round the world" at Lexington and Concord ignited the conflict. Eaton overheard firsthand tales of Tryon's brutal raids on the Connecticut coast, when drunken cursing British soldiers were said to have threatened colonial mothers: "Shall we bake your baby into a pie?" Eaton, at age fifteen, reckless and patriotic, ran away from home to join the Continental Army, but instead of dodging bullets, he was dodging dishrags; he found himself waiting tables for the officers in Major Dennie's Connecticut Brigade. Thomas Paine's classic line "These are the times that try men's souls" is followed by a less well-remembered sentence. "The summer soldier and the sunshine patriot will, in this crisis, shrink from the service of their country."

Young Eaton clearly wanted to be a *year-round* patriot; he reenlisted for a new three-year hitch in the Connecticut Brigade. Private Eaton drilled in 1782 before General George Washington, who would

become Eaton's demigod. (He later wrote embarrassing doggerel cele-
brating the commander in chief.) Eaton saw enough combat to receive a
leg wound, although no details have survived of the incident. When
General Washington's victorious armies were disbanded in 1783, Eaton
left as a sergeant.

The leg wound must have healed quickly because Eaton soon was
judged far and away the fastest runner at Dartmouth College. A fellow
alumnus, in a brief sketch, remembers Eaton giving a rival a "two-rod"
head start, then catching up to him, *somehow leapfrogging over him* and
beating him in the race.

From his army discharge to his graduation seven years later from
Dartmouth, a picture emerges of a poor farmer's boy, relentlessly pursuing his education despite numerous financial setbacks. The *parents* of his
classmates paid their bills. He, on the other hand, wrote to the president
of Dartmouth College, requesting permission to drop out for a semester
to earn money. "I have no resource but industry and oeconomy, have not
rec'd six shillings assistance since I have been at College, nor do I expect
any." He tutored, took odd jobs, and displayed a persistence he would
show all his life.

One time, unable to afford stagecoach fare back to school, he
plunked a staff over his shoulder with a bag of trinkets to sell and walked
175 miles from Mansfield, Connecticut, back to Hanover, New Hampshire. Dartmouth in those days graduated about thirty students a year,
and the three full-time faculty members specialized in Latin, Greek, He-
brew, rhetoric, arithmetic, philosophy, civil and ecclesiastical history, natural and political law.

One of Eaton's classmates described him as likable and a bit unusual.
"He was odd, precise in his language—full of decision—sometimes a little morose . . . suffered bouts of melancholy." (All his life, in periods of
lull, he would gravitate toward gloom and anger, while in moments of action, his bullheaded optimism would tow others along.) As for his aca-
demics, in his Classical Studies, Eaton favored tracts on war, devoting
himself to memorizing passages from Caesar's *Commentaries* or
Xenophon's *Retreat of the Ten Thousand Greeks*. Eaton also showed a certain wit . . . well, rather a certain collegiate wit circa 1790.

Always trying to make money, Eaton was hired to haul back to campus the college bell, which had been repaired. In transit, he hung it under the farm cart, and so it pealed throughout his return journey. A classmate asked: How did you feel making so much noise? "I felt <u>bell</u>-igerant," he replied. A professor scolded him for alarming the townspeople and asked, "Do you not forget your reputation as a student at the college?" Eaton answered: "I did not forget, Sir, but I am a member of the Dartmouth <u>belles</u>-lettres society." Eaton told a friend who saw him riding into town with the bell clanging: "I am resolved not to go through the world without making a noise in it."

Dartmouth granted Eaton his long-sought degree of Bachelor of Arts on August 25, 1790, and soon after he landed a job as clerk in the Vermont House of Delegates. But that position was a mere stopover on Eaton's newly chosen career path to join the military. At the State House, he met one of the first of his Federalist patrons, General Stephen R. Bradley, senator from Vermont, who used connections to gain for the twenty-six-year-old Eaton an appointment as captain in the United States Army. (In those early days, the nation was quite divided over the need for a standing federal army; Jefferson's Republicans then used to ask: Couldn't state militias handle the job without the nation running the risk of some charismatic general trying to subvert democracy?)

Around this time, Eaton joined the Freemasons, a secretive society full of high-ranking Federalists. At his swearing-in ceremony, Eaton chose a telling "makr," or personal motto: "I will spare the vanquish'd and pull down the proud." (Eaton's targets for the latter half of that motto would include: Reverend Clark Brown, Commodore Richard Morris, Captain James Barron, Bey Hamouda of Tunis, Bashaw Yussef of Tripoli, Admiral Murad Rais, Army Captain Butler, Army Colonel Gaither, diplomat Tobias Lear, and President Thomas Jefferson, among many others.) William Eaton clearly had a problem with authority.

In August 1792, the newly minted young captain in his smart blue uniform married General Danielson's wealthy young widow, honeymooned with her about a weekend or so (long enough to get Eliza pregnant), then hurried off to join his army unit. Captain Eaton's mission called for him to serve under General "Mad Anthony" Wayne on his campaign to subdue the Indian tribes in the Ohio Valley wilderness. This mission would magnify Eaton's love of country and would hone his military skills beyond reading Caesar's *Commentaries* and washing Revolutionary War dishes. Ever the daredevil, he took frequent unassigned scouting excursions on the west or "Indian Side" of the Ohio, where he saw "tracks of dear, bear and buffaloes . . . and here and there a moccasin." The spectacular grandeur of unspoiled nature—"sycamore, elm, beach, aspin, hickory, walnut, maple . . . large beyond credibility"—intoxicated Eaton with the opportunities for national expansion.

During this campaign, Eaton tasted more combat—skirmishes and ambushes—than during his three and a half years in the Continental Army. He helped oversee General Wayne's building of Fort Recovery, which stood on the site of one of the worst U.S. losses—and greatest Indian victories—in American history: General St. Clair's defeat by Chief Little Turtle when one-third of the American force of 1,748 was killed, including 57 women following the troops.

Eaton idolized forty-seven-year-old General Wayne and would model his own style of command after Wayne's. Some generals speechify then retreat to a hilltop to drain a pot of coffee. "Mad Anthony" personally led the troops. "When in danger, he is in his element," Eaton wrote, "and never shows to so good advantage as when leading a charge." As to his character, Eaton described him as "industrious, indefatigable, determined . . . not over accessible but studious to reward merit." Eaton noted flaws as well: "He is in some degree susceptible to adulation, as is every man who has an honest thirst for military fame." Tellingly, Eaton added: "He endures fatigue and hardship with a fortitude uncommon to men of his years; I have seen him in the most severe night of the winter of '94, sleep on the ground like his fellow soldier, and walk around his camp at four in the morning with the vigilance of a sentinel."

Eaton, though raised in farm country New England and refined at bookish Dartmouth, forced himself to toughen up like Wayne. "[I have] slept more than a hundred nights in that same wilderness, and as many miles back from the Ohio, on the naked, sometimes frozen ground with nothing but a cloak or a blanket, frequently in hail, rain and snow—amidst the yellings of wolves and savages."

(This training in outdoorsmanship in the American wilderness would one day save Eaton's life and the lives of his men in the Libyan desert.)

No episode of Eaton's life, however brief—his stint with Wayne lasted less than two years—could unfold without some personal conflict. Despite all his talents, Eaton's personal combativeness repeatedly undermined his chances for advancement. A superior officer, Captain Butler, gave Eaton what Eaton perceived as conflicting orders for drilling the infantry. He refused to obey certain commands on the parade ground with a thousand men and General Wayne in attendance. Captain Butler on horseback, sword raised, charged Eaton, who grabbed an espontoon, a military half-pike, and awaited the attack. General Wayne personally halted the fight, shouting, "Gentlemen, this is neither the time nor the place."

Eaton issued an immediate challenge to Butler, who in the calm of the barracks decided to submit the altercation to a committee of friends to rule on it. All was eventually patched up without bloodshed, and one senses that Captain Butler wanted no part of ten paces and firing pistols with Eaton. (Dueling was then common among officers in the American military, especially in the navy.)

Eaton soon returned to New England (and yes, he impregnated Eliza) before shipping out to his next assignment: the Georgia border, north of Spanish Florida. Sometime during his travels, Eaton met his next Federalist patron, the secretary of war, Thomas Pickering. (An ultra Federalist, Pickering would help found West Point Academy, and his disappointment with Thomas Jefferson would mount so high that he would lead the almost forgotten New England secession movement during the president's second term.)

In Georgia the main mission of the federal troops was to overawe the Indians into friendly relations with American settlers. However, sharp practices by American land speculators (and well-placed bribes by authorities in Spanish Florida wanting a buffer zone) complicated the situation. Eaton, with 160 men under his command, erected a fort at Colerain on St. Mary's River. He wrote to the secretary of war and told him that he had called it "Fort Pickering" . . . but "not however, that I might satirize a good man by erecting his monument in mud."

Eaton, scouting again and learning Indian dialects, acted as a spy for Pickering. He sent him secret reports on the dangerous situation at the border, and he named names of the worst land speculators and fearlessly included his own commanding officer on that list. Land speculation—much of it corrupt, with false property descriptions—fulfilled the financial gambling needs of many early Americans, much as the stock market does today. Fortunes hinged on the validity of a title.

Eaton said that Colonel Henry Gaither had offered him a shady land deal for 500,000 acres of dubious title at $35,000 but that he had turned it down. Eaton also pointed out that Gaither had selected a swampy, unhealthy site for the key Georgia trading post because it suited his holdings. Colonel Gaither ordered Eaton to cease making reports to Pickering; Eaton refused.

Not long afterward, Gaither had Eaton court-martialed on charges ranging from profiteering by selling jackets to the troops, to pocketing sign-up bounties, to disobeying orders and hoarding rations. A fellow officer wrote supportively to Eaton, saying: "[Gaither] is an ignorant, debauched, unprincipled, old batchelor . . . willing to sacrifice the purest character to gratify the spleen of his soul."

The five-member army jury during the two-week-long court-martial rejected most of their commanding officer's accusations, but Gaither nonetheless ordered Eaton suspended from command and jailed for a month inside Fort Pickering. More than two dozen heads of family in Georgia signed a letter in Eaton's favor, thanking him for preserving them from plunder by undisciplined federal troops. ·

Eventually bowing to pressure, Gaither allowed Eaton to go to Philadelphia to deliver the court-martial findings personally to Secretary of War Pickering. Eaton's Federalist patron immediately overturned the verdict and reinstated Eaton as captain in good standing. His entire army unit, however, was disbanded soon after.

Eaton now found himself unemployed long enough to spend almost six entire months in and around Brimfield (daughter Almira would arrive from this visit). Pickering, whom President Adams had appointed secretary of state, gave Eaton a confidential mission to investigate a conspiracy by three influential men, including Governor William Blount of the Southwest Territory, to mount a private paramilitary force of Indians and frontiersmen to drive the Spanish from Louisiana and Florida. This was almost a decade before Jefferson's Louisiana Purchase, and while many Americans hungered for the departure of the Spanish, the administration chose not to pursue it with an unlicensed band of adventurers. (Aaron Burr about a decade later would launch a similar conspiracy to drive out the Spanish and would try to recruit William Eaton.)

Eaton swiftly arrested the main New York conspirator, a controversial doctor named Nicholas Romayne (1756–1817), who helped found Columbia's prestigious College of Physicians and Surgeons. Eaton left Philadelphia on July 10, captured Dr. Romayne with all his secret papers in New York City before 3 A.M., and delivered him back to the nation's capital by 2 P.M. on July 12. Pickering was impressed.

Eaton's loyalty and efficiency were soon rewarded. Pickering in 1798 chose Eaton as the new consul to Tunis to stand up for American rights and keep tribute payments as low as possible. Unsurprisingly, Eaton, New England patriot, defier of authority, was appalled within moments of arrival on the north coast of Africa. "Can any man believe that this elevated brute," he wrote of the Dey of Algiers, "has seven kings of Europe, two republics and a continent tributary to him, when his whole naval force is not equal to two line of battle ships? It is so." Even before he arrived, former Captain Eaton preferred a military solution.

* * *

On April 30, 1804, with green leaves starting to bud on the family trees in Brimfield, Eaton—entrusted with a mission to overthrow a Barbary Coast government—said good-bye to wife Eliza. Judging from his ensuing letters, this farewell was probably quite frosty. Family finances were tight, and he warned her to keep an "exact account of all receipts." He was also taking her teenage son to go to war. His diary reveals that he was once again in possession of that Diana vestal virgin chastity ring he had given her—either she had returned it or he had reclaimed it. That spring morning, the snows of a long hard winter having finally melted, he hugged his youngest two daughters and motioned to his two stepsons to mount up for the twenty-five-mile ride to Springfield.

The forty-year-old man, along with seventeen-year-old Timothy (college bound) and fifteen-year-old Eli (soon to be midshipman), had a pleasant day-long ride, accompanied by a handful of young men from Brimfield, friends of his stepsons.

In a rare simple, happy entry in his diary, Eaton noted: "Dined together in great hilarity and parted with mutual wishes of prosperity."

After a couple of days in Springfield handling business matters, Eaton sent Timothy back home to deliver some valuables—a gold watch, a jeweled snuffbox—to Eliza to help pay off their debts and keep her Danielson properties from being sold.

William and Eli traveled to New Haven and boarded Lane's Packet to head to New York, and then they continued south on their weeklong trip to Washington City.

Once there, Eaton, in a buoyant mood, splurged $24 to buy six heavy volumes to fill the long days and nights of the transatlantic voyage. His selection reveals his tastes: Adam Smith's *Wealth of Nations, Herty's Digest of the Laws of the United States, Conductor Generalis* (British criminal law procedures), Millet's *General History, Life of Washington* (Parson Weems), *Telemachus.* While Eaton was earnestly choosing his new books, he had no idea that President Thomas Jefferson had received a letter from the Mediterranean and was now having grave second thoughts about sending Eaton on the mission.

CHAPTER 5 *Tripoli: Decatur's Raid*

I shall hazard much to destroy [the Philadelphia*]—it will undoubtedly cost us many lives but it must be done. I am surprized she was not rendered useless, before her Colours were struck.*

—COMMODORE EDWARD PREBLE (USS *CONSTITUTION*, SYRACUSE HARBOR) TO SECRETARY OF THE NAVY ROBERT SMITH, DECEMBER 10, 1803

ON CHRISTMAS MORNING, one hundred and fifty of the American prisoners, slaves on the coast of Barbary, marched through the eastern gate of the city, passed the shriveled severed hands and feet, and headed out along the shore. Rousted just before dawn, they had not yet tasted a morsel of food. Blustery forty-five-degree winds, typical Tripoli winter weather, chilled the men, clad only in long pants and a shirt; most of them walked barefoot. Veering into the low winter sun, these men, not allowed to celebrate their Christian holiday, cast long weary shadows on the sands.

Turbaned overseers, swinging sticks, hurried the men to a decrepit wreck of a boat, half buried, stuck just offshore. This was not the *Philadelphia,* then in almost perfect repair in the harbor, but some discarded merchant vessel. For marine private William Ray, this Christmas day ranked high on the list of most miserable days of his life. "It was the coldest season of the year," he wrote. "We were almost naked, and were driven into the water up to our armpits. We had to shovel sand from the bottom of the water and carry it in baskets to the banks."

Stooping over in the seawater, the Americans lugged the dripping loads up onto the beach. Over and over again.

"The chilling waves almost congealed our blood," wrote Ray. "The Turks seemed more than ordinarily cruel, exulting in our sufferings. We were kept in the water from sunrise until about two o'clock, before we had a mouthful to eat, or were permitted to sun ourselves."

The guards then ordered the kitchen-help prisoners to bring out some loaves of coarse black bread, some water, and a jug of *aqua-deut* to pass around. The men, during their break, ran in place, clapped hands, and did everything to get warm. The guards then forced them again into the water to work until sunset, when they were marched soaking wet into the glare of the setting sun back to the prison barracks. Since none of the prisoners had a change of clothes, they all slept in an inescapable dampness curled on the ground without any blankets. That night, William Ray prayed to die in his sleep "that I might never experience the horrors of another morning."

This grim routine continued, made grimmer by the handful of turn-Turks in their midst. The men found it easy to hate the five renegades who wore Moslem clothes and ordered them about. But there was another kind of villain in their midst as well, a subtler one.

Carpenter William Godby, the same man who had mishandled the scuttling of the ship, had accepted the Bashaw's offer to work for wages. (The Bashaw didn't force any of the officers to do labor; almost all refused, preferring idleness to indignity. Bainbridge and Porter opened an informal school for the midshipmen; they also put on theatrical skits to pass the time.) Godby, whether building gunboats for the Bashaw or repairing wrecks, rode the crew hard, "as cruel to our men . . . as any of the other drivers," according to Ray.

Godby earned more than $100 for his various services; one night he came back to the officers' quarters a bit tipsy and started bragging about his pay and privileges. U.S. Marine Sergeant David Irving and two others ragged Godby over helping the enemy. Insults led to blows, and the threesome beat up Godby. The following morning, the carpenter asked for an audience with the Bashaw. Turbaned Swedish turncoat John Wilson translated the man's complaints. (Aboard ship, Sergeant Irving had once ordered Wilson lashed for interfering with a sentry on duty, so Wilson no doubt magnified Irving's crimes.) The Bashaw ordered all three Americans immediately bastinadoed. "They were all most unmercifully beaten on the soles of their feet and on their posteriors," wrote Ray, "and then hampered with a huge chain at each leg and sent to prison with us where they remained for one night."

Disgusted, Private Ray observed that while the crew was "compelled to work or perish in tortures," Godby, on the other hand, "was under no compulsion but solicited the undertaking."

This distinction raises an interesting point, one close to the heart of hard men like William Eaton and Edward Preble. The generally accepted rules of warfare at the time called for enemy combatants taken in war to be held as prisoners, to be exchanged at a later date. Part of the reason the Barbary Coast pirates instilled such fear was that they refused to treat captured enemy soldiers as prisoners of war but instead called them "slaves," forcing them to work and often threatening to auction them off.

On February 15, a remarkable month-old letter from Commodore Preble arrived in Tripoli, addressed to the entire crew of sailors and marines. (Preble gave Captain Bainbridge discretion as to whether or not to deliver this letter.)

The United States was a young country founded on precedent-breaking ideas, with a strong strain of not wanting to follow the tired lead of Europe. The commodore here displays a staunch New England demand for resistance, in tones reminiscent of Consul William Eaton when he declared he would rather be "impaled" than run an errand for the Dey of Algiers.

Preble wrote:

> *Altho' the fortune of War has made you prisoners to the Bashaw of Tripoly, it has not made you his Slaves—Whether you will be Slaves or Not, depends on yourselves. Your determination not to work will be proper, and if the Bashaw should attempt compulsion by punishing you for a refusal, I shall retaliate on his Subjects which I now have and which may hereafter come into my possession.*

If you conduct [yourselves] properly, you will in due time be redeemed and restored to your friends, and entitled to receive full pay from the time of your capture to your arrival in the United States. In the mean time every proper means will be taken for clothing and keeping you as comfortable as circumstances will admit of, but should any of you voluntarily engage your services to the Enemy, and afterwards fall into the hands of your justly incensed Country Men you will undoubtedly suffer death agreeable to the laws of the United States.

You ought not to let the threats of those, into whose hands you have unfortunately fallen, intimidate you, but obstinately persist in your rights of being treated as prisoners and not as Slaves. I shall write to the Bashaw immediately and acquaint him that all those Americans who suffer themselves to be compelled to work for him, will be considered as having alienated themselves from the United States, and of course our Governm.t will not consider it under any obligations to ransom them. Behave like Americans, be firm and do not despair. The time of your liberation is not far distant.

I am with Sentiments of regard & Consideration
Your friend,

Edw.d Preble

Captain Bainbridge, on the day after receiving it, decided *not* to deliver Preble's inflammatory letter to the men. Preble's bold gambit would have certainly brought misery and perhaps even martyrdom to some, but it could have also set an extraordinary precedent on the coast of Barbary. Bainbridge promised to explain to Preble his reasons for withholding the letter but never did in writing.

That same night, February 16, the prisoners all went to sleep soon after dark. A few hours later, an overwhelming torrent of noise woke them up. Edward Preble had decided to send another message of defiance, one that Captain Bainbridge could not intercept.

"About 11 o'clock at night, we were alarmed by the screeches of women," recalled Private Ray, "the clattering of footsteps through the prison yard, and harsh loud voices of men, mingled with a thundering of cannon from the castle which made our prison tremble to its base." The former schoolteacher added: "Tumult, consternation, confusion and dismay reigned in every section of town and castle. . . . In the confusion of voices we could often hear the word 'American,' and therefore hoped that some of our countrymen were landing to liberate us; but the true cause of so much clamour we did not learn until morning." The 270 prisoners in a cramped barracks, with four square feet each to stand in, spent the night in the dark, enveloped in all that noise. They would soon learn that it was Stephen Decatur on a mission to burn the *Philadelphia*.

* * *

Just before Christmas, Lieutenant Decatur, commanding the *Enterprize* and sailing in tandem with Commodore Preble in the *Constitution*, had stumbled onto an unknown sail off the coast of Tripoli and given chase. Decatur, over a lifetime in the U.S. Navy, would rise to the rank of commodore and would become arguably the greatest living military hero in the nation for more than a decade; he would repeatedly show himself to be daring but would also reveal a bit of a prickly streak that would lead to his involvement—as principal or second—in numerous duels.

Decatur succeeded in driving the other ship, which was flying the colors of the Ottoman Empire, toward the massive 44-gun frigate *Constitution*. Per earlier agreement, both Preble and Decatur were flying the Union Jack of England. The charade continued while a boat carried the other ship's captain to the *Constitution* and while a search party examined the other ship's cargo. Once Preble was convinced the other ship, *Mastico*, was to some extent sent by the government of Tripoli, he ordered the Stars and Stripes to be raised, which caused "great confusion" on the deck of the other ship.

As so often happens with captures of this sort, especially in the Mediterranean, it was very difficult to determine the exact nationality of the at-mercy ship. She was a ketch-rigged, two-masted vessel of about 70 tons burden, carrying about 70 people: a Turkish captain, seven Greeks, and four Turks as sailors, a Turkish officer, two officers, and ten soldiers of Tripoli as passengers, and thirty young "fine" black female slaves and a dozen black slave boys shipped at Tripoli, most of whom were intended as presents for the Grand Sultan of Constantinople. The ship also carried two cannons and a cache of muskets and pistols, as well as $1,000 in foreign currency.

The captain presented papers in Arabic, which Preble couldn't read, and one brief sheet that he could decipher. "The Turkish Officer alone had a Passport from the English Vice Consul," wrote Preble in his diary, "specifying that he was to take passage in a vessel with Turkish colors but neither the name of the Vessel or Master was mentioned in it." The technicality facilitated capture, as did some eyewitness testimony.

By chance, an Italian doctor on board the *Constitution* knew several of the prisoners. He said the two Tripoli officers were of the highest rank and that they and their soldiers had participated in the capture of the *Philadelphia*. The doctor, who had been in Tripoli at the time, said that this ship's captain, a Turk, had raced out to the beached *Philadelphia* and grabbed a few souvenirs. (Lieutenant David Porter's sword and belt would later be found among the captain's possessions.)

So Preble decided to keep the prisoners and send the *Mastico* into Syracuse in Sicily, where her papers could be translated, and then eventually an admiralty court could judge whether she was a legitimate prize. (Thomas Jefferson was not at all pleased when he learned months later of Preble's aggressive action seizing a cargo intended for the Ottoman Empire, a country that had been generally friendly to U.S. interests. "I am not without hope," wrote Jefferson in that barely concealed tone of oh-god-why-do-you-surround-me-with-fools, "that Preble will have the good sense [to send off] . . . at our expense the presents destined by Tripoli for the Grand Seigneur, and intercepted by us.") International politics were muddying Preble's simple resolve.

The commodore, whose main source of information about the *Philadelphia* loss had been letters from Bainbridge, grew deeply disgusted when the Italian doctor gave him new details. He told him "it was 4 hours after the *Philadelphia* struck the ground before the gunboats came out to attack her, that for several hours they continued firing without one shot hitting the *Philadelphia*—that she struck her colors & the enemy were afraid then to come alongside until Captain B. & officers left the ship & landed; when they boarded her finding every man on board drunk & laying about the decks like dead men. The moment the officers landed they were stripped to the buff. Thus (if this information be true & we have no reason to doubt it) one of our finest frigates was deserted, without even making a defense to be expected from an American cockboat."

Ever since Preble had learned of the *Philadelphia* fiasco, he had yearned to make certain the Bashaw would never turn the frigate's three dozen guns on American targets or sell the vessel for an immense profit. It was now on Preble's storm-battered ship in the southern Mediterranean that the commodore began to refine his plan for revenge, but as a key first step, he needed to legitimize his taking of the prize ship *Mastico*.

Unable to find a trustworthy Arabic translator in Syracuse, he sailed ninety miles to Malta. After three annoying days waiting for an English rendition, the American commodore on January 20 did not receive the results he craved. He learned that the basic story of the Turkish captain and officers was true. An officer of the Bashaw of Tripoli was commissioned to pick up goods in Bengazi and then deliver those items along with twenty slaves to Constantinople; the other twenty-three slaves were to be auctioned there. The ship was registered in Crete, part of the Ottoman Empire.

This failure to discover lawful grounds for keeping the ship would severely hinder Preble's secret plans . . . since at that moment he needed a Tripolitan Trojan horse, that is, a Moslem vessel capable of sauntering into Tripoli harbor and not arousing suspicion.

Then Preble caught a break.

In Syracuse a week later, he made the acquaintance of an Italian captain, a veteran pilot, one Salvatore Catalano of Palermo, who said that he had been in Tripoli when the *Philadelphia* was captured. Catalano, under oath in the Royal Vice Admiralty, swore that this captured ship, *Mastico*, had been in Tripoli harbor and had dropped its Ottoman colors, hoisted the Tripoli flag, then loaded aboard dozens of armed men and sailed out to subdue and plunder the *Philadelphia*. This version of events amounted to far more than a few curious officers sightseeing at a capture.

Preble decided that this testimony made her an enemy vessel and a legitimate prize. "The Captain and Crew having acted hostile towards our Flag, under enemies colours, I cannot release either the vessel or them," he wrote.

Then, in an inspired moment, Commodore Preble chose the new name *Intrepid* for the *Mastico* prize, and he ordered her fitted out for a cruise. In a transaction typical of seamen's lives in the 1800s, the seven Greeks in the crew, technically slaves of the Bashaw of Tripoli, were allowed to join the crew of the USS *Constitution*. Also typical of the era, the forty-three blacks were landed at Saragosa and locked up as slaves.

On January 31, 1804, Preble gave the most memorable orders of his career to Lieutenant Decatur, who would command the *Intrepid*, and to Lieutenant Charles Stewart, who would command the 16-gun brig *Siren*. Lord Admiral Nelson, no mean judge of nautical talent, would call their mission "the most bold and daring act of the age."

Preble ordered Decatur to take the *Mastico/Intrepid* and sail directly to Tripoli, enter the harbor at night, board the *Philadelphia*, burn her, and then retreat. "On boarding the Frigate, it is probable you will meet with Resistance, it will be well in order to prevent alarm to carry all by the Sword." Obviously, silent throat-slitting would delay detection. Not wanting to take any chances that *Philadelphia* might survive again, he ordered that once the ship was on fire, the men should lug two eighteen-pounder cannons over to the main hatch, point them straight down, "and blow her bottom out." Hoping to inflict even more harm, Preble added that, if feasible, Decatur, instead of retreating aboard *Mastico/Intrepid*, should ignite that vessel as well and send her in among the Bashaw's fleet as a "fire ship" to burn as many Tripoli vessels as possible. They should then make their retreat by oar in small boats to the *Siren*.

This was an insanely daring plan, since the *Philadelphia* sat nestled deep in the Bashaw's tricky harbor, next to a dozen other armed ships under the castle's heavy batteries. Preble gave Decatur five midshipmen from the *Constitution* and told him to see whether any of the 70 crew and officers from the *Enterprize* would volunteer. This mission was strictly optional, and Preble offered to make up any shortfall in the complement of men. Instead, Decatur was engulfed by men willing to risk their lives. Too many volunteered. Lieutenant Charles Gordon, for one, sent a note to Preble begging the favor "to let no opportunity escape wherein I can render my country any service."

After months of little action, certainly the chance for danger appealed, but in addition, something about twenty-five-year-old Stephen Decatur inspired confidence and swept other men along. Tall, athletic, handsome with wavy hair, he was a strong, warm commander who maintained discipline not through fear of punishment but through loyalty and fairness. Decatur, as a young man, was credited with several daring rescues, including swan-diving from the yardarm to save a drowning sailor. He grew up in a seafaring household and was always more mechanically than academically bent. His father, Stephen Decatur Sr., veteran sea captain, was actually the first commander of the frigate *Philadelphia* after it came off the blocks.

Despite the choppy seas, the navy men were eager to depart for Tripoli. Ralph Izard Jr., a midshipman from the *Constitution* allowed to go on the mission, wrote home to his mother on February 2, 1804, from Syracuse harbor. "Before this day [next] week, I am in hopes we shall have the happiness of seeing the *Philadelphia* in flames—We shall astonish the Bashaw's weak mind with the noise of shot falling about his ears. Perhaps some 'more lucky than the rest may reach his heart' & free our countrymen from Slavery."

The *Mastico/Intrepid* and the *Siren* set sail for Tripoli, but within days, gale winds forced them off the plan. The first crack at a rendezvous on February 8 outside Tripoli harbor fell through when violent seas made it impossible for the *Siren* even to weigh anchor, and instead was forced to cut the anchor cable. "The men [were] several times knocked down by the capstan bars and several much injured," wrote an officer.

The captains of the two vessels had to tie up their sails and ride out the storm. Aboard both ships, the whistle of the winds mixed with the ominous sound of men sharpening steel.

On the night of February 16, they tried again. The *Siren* waited just outside Tripoli harbor. The *Mastico/Intrepid* slowly proceeded in the dark into the harbor and approached the *Philadelphia*. When the Tripolitan guards aboard the *Philadelphia* noticed the other ship, they took the tompions out of the cannons, making ready to fire. The American sailors crouched belowdeck, with hatchets, daggers, cutlasses at the ready. Salvatore Catalano of Palermo stood on the deck with a handful of Americans disguised as typical Mediterranean sailors. He hailed the *Philadelphia* and spoke to the guards in Lingua Franca, mixed with some Arabic from a lifetime at sea: "We come from Malta and have lost our anchors in the storm. Can we make fast to you for the night?"

The unsuspecting guards on the *Philadelphia* tossed over a thick hawser rope. The disguised crewmen pulled the two ships close to each other. The instant before the two vessels touched, Decatur gave the signal, and 60 concealed Americans sprang up, edged weapons in hand, and boarded the *Philadelphia*. "The Tripolitans on board of her were dreadfully alarmed when they found out who we were," wrote middie Ralph Izard Jr. "Poor fellows! About 20 of them were cut to pieces and the rest jumped overboard."

The ambush ended quickly, but not quickly enough. "The whooping and screaming of the enemy being boarded and defeated drew an almost instantaneous and continued fire of small arms from two xebecs lying near," wrote surgeon's mate Lewis Heerman. Now the 60 boarders raced about the long deck of the *Philadelphia*, following Decatur's detailed plan, and they climbed belowdeck to scatter combustibles. "I immediately fired her in her Store Rooms, Gun Room Cockpit and Birth [Berth] Decks," wrote Decatur in his official report. "And remained on board until the flames had issued from the Spar Deck Hatchways and Ports."

If the *Philadelphia*'s gunpowder caught fire, Decatur and others would be launched skyward. The stragglers literally outraced the flames to reboard the ketch *Mastico/Intrepid*. The mission was completed within fifteen minutes, but in the confusion, the *Philadelphia*'s shore boat, which the Americans had hoisted down, drifted away, carrying a flag of Tripoli, a trophy.

The *Philadelphia*, strategically drenched in combustibles, roared up in flames, garishly illuminating the harbor. The *Mastico/Intrepid* lay two feet downwind of this inferno. Now, a not so strange thing happened. It was as though currents of air "were rushing from every side toward the flames," pulling everything into the blaze, according to Heerman, surgeon's mate. Fire needs oxygen, and the *Mastico/Intrepid* was being sucked closer to the *Philadelphia*.

Decatur had no hope whatsoever of sailing away. The castle cannons began shooting; a ball pierced his topgallant sail.

Decatur ordered two oared boats in the water, with tow ropes tied to the *Mastico/Intrepid*. The men literally pulled for their lives, hauling the ship inches, feet, yards away from the burning *Philadelphia* and toward the mouth of the harbor. Meanwhile, as the men rowed, they heard an enormous broadside. Many of the forty-four cannons of the *Philadelphia* were mounted and loaded with powder and shot; the flames ignited the charges and sent cannonballs hurtling toward the town. The fat anchor cable soon burned through, and the vessel flambé began to drift deeper into the harbor and toward the Bashaw's castle.

The Americans pulled harder to escape. In freshening winds and choppy surf, they pulled for almost two hours before reaching the edge of the harbor. There, in the dark, they stumbled onto another boat. They were stunned and ready to attack until they realized it was the *Siren*'s boat come to help.

Sometime after midnight, the two ships rendezvoused, along with the small boats, and sailed back toward Syracuse. Not a single man was killed, only one slightly wounded. They could see *Philadelphia* burning for miles.

From the letters of the Dutch consul Antoine Zuchet, there emerges a view from inside Tripoli looking out to the harbor, and, more particularly, an intimate glimpse of how the Bashaw reacted to the raid.

"The Americans have just partially erased the shame of Captain Bainbridge's easy surrender of the frigate *Philadelphia*," wrote Zuchet to the foreign ministry in Amsterdam.

> *It was the evening on the Feb. 16 around 10 P.M. that by a very determined bravery they burned the frigate that was anchored in the middle of the harbor. Despite all efforts, the Bashaw could not slow the voracity of the flames which continued for 36 hours, leaving almost no remnant of the incineration.*
>
> *Into what fits of rage did this gallant enterprise throw the*

Bashaw; it was necessary that this prince unleash his fury on someone.
So it was the poor artillerymen [of the castle cannons] who felt the sad
effects of his rage. He beat them upside down and sideways; except
those lucky ones who dared to seek refuge in the mosques.

The Bashaw . . . who had preened over the capture and had
expected to use the frigate to lay down the law to the entire universe,
was deeply hit by this misfortune; but his political side required him to
try to hide his chagrin and he forced himself, as much as he could, to
try to show indifference over the loss, saying that it was only a
punishment of Heaven and had nothing to do with the valor of his
enemies.

The American officers who a few days prior to the burning of the
frigate had been allowed to walk in the countryside . . . were once
again confined in their prison, and their guard was doubled and
soldiers were posted on the roof of their building. Yussef, still not
satisfied with these precautions, commissioned a new prison house
built inside his castle; he ordered an iron grill placed at roof level over
the [tall] interior courtyard. He apparently fears that, in imitation of
Daedalus, they might escape by flying away upon the air.

While the officers lost promenade privileges, the crew suffered much
more in the wake of the raid. "Early in the morning and much earlier
than usual," wrote Private Ray, "our prison doors were unbolted, and the
keepers like so many fiends from the infernal regions, rushed in amongst
us, and began to beat everyone they could see, spitting in our faces and
hissing like serpents of hell. Word was soon brought that the wreck of
the frigate *Philadelphia* lay on the rocks near the round fort, almost consumed by fire. We could not suppress our emotions, nor disguise our joy
at the intelligence, which exasperated them more and more, so that every
boy we met in the streets would spit on us and pelt us with stones; our
tasks were doubled, our bread withheld, and every driver exercized cruelties tenfold more rigid and intolerable than before."

Bashaw Yussef, receiving spy reports from Malta that the U.S. Navy
was planning to bombard or even invade his city, stepped up his efforts to
fortify Tripoli's defenses. The crew of the *Philadelphia*, under the orders

of Carpenter Godby, "who to court favour from the Turks struck several of our men," worked at salvaging the metal work, bolts, spikes, copper sheathing, from the charred remains of the frigate. The Bashaw was growing desperate. Unable to locate enough lumber for shipbuilding, he ordered the town's olive presses dismantled for planks for gunboats.

About two weeks after Decatur's daring raid, the thirty American officers were marched through the prison yard of the crew on their way to their new unpleasant accommodations inside the castle. The guards ordered silence. "Captain Bainbridge, however, bid us be of good heart," recalled Private Ray, "although he looked very much dejected himself." (Bainbridge was indeed gaunt and emaciated despite access to a steady diet with meat.)

On March 4, the bodies of two of the Tripolitan soldiers who had been guarding the *Philadelphia* washed ashore. Bashaw Yussef personally examined the corpses and declared that they were so hacked up, it looked as though they had been "massacred." He ordered harsher guards assigned to the prison of the American officers. One of them took an especial dislike to Lieutenant David Porter, who set about trying to plan an escape. Captain Bainbridge for the first time tried to write a letter to Commodore Preble with portions concealed in invisible ink. "By writing with lemon juice or milk it cannot be discovered until it has been heated over the fire," he informed Preble. Bainbridge hoped to be able to give the commodore secret tips on negotiating the best deal with the Bashaw.

On March 26, a frigate with an American flag sailed into the harbor, a white flag flying. A negotiator, Richard O'Brien, former U.S. consul to Algiers, was ready to make an offer.

CHAPTER 6

Alone at Sea

WILLIAM EATON, TOWING along his fifteen-year-old stepson, Eli E. Danielson, shook off the dust of the Baltimore stagecoach and alighted in Washington City, ready to gather supplies and go on his mission. With Congress not in session, the nation's capital on May 10, 1804, appeared even emptier and odder than usual. The deep brown of springtime mud defined the place far more than marble white.

Eaton headed away from the few half-built government buildings and over to the navy yard on the eastern branch of the Potomac to drop off his stepson. Thanks to the renewed war effort, the navy yard was the one business thriving in Washington besides politics.

Although Eaton had passed more than a month visiting his family, the squadron still remained nowhere near ready to embark. This lag time allowed reports—troubling reports about Hamet—to flow to President Jefferson, who was now having serious misgivings about Eaton's mission.

Again it was a case of important news traveling fitfully. This time the slowness was due to a sleazy agent in Malta, who had hoarded letters for months. Commodore Preble, when visiting Malta in February, had discovered that the U.S. Navy agent there, Joseph Pulis—who spoke no English and who had previously served as consul for Tripoli—was stashing all the U.S. mail and not delivering it. Among three sacks, Preble found dozens of letters written by loved ones in the United States to the men imprisoned in Tripoli that Pulis, probably bribed, had refused to deliver.

Among the letters that Preble forwarded to Washington City was one written in November by a man named Richard Farquhar, a somewhat shadowy figure, a conniving Scotsman who wanted to act as point man for the United States in delivering money and supplies to the older brother, Hamet. He was volunteering to be a business agent for America. In the long letter he wrote to Jefferson, he mentioned in passing that Hamet, since "finding his Brother's troops arrive daily from Tripoli & no assistance from America," had been forced to flee from his army base in Derne in eastern Tripoli to neighboring Egypt.

Also, around this time, a report dated January 17, 1804, arrived from Commodore Preble to the secretary of the navy. He confirmed that Hamet had fled to Alexandria, but Preble tried to put a positive spin on the developments. "He has all the Arabs & a number of Mamelukes at his command, and wishes to march to the siege of Tripoly." Preble met at Malta with one of Hamet's representatives. "[Hamet] wants 50 barrels of powder Six Brass 4 & 6 pounders and Eighty or Ninety Thousand dollars. This he thinks with our assistance by sea would put him in possession of Tripoly; and I am very certain that it would in less than two months." Hamet, through his representative, promised perpetual peace with the United States, the freeing of the American hostages, and the option for the United States to hold as security the main fort in Tripoli harbor. "I wish earlier notice had been taken of this man," stated Preble.

But Jefferson reacted differently from Preble. The president interpreted both letters, according to Eaton, to mean that Hamet's chances were considerably poorer and that the aid effort would cost far more than previously thought.

"On the first symptoms of a reverse in his affairs, discouragement superceded resolution with our executive [Jefferson], and economy supplanted good faith and honesty." Jefferson decided that it was no longer a viable risk to spend $100,000 in cash and weapons (pistols, muskets, artillery, and gunpowder) to aid a fugitive in Egypt. For Eaton, it was déjà vu betrayal. Just as Captain Murray had abandoned Eaton's Hamet scheme in 1802, now Jefferson was preparing to do so in 1804.

"The auxillary supplies, now supposed in readiness, are withheld," Eaton later wrote in a long sardonic letter to a Federalist friend in Springfield, Massachusetts, also describing his meeting with top officials.

"The President becomes reserved. The Secretary of War <u>believes we had better pay tribute</u>. He said this to me in his own office. Gallatin, like a cowardly Jew, shrinks behind the counter. Mr. Madison <u>leaves everything to the Secretary of the navy department</u>."

On May 26, 1804, President Jefferson met with his Cabinet (secretary of war, secretary of the navy, secretary of treasury, secretary of state, and attorney general). Very little evidence has survived of that meeting except for a scrap of paper of the president's notes that Jefferson, in his seventies, saved while organizing his papers for posterity.

The snippet is a sort of Rosetta stone to decipher the meeting *and* Jefferson's policy. The first part of the four-sentence note states: "What terms of peace with Tripoli shall be agreed to? If successful, insist on their deliverg. up men without ransom, and reestablishing old treaty without paying anything."

Jefferson was evidently hoping that the United States would defeat Tripoli, and thereby not pay any ransom or tribute. From his other writings, it's clear he also aspired to the higher purpose of teaching the Barbary pirates and all of Europe a lesson by defying extortion. (The phrase "state-sponsored terrorism" didn't exist yet.) The president might have had another, subtler motive for wanting a military victory. The Federalist press had been needling him for years over what his critics called a moment of personal cowardice.

During the Revolutionary War, when he was governor of Virginia, Jefferson learned that an entire troop of British cavalry was headed for Monticello. With no American forces nearby, he retreated with his family via horse and carriage. "Would it be believed . . . ," Jefferson acidly wrote years later, "it has been sung in verse and said in humble prose, that forgetting the noble example of the hero of La Mancha and his windmills, I declined a combat singly against a troop, in which victory would have been so glorious?" Maybe he did crave a military victory to erase the slander.

The next part of Jefferson's cryptic little note deals with what to do in the event of defeat.

"If unsuccessful, rather than have to continue the war, agree to give

500 D[ollars] a man (having first deducted for the prisoners we have taken) and the sum in gross and tribute before agreed on."

That meant that the Cabinet was setting $500 a man as the maximum ransom—in the event of military loss—and the United States would also pay a one-time sum and an annual tribute agreed to at an earlier Cabinet meeting. Back on April 8 of 1803, reeling from ineffective efforts by the U.S. Navy, the Cabinet had set a *secret* price for buying peace. They had agreed that Madison should write a letter giving the then U.S. consul James Leander Cathcart the go-ahead to offer Tripoli $20,000 for peace and $8,000 to $10,000 a year after that. Madison, however, also emphasized: "The arrangement of the presents is to form NO PART of the PUBLIC TREATY, if a private promise and understanding can be substituted." In addition, Madison's letter to Cathcart was to be kept secret.

The administration was trumpeting its war effort while secretly being willing to pay off Tripoli. Clearly, if the United States ever paid tribute, the Jefferson administration preferred that no one know anything about it. That dreaded word *tribute* hit some raw nerve with the nation and with Jefferson. The wildly popular slogan "Millions for Defense, Not a Cent for Tribute" had originated a half decade earlier when the United States had refused to pay bribes to government officials in France; the very origin of the United States was inextricably bound to the colonists' fight against paying excessive taxes to England. Yet Jefferson—determined to avoid open-ended war expenses—was willing to pay a small amount of tribute, preferably in secret. In Jefferson's internal tug-of-war, "Economy" might yet win out over the desire to crush "lawless pirates."

The last snippet of Jefferson's note on the meeting dealt with Hamet.

"Shall anything be furnished to the Ex-Bashaw to engage cooperation? Unanimously 20,000 D[ollars]."

The Cabinet was voting—somewhat stingily—to earmark $20,000 for aid to brother Hamet. This represented a steep drop from a month earlier. To further tighten the purse strings, the navy's new commodore, Samuel Barron, would have total discretion to decide whether Hamet would receive *any* money or aid. And it still wasn't confirmed that Eaton would even be sent. The Cabinet passed along that decision to the navy.

Eaton's last hope to go on the mission rested with his new friend, Secretary of the Navy Robert Smith. Despite apparent pressure from within his own party against Eaton, Smith decided to allow him to go. Later that same day of May 26, 1804, Eaton officially received his nebulous title as "Navy Agent for the Several Barbary Regencies." He was told he would report to and receive orders from Commodore Samuel Barron, and that his salary would be $1,200 a year, with rations of a lieutenant. Despite being on the verge of financial ruin if the government ruled against his Tunis expense account, Eaton turned down his salary. With typical bravado, he stated it would be his privilege to fulfill this mission. (Mrs. Eaton's reaction to all this is unfortunately lost.)

Now comes a twist that could be mere oversight or could be the workings of the master puppeteer Jefferson. When the secretary of the navy relayed orders to Commodore Barron on June 6, he failed to mention the $20,000 that Barron was allowed to spend on Hamet. He stated the Hamet plan vaguely with little apparent enthusiasm: "With respect to the ex-Bashaw of Tripoli, we have no objection to you availing yourself of his co-operation with you against Tripoli—if you shall upon a full view of the subject after your arrival upon the Station, consider his co-operation expedient. The subject is committed entirely to your discretion. In such an event you will, it is believed, find Mr. Eaton extremely useful to you."

In other words, fact-find carefully before doling out a penny.

In contrast, Secretary of State Madison relayed the $20,000 budget for the Hamet project to the new consul general, Tobias Lear, a man who despised the Hamet plans from the start and who would never encourage Commodore Barron to spend a penny on it. That means that either Madison was paying more attention during the Cabinet meeting or Secretary Smith rates as a sloppy writer—or this is exactly how Jefferson wanted it handled.

William Eaton, a man *perhaps* on a mission, left Washington on May 31, and proceeded to travel ten days to cover the 250 miles to Hampton,

Virginia, staging station for the U.S. Navy. Eaton's succinct observation on Virginia: "multitudes of black skins and black coats, [that is] negroes and methodist preachers." His trek was enlivened by a stay at the Merry Oaks tavern in Hanover where "a charming accomplished young lady sang with excellent taste and judgement and a very agreeable voice." But soon after he arrived in Hampton and had booked himself into Jones Tavern, he discovered that his stepson Eli had fallen extremely ill aboard ship.

Eaton immediately gained permission to take Eli ashore to stay with him. "He lodged in the same chamber with myself," Eaton later wrote to his wife, "and I confess it moved my sensibility to hear him repeatedly call on 'Ma' in the melancholy reveries of sleep, nature thus confessing in its dreams what his manly soul disdained to acknowledge while waking." Ashore under care, the boy soon rallied and repeated his desire to go fight the Barbary pirates. "I believe you must be reconciled to give this son to his country and to the achievements of war." (Eli would not live to see his twentieth birthday.)

Eaton stayed in bustling Hampton and watched this magnificent fleet arrive. Hardly an armada, nonetheless this squadron of five ships would eventually link up with the six Mediterranean ships under Preble to represent the largest U.S. Navy fleet assembled under Thomas Jefferson. The State Department issued a circular to all American consuls in Europe, stating: Congress has appropriated "a million of dollars . . . to enable the President to impart such vigor to the conduct of war, as might at once change the exultation of the enemy in his casual fortune into a more proper sentiment of fear and prepare the way for a speedy and lasting peace with Barbary."

Eaton watched the barrel makers and canvas stitchers and beef salters at work; he glimpsed a seemingly endless parade of supplies readied to be loaded to feed two thousand men for several months: salt pork, peas, butter, cheese, biscuits. (On board ship, the salt meats would be delivered to the cook at sunset, he'd soak them in clean water, changing the water every four hours to cut down the salt, then boil and serve them the following noon.) In theory, each man could expect almost a pound of meat a day. Barrels of beer, rum, and water were rolled to the docks.

Closer to Eaton's heart, he saw the careful hoisting of barrels of gunpowder and stacks of muskets, pistols, and hatchets.

Eaton watched the *Congress,* under the command of Captain John Rodgers, arrive carrying thirty-six guns. A large three-masted frigate, built at Portsmouth, New Hampshire, with a crew of 340 men, the ship measured 165 feet long and 39 feet wide. On Thursday, June 13, the largest frigate, the flagship, the *President,* arrived. Its mainmast towered 100 feet, and when fitted with topmast, topgallants, and royals, the whole extended a heroic 230 feet, a fine perch for the commodore's 120-foot-long red-white-and-blue pennant. Commodore Samuel Barron's ship would carry 400 men. Next came the *Essex,* built at Salem, Massachusetts, a frigate about twenty feet shorter than the *Congress,* carrying twenty-six twelve-pound guns and ten six-pound guns. Next sailed in *John Adams,* built at Charleston, South Carolina, a bit smaller than the *Essex.* Finally the *Constellation,* similar to the *Congress.* Even in an age accustomed to the sight of fighting sail, the array of five tall three-masted ships, with their dozen-plus sails each, aroused admiration onshore.

But all was not well with this fleet, so hastily convened. Besides some shoddy supplies and even rotted woodwork, the men were more restless than your average underpaid overworked sailors. Blame the spirit of the times—American Revolution, French Revolution, the mutiny on the *Bounty* in 1789, the more bloody one on the *Hermione* in 1797—or blame one man, Robert Quinn. The word *mutiny* was whispered on the flagship *President.*

The U.S. Navy prided itself on being more humane, more fair than the British Royal Navy. Quinn disagreed. He secretly wrote a note, which he signed "UNHAPPY SLAVES," and had it delivered anonymously to Commodore Barron. Quinn stated,

The horrid usage that has been carried on in this Ship of late by the principal officers is enough to turn every Mans heart to wickedness, we are Kept on Deck from 3 O'Clock in the morning till 8 at Night [seventeen hours]. There is no regulations in any one thing, we have been on deck several days without one bit of Victuals, and durst not look for it, we cannot wash a single article for fear of being cut in two.

You expect everything done at a word, there is no allowance made for our friging [moving about] day & night, but the time will come, when you will drive all thoughts of fear out of our minds. Tyranny is the beginning of mischief . . . any Commander or Captain that had the least feeling or thought, would not suffer this horrid usage, it is almost impossible for us to live. The President is arrived to such a pitch as to exceed the Hermione, some of our friends in America & other parts shall know of this shortly and in time we hope to get redress. Death is always superior to slavery.

This rousing speech—unfortunately not Patrick Henry to King George III—roused Commodore Barron to action, no small feat. He demanded that John Rodgers find out the identity of the letter writer and then convene a court-martial and ask William Eaton to serve as judge advocate. Four efficient days later, on June 23, the court passed sentence on Quinn: "to have his Head & Eye brows shaved, branded in the forehead with the Word MUTINUS—to receive three hundred & twenty lashes, equally apportioned along side of the different ships of the Squadron, with the label MUTINEY in large capital letters inserted on its front, & to be Drum'd on shore under a Gallows in a Boat tow'd stern foremost by a boat from each ship in the Squadron as unworthy of serving under the Flag of the United States."

On Monday, June 25, at 8 A.M., a scant week from writing the letter, Quinn received the horrific punishment. In that era, punishment was always performed in public so as to deliver a cautionary spectacle, a deterrence. Sailors neatly dressed in blue and white pulled at the oars of five boats, from the stern of which five ropes extended to the stern of one boat. The tow lines like arrows pointed to Quinn and to the boatswain's mates, there to swing the cat-o'-nine-tails. A doctor and a chaplain also attended.

Aboard each of the U.S. warships, the men, with black neckerchiefs tied at their necks and long hair neatly pulled back in ponytails, stood rigidly as the whipping boat hove alongside. It is not recorded whether Quinn screamed much or little. Few men could survive such a savage beating without becoming crippled for life. Three hundred and twenty blows would have created puddles of blood when, at the end, to the sound of drums, Quinn's barely conscious body was towed ashore under the gallows.

This extended loud bloody spectacle delivered perhaps an even sterner warning to the various crews than a simple hanging.

Amid all this drum beating and misery, amid all this spread of canvas and lethalness of exposed cannon, Eaton could not help but dwell on what had happened to his mission. He stood there in civilian clothes in the middle of this sea of epauleted, gold-buttoned naval officers and blue-jacketed marines and sailors. Though allowed to board the ship heading to the Mediterranean, he had received absolutely no commitment of men, weapons, ammunition, supplies, or money. His orders to coordinate with Hamet in the overthrow of the Bashaw of Tripoli were never put into writing. The president and the Department of State had even refused to give Eaton letters of introduction to any allies; they had written nothing to Hamet.

As the flagship *President* headed out to sea on July 4, 1804, Eaton found himself *almost* shaking with anger. The administration, he believed, was close to turning his effort for Hamet into a rogue mission, or an afterthought. In a long letter to a Federalist friend, Colonel Thomas Dwight, Eaton characterized Jefferson's actions as supremely devious. He explained: If Eaton succeeded, Jefferson could draw to himself the praise for this "miracle." However, if Eaton failed, no documents existed to show the United States ever supported a mission to overthrow a foreign government. "[The president] evades the imputation of having embarked in a speculative, theoretical, chimerical project." And Eaton added: "This [blame] will fix on me."

Jefferson was in effect demanding deniability (before the term existed), and he was nullifying the reputation of the operative as irrelevant. That's standard procedure for covert ops nowadays. Eaton was outraged that Jefferson wanted both deniability and moral high ground, and so have all the presidents ever since.

In his letter, Eaton recapped his situation of going on a solo mission, with almost no support, to find an outcast in Alexandria named Hamet and then to overthrow the government of Tripoli and thereby cripple

Barbary piracy. "Though the adventure . . . be as forlorn, and, perhaps, as hazardous as any one ever successfully undertaken by an individual, I will carry it into execution or perish in the endeavour. I am convinced that our captives cannot [by any other means] be released without ransom; and, as an individual, I would rather yield my person to the danger of war in almost any shape, than my pride to the humiliation of [negotiating] with a wretched pirate for the ransom of men who are the rightful heirs of freedom."

As the coastal breezes pushed the broad canvas and the woven ropes stretched and the frigate crested eastward, Eaton also found time to write a letter to his wife, one that was warmer than his previous ones, which had been harsh and businesslike. "We are now standing to sea before a beautiful breeze and under a full crowd of sail. And in about four hours I shall lose sight of the American shore. When I shall see again this land of freedom, or whether ever, is an event yet concealed in the bosom of infinite wisdom. You may rest assured that I shall use all my exertions to render my absence as short as possible." He closed a bit more affectionately than had been his recent custom. "I wish you the smiles of Heaven, and am, Madam, with suitable consideration, yours, William Eaton."

With not a cloud in the sky, steady breezes propelled the squadron of four U.S. frigates eastward for an uneventful two weeks. Restless William Eaton was confined to the hundred or so feet of deck space on the *President*, careful never to enter the windward side of the quarter-deck unless invited by Captain Barron. Eaton channeled his excess of energy into writing vitriolic letters to Federalist comrades, critiquing Jefferson as a loather of the military. With so much time to pass, Eaton copied passages out of his various books and into his notebooks. Under "Patriotism" he wrote: "Piristratides, going with some others [as] ambassador to the King of Persia's lieutenants, was asked whether he came with a public commission or on their own to court? He answered, 'If successful, for the public; if unsuccessful, for ourselves.'" And Eaton wrote just below the quotation: "Such, I think, may be my commission to the Barbary Coast."

At 6:30 P.M., on July 11, aboard the *Congress* under Captain Rodgers, six men stood on the rope behind the main topsail yardarm, about 150 feet above the deck; they untied the points (plaited ropes) that held the topsail, when a gust of wind suddenly filled that sail. The men couldn't hold their grip; three fell into the sea and drowned, though an instantly dispatched cutter searched for them. Three crashed onto the deck, two of them died. Many of the sailors now suspected that this voyage might be jinxed.

The extraordinary run of fair weather snapped abruptly on July 21 as the ships reached Pico in the Azore Islands; for the next forty-one days—except for a dozen hours near Gibraltar—contrary winds stymied their race to join Preble at Tripoli for a combined summer campaign.

Not only did headwinds force them to tack hundreds of miles off direct course, but a dead calm set in. The surface of the Mediterranean turned to glass; the ship did not rock. On August 20, off Cape De Gat, while some men fished, William Eaton performed an experiment. He took a "Queen's Ware" plate, tied it to a log line, and lowered it into the water. He reported that the plate was clearly visible at a depth of 148 feet.

In this heat and calm on this stalled ship, William Eaton finally succeeded in gaining a private audience with Commodore Barron to advance his Hamet project. Barron, at forty-one, was Eaton's contemporary in age, but Barron hailed from Jefferson country, Hampton, Virginia. And his military career, unlike Eaton's, showed no disciplinary spikes, no major victories, just a steady climb through seniority. A calm demeanor, a demand for protocol, and a cautiousness seemed his dominant traits. He, like many fellow naval officers, showed a preoccupation with reputation.

For six shipboard weeks Eaton had refined his pitch, and he now came prepared with one dozen crisp reasons: half showing the benefits of backing Hamet and the other half showing the disadvantages of *not* backing him.

Eaton, in civilian clothes, addressed the commodore. In essence, this veteran of the United States Army was contrasting the benefits of a land attack to that of a naval bombardment. Eaton, though polite, was clearly impolitic in framing the argument that way and pitching it to a lifelong navy man.

Benefits of cooperation:

1. A land attack from the rear will cut off the Bashaw's retreat and his supply lines.

2. Dread of retaliation from more land attacks will deter the enemy from hurting the American prisoners.

3. Oppressed residents of Tripoli, seeing themselves besieged, will open the gates to their liberator.

4. Perpetual peace with no ransom is already agreed to by Hamet.

5. Aiding Hamet is a relatively inexpensive experiment.

6. The United States, through Eaton in 1802, pledged aid to Hamet and must not break its word.

The corpulent commodore, weary in the heat on the listless ship, nodded as implacable Eaton continued to make his case. Disadvantages of not cooperating:

1. Batter down the town (with naval cannon), but Yussef can always retreat.

2. U.S. prisoners can be placed on the castle walls.

3. Even in naval victory, U.S. prisoners can be carried south to the mountains.

4. Even with a new peace treaty, no guarantee Yussef will honor it.

5. Expensive in both blood and money.

6. To abandon Hamet would harm the reputation of the United States.

Commodore Barron listened intently; he was unfailingly polite and seemed sympathetic. However, he did not show his hand; he did not explicitly promise any aid. Eaton, jotting in his notebook, tried to write positively of his prospects. A slip of the pen, however, probably exposed his truer feelings. He wrote after his meeting: "If this plan succeeds (which will certainly have the full coincidence of the Commodore) and treaty should follow . . ." He no doubt intended to write "have the full *confidence* of the Commodore." But his quill slip would prove prophetic. About all he would gain was the "coincidence" of Barron.

Two days later, on Thursday at 3:30 P.M., while the commodore and the *Constellation*'s captain Hugh Campbell and Navy Agent Eaton were still dining on the *President* in the commodore's cabin, the ship, then traveling at a dull three knots, suddenly lurched hard, as if it had struck a reef. Glasses and plates clattered to the floor. The ship then seemed to jolt upward about a foot in the air, then drop back down. Several times over the next forty seconds, this unnerving foot-high jump recurred. The officers raced to the ladders to climb on deck, ordered plumb lines heaved. The odd part was that the *President* stood about seventeen miles west of Cape De Gat, well out in the Mediterranean. No one saw rocks or shoals anywhere.

The *Constellation,* about a mile away, sent over a boat to inform its captain that it had hit a rock. About a league away was a Spanish merchantman. The U.S. ships approached it and asked how she sailed. She too said she had felt a "shock." Comparing stories, they discovered that all three ships had felt the jolt at the same time, and the officers reasoned that it must have been an earthquake. At about 5 P.M., they felt a one-minute aftershock and then a milder one the next day. "The effect . . . on the ship's people was also remarkable," wrote Commodore Barron to a British diplomat at Malta. "The alarm, agitation and amazement appeared much greater than . . . had the ship been actually aground." Sailors sensed more trouble ahead.

The squadron reached the vicinity of Sardinia on September 2, 1804. For William Eaton, this island provoked in him the memory of Anna Porcile, the Italian slave girl whom he had rescued in Tunis in 1799; more germanely, he thought of her father's debt to him of $5,000. Chevalier Antonio Porcile had owed him the large sum of money for four years. Eaton could only stare longingly as they glided by; the squadron was late for its rendezvous with Preble. Summer was the best season to fight in Tripoli harbor—no dawdling for debts.

It is never easy to pin down a commodore; he is god upon the seas and indeed for a while answers to no one but God. Eaton, a very direct man, tried to pin Commodore Barron down on the issue of supplies and money. Barron, when he responded at all, tantalized Eaton with polite vagueness.

The fleet reached Malta on the evening of September 5, 1804. Malta, now under British rule, was a tiny outpost of sophisticated Europe, a strategically located oasis just far enough away from the Barbary Coast and Sicily. Gone were the days of the Catholic Knights of Malta, who, needing a mission after the Crusades, had terrorized Moslem ships and enslaved Moslems from 1530 up until 1798 when Napoleon had captured the island on his way to Egypt. The main port, La Valetta, combined the seaside charm of white sandstone houses with the cosmopolitan allure of theaters, restaurants, and gardens.

On September 6, 1804, Eaton wrote to the secretary of the navy, describing how he was confident he could succeed with Hamet, *if given supplies*. "The Commodore is not decided whether any construction of the President's instructions extends to a discretion of procuring and furnishing [supplies]." Then Eaton added: "He will probably express himself on the subject after having fixed on his plan of operation."

It was finally dawning on Eaton that Commodore Barron was not fully aboard on the Hamet project, and that, even if sympathetic, the commodore might choose a narrow interpretation of his orders and refuse to hand over any money. So, at its simplest, Eaton needed money, a solid sum to buy field artillery, muskets, pistols, and food, to pay mercenaries, and to rent camels. And Eaton's best shot, really his only shot, at that moment was the $5,000 owed him by Anna's father, the painfully courteous and constantly penniless chevalier of Sant-Antioco.

Eaton needed to pursue his money quest, but that was easier said than done. He couldn't lift a telephone or tap a telegraph key; even worse, the British medical authorities in Malta refused to let the Americans go ashore, since the U.S. frigates, in transit, had stopped a Tunisian vessel, a possible carrier of disease. They were placed in quarantine for at least seven days. (The very word *quarantine* derives from the Latin/Italian *quaranta* or *forty* as in "forty days" to make sure the ship isn't carrying some still-aborning disease.) However, letters could be exchanged and harbor boats could row nearby for some full-throated conversations.

One such boat that visited the *President* carried Richard O'Brien, the former consul to Algiers. When captain of the *Dauphin,* he had been captured by Algerian corsairs in 1785 and was kept a prisoner for ten years before being ransomed. He had courageously returned as consul, but his diplomatic style was far more pragmatic (i.e., pay something) than Eaton's fierce patriotism (pay nothing). In a comic-opera quirk, O'Brien's love life had accidentally undermined U.S. diplomacy in the region and led, albeit indirectly, to Tripoli declaring war on the United States. James L. Cathcart—the U.S. consul to Tripoli, a testy, arrogant man—had hired a young Englishwoman to be a traveling companion for his fifteen-year-old pregnant wife. A fellow traveler described the companion as "of good appearance . . . about 20 years old." Cathcart referred to her as his wife's "humble friend" and allowed her to dine at their table. The young woman, Betsy Robinson, had fled a vicious stepmother in England to come to Philadelphia to search for her only brother. Said brother, however, was gone to China, so she had taken a job. Now, after thirty-six days of sharing cabin space with the husband and wife on the trip to Tripoli, the young woman, Miss Robinson, decided that Cathcart was no gentleman, and she resolved to leave the ship at the next port, which happened to be Algiers. There, the American consul, O'Brien, knowing none of this intrigue, invited them all to dinner. In the drawing room, O'Brien asked Cathcart to escort the young lady to the table. Cathcart, furious at Betsy, declined and called her "his maid." An eyewitness reported: "The confusion, mortification and indeed distress" caused Betsy to burst out crying. The next day, she informed Cathcart that she would not proceed with them to Tripoli. "A storm arose . . . of thunder and smut," recalled this eyewitness. Cathcart called her "choice names." She said that his words proved indeed that he was not a gentleman. He called her more choice names.

When all was calm, Consul O'Brien, a forty-seven-year-old bachelor, agreed to allow her to stay in Algiers to catch a ship back to America. Cathcart, enraged, swore he would send a report to the Department of State, stating that "O'Brien had seduced his maid from him."

On March 25, 1799, about six weeks after meeting her, Richard O'Brien married Betsy Robinson. "The Lord give you many days and

<u>nights</u> of happiness," Eaton had written, congratulating him. O'Brien's good fortune further angered Cathcart against O'Brien, who was then consul general for the Barbary Coast and Cathcart's superior. O'Brien soon refused to respond to any of Cathcart's letters. All mail between the two men had to be filtered through Eaton in Tunis, a very time-consuming detour sometimes involving desert foot messengers; ultimately, Cathcart, an abrasive diplomat, took no guidance from O'Brien and little from Eaton. With little diplomatic coordination, Cathcart botched relations with the Bashaw and war with Tripoli ensued.

(For O'Brien, two daughters ensued as well, followed by a son in February 1804.)

On September 6, 1804, O'Brien sat in the boat, yelling up to Eaton. The naval agent, whose first three children were girls, joked to merchant captain O'Brien about their wives always giving birth "to a transport, not a frigate." Now he congratulated O'Brien on the recent arrival of a frigate, i.e., a fighting vessel, a son.

These two veterans of the Barbary Coast discussed many topics for an hour. O'Brien had resigned his post as consul general, and he described to Eaton his replacement, Tobias Lear, a forty-two-year-old former personal secretary to George Washington. Both men had met Lear, and neither Eaton nor O'Brien especially liked the man and his affected courtly manners. Lear had made a bad first impression on O'Brien by telling him the unlikely story that he had once turned down the position of secretary of state under Jefferson.

O'Brien told Eaton that over the past year the Jefferson administration had authorized him to offer $8,000 annual tribute to Tunis and, more important, to shell out $110,000 for peace and prisoner ransom to Tripoli. Both offers had been rejected. Eaton, in character, was appalled at the dangling of cash to extortionate sea robbers.

O'Brien passed to Eaton a sheaf of documents regarding U.S. policy in Barbary, and Eaton, as though compiling a case against Jefferson for offering to pay "tribute," copied out twelve pages. The conversation eventually shifted to Eaton's mission. The New England zealot complained that he was having a hard time securing supplies from the commodore, and he mentioned that he pinned his hopes on Anna Porcile's ransom debt to provide seed money for the mission. O'Brien said he had heard that the U.S. Navy agent Joseph Pulis had some documents involving Anna. He would look into it. The next day, the harbor rats rowed O'Brien under the *President*'s stern, where Eaton could lean out and talk to him. O'Brien handed up to Eaton a letter dated "22 Juillet, 1804" from Chevalier Antonio Porcile to His Excellency, the President of the United States.

Eaton had been chasing his money for years. When banished from Tunis, he had given last-minute instructions to the next American consul, Dr. George Davis, to refuse to allow Anna to leave the country until the debt was paid. Since that time, Eaton had learned that the French government had intervened and negotiated a $100-a-person ransom to free close to a thousand slaves from San Pietro. He didn't know whether Anna had been allowed to return last June to her homeland with the others.

Eaton, quarantined in Malta harbor, opened the copy of the letter from Count Porcile, and from the first obsequious sentence he smelled problems.

The count conveyed to Jefferson "sentiments of perfect gratitude" for the "liberation of my daughter" and for the "kindness which preserved the honor of a young lady, exposed among a ferocious people insensible to all feelings but those of violence and brutality." He thanked him for "the kind offices of this illustrious nation of the New World which excites the admiration of all Europe."

Sifting through the high-flown language, Eaton discovered that Anna had departed Tunis and was now reunited with her family in Cagliari in Sardinia. The count praised the United States for granting him "unmerited favors as great as they were unexpected." Chevalier Porcile added that he hoped that Jefferson might try to force the Bey of Tunis to restore $2,000 worth of jewels, confiscated from Anna before she departed. "The embarrassed state to which the pillage of my house has reduced my fortune compels me to be careful even of trifles."

How could a beautiful teenage girl amass those jewels while in Tunis? Very few scenarios—besides manipulating the lust of Moorish suitors—sprang to Eaton's mind. The count then offered to act as the American business agent for Sardinia.

Eaton was flabbergasted. He scribbled in his notebook: "The foregoing letter, written in barbarous French, was handed to me as an equivalent for seventeen thousand piasters of Tunis which I disbursed years ago. . . . —It is to me altogether enigmatical—I never spoke [with] the President on the subject. Yet it would seem he must have forgiven Porcile the debt and made the transaction a matter of national generosity."

Eaton thus added another perceived outrage to his list of complaints against the Jefferson administration. (Eaton would later learn that Consul George Davis had written to the Department of State asking advice on what to do with Eaton's beautiful young Italian prisoner-slave . . . should he keep her? Sell her? Let her go? Madison had replied in December of 1803: "Whatever may be Mr. Eaton's individual claims upon the Sardinian lady he ransomed, you will carefully abstain from representing either to the Regency of Tunis . . . that the United States possess any right or claim to hold her in the condition of a slave.")

Eaton had yet again been disappointed in trying to secure financing for his mission. He didn't even have time to dash off a reply (in French) to Count Porcile before Commodore Barron ordered the *President* as well as the *Constellation* to head immediately to Tripoli. Barron was taking over command of the squadron. Very soon he would have the *President, Constellation, Constitution, Argus,* and *Vixen* standing before Tripoli. Another six navy ships, the *Congress, Essex, Siren, Nautilus, Enterprize,* and the *John Adams,* roamed elsewhere in the Mediterranean and would also come under his command. "With this force," Barron's original orders stated, "it is conceived that no doubt whatever can exist of your coercing Tripoli to a Treaty upon our own Terms."

The government of the United States expected a military victory.

As Eaton and Barron were finally heading to the scene of combat, Commodore Preble was making a last-ditch effort at Tripoli to end the war. Preble's final risky gambit would sear a horrific image on the minds of some of the enslaved *Philadelphia* crew. They would see American corpses gnawed at by stray dogs.

CHAPTER 7

Yussef

BY LATE SUMMER, Commodore Preble's patience had run out. For months he had been expecting Barron and reinforcements to arrive for a final attack. Hard autumn winds would soon whip the southern Mediterranean and make close-to-shore activities too dangerous. Where was Barron?

Now, on September 2, Preble decided to attempt the death blow on his own; he ordered the men to fit out a bomb-ship, an "Infernal" in sailor slang, to be loaded with 100 barrels of gunpowder and 150 bombs. The American sailors would try to slip this volcanic intruder into the harbor at night, nestle it among the Bashaw's fleet, light a fifteen-minute fuse, then row away, their lives depending on each oar stroke.

Over the course of the previous month Preble, with a handful of navy ships, had tried (but failed) to torment the Bashaw into agreeing to a bargain-price ransom and a tribute-free peace. He had orchestrated a naval bombardment from the long guns of his frigates; he had daringly sent smaller vessels into Tripoli to board the Bashaw's gunboats. Nothing had worked well enough for victory.

Preble himself, parading on the deck of the *Constitution,* once spent 54 minutes within musket shot of the shore batteries, venturing that close to unleash broadsides on the town and the corsair fleet. This was Eaton-style attack: reckless and righteous. The shore batteries hit the *Constitution* with nineteen shots, including drilling a perfectly round hole through the mainmast, which miraculously did not topple.

On August 2, Stephen Decatur's brother James had led a gunboat into the harbor and furiously attacked a Tripolitan vessel, forcing it to surrender. In the moment of victory, James was treacherously shot. Brother Stephen became so enraged that, with only ten men, he attacked a gunboat with twenty-four scimitar-wielding defenders. While Decatur was fighting hand to hand against the Tripolitan vessel's gargantuan captain, an enemy sailor sneaked up behind him and raised his sliver-moon blade to slash Decatur. According to lore, sailor Reuben James intercepted the blow with his head, sacrificing his life to save Decatur's.

Bashaw Yussef Karamanli of Tripoli had a ringside seat for watching these battles: the terrace of his castle, which overlooked the harbor. He could hear the percussive thunder of his cannons, followed by the whoosh of cannonballs hurtling through the air. No daredevil, the Bashaw didn't take any risks with his own personal safety; he always made sure to have his marabout holy man slip a scrap of paper under his turban, a script from the Koran, which would protect him from harm. "If a Turk gets wounded or killed, it is supposed the blessed paper is too old or not placed in a proper manner," noted a Christian traveler.

At 4 A.M. on Tuesday, August 28, Preble and the other captains had begun bombarding the town, raining down *eight hundred* balls and shells in two hours. *Constitution* purser John Darby thrilled to the courage and rigid discipline of the American Navy. "The Commodore's ship when standing in and during the engagement was the most elegant sight that I ever saw; she had her tompions [cannon plugs] out, matches lit and batteries lighted up, all hands at quarters standing right in under the fort & recei.g a heavy cannonading from their Battery. . . . As soon as [Preble] got within pistol shot, he commenced firing his bow guns and immediately laid his starboard side parallel to the castle and gave them a broadside."

The cannonballs fell willy-nilly in the town, inflicting little damage on the stone buildings, but one of them almost killed the most candid diarist.

"The moment . . . the Americans started firing, I leapt from my bed in my nightshirt," wrote Dutch consul Zuchet, "by what presentiment, I don't know, and without stopping grabbed my clothes under my arm and left my bedroom. I was halfway down the stairs when a cannon hit the wall in my bedroom and skimmed along my bed to the pillow and then embedded itself in the wall opposite causing more damage . . . I would have been cut in half."

Although Preble had failed in August to coax the white flag from Tripoli, he had left the enemy a bit perplexed. Prisoner Ray wrote that the surrender of the *Philadelphia* "to one gunboat without bloodshed" had led the people of Tripoli to believe that Americans were all cowards. They were then surprised by this summer onslaught. "The Turks told us," Ray wrote, "that the Americans were all drunk, or they would not have ventured as they did, and fought so furiously."

Now, on the evening of September 2, Preble hoped to deal the deathblow and demonstrate that the United States could indeed crush Tripoli. Wrote Consul Zuchet:

> At 9 P.M. a blaze could be seen between the reefs that frame this port, as if a barrel had caught fire. An explosion was followed by a noise as though several enormous bombs had blown up simultaneously and at the same instant, the air was filled with grenades. The force of this noise was so horrific that it caused the earth to tremble for two miles around the city. At first, we didn't know what to make of it all; the next day, we were assured that it was a small boat that Commodore Preble had tried to slip into the port with the idea, possibly, of destroying all the Bashaw's sloops and gunboats, that were tucked under his castle and also to make the castle itself flip in the air. It's impossible to know how the fire got started on the boat which is here dubbed an "Infernal"; apparently it was accidentally caused by those who guided her. The Bashaw, who went to the spot where the fire was seen in order to try to figure out what had happened, saw there the hulk of the boat sunk to the bottom. The Tripolitans also retrieved 14 dead bodies, including a mutilated one, discovered willy-nilly along the border of the reefs.
>
> The Bashaw ordered all of the bodies transported to his arsenal. There, from his balcony, he amused himself by watching his people hurl curses and insults at the corpses. He wanted to share this spec-

tacle with Captain Bainbridge under the pretext of letting him see whether he recognized anyone among the dead. Bainbridge identified an officer [Richard Somers] and begged the Bashaw for permission to bury him in a grave. The request was refused. The remains of these human beings were not buried until after three days later, when the greater part of them had been devoured by dogs.

Preble had failed; Yussef Karamanli of Tripoli was still unrepentant. Zuchet, a longtime observer, felt the Bashaw was becoming even more mercurial and violent. "One never knows what to expect from a prince with such a personality as this . . . one hears of nothing but murders and the most atrocious outrages. . . . Who can feel safe after these fine exploits of his? and after he has bragged, even publicly, that there are easy ways for him to avenge himself on anyone, indeed that he can cause *accidents* to occur without it ever being attributed to him."

The United States had found a surprisingly resilient enemy in Bashaw Yussef. His knack for brutality and duplicity, while certainly a hallmark of most petty despots, amounted to something of a Karamanli family tradition. Yussef's great-grandfather, Ahmed I, in fact founded the family dynasty in 1711 through a brutal trick.

For almost two millennia, this region (Tripoli in Jefferson's day, Libya today) was juggled about by various foreign interlopers: first Greeks, then Romans, Goths, Arabian Moslems, and then, among others, neighboring Tunisians, Sicilian Normans, and Maltese knights, until finally the Turks of the vast Ottoman Empire subdued the territory in the 1550s. The Grand Sultan in Istanbul appointed a pasha (bashaw) and sent Janissaries (the Turkish elite warrior class) to maintain his grip; tribute would be squeezed out and siphoned to Istanbul.

Then came Karamanli. The leader of a small local army, Ahmed Karamanli had won a violent civil war in 1711 and claimed the throne. However, he knew his hold on power remained tenuous so long as the Turkish Janissaries still thrived and swore loyalty to the Sultan. So, pretending to crave their blessing for his rule, he invited them to a peacemaking banquet.

The turbaned Janissaries, aboard jeweled mounts, toting silver-hilted scimitars, arrived at Bashaw Ahmed's summer palace. In typical North African style, high windowless walls surrounded a central courtyard, where Ahmed, with salaams upon his lips, graciously greeted his guests. The loud thump of drums and squeal of stringed instruments, signs of a raucous party, drowned out his words of welcome. The smell of delicately spiced lamb enticed the guests inward. Each Janissary passed from the courtyard into the hallway that led to the banquet rooms. The doors shut behind them. There in the shadows lurked the Bashaw's black slaves, his loyal palace guards, who quickly strangled each Janissary and dragged away the body. More guests arrived, more corpses slid along the tiled floors. That night, three hundred Janissaries died, and Ahmed gained a lock upon power for his family that would last more than a century. He looted all the officers' homes and shrewdly shipped half the booty to Istanbul to placate the Sultan.

For the next two generations in Tripoli, succession flowed easily, and the nation thrived. Then came the three current brothers: Hassan, Hamet, and Yussef. All grew up as pampered princelings; when Hamet married a Circassian bride, the jewels laced into her hair weighed so much that they kept tipping her head backward.

In 1790—when Yussef was twenty, Hamet twenty-five, and Hassan twenty-eight—Yussef, who had already feuded with both his brothers, pulled off a deception worthy of the dynasty founder. In one act, he shamed his religion, his mother, and the sacred laws of the harem. Yussef contacted his mother in late July and told her that he wanted to reconcile with his oldest brother. Could she arrange a meeting in her apartments in the castle? The brother promised to show respect for the sanctity of the harem and arrive unarmed. She led them both to a sofa and sat between them, holding each of their hands, and she later told the sister of the English consul "that she prided herself on having at last brought them together to make peace at her side."

To seal their reconciliation, Yussef said they should swear an oath on the Koran. The eldest replied, "With all my heart." Yussef stood up and called loudly for a Koran. That was the signal. A eunuch entered and handed him two loaded pistols. His mother tried to deflect the first shot, and several of her fingers were shattered. The ball entered the eldest's side, but he grabbed a scimitar by the window, shouting at his mother, "Ah! Is this the last present you have reserved for your eldest son?"

Yussef's next shot hit Hassan in the chest, and he fell bleeding. At the sound of shots, Hassan's wife, who was eight and a half months pregnant, rushed in and sprawled herself on his body to protect it. Yussef's black slaves dragged her off by her hair and finished the assassination, firing nine more pistol balls into Hassan and then hacking and emasculating the body.

Such a wanton crime set Tripoli in an uproar. Would the elderly Bashaw punish Yussef, who had surrounded himself with a small army? Would middle brother Hamet attack Yussef? No one had the nerve to confront Yussef. The Bashaw promptly pardoned Yussef and cravenly demanded that Hamet go unarmed to ask his *younger* brother's permission to be appointed as the new rightful heir to the throne. But before leaving the castle, amid all this turmoil, Hamet fainted onto his sofa, and word of his weakness spread.

The sister of the English consul, Miss Tully, left an extraordinarily intimate memoir of her ten years in Tripoli. She describes meeting Hamet a few months after his brother's murder. The portrait is of a gracious gentleman. "His behaviour was mild, polite, and courteous . . . his manners to his family were not less affectionate and delicate than those of the most polished European." Miss Tully was at once amazed by one trait, quite unusual in a Moslem man of that era. "He converses with his wife and sister in a manner which shewed he considered them as rational beings."

Yussef, the most feared man in the nation, remained in the countryside, training an army, building allegiances among the tribes, while Hamet lived a sheltered life in the palace. His father grew so disgusted with Hamet that he cut off his allowance, and when the Jewish moneylenders refused him credit, he went politely begging loans from the foreign consuls.

Yussef readied his forces to attack to claim the throne. By his twenty-third birthday, all was in readiness; then, out of nowhere, a fleet of Turkish ships appeared in the harbor, and one Ali Bourghol, a mercenary, claimed the Sultan had appointed him the new Bashaw of Tripoli.

Within days, the aged Bashaw and his son Hamet slunk away to Tunis. Yussef remained, plotting resistance.

Ali Bourghol set about looting and pillaging the country. Soon, not a female or a Jew dared to walk the streets. The mighty fell. The favorite consort of the old Bashaw was an "immensely fat Jewess," dubbed "Queen Esther," who would tell the Bashaw stories every night at bedtime. She was described as mischievous, happy, and very rich from wielding influence at the castle. Ali Bourghol locked her up in a cell, demanding a ransom of $15,000. The woman's son arrived at the British consulate, distraught. He said the tight manacles on his mother's blubbery wrists and ankles chaining her to the dungeon wall would kill her, and he remembered once seeing oversize manacles and a long chain in the consulate's prison. Could he borrow them?

Esther was apparently huge; Miss Tully reported it took several strong men to lift her onto a donkey, and slaves always walked alongside to make sure that she didn't fall. A wry Italian traveler visiting Tripoli around this time commented: "If a camel is necessary to carry her, she is considered a superior beauty . . . any woman who cannot move without leaning on two slaves can have only modest pretensions."

Consul Tully lent the chain, and Esther's life was saved. Many of the wealthiest Jews, however, did not survive. Two brokers for the Dutch consulate were burnt to death by "slow fire."

Yussef allied himself with the ruler of Tunis and with his brother Hamet to mount a resistance against Ali Bourghol. The Jews of Tripoli helped finance the mission. The well-trained troops of Yussef and an army from Tunis attacked Tripoli. The end was swift.

"The pacha usurper [Ali Bourghol] departed as he had arrived, a pirate," stated the French consul. "He wanted to squeeze the last drop out of the sponge but the enemy was already firing bombs into the city." Bourghol began to massacre hostages, decapitated eleven Christian slaves, and even killed his own officers to take their loot; he departed around 3 A.M. on January 16, 1795, taking a French merchant ship with him. "One could compare the flight of the pacha to the end of a plague, as the aftermath was so sweet."

On January 19, Hamet and his brother Yussef entered the city triumphant; the people of Tripoli welcomed them enthusiastically "with expressions of joy as lively as sincere." The ruler of Tunis had convinced the old Bashaw to step down, and Hamet, twenty-nine years old, found himself proclaimed Bashaw of Tripoli.

He discovered the treasury empty. Ali Bourghol had stripped the palace down to the last stick of furniture. With no money to pay the army and with the Bedouin camped outside the city threatening to attack, Hamet was forced to borrow 60,000 Venetian sequins to bribe the Bedouin to leave. Hamet also begged the foreign consulates to lend him furniture, and he received, for instance, from the British: silver candlesticks and snuffers, an English sofa, some chairs, a mahogany dining table.

The English consul, Simon Lucas, was not the least bit impressed with the new ruler, Hamet. "The Bashaw Sidy Hamed, having at best a weak understanding, gave himself entirely up to his pleasures, was almost in a constant state of inebriation and consequently neglected the government. Sidy Joseph (Yussef) who is quite the opposite character of his brother neither drinks nor smokes and, having studied for some years in the school of adversity, acquired a thorough knowledge of the constitution of the government and of the disposition of his subjects, who love him almost to adoration, and had been frequently applied to in private by the principal people to salvage his country from total ruin by wresting the reins of government out of his brother's hands."

(An earlier French consul disagreed; he described Hamet as "very affable" and said most diplomats dreaded that Yussef, "sanguinary and ferocious," might one day rule.)

On June 11, Hamet invited his brother to go gazelle hunting with him in the dunes by the city. (Hamet never left the city without his brother, for fear of treachery.) Yussef accepted the invitation but after leaving with his brother, secretly doubled back, killed the gatehouse guards, and ordered the city gates shut. Cannon fire announced the betrayal.

Hamet fled. Bedouin sheiks honored the laws of hospitality but would not rally to his cause. Hamet put up no fight. Yussef offered Hamet a choice: return to Tripoli and live a retired life with his family under house arrest or take the governorship of Derne and Bengazi, rich provinces to the east. Hamet accepted the governorship, but for the time being, Yussef kept Hamet's family—his wife, Lilly Howviva, and his three sons and two daughters—as hostages. A storm forced Hamet's ship to Malta, and fearing treachery, he decided to flee to Tunis. So began the captivity of Hamet's family inside the castle of Tripoli, and Hamet's exile.

For the past nine years, Yussef had ruled Tripoli with an iron fist, establishing law and order, restoring the Jews to revive commerce, and revamping the corsair fleet to extort tribute money from European governments. He gradually repaired the castle and replenished the treasury. The French government, post-Revolution, sent him a shipload of trinkets looted from the homes of aristocrats: carpets, mirrors, chandeliers. Yussef was using a bidet as a fountain until the English consul informed him of its proper function.

Over the years, Yussef married a second wife, an African, to go along with his first wife, a cousin who at age twelve had given birth to his first child. By age twenty-one she had given birth to three sons and three daughters. His black wife had given birth to one son and two daughters.

Now, on this day in early September of 1804, Yussef was fulfilling the family tradition of ruthlessness. He encouraged his people to hurl insults at the corpses of the American sailors; he let stray dogs gnaw on their bodies. His brother Hamet's family remained hostages in the castle, scorned, disgraced. And weak wandering Hamet—on whom American hopes were pinned—was nowhere to be found. Rumor had him somewhere in Egypt.

CHAPTER 8

The Mission: Eaton Unleashed

JUST AFTER DAWN, Commodore Samuel Barron in the privacy of his cabin aboard the USS *President* off the coast of Tripoli handed a set of orders to Isaac Hull, the thirty-one-year-old captain of the brig *Argus*. William Eaton stood nearby and recorded what happened next in an entry in his notebook under the heading "Secret Verbal Orders of Commodore Barron to Captain Hull . . . in the presence of the undersigned . . . Sept. 15, 1804." Both Eaton and Hull later signed it as witnesses, and Eaton gave three additional signed copies to officers to carry home to the United States.

Eaton stated that Commodore Barron said the following to Isaac Hull.

Sir,

> The written orders I here hand you to proceed to the port of
> Alexandria or Smyrna for the purpose of convoying to Malta any
> vessels you may find there, are intended to disguise the real object of
> your expedition, which is to proceed with Mr. Eaton to Alexandria in
> search of Hamet Bashaw, the rival brother and legitimate sovereign of
> the reigning bashaw of Tripoli, and to convoy him and his suit[e] to
> Derne or such other place on the coast, as may be determined the most
> proper for co-operating with the naval force under my command. . . .
> Should Hamet Bashaw not be found at Alexandria, you have the

discretion to proceed to any other place for him, where the safety of
your ship can be, in your opinion, relied upon.

The Bashaw may be assured of the support of my squadron at
Bengazi or Derne where you are at liberty to put in, if required. And
you may assure him also that I will take the most effectual measures
with the forces under my command for co-operating with him against
the usurper, his brother, and for re-establishing him in the regency of
Tripoli.

William Eaton appeared finally to have a U.S. Navy ship ready to take him to his first destination in search of Hamet. However, conspicuously absent from Hull's "Secret Verbal Orders" was any mention of supplying arms, ammunition, or money. Barron was, in effect, approving the transporting of Hamet with naval support for Hamet's war efforts. Eaton and Captain Hull left the *President* and at 8 A.M. boarded the *Argus*, which set sail for Malta. They arrived about forty hours later at midnight on September 17.

Now Eaton had a ship, and according to his notebook entries, he fully expected to leave for Alexandria within a day or two. But he still had no money. He dashed off a furious letter to Don Antonio Porcile. He opened with no chitchat or gracious greeting but launched very abruptly with the words: "It seems you have wholly mistaken the intentions of my government in consenting to the release of your daughter Anna." Then Eaton stated he had drawn a bill of credit upon one Charles Wadsworth for the sum of $8,354 (the loan plus interest), payable on sight, "which I have no doubt you will honor." (It was a bluff for money on Eaton's part, and Wadsworth, a U.S. Navy purser, would never secure a penny from Porcile.)

Eaton, still furious over his lack of funds, also scribbled a testy note to Secretary of State Madison, also beginning abruptly: "I request you will be pleased to cause information to be forwarded from the office of the Department of State by which I may learn on what grounds . . . the Chevalier Antonio Porcile of Sardinia founds a pretext of having been released." Eaton explained that he had been counting on that money to finance his mission. "This disappointment embarrasses exceedingly my calculations as I am left wholly without an alternative."

Exasperated, Eaton also complained in a letter that same day to the secretary of the navy. "Commodore Barron declares he does not consider any construction of the President's instructions will justify him in furnishing cash, arms and ammunition to Hamet Bashaw." Eaton added that therefore, he must reluctantly retract his offer not to receive a salary and requested that he be allowed to draw his salary of $1,200 to use to finance his mission.

Eaton's frustrations boiled over. "I cannot forbear expressing on this occasion the extreme mortification I suffer on account of my actual situation: destitute of commission, rank or command, and I may say, consideration or credit."

Despite the hurdles, Eaton remained doggedly determined. "I hope to be organizing my saracen militia on the plains of Libya in order to bring them to the field next spring," he wrote to a Federalist friend, Colonel Dwight. And he stated if Barron denied him supplies, "I shall be compelled to draw on the enthusiasm of Arabian resentment . . . as a substitute for field artillery, muskets, cartridges, flints, &c.—for I shall not abandon the object."

On the verge of embarking, Eaton suddenly lost his one firm asset: the ship. The *Argus*, after a season in the winds off Tripoli, needed caulking, but no caulkers were to be found at Malta or Syracuse. So it was decided that the *Argus* would sail to Messina in northern Sicily. Also, Commodore Preble (the honorific title *Commodore* remains for life) wanted to return eight gunboats and two bomb boats he had borrowed from the King of Sicily. Preble requested that Hull in the *Argus* shepherd the loaner vessels to Messina. Since the caulking would take a week or more, the senior officers decided instead of sailing and killing time in Messina, they would take a little excursion to see Europe's tallest active volcano.

So crusty Preble, dashing Decatur, dogged Eaton, along with two other officers and an Italian hotel owner, set out to make a 95-mile overland trip from Syracuse to Messina.

Eaton, who wanted nothing but to train an army, found himself on a weeklong tourist trip on horseback on deeply rutted Sicilian roads. Preble complained about "the torments sufferd from bugs & fleas." Eaton barely mentioned seeing Mount Etna, Europe's largest active volcano, and spending a day at Lake Lentina. The edgy patriot made a bad tourist. This New Englander's longest comments dwell on being appalled by the poverty and ignorance of the deeply religious Catholic peasants. He notes that only a revolution will rid the region of the wealthy priest class. More cheerfully, he mentioned enjoying the company of Edward Preble and Stephen Decatur, and he clearly spent hours asking them about their summer naval exploits off Tripoli. (A month later, Eaton would produce a 10,000-word account of naval operations, complete with a swashbuckling version of Decatur wrestling the huge Turkish captain.) The friendship with Preble, which would continue until Preble's death, would prove crucial to Eaton's pursuit of his mission.

With an early morning start on October 5, the group reached Messina, an ancient port on the tip of Sicily, and found that the navy ships had already arrived for repairs.

For a week, the harbor echoed with the sound of hammers striking the flat-bladed caulking irons to drive the tar-laced hemp deeper into the seams. Once the Italian shipworkers had embedded caulk in every seam of the brig, the hull had to be sanded smooth, then painted. No fires were allowed anywhere near the oil-based paints.

Finally, on October 18, the *Argus* was ready to sail from Messina to Syracuse, where she would spend a few days while Preble handled government business there. Syracuse, an impoverished port full of devout peasants and one glorious opera house, often served as unofficial U.S. Navy headquarters for the region. Eaton, with no ability to order *anyone*, had no choice but to go along and wait.

Some of the wait was endured by visiting the British consul, Mr. Gould Leckie, who happened to have as a houseguest an odd pudgy entertaining young man, Samuel Taylor Coleridge. The poet had already written "Rime of the Ancient Mariner" and "Kubla Khan," but there's no indication that the Americans knew they were in the presence of literary genius. None of the Americans were impressed enough to include

Coleridge in their notes or letters; the poet, however, would mine material, especially from Decatur and Eaton.

Coleridge, about to celebrate—morbidly, of course—his thirty-second birthday, had come to Malta and Sicily to escape his dejection back in England over marrying the wrong woman. "He has had no calamities in his life," once commented Robert Southey, the poet laureate, "so contrives to be miserable over trifles." Perhaps that assessment was a bit harsh. Coleridge was deeply in love with one Sara Hutchinson, and he was still fighting a constant battle against opium addiction. He arrived in Malta earlier that year in May 1804, eventually took up lodgings in the palace headquarters of the British governor, Sir Alexander Ball, and by October was well into a three-month "working holiday" in Syracuse. He clearly wasn't winning all his battles with opium. In one Syracuse diary entry, he devotes an entire page to describing how he could squint his eyes while looking through mosquito netting and make the "french grass-like streaks" on the netting multiply and multiply on the walls.

On October 19, Eaton and the Americans chatted with Coleridge, who made notes about a story that Decatur told. A pair of Indians had ambushed an American family, massacring everyone except two boys, aged nine and eleven, whom they hauled toward the Indian camp. They passed the first night on the road, and the Indians drank a bottle of wine and fell asleep. The older brother "put up the musket to the ear of one of the Indians, & placed his little brother there to fire it off." The eldest stood with a tomahawk over the other Indian. He gave the signal; the little one pulled the trigger, the elder swung the hatchet, and the boys escaped. Orphaned, they went to sea and wound up serving under Decatur, who told Coleridge he would introduce him to his cabin boys.

The following day, Coleridge marked his birthday. "O Sorrow & Shame! I am not worthy to live—Two & thirty years.—& this last year above all others!—I have done nothing."

Eaton—ever trying to do something—dashed off an angry letter to an *old* enemy, Captain Alexander Murray, the one who had refused years earlier to aid him in the Hamet scheme. In the United States, Murray had apparently refused to fight a duel with him, so Eaton informed him that he would take his revenge another way. He would write a history of the Tripolitan War that would expose Murray as a coward and a hypocrite.

Preble finished his business, and the *Argus*, carrying Preble and Eaton, traveled to Malta, arriving on the night of October 23. The port of La Valette boasts one of the finest natural deep-draft harbors in the world, running inland almost two miles, with the city on a high spit of land. The harbor throat, or entrance, a mere four hundred yards wide, is flanked by huge batteries of cannons. The land surrounding the harbor is steep enough "that the largest ships of war might ride out the stormiest weather almost without a cable," according to an American officer. The city, built on a hill, contained streets so nearly vertical that steps had to be carved into the stone. The sun glinted blindingly off the white freestone houses.

British quarantine rules, which required seven days' wait for all ships coming from Sicily, kept restless Eaton on board ship in the harbor. He took the time to read the logbooks to help him on his history of the naval war. He planned to write of Preble's heroics, which would glow in sharp contrast to the laziness and cowardliness of Eaton's enemies, Murray and Morris; each word of praise would be a dagger to Murray.

Eaton, after all the waiting and forced sightseeing, expected to leave any day for Alexandria when Commodore Barron suddenly decided on October 27 to dispatch the *Argus* to go look for the ships on blockade duty: *Congress, Constellation,* and *Nautilus*. Barron had received news of a severe gale off Tripoli and wanted the *Argus* to check for damage and replace any ships, if necessary. Eaton's mission clearly rated bottom end.

To make matters worse, Eaton discovered that Barron was deathly ill and growing almost incapable of making decisions. Barron had already spent ten days onshore in Syracuse trying to recuperate; he had tried reboarding his ship, but he only grew worse from what was described as "an affection of the liver." The commodore who, when well, had been vague and polite toward Eaton, was now so ill that he could hardly think straight. Eaton, never the most politic one, didn't hesitate to write the truth to the secretary of the navy: "The physician Doc Cutbush has been under serious apprehensions of alarm . . . and I much fear [Barron] will not have sufficient health to transact the business . . . preparatory to the operations of next spring and summer."

At the end of October, Eaton found himself marooned in Quarantine Harbor of Malta, awaiting the return of the *Argus*. He grew even crabbier; everything set him off. He scribbled in his notebook that while his friend Dr. Babbit, also of Massachusetts, had just received a letter from home dated September 2, he hadn't received any mail from his wife, Eliza. He had sent her a letter "three months and six days" earlier. "Why not an answer!" he fumed in thick letters, etched deep in his notebook.

Around this time, Colonel Tobias Lear, the new U.S. negotiator for Barbary, who with his wife had taken up residence in civilized Malta, paid Eaton a visit. Lear had himself rowed out in the harbor. The meeting was conducted politely, but the men barely concealed their disdain for each other. From Eaton's point of view, Tobias Lear during that visit looked Eaton in the eye and told him a bald-faced lie. He informed Eaton that Thomas Jefferson refused to grant permission to American consuls to pay tribute to Tunis or Tripoli. (Eaton, of course, had already read the April 9, 1803, State Department document allowing tribute, preferably in secret.) "I have sometimes seen a brave man dishonest," wrote Eaton of Lear. "I never saw a coward who was not."

Eaton and his new friend, Preble, were Old Testament on the subject of tribute: The honor of the United States forbids the payment of a single penny to Barbary pirates in public *or in private*. He railed in his notebook that Jefferson was abandoning his own position on not paying tribute. "To secure himself in the secrecy of this disgraceful secession, [he] has placed his entire confidence, relative to our diplomatic intercourse with Barbary, in a man who has only distinguished himself for his treachery to the memory of the man who created him." Eaton was referring to the fact that Lear had jumped from working for George Washington, the king of Federalists, to serving Jefferson, arch-Republican. Eaton, in quarantined limbo, seemed to be becoming a bit unhinged. Across the top of one page, he scrawled: "Colonel Lear not to be leered at!!!" Three exclamation points and two underlines.

Lear, for his part, despised Eaton as well. On November 3, Lear in a long letter to Secretary of State Madison wrote a starkly negative assessment of Eaton's mission. "I presume the co-operation of the Brother of the Bashaw of Tripoli will not be attempted. Our force is thought sufficient to compel him to terms without this aid, and in any event it is very doubtful whether he has it in his power . . . to render us service. He is now in Egypt, driven by his brother from Derne, where it is presumed he might have made a stand, had he been a man of any force or influence; which from the best accounts I can collect, he is not.

"Indeed I sh^d place much more confidence in the continuance of a peace with the present Bashaw, if he is well beaten into it, then I sh^d have with the other, if he should be placed on the throne by our means."

Lear stated that the *rumors* of the U.S. naval preparations appeared sufficient to bring Tripoli around to negotiate a reasonable peace treaty and ransom. He mentioned that in the spring he expected to accompany Commodore Barron to Tripoli "in order to be ready to treat with the Bashaw, if he sh^d desire it; before we make an attack." (The word *before* would prove ominous and prophetic.)

Barron and Eaton shuttled back to Syracuse, a place where lax quarantine laws would allow them to go ashore immediately. Barron's health was worsening, and he wrote to Captain Rodgers, "I am so unwell to Day that I can scarcely write at all & am totally unfit for business—God knows how it will End."

Finally on November 10, Commodore Samuel Barron, thinking himself near death, issued orders for the *Argus,* which had returned, to carry William Eaton to Alexandria. Barron had received some favorable reports about Hamet and, *amazingly,* he ordered Captain Isaac Hull to aid Eaton. "If on your Arrival in Egypt it should be found necessary to furnish any Stores, Ammunition, Money &c. for the Service of the United States, in aid of the intended cooperation with Hamet Bashaw, you are hereby Authorized to supply Mr. Eaton with such as may be wanted for that purpose, and can be spared from the *Argus* Brig under your command—taking his receipts & Vouchers for the same."

A smallpox outbreak on board the *Argus* slowed the ship's exit. Some of the sick men were ferried ashore to a new U.S. hospital that Barron was setting up in Syracuse. The ship was fumigated, and at least one sailor, Lev White, died and was consigned to the deep outside the harbor. (No one wanted the corpse to wash ashore.)

Eaton took advantage of these last few days prior to leaving. First off, he made certain *not* to visit Barron, who was recuperating at a country house outside the city. Eaton must have been afraid that Barron would change his mind. Eaton's excuse, given a week later to Barron, is completely unconvincing. Eaton, who had trekked alone on the Mississippi and scouted Indians in Spanish Florida, claimed that he tried twice to find Barron's house in the evening and once missed to the left and the next time to the right.

One can easily find another motive in Eaton's avoiding Barron. The New Englanders, Eaton and Preble, were cooking up a little end run to help Eaton embark on his mission. Preble wrote a note to Sir Alexander Ball, British governor of Malta, a longtime friend. (Preble had once commissioned a fishing boat to be built in America and sent to Ball by way of thanks for help in fighting Tripoli.) Preble wrote: "Commodore Barron being at present sick in the Country for the recovery of his health, I take the liberty of introducing to your Excellency William Eaton, U.S. Naval Agent for the Barbary States. Mr. Eaton is going to Egypt, and wishes to obtain a letter of introduction from your Excellency to some Character of your acquaintance. Any attentions you may please to shew Mr. Eaton will be considered as an additional obligation to the many which your Excellency has already confered on . . . Edward Preble."

With the French long evacuated from Egypt and the eastern Mediterranean, Sir Alexander Ball ranked among the most powerful men in the entire region.

Eaton, ready to depart early the following day, took one last crack at landing more supplies. (He clearly knew that the brig *Argus*—carrying 140 men—held but a trifle of what he needed, and that Barron might be delirious.) Eaton yet again wrote to the secretary of the navy.

On further consideration, I am of opinion that the supplies of arms
and ammunition to be loaned [to Hamet] should come out from

America. . . . Brass field pieces, well mounted, and excellent french
arms are ready at Springfield; and as this place is in the vicinity of
Hartford, the best port in the United States, perhaps for shipping salt
beef, 14 brass 4p^{rs} and 500 or a thousand stands of arms may be sent
out from thence. Good muskets, powder, flints and balls; and suitable
ammunition for the Artillery will be necessary.

Presuming on the perseverance of Government in the resolution
you expressed to me last spring of furnishing those supplies I shall
assure the Bashaw accordingly. If cash be loaned him, of which he will
stand in need, I desire it may be under regulations which will impose
no responsibility on me.

That last sentence marks one of the very few times that William
Eaton showed any fiscal caution. At that moment, under tentative calculations at the Treasury Department, Eaton owed the enormous sum of
$40,000 to the government. He clearly did not want this new mission to
put him any further in debt; in fact, his best chance for escaping ruin was
a victory by Hamet, which would halo Eaton.

At 6 A.M., on Wednesday, November 14, Captain Hull maneuvered
the *Argus* out of Syracuse harbor. Eaton had agreed to take two men
along on his mission: Richard Farquhar, the scheming entrepreneur with
vague ties to Hamet, and Salvatore Busatile, consul in Sicily for Hamet
Bashaw. Farquhar had been sending on average a letter a month to a U.S.
official or even to the president himself, offering to help in aiding
Hamet. His last letter of October 15, this one to Commodore Barron,
reported that a famine in Derne and Bengazi made those two locales ripe
for insurrection. He offered to arrange for boats or supplies or men. On
board ship, he told William Eaton that his spies had told him that a vessel bound with grain for Tunis was actually smuggling arms and ammunition to Tripoli. The other passenger, Busatile, had written a letter to
Commodore Barron on November 1 stating that Hamet had a large army
ready to cooperate with the United States, that the United States could
keep all prize ships captured, and that he would pledge eternal peace
with the United States and would repay any money advanced to him.

More immediately, the consul relayed that Hamet requested $10,000 to enable him to capture Derne and Bengazi. (Barron never replied; around this time, Midshipman William Allen in a letter home wondered whether Barron would live or not.)

At midnight on November 15, the *Argus* traveled south and arrived in Malta. British quarantine officers refused to let the men of *Argus* ashore, and the following day, Eaton sent Preble's note, via shore boat, to Sir Alexander Ball. The secretary receiving the note was apparently none other than Coleridge, who had returned to Malta to take a low-level post in Ball's administration. Later that same day, Eaton received Ball's prompt reply, which included letters of introduction to Samuel Briggs, British consul at Alexandria, and to Major E. Missett, the British "resident" (agent) at Cairo.

The letters from Ball were quite strongly worded. "I request that you will assist him and do everything in your power to accelerate his business. Every attention paid him will be considered an obligation conferred on   your very faithful and obedient servant Alex. Jn.o Ball." Ball also sent a package and some letters for Eaton to deliver to these civil servants in Egypt.

So while Eaton had not a single piece of paper from his own government authorizing him or even introducing him undercover, he carried two very potent British letters. These two documents—and the welcome they engendered—would facilitate and without a doubt save Eaton's mission on several occasions.

Eaton had one last matter to attend to before the *Argus* departed from Malta. "It was my intention to have taken along with us Hamet Bashaw's Consul," he wrote to Barron, "but on a closer inspection, I don't like him. There is too much wood about his head and beef about his ankles either to advance or retreat handsomely."

One last American visitor was rowed alongside the *Argus*. Tobias Lear had received a letter from Commodore Barron informing him that Eaton was going forth on his mission. Barron had downplayed the level of his commitment, telling Lear that the mission was mainly for fact-finding and providing transportation for Hamet to take Derne and Bengazi. By way of lukewarm endorsement, Barron concluded in a note: "It may have a good effect on his brother, it cannot, I think, have an ill one." Barron promised to inform Lear before taking any "ultimate measures."

Saturday evening, Tobias Lear neared the *Argus*. The two men spoke. Whatever Eaton said did not change Lear's opinions. "I am not at all sanguine in the expectation of ultimate good," he quickly wrote to Barron.

The *Argus* weighed anchor and headed east, smack into a gale off Crete. They had to reef the sails and wait it out. Perhaps it was appropriate that Eaton sailed in the *Argus*; was he not like the mythic Jason who sought the Golden Fleece? Eaton's quest—though without dragons—often seemed equally daunting. Eaton, aboard the pitching vessel, concentrated hard to copy letters into his notebooks. He now had a ship, a sympathetic navy captain with a small amount of supplies and cash available, and two British letters of introduction. All he needed to do was to find Hamet.

CHAPTER 9

Hunting Hamet in Egypt

ON NOVEMBER 25 around noon, an American sailor aloft aboard the *Argus* spotted far off a faint vertical line, a kind of reddish finger extending skyward. He was pretty certain that he was looking at "Pompey's Pillar," the first Egyptian landmark visible from sea. He called down to the officers on deck. William Eaton, hearing the words, was eager to get onshore.

Captain Hull, however, approached this coastline near Alexandria very gingerly. The nearby silty outpourings of the Nile create hard-to-read inbound currents and shifting shoals. Perhaps no other supremely successful trading mecca, certainly not one that once brokered goods from Africa, Asia, and Europe, was ever saddled with such a rotten approach. The famed Lighthouse of Alexandria, the Pharos, which has received centuries of favorable press for its mechanical ingenuity and architecture, served a supremely utilitarian function: It helped guide ships in on this dangerous low-lying coast.

Circa 1804, lookouts had to make do with Pompey's Pillar, which stands 70 feet tall and 8 feet thick, a *solid* piece of polished red granite. (This column, despite its snappy nickname, was built in the fourth century A.D. and has nothing to do with the Roman general Pompey.)

At 4:30 P.M., Hull ordered a salute gun fired and flags hoisted to call for a pilot to sail out to help navigate the *Argus* into the harbor. No one ashore noticed, or no one cared. The sun set, and the *Argus*, taking no chances, tacked offshore, at times hauling up the mainsail. William Eaton waited.

At dawn Hull eased shoreward; this time he hoisted an English flag after firing his salute. An Arab pilot, at the bidding of the English consul, sailed out. That afternoon the man guided the *Argus* westward through the tricky opening of the Old Harbor of Alexandria. Sea-savvy travelers routinely complained that the casual dumping of ballast by lazy crews threatened to choke off access. The challenging entry, in any case, allowed harbor pilots to increase their fees. A Turkish man-of-war and six frigates were anchored there, dwarfing the brig *Argus*.

The pilot, at the bidding of the British consul, informed Captain Hull that the Turks, then nominal masters of Egypt, would answer any salute, gun for gun. So the Americans reeled off the steady, very respectful seventeen-gun salute, which was reciprocated by the Ottoman admiral. (Eaton, ever ready to perceive a slight, counted thirteen in response; Captain Hull counted seventeen.) The sailors of the *Argus* dropped anchors fore and aft in six and a half fathoms of water. Soon after, the English consul, Samuel Briggs, and a handful of Turkish port officials were rowed out and they climbed aboard.

Pleasantries completed, Eaton presented his letter of introduction from British governor Ball of Malta to Mr. Briggs. This single piece of paper pried open entrée into Egypt, a country then wracked by civil war and paralyzed in many locales by conflicting factions. Before leaving the ship, Briggs, an energetic merchant in addition to being British consul, promised to provide any assistance within his power.

All the foreign consulates raised a polite flag of welcome to greet the Americans, except for the houses of France and Spain, then at war with England. (In fact, the French consul, a Piedmontese named Signore Drovetti, would soon start spreading rumors about Eaton that would endanger Eaton's life . . . and then later Drovetti's, once Eaton learned about it.)

That night, Consul Briggs sent a letter to the Americans, informing Eaton and Captain Hull that at 9:30 A.M. the following morning both the governor of Alexandria and the Turkish admiral would receive visits from them. Briggs and his interpreter would meet them at Admiral's Wharf and accompany them.

The standard means of ground transportation in Alexandria in 1805 was by short ass. "They make use of asses to go from one part of town to another, of so small a size, that the legs of the rider nearly touch the ground," noted Ali Bey, a seasoned traveler. Ali Bey measured several at thirty-nine inches tall to the crown of head, and he suggested this beast, which ate one quarter as much as a horse, might revolutionize the daily commute to work in Europe. He added that the animals stepped very lively and that bystanders enjoyed the pratfall comedy of the slipper-wearing overseers, skiddering around trying to keep up with their asses.

William Eaton did not want to be a tourist; he wanted to pursue his mission, but even he couldn't help but notice the decline of one of the greatest countries in the history of mankind.

Egypt lay in ruins. Egypt's ruins lay in ruins. The latest conquerors—French, British, Turkish, Albanian, Mameluke—cherry-picked the antiquities; their unpaid troops vandalized and pillaged; the local elite still borrowed Roman columns for their summer homes. The magnificent baths of Cleopatra have disappeared under the rubble. Caliph Omar burned the Library long ago. The desert sands encroach the remaining gardens. A gorgeous metropolis that once housed one million people and dictated fashion and literature to the world has disappeared. Now, a mongrel town of 5,000 Arabs, Copts, Italians, Turks, Albanians, Jews remains on the same geographical spot; the inhabitants bark out a bastardized version of Arabic and Lingua Franca. It is said most Alexandrines speak four languages—badly. And to think that Cleopatra once defined a "barbarian" as an uncouth person who could not speak a neat version of Greek.

Alexandria was no longer a Grande Dame.

The governor and admiral, the two most powerful Turks in Alexandria, welcomed the Americans—Hull in a naval uniform and Eaton in civilian clothes. Slaves sprinkled them with rose water and served them coffee. The elaborate ceremony dragged on. The instant that Eaton was able to corner Briggs for a moment of privacy, he asked him about the location of Hamet, the exiled prince of Tripoli. Briggs replied that he had heard vague reports that Hamet was somewhere *far to the south*, hundreds of miles below Cairo, and that to see him, Eaton would need to pass through battlefields filled with fierce Mamelukes and other armies waging war there.

The news gut-punched Eaton. It was one tiny step short of Hamet being dead or in prison. Egypt lay in tatters, checkerboarded by rival factions. Some of the Turkish troops had disintegrated into roving bands of Albanian deserters; several large armies of Mamelukes and rival Mamelukes and Turkish mercenaries under Muhammad Ali each claimed huge swaths of territory; predatory Bedouin tribes preyed on any stragglers, while French and English soldiers—stranded from preceding wars—joined up here and there. To reach Hamet, Eaton must sidestep the warring camps, survive the outlaws, and do so with a force of a dozen men. It would be days before he would even understand the loyalties of all the various groups.

Everyone—from Consul Briggs to the governor of Alexandria—strongly advised against going south at this time. Eaton decided to leave immediately.

He also decided that to facilitate this excursion south, his small group would masquerade as American officers on vacation, eager to see the wonders of Egypt. As for Eaton himself, he would impersonate an American general on holiday. (Indeed, a week later, he would allow himself to be introduced as "General" to a high-ranking Turkish official.)

To complete his charade, he donned a military uniform of some sort, perhaps his old U.S. Army captain's uniform.

Eaton prepared to head out the following morning.

Since no soldiers had been assigned to him in advance, he now had to ask permission of Captain Hull to borrow a few able-bodied recruits. Eaton convinced Hull to loan him four officers: Lieutenant Joshua Blake of the navy, Lieutenant Presley O'Bannon of the marines, Midshipman George Washington Mann, and Eli E. Danielson, Eaton's own stepson. The choice of Lieutenant O'Bannon proved especially fortunate; O'Bannon was a high-spirited brave Kentuckian who carried his fiddle everywhere and had been known to lighten things up with "Hogs in the Cornfield." Eaton also took Richard Farquhar, the wily entrepreneur who was trying to hitch his fortune to Hamet, and Seid Selim, a Janissary. A man named Ali would serve as the group's dragoman, a kind of all-purpose tour guide, a fixer.

Eaton rushed to borrow some weapons and ammunition from the *Argus* and to purchase supplies on credit in Alexandria and have them all toted aboard the boat he hired to go to Rosetta. With typical energy, Eaton was ready to leave that same day, November 28, but the winds conspired against him. To increase his odds of finding Hamet, he sent a messenger ahead by camel to look for the ex-Bashaw. Finally, on November 30, Eaton with seventeen men playacting as a tourist party headed east along the coast in moderately favorable wind.

The trip from Alexandria upriver to Cairo, a famed route along the Nile, is a surprisingly difficult journey. First, Eaton would need to weather thirty miles east along the African coast to reach the dangerous waters where the inbound Mediterranean batters against the outbound Nile. Past there, he would head south a ways then change from a coastal vessel to a boat more suited to upriver Nile travel, which sometimes required sailors to hop ashore and haul them forward. These were the natural dangers and difficulties; add to this that the area south of Rosetta was a lawless zone infested by Bedouins and by bands of Albanian deserters from the Turkish Army.

That first afternoon, they reached Aboukir Bay (Abu Qir) on the coast, the site of one of the world's most famous naval battles. On August 1, 1798, Admiral Nelson had wiped out the entire French fleet there, stranding Napoleon and his conquering army amid the pyramids.

The Americans skirted to the far end of Aboukir around 4 P.M., and the ship's captain decided that too little daylight remained to risk crossing the bar of the Nile. While the sailors fished for mullet, Eaton, acting the tourist, decided to go ashore to visit the fields where the French had fought a land battle against the British invading army. "The battlegrounds there," wrote Eaton, "we found still covered with human Skeletons." He walked amid the bones and later called them "ghastly monuments of the savage influence of avarice and ambition."

He returned to his vessel and, with the American flag flying, embarked early in the morning for the Nile. Around midday, they reached the rough Boghase, the entrance bar of the Nile. "The billows are generally very strong," wrote one traveler. "For it is a bank of sand, against which the waters of the Nile beat with prodigious force. Ships find very little water; and the straits which are passable shift constantly, so that there is a boat stationed upon the bar to indicate the passage. It requires ten minutes to cross it and boats hardly ever pass over it without touching the sand three or four times."

In crossing the bar, Eaton experienced one of the most amazing transformations of landscape on the face of the earth, going from the sandy brininess of the coast to the lushness of the Nile. Travelers have compared this transit to moving into a kind of dream world. The water shifts color from Mediterranean blue to Nile red. The voyager begins to see verdant fields, rice plantations, palm trees, orange groves. The air hangs heavy with scent; suddenly dozens of vibrant-hued species of birds wheel above. Eaton entered the Nile at 1 P.M.

Around 2:30 P.M. a large Union Jack came into view. The barge of the British Rosetta consulate with Union Jack awnings approached. Word had already reached them via foot messenger of Eaton's impending visit, and they came to greet him. Eaton and Lieutenant Blake boarded the large British vessel for the half hour remaining to reach Rosetta.

Each minute heading south, Eaton became more impressed by the fertileness of the Nile delta. Rosetta served as the stopover point for travelers switching from a seacoast vessel to a Nile boat. The Arabs called the town "Rashid," and it was one of the more beautiful and prosperous places in all Egypt, with ambitious gardens, groves of orange and lemon trees, and smart five-story brick houses. An Albanian governor, with a force of three hundred Albanians, kept the town safe for the Turks.

Major Missett, the British resident agent at Cairo, greeted Eaton at the Rosetta landing. (Missett had abandoned Cairo to avoid the conflict raging there.) Eaton handed him a letter of introduction. The two men quickly found they enjoyed each other's company. "You will find in Major Missett all that can be comprized in the term of a Gentleman, with the frankness of an old soldier," wrote Eaton to Captain Hull.

Also greeting him was Doctor Mendrici, whom Eaton had met in Tunis. Mendrici, family physician to the Bey, had often shared secrets with Eaton, and Mendrici, like Eaton, had been eventually banished from Tunis. Mendrici's offense, Eaton described somewhat cryptically, was "possessing dispositions congenial to the interests of the Bey's wife." The good doctor had thrived since, and was now chief physician to the highest ranking man in Egypt—Viceroy Ahmet Pacha—and also on call to the British consulate. Eaton was thrilled to see Mendrici, who spoke Lingua Franca and Arabic and knew Hamet from Tunis.

The Americans stayed in the British consular house in Rosetta. Although Eaton found the surroundings magnificent, he wanted to head south immediately to Cairo and continue his hunt for Hamet. Unfortunately, the fast of Ramadan began that night, and a religious sheik traveling with a huge entourage had commandeered all the Nile boats in Rosetta. Eaton found himself with two days to kill before another boat would arrive. He spent the time with Major Missett, both lamenting the lack of port and Madeira. Missett filled Eaton in on the warring factions and complex political situation roiling Egypt. If attacked, Eaton might at least have a glimmer of understanding of the adversaries involved.

The Turks and Mamelukes had uneasily shared control of Egypt for almost three hundred years, from 1517 to the French invasion of 1798. Despite being fellow Moslems, the Turks amounted also to foreign invaders. To Westerners, the Mamelukes were an odd class of warrior-slaves to comprehend. They originated when the Turks bought Greek Orthodox Christian slaves, often fair-skinned, from regions of Georgia or Circassia, trained them in military arts, then freed them and converted them to Islam to act as an elite corps of Mamelukes. Over time, these warriors tired of their subservient role and seized control of Egypt, and developed great houses of Mameluke beys. Since generations of Mamelukes were handpicking the slaves that would refill their ranks, the Mamelukes were often strikingly handsome and athletic. They wore extremely baggy trousers (which would reach the chin if pulled up), a large sash, and yellow stockings and slippers. They always went about heavily armed with at least a curved scimitar and two pistols, and roamed the country, exacting taxes and inflicting justice.

Napoleon changed all that; he invaded in 1798, claiming he had the blessing of the Ottoman Empire to free Egypt from the oppression of the Mamelukes. His victory crumbled when Nelson left him ship-less, but the French ruled for a couple of years before British forces teamed up with the Turks to drive them out. (On December 2, while Eaton was chatting with Major Missett, Napoleon was crowning himself emperor in Notre Dame in Paris.)

The British Army eventually departed also, and by 1804 Egypt was a lawless mess. The Sultan in Istanbul appointed a pacha who in theory ruled all of Egypt but in reality controlled mainly the north near Alexandria. The Turks had used Albanian troops under a commander named Muhammad Ali, but he had branched out and claimed Cairo for himself. Bands of Albanian deserters raped and pillaged outside the main cities. And the Mameluke beys, having hired all the local Arab tribes, controlled Upper Egypt (i.e., south of Cairo), where Hamet had taken refuge. Further complicating matters, there were twenty-four Mameluke beys, and many of them hated one another. At that moment, the Turkish forces of mostly Albanian troops (with a few leftover Frenchmen) were attacking the Mamelukes south of Cairo. Further stirring the pot, diehard enemies England and France were sending spies to various camps, trying to align themselves with the eventual winner . . . whoever that might be.

As Eaton understated it in a later report to the secretary of the navy: "The interior of this country being in a state of general revolt renders traveling somewhat dangerous." The current main threats: Albanian deserters "who restrained by no discipline ravage and murder" and Bedouin tribes "who prey on the defenseless."

After two days together, Eaton decided to reveal his entire Hamet mission to Major Missett, and the British officer insisted that the consulate's heavily armed boat accompany Eaton to Cairo. Missett also found a trusty courier to try to deliver another message to Hamet.

Eaton hired a *marche,* a smallish boat with triangular sails and a small cabin built onto the deck. The larger British vessel, with its canopy flags, had two swivel guns mounted. Each craft carried about a dozen men armed with muskets, pistols, and sabers.

Cairo lies 115 miles upstream from Rosetta. They embarked at 3 P.M.

on December 4, passing innumerable little villages, watching a timeless agrarian scene unfold along the shores. Egyptian women toiled in the fields guiding plows pulled by donkeys. Their faces were covered, but suprisingly their breasts were sometimes exposed, as their head-to-toe garment featured long side slits allowing free arm movement for farmwork and easy access for nursing. (Exposing the face was considered more scandalous: A traveler once observed a group of women, when surprised by marauders, flinging their dresses up over their heads to remain modest.)

The following day, headwinds caused the parties to disembark. Eaton succinctly noted "inhabitants oppressed and miserable." He dined in a garden near a village called Fuor. The villagers along the Nile sometimes supplemented their incomes nicely from boats delayed heading upriver. "In many of the villages are women for the convenience of strangers, a part of whose profits is paid to the government," wrote William Browne, who passed that way about a decade earlier. He added somewhat oddly: "I didn't notice that the nature of their calling created any external levity or indecency of behavior."

While Eaton made no mention of visiting any brothels, he did find time during his stay at Fuor to put on a shooting exhibition for the locals. Consul O'Brien's nickname for Eaton had been "Captain Rifle." Eaton placed an orange in front of a large tree and paced off a hundred feet. A crowd of peasants gathered. With their rusty muskets, they knew they'd be lucky even to hit the tree. Eaton raised his rifle to his shoulder and squeezed the trigger. His shot smacked the orange, which spun in the dust. He reloaded and hit the pulpy target again. His third shot split the orange in half and "astonished the inhabitants."

Thanks to tow ropes and some decent wind, Eaton and company made some progress up the Nile, but again on the following day they were forced to go ashore. Eaton walked around the village of Sabour, which resembled a ghost town. Two days earlier, a troop of five hundred Albanian deserters had consumed or destroyed nearly everything of value. Torched buildings teetered next to piles of rotten food. The villagers told the Americans that the Albanian banditti appeared headed eastward toward the Damian branch of the Nile, but they warned that a

Bedouin tribe was still prowling the area, lingering about four miles to the south. They said they prayed for the return of the English to bring some law and order.

Eaton, his stepson, and the others reboarded their vessels and headed south. From the vantage point of the midriver railing, they saw a group of mounted Arabs swoop down upon a village's herd of camels, buffalo, and cattle and drive off a half dozen animals. The terrified villagers did nothing but shriek and offered no resistance. "The Arab camp were within half a league [of our boats] but the fire we raised from our fowling pieces upon the vast numbers of pigeons and other small fowl in its environs must have deterred them from attempting to examine our baggage," Eaton wrote. The expression "examine our baggage" shows his dry wit returning; it's as though each moment of danger revives him, draining away some of the bile of inaction.

At 6 P.M. the British and American vessels reached Bulac, the port town serving Cairo. They had successfully avoided the Albanian banditti and the Bedouin marauders, but as they came to anchor, a Turkish boat full of armed men and officers approached. Eaton's dragoman and his Maltese servant, nicknamed "Lewis," began the parley for permission to pass into the harbor. The loud gutturals, commonplace in Arabic, grew louder and more guttural. Lewis, a wily, resourceful man but hotheaded, grew more agitated. The Turks insulted this servant of a Christian. Lewis fired his musket into the water just ahead of the Turkish boat. Would the Turks open fire? Eaton and the British Captain Vincent made elaborate gestures for calm. The irate Turks, swords in hand, boarded. Eaton and Captain Vincent offered apologies and, with some coins backing their words, placated the Turks.

William Eaton now found himself one step closer to Hamet, having reached the great metropolis of Cairo, the jumping-off point for travelers heading farther south on the Nile. Eaton noted in letters that he expected to remain ten days at most in Cairo; he instead would find himself stranded there a bit longer.

Cairo—with a ployglot population of 400,000 Egyptians, Turks, Albanians, Syrians, Copts, Jews—once thrived as the hub for commerce from two continents. Twice yearly from time immemorial, massive African caravans of thousands of slaves, spices, and ivory arrived from the desert. In earlier centuries the wealth of the Indies, which by Eaton's time passed by ship around the tip of Africa, used to go through Red Sea ports and then be siphoned through Cairo. To Turks and Egyptians, Cairo was "Misr el Kahira," "Misr, without an equal, Misr, the mother of the World." To monomaniacal Eaton, it was the gateway to Hamet.

Cairo was nominally under the control of Ahmet Pacha, a viceroy appointed by the grand sultan. Actually, Muhammad Ali, a cunning thirty-five-year-old Albanian warlord with an army, controlled the city; however, it suited Ali's interests for the time being to allow the Pacha to rule in grand style. (By the following year, Muhammad Ali would crush the Mamelukes and have himself appointed by the Sultan to replace this viceroy; he would found a dynasty that would rule Egypt for a century and a half until lust-crazed King Farouk and his *ninety-five* offspring would kill it off.)

At that moment, Muhammad Ali was bivouacked to the south, fighting the Mamelukes. The Pacha sent horses and an armed guard to escort Eaton and his party into the city. A huge crowd gathered along the route. "We passed as American officers of the Army and Navy whom curiosity had brought from Malta to Egypt during the winter's suspense of operations."

Major Missett had kindly offered to allow the Americans to stay at the British House. Dr. Mendrici paid a quick personal visit to the Pacha, his patient, and put in a good word for the Americans. In the late afternoon, the Pacha's interpreter came to welcome the Americans and told them the Pacha would be pleased to entertain them at the palace at nine o'clock *the following night*. He explained that the late hour was chosen because the fast of Ramadan had begun.

During Ramadan, the ninth and holiest month of the Moslem lunar calendar, Moslems must refrain from eating or drinking or having sexual intercourse from sunrise to sunset. Some theologians call the daylight hours a time for atonement for sins; all state that the fasting shows obediance to Allah's command.

The Americans, though only masquerading as tourists, were fortunate to be in Cairo during Ramadan because the requirements of following Islamic law created a beguiling nocturnal spectacle.

Endless torches and bonfires illuminated the streets, mosques, and courtyards far into the night as turbaned men and veiled women celebrated outdoors. "Hundreds and thousands of lights may be seen in the great salons of the rich," wrote traveler Ali Bey, "which consist of plain crystal or coloured [oil] lamps suspended from the ceiling. They produce a charming effect and no unpleasant smell, for the smoke passes out of ventilators."

He added: "It is well known that the rich observe [Ramadan] by living in a manner completely opposite to their general mode, that is, by sleeping all day and amusing themselves during the night."

William Browne, a British traveler who visited Cairo during Ramadan a decade earlier, chronicled the routine for the postsunset festivities. A long prayer was first recited, followed by a sumptuous feast. After that, oiled Egyptian wrestlers grappled for prizes, then came storytellers, many reciting tales from *A Thousand and One Nights*. Next came the comic wits who "wrestled in similes"; their performance often degenerated into insult contests: "You are like the city ass; you look sleek and carry dung." Then, deeper in the night, appeared the female singers, sometimes to the accompaniment of stringed instruments; finally, the main attraction, the female dancers, notorious for their belly dancing.

While the lure of such entertainment would have thrilled a true tourist, Eaton looked forward to breaking fast with the Pacha only to learn about Hamet; indeed, he spent his first day in Cairo inquiring of the servants at the British House if any knew of Hamet supporters in Cairo. And Eaton succeeded in meeting with three former officials of Hamet's exiled government: a secretary of state and two ministers. He described them as "destitute of everything but resentment, for even hope had abandoned them."

Eaton discovered from them that the rumors were indeed true: Hamet, "after a series of vicissitudes and disasters," had joined the Mamelukes; that he commanded a few loyal Tripolitan soldiers and some Arab mercenaries; and that Hamet was besieged with the Mamelukes inside Minyeh in Upper Egypt. *Besieged* meant that the city in which Hamet stayed was ringed by 8,000 Turkish and Albanian troops. Minyeh lay 140 miles south, upriver, a five-day journey from Cairo. Eaton later wrote a letter to the secretary of the navy, detailing the obstacles: the near impossibility of a small Christian force passing through a war zone to reach Hamet, the difficulty of even sending a Moslem messenger to him, the unlikelihood of obtaining a letter of safe conduct from the viceroy for Hamet to travel, and finally, the fatal risk of Hamet appearing a traitor to the Mamelukes if he tried to flee Minyeh.

Eaton weighed his options and decided his best chance lay in trying to convince the viceroy, that night at the reception, to help Hamet to abandon the rebel Mamelukes and leave the country. Eaton blithely added: "These obstacles overcome, everything else seemed feasible."

At 8 P.M. a small detachment of mounted uniformed Turkish officers and attendants on foot entered the courtyard of the British House, leading six Arabian horses, richly caparisoned with the finest jeweled saddles. Eaton, in some kind of homemade general's uniform, Presley O'Bannon, in the blue coat with scarlet collar and lace cuffs of a U.S. Marine lieutenant, and two blue-coated midshipmen with gold lace at their collars mounted up alongside Captain Vincent and Dr. Mendrici. The dozens of men on foot carried large flaming torches; immense crowds lined the mile-and-a-half path. Spectators, wrote Eaton, were curious to see "the men who had come from the New World." (Presumably, they expected Native American Indians, not officers who resembled Europeans.)

At the gate of the citadel, more servants, grooms, and guards stood ready to help the men down from their horses and guide them inside the courtyard. The Pacha intended an ornate welcome. Albanian soldiers, in full uniform with a kind of chain-mail waistcoat and high leather buskins and red caps, paraded in the courtyard. The grand staircase to the Hall of Audience at the Citadel was lined with young turbaned Turkish officers in dazzling uniforms, carrying jeweled swords.

Eaton described the primary room of the court as surpassing in "magnificence" anything he had ever seen of this kind, that is, more sumptuous than those in Algiers or Tunis. The viceroy invited William Eaton, taking him by the hand, to join him on a large sofa of "embroidered purple and damask cushions." Also attending were a host of long-bearded advisers comprising the government *divan,* or council.

First came elaborate hospitality and salutations: coffee, followed by pipes and sherbet. Since Islam forbade liquor, the drink on *public* occasions must be coffee. Many travelers crowned the Turks—in an age of heavy tobacco use—as the world's leaders, with a pipe in their mouths most waking hours. As for the pipes used at the palace, these were no hubble-bubbles, but rather six-foot-long delicately carved poles of scented wood. "The tobacco of Turkey is the best and mildest in the world," wrote one French traveler. "It has not the acrid taste which in our countries provokes a continual spitting; the length of the shanks in which the smoke rises, the odoriferous nature of the wood, the amber tube that is held in the mouth, the aloes wood with which the tobacco is scented, contribute to make it still milder and to render the smoke of it not unpleasant in a room."

Eaton ate his fruit sherbet in a salle redolent of Arabian coffee beans and Turkish tobacco. An always quick—and often biased—judge of character, Eaton decided that the Turkish viceroy "was a man of much more frankness and liberality than commonly falls to the character of a turk." Showing a genuine curiosity, the viceroy peppered Eaton with questions about the ongoing British-French war, the history of the United States. Is the United States at war or peace? With whom?

The viceroy decided to dismiss the courtiers and servants, and Eaton found himself alone with the viceroy and his interpreter. Eaton spoke in French, and the interpreter translated to Turkish. The viceroy, with a smile, told Eaton that he doubted that Eaton's purpose was merely tourism.

Eaton, making a snap decision, decided to confide in the Pacha his true mission, even though Hamet was at that moment fighting along with the rebel Mamelukes.

Eaton labored to explain the entire history of U.S. diplomatic relations with Tripoli and the Barbary war, stressing Yussef's betrayal of the treaty. Eaton artfully contrasted the duplicity of the Barbary rulers with the honorable conduct of other Turkish princes. (Nominally Algiers, Tunis, Tripoli, and Egypt were all regencies of the Ottoman Empire.) Eaton, laying it on thick, drew parallels between Islam and American

Christianity: "Both taught the existence and supremacy of *one* God," encouraged charity, and "forbade unnecessary bloodshed." The viceroy agreed.

Eaton then explained that his mission was to restore Tripoli's legitimate sovereign to the throne, and in so doing prove to the world "We do not unsheath the sword for conquest nor for spoil but to vindicate our rights."

The viceroy replied that he had met Hamet and had even helped him out in time of need. (Hamet seemed to teeter from one handout to the next.) He said that he would like to help Eaton on his quest, but he added that if Hamet had indeed joined the Mamelukes, it would greatly complicate the situation. Eaton replied that it was holier to pardon a repenting enemy than to punish him.

The viceroy agreed to send couriers to search for Hamet, and Eaton sent couriers as well, adding to the two messengers he had already sent from Alexandria and Rosetta. Eaton in all his messages suggested that Hamet hurry to Rosetta to contact Major Missett at the British House. He signed his notes "Agent General of the United States."

The day after leaving the meeting at the palace, Eaton was optimistic that the viceroy would help. Then an unexpected difficulty arose. The French consul, Signore Drovetti, informed the viceroy that the American party were actually spies working for the British. Drovetti explained that the Hamet tale was a smoke screen to allow the Americans to reach the Mamelukes and help cement an alliance with Great Britain. In crazy-quilt Egypt, anything made sense. "I found the means however (the means that move every thing in his quarter of the globe) to remove this difficulty," Eaton wrote. The "means" are easily explained: Dr. Mendrici approached the viceroy's interpreter to offer him a bribe. Whether the money reached the viceroy didn't concern the Americans.

Eaton needed cash right away for the bribe, so he borrowed it *from the British,* promising them that the United States would repay the loan. By simply not asking in advance, Eaton thus avoided the risk that the U.S. Navy would turn him down. Then, the following week *after the fact,* Eaton wrote Captain Hull that he had borrowed $2,000 on the Briggs Brothers credit and that Hull should reimburse them in Alexandria.

Eaton secured Dr. Mendrici by appointing him "Commercial Agent" for the United States at Cairo. Of course, Eaton had absolutely no authority to make the appointment, but he did add the proviso that Mendrici would remain "until the pleasure of the President shall be expressed on the subject."

On December 16, Eaton confirmed from a reliable source that 8,000 Albanian and Levant troops serving the Turks had indeed surrounded the 3,000 soldiers of the Mameluke beys at Minyeh. Both sides were digging in for a long seige, which didn't bode well for Eaton passing through the lines.

That evening after sunset, Eaton once again had an audience with the viceroy. After the usual ceremonies, Ahmet Pacha gave Eaton an earful on the errors of Hamet's ways in joining the Mamelukes. However, thanks to the bribe, he granted Hamet "a letter of amnesty and permission to him to pass the Turkish army and leave Egypt unmolested." Eaton added: "It now remains to detach him from the rebel Beys."

The following morning, Eaton sent four separate couriers, each carrying a copy of the viceroy's amnesty and safe-passage. Three of the messengers were Maltese, disguised as Arabs. "God has ordained that you should see trouble," Eaton added in an accompanying note to Hamet. "We believe he hath ordained also that your troubles shall now have an end." It was crucial that Hamet learn about the pardon before the Mamelukes did, who might kill him. The couriers had orders that, if captured, they should destroy the pardons.

Now all Eaton could do was wait for an answer. The New Englander, however, was not adept at wasting time; he decided to go with his stepson and his fiddle-playing marine and do some actual sightseeing. He hoped for an answer from war-ravaged Minyeh, 140 miles upriver, within ten days.

Next morning, Eaton and friends visited the famed Nilometer on Rhoda Island in the Nile at Cairo. The Nilometer, built in 861 A.D., was more than just a large ornate carved column for measuring the water level of the Nile. The annual reading there during a vast public festival delivered a thumbs-up or thumbs-down for the country's future. If the river level reached 16 cubits (about 24 feet), a fine harvest would be guaranteed, but 18 cubits heralded flood, and a mere 12 cubits drought.

Eaton crossed from the island to the western shore and continued into the ruined city of Giza, which had a decade earlier housed the magnificent Mameluke palace of Murad Bey. "I had been told that it was a delightful spot," wrote a traveler, "on account of its country houses and gardens . . . it is now a miserable abode filled with Arnaut [Albanian] soldiers who conduct themselves like banditti." From Giza, the pyramids and the Sphinx loomed in the distance. However, Bedouin marauders had taken over the turf in between, swaying Eaton to skip taking a closer look.

From his vantage point, the pyramids would have appeared like God's discarded playthings, casually tossed in front of the Mokattam mountains. Eaton remained unimpressed. "Ruined temples, pyramids, and catacombs, monuments of superstition, pride and folly of their founders disgust my sight; for with their magnificence I cannot but couple the idea of the slaves who must have groaned under the oppressive folly of their fabrication."

Even the Nile didn't move him. "When I contrast the pure currents, healthful margins, and delightsome landscapes of our Susquehannah, Delaware, Hudson and Connecticut [Rivers] with the muddy waters, miry or parched banks and eternal deserts of the [Nile]; and the intelligence, freedom and felicity of the citizens [in America], with the stupid ignorance, rivited vassalage and hopeless misery of the peasants here, I almost lose sensibility of pity in the glad reflection that I am a citizen of the United States."

The irritated tourist returned to his lodgings at the British House and to his preferred pastime: the mission. There he found two more men who had been close followers of Hamet, and both promised Eaton that it would be possible to recruit a troop of three hundred to five hundred men to march from Egypt. Eaton, upbeat, wrote to Hull to inform him that provisions should be gathered in Alexandria for at least one hundred men. He also warned him that he would need more money: about $4,000 or $5,000. "If Government should reprove our arrangements, we will reimburse them from the spoils of Bengazi [a large port city in Tripoli], which I already calculate upon as ours, nothing will hinder but unforeseen disaster." (Eaton's life sometimes seemed like a string of unforeseen disasters.) Eaton eagerly awaited Hull's reply, since Hull controlled the purse strings.

Perhaps the French consul was not so far off in describing Eaton and friends as spies for the British. Eaton did indeed write a detailed note to Major Missett, in Rosetta, but apologized that he couldn't find any fresh reliable news about the Mameluke-Turkish war in Upper Egypt. "We are more perplexed with contradictory reports, than were there free presses for the parties," he added, no doubt thinking of the severely biased accounts in rival Republican and Federalist papers back in America.

Once again Eaton was forced to wait. So, on Thursday, December 20, instead of viewing more pagan artifacts, Eaton sought out a Christian shrine. New Testament lore places the Holy Family with the baby Jesus wandering to Cairo. On the way, Jesus is said to have miraculously caused a spring to appear in a Jewish community called Ain Shams. (Mary took advantage of the sudden water to wash Jesus' clothes.) True believers are convinced that the balsam plant took on healing properties by being nourished at the Jesus spring. (Copts for centuries have been peddling balsam-laced consecrated oil, called "chrism.")

The Holy Family then trudged into Old Cairo where, legend has it, Jesus' arrival caused all the idols to topple and prompted the Roman governor to order the Christ child killed. The Holy Family fled.

So did Eaton after a morning in Old Cairo. He had seen pagan and Christian; now he visited an Islamic site. He traveled to the nearby village of Daerteen and was allowed into the Mosque Atarenabee. He and his party must have seemed less than enthused because a guide offered to let them "view all the ladies of the village." Though Eaton doesn't specify what exactly their "view" entailed, he closed this diary entry: "Omnia vincit argent," as in "Money conquers all."

And Eaton waited. On the agenda for this Friday night was dancing girls. Egypt was world famous for its belly dancers, and someone in the American group hired a few to perform. William Browne, a decade earlier in Cairo, had witnessed a similar spectacle. "They are always attended by an old man and an old woman who play on musical instruments, and look to the conduct of the girls that they may not bestow their favors for an inadequate reward; for though not chaste, they are by no means common."

French traveler Charles Sonnini de Manoncourt offered more details on the entertainment. The dances "consist chiefly of very quick and truly astonishing movements of the loins, which they agitate with equal suppleness and indecency, while the rest of their body remains motionless." The women sometimes danced in gyrating pairs and sometimes wore little metal cups on their fingers, which they clacked like castanets.

Eaton, with his patriotic blinders, was less impressed. "At evening an exhibition at the English house of the *almee,* dancing women: Haggard prostitutes, disgustful, obscene monsters who exhibit savage nature in jestures of studied and practised depravity: something resembling the Spanish *balario* [bolero], from which the latter probably originated."

Up north in Alexandria harbor just before Christmas Eve aboard the *Argus* Captain Isaac Hull found time to write a reply to William Eaton, down in Grand Cairo. The note was meant to douse the fire of Eaton's optimism.

"I have made arrangements for paying Mess.rs Briggs the Thousand Dollars, which you inform me you had drawn for, but as for the four or five Thousand you say you shall want—God Knows how we are to obtain that, unless you have the means at Cairo, for I know of none here.—I am already pennyless." He mentions not even having enough money to pay off the debts incurred for the *Argus.* Then he wonders what exactly Eaton means by asking him to provide provisions for one hundred men, and warns that he cannot possibly carry them to Rosetta at this time of year.

"The plan you have formed of taking Derne, I think rather a Hazardous one, unless the Bashaw can bring into the field from Eight Hundred to one Thousand Men, particularly as we are destitute of every article necessary for an expedition of this kind." He states that "the most we can do" is transport the Bashaw to Syracuse, try to get supplies and troops, and then set off anew for Derne or Bengazi. "You must be satisfied that it is my wish to do everything in my power before we return, but when I look at the situation we are sent here in, I lose all patience.—

With a little Vessel, without friends, without authority to act . . . in short without everything that is absolutely necessary to insure success to an Enterprize."

Hull repeats that it would be best to find Hamet, bring him out of Egypt, then look for a new plan with proper backing. "I say as I have said before that I do not see that anything more than getting the man can be done."

Eaton would receive this dismal Christmas present within a week. A less stubborn man might have been deterred.

CHAPTER 10

White Christmas in Tripoli

THE AMERICAN PRISONERS, hungry and overworked, were expecting an extraordinary treat for Christmas: a dinner of meat and vegetables, two loaves of bread per man, all to be washed down by a *quart* of wine each. The men hadn't tasted a morsel of meat in two months, and a grain shortage had pinched their diet further. "The American sailors, it is a pity to see them," wrote Dutch consul Zuchet. "They sometimes go two to three days without even the miserable barley bread that the Regency gives them and no one thinks to exempt them from the hard work they are forced to endure."

But for Christmas, the unpredictable Bashaw had agreed to let them take the day off, even though it fell on a Wednesday. After more than a year in captivity, the prisoners welcomed the feast with an intensity difficult to imagine. Then Christmas morning, a routine inspection revealed dozens of ropes and other supplies missing from the Bashaw's naval stores. The guards entered the American prison and announced: No food at all would be brought until someone confessed to the crime. Christmas—like the rest of their lives—was on hold.

Ever since Preble's bombardments in late summer, conditions had worsened for the American prisoners. Since their own captain had delivered scant aid, they had smuggled a poignant letter out of Tripoli in early November to the commodore, asking for help. "They send us to work rain or shine like horses in the cart, some carrying large large stones, some plastering and repairing the fort and castle, others transporting guns that came out of the frigate . . . seven or eight savages to every 20 or 30 Men with large sticks to beat us along and very often no bread nor oil for 2, 3 & 4 days."

The anonymous letter writer—no doubt funneling hollered suggestions—especially noted that the five U.S. servicemen who had renounced Christianity were "worse to us than the Turks." He added: "I hope when we get released we will have the pleasure of stretching their Necks a little longer."

By mid-November, the food shortages had grown so brutal that many of the men, despite winter's onset, sold their clothes to Jewish rag merchants to get a few coins to purchase nourishment.

On December 7, Dr. Cowdery, the physician to the ruling family, overheard the Bashaw ordering his taskmasters to abuse the American prisoners to spur complaints and speed up a hefty ransom from Jefferson.

After suffering through three consecutive days of beatings and no food, the prisoners went on a hunger strike, that is, a strike against hunger. On the morning of December 10, the guards unlocked the prison and, banging their sticks, shouted the usual: "*Tota Fora*" ("Everybody Out" in Lingua Franca). None of the 275 Americans moved. The guards grabbed the men who slept on the floor and began thrashing them with sticks. The men refused to work without food. The guards threatened to bring soldiers to shoot them. "The wardens whipped them until they were tired," wrote Dr. Cowdery, "and then went to inform the Bashaw." A compromise was reached. Work till noon, then be fed a loaf of black bread with a half gill of oil.

The Bashaw's own soldiers were also mulling rebellion, angry that they hadn't received their Ramadan bonus of extra rations and money. Cornered by adversity, the Bashaw grew more defiant. He told the Dutch consul that the Americans could bring twenty frigates and that he wouldn't surrender, and he vowed he'd convert to Judaism before accepting $1,000 a man as ransom.

The starving American prisoners decided that it was time to take their fate into their own hands. Four officers, who had been allowed to live with the crewmen, devised a plan for taking over the castle. The idea was that at the moment the prison gates were opened at dawn, the 275

American slaves would overwhelm their guards, rush to capture the castle armory, and hold the Bashaw and his family as hostages. They'd then free the other American officers and point the castle cannons toward the city. Marine Private Ray called the plan "preposterous" without naval support. He said that they'd soon run out of food and be forced to surrender. In any case, before they could try it, someone ratted them out, probably one of the turn-Turks.

The Bashaw was, of course, furious when he discovered American designs on his castle. His irritation mounted even higher when he learned—probably from a spy in Malta—that some Americans were in Egypt trying to find his older brother to bring him to launch a civil war. Ever cunning, the Bashaw ordered his middle son to marry Hamet's twelve-year-old daughter, who was still a hostage. The marriage was celebrated on December 21, 1804, and humiliated Hamet in the eyes of the people of Tripoli. Now she would show her loyalty to her husband's family and battle lines in a civil war would be blurred.

When Captain Bainbridge somehow learned of Eaton's plans to vault Hamet onto the throne, he, too, sprang into action. He wrote several long letters in lime juice to Consul General Tobias Lear, expressing his outrage. Flames brought the invisible words to life. "I can't conceive that the least benefit could derive to the U.S. from pecuniary or other aid given to the poor effeminate fugitive brother of the Bashaw of Tripoli."

Bainbridge, from his prison keep, reported that the people of Tripoli despised Hamet. "He was placed by his Brother in Command at Derne, the most favorable province for his attempting a Counter Revolution. The present Bashaw suspecting that he was not conducting himself properly, drove him from that situation, only by an Order without sending troops against him. What can be expected from such a pusillanimous being?"

Just before Christmas the desperate prisoners had convinced Captain Bainbridge to garnish their future wages to pay Danish consul Nissen to cater a Christmas feast. Nissen, a genuinely generous soul, had rushed his orders to the butchers and the bakers. His own wine cellar held the cask. All had appeared so promising . . . but now on Christmas morning, with the Bashaw still irate over the theft, the 275 American prisoner-slaves, along with about 50 Neapolitans, moped in their jail. The feast was nixed. The slaves wistfully daydreamed of home and family and of ample meals. The ill-clad men in the warehouselike prison sprawled on their cots, which had been ingeniously slung one on top of another, five levels high. Then a surprising thing happened. The Bashaw's investigator found the stolen ropes and supplies in a Tunisian's warehouse. The merchant admitted buying the cordage from Selim, the Bashaw's son-in-law.

Though late, Christmas dinner was served to the Americans; the cask of wine arrived. William Ray certainly enjoyed every mouthful. Camel or lamb, it tasted good.

By nightfall, the prisoners, with a gut full of wine, were singing songs. The crewmen were perched upon their bunks—lamps glowing. Ray wrote down the lyrics of one song that he had adapted from the rousing tune of "Madam, You Know My Trade Is War."

The men, many bearded and unwashed, exhausted and enslaved, sang with all their hearts. Ray was moved. The song was called "Adieu, Blest Liberty."

> *In helpless servitude, forlorn,*
> *From country, friends and freedom torn,*
> *Alike we dread each night and morn,*
> *For nought but grief we see;*
> *When burdens press—the lash we bear,*
> *And all around is black despair,*
> *We breathe the silent, fervent prayer,*
> *O come, blest Liberty!*
>
> *And when invading cannons roar,*
> *And life and blood from hundreds pour,*
> *And mangled bodies float ashore,*
> *And ruins strew the sea;*
> *The thoughts of death or freedom near*
> *Create alternate hope and fear!*

Oh! when will that blest day appear,
That brings sweet Liberty?

Just after dawn on December 26, the American sailors trudged to work as usual; their hopes and dreams rested on the U.S. Navy fleet arriving in springtime, or on a negotiator coming with sacks full of money. They had no idea about the machinations of Jefferson's secret agent.

WILLIAM EATON STUBBORNLY waited in Grand Cairo for a message from elusive Hamet. Rumors poured in: *Hamet had an army of Arabs; he had no army; he was a prisoner of the Mameluke beys; he was dead.* After three long weeks Eaton was convinced that a messenger would arrive any moment; he and the others had given up sightseeing. They often spent days in the vicinity of the British consul's house, listening for the clip-clop of a rider or for a courier pounding on the gate. "I confess I do not feel altogether at my ease remaining so long in a state of uncertitude," wrote Eaton to Hull on December 29, characterizing the feeling as "something worse than suspence." He conjectured that maybe Hamet, after being tantalized so many times by promises of American aid, simply doubted their commitment and refused to respond.

Eaton knew, as they all did, that at some point Captain Hull's patience would have to run out, that he couldn't endlessly feed an idle crew in port, and that he would then order his navy officers back to ship, leaving Eaton in Egypt to pursue his quest alone. He informed Hull that if no message arrived soon, he would indeed head south, try to cross the Turkish lines, and slip into the Mameluke camp. "The undertaking will be hazardous," he wrote with customary bravado, "but this is a world of adventure, in which little is to be expected without enterprize and perseverance, and not a great deal to be realized with them."

An edginess seemed to infect the entire party. The restless Americans passed the time gambling, playing billiards, drinking, visiting brothels. A

42-gallon cask of Madeira and a 72-gallon cask of wine showed up on the expense account for Cairo.

On the night of December 29, in a run-down billiard hall, as outcasts from a dozen nations looked on, Robert Goldsborough of the U.S. Navy and Richard Farquhar, the ambitious Scot, played several games of billiards; the bet was a half-pint bottle of attar of roses, a perfume easily available in Cairo.

Goldsborough, a cocky young man from a prominent Maryland family, had arrived in Cairo to deliver a query from Hull and had stayed to await a definitive reply from Eaton. The two billiards players, both drinking, argued over the tally in the game; they insulted each other. A choice word from Farquhar provoked Goldsborough, who threw the first punch. Standing toe to toe, they exchanged blows, with each man receiving a black eye. Then Farquhar wrestled Goldsborough to the floor and began pounding him. The crowd, apparently deciding that the American was in the wrong, was ready to let the Scot "break his bones" as one witness later put it. But Selim, the jack-of-all-trades Janissary hired by Eaton, jumped in and rescued the young American officer.

Eaton was not at the billiard hall and so only learned of the "fisticuffs" the following morning. Eaton interrogated various officers and found out that Goldsborough was probably guilty of much more than one single brawl. He was accused of cheating at cards at "the most respectable Christian house in Grand Cairo," and also of drunkenly wandering the streets of Cairo lifting the veils of women. (It's a minor miracle that a jealous husband or brother hadn't killed him.)

Goldsborough was apparently willing to risk his life to view beautiful plump women. "Her face is like a full moon," ran one Egyptian proverb on beauty, "her haunches are like sofa cushions." This metropolis, coveted by so many foreign conquerors, had another proverb, germane to the next accusation against Goldsborough: "Choose a blond woman for your eyes; choose an Egyptian for pleasure."

Eaton wrote that Goldsborough, the *Argus*'s purser, was also accused of "what is somewhat more base, [that is,] of bilking his Courtezan in a Brothel." Eaton was mortified that the first appearance of American officers in the famed city of Cairo should result in such boorish behavior.

"Good God," wrote Eaton, "when will our young men learn the weight of respect which ought to attach itself to a Uniform and a Sword?"

Goldsborough, when he found out the exact charges, denied everything. Eaton, although he was not Goldsborough's superior officer, strongly advised the young man to return to Alexandria the following day, which happened to be New Year's Eve. Goldsborough reluctantly agreed. (He would later demand an apology from Eaton, who instead would recommend him for court-martial.)

Eaton decided that he had better show Captain Hull some progress of some kind, so he dispatched Richard Farquhar to go to Alexandria with a ragtag bunch of recruits, lined up in Cairo for the Hamet mission. He gave Farquhar orders to feed them and retain them "conditionally," and to look for more "conditional" Christian troops in Alexandria.

In addition, Eaton around this time signed up another recruit, an extremely unusual fellow. Thirty-six years old, a muscular 5'9", he told them he had already led many lives under many names: He claimed to have served in the Austrian, French, and Turkish armies and deserted from all three; he said he had run a British coffee house in Cairo, had joined the Capuchin monks, had become a Moslem dervish after publicly circumcising himself, and had visited Mecca. No one knew whether any of it was true, but Jean Eugene, as he now wanted to be called, spoke many languages, and he was enough of a military engineer to know about land surveying. Perhaps every covert op needs a multilingual, pathological liar.

While Eaton lingered in Cairo, it looked as though the war might come to him, just not the right war. The Nile-drenched valleys in Upper Egypt had finally dried, and the Mameluke army was reported "approaching Cairo with imposing strides." As hoarding began, shortages hit the city; a huge camel caravan full of supplies coming from Suez was waylaid by Bedouin, worsening the situation. On Wednesday, January 8, Eaton received another impatient letter from Hull. "At all events it is time to determine on something, for it is impossible for us to remain here long." The *Argus* was running out of food, he wrote, and no cash remained to buy any more. He politely suggested that if Eaton needed any more money, he should draw on the U.S. Navy or the State Department but not on Isaac Hull or the *Argus*. "I do not think I have any authority to draw money for any other purpose than paying [the *Argus's*] disbursements."

Hull, however, didn't relish hamstringing Eaton. "You will pardon the hints I have given in this letter." Eaton dashed off a reply. He stated he planned to leave Cairo in two days—not to return to Alexandria—but rather to head south with Presley O'Bannon and try to survive "wild Arabs," "Arnaut Turks," and Mameluke beys. "If we fail . . . , you will do us the justice to believe us Martyrs to a cause in which we feel the honour and interest of our Country deeply involved—Release of our Prisoners without Ransom and peace without the disgraceful condition of Tribute."

Whatever Eaton's love of glory, he returned time and again to this root motive for his mission: The honor of the United States demanded zero toleration of extortion and insult by Tripoli.

(Eaton didn't realize it, but on that exact day, one-third of the way around the world in Washington City, Thomas Jefferson was reaching a more pragmatic conclusion. After a Cabinet meeting, he wrote in his notes: "Not to give a dollar for peace. [However], if the enterprise in the Spring does not produce peace & delivery of the prisoners, ransom them." The president, though, clearly wanted to test the military option first.)

Standing at the front gate of British House, Eaton sent off the courier to carry his letter to Hull in Alexandria. He was forcing himself to envision the prospect of a long, dangerous trek south.

Moments later, an Arab, dusty from the desert, arrived at the gate . . . with a message from Hamet. Finally. Eaton rushed to find Selim to translate it from Arabic. (Hamet spoke Arabic, Turkish, and some Italian; Eaton spoke English, French, and some Italian.) It turned out that only by the thinnest of margins had one of Eaton's letters reached Hamet. The Maltese couriers, disguised as Arabs, had been captured as spies by the Mameluke troops, who sentenced them to die on the following morning; that night, they slipped liquor to their Moslem guards, who became drunk. They were able to escape and found Hamet the next day.

Hamet's encouraging letter read:

To our friend, the very good friend of our Highness, the American
General, Mr. Eaton:

> *We have received your letter and . . . gave thanks to God for*
> *having preserved your health. Know that I am ever the same as you*
> *knew me at Tunis, my friendship is constant and uniform, but you*
> *have been tardy—We must however make the delay serve a good*
> *purpose. From the date on this [28 Ramadan/January 3] I leave this*
> *[place] for Behira [a region in the northeast that includes Alexandria]*
> *and shall take quarters at the house of the Arab Chief Abd'el giver el-*
> *Be Kourchi, where I propose to you to meet me.*
>
> *I have written to my subjects and to my minister Mahmoud Kogea*
> *and also to the Governor of Police, Muhamed, son of Abdelrahman,*
> *that they may treat [negotiate] with you; and whatever you conclude*
> *with them will be ratified by me.*
>
> *Your operations should be carried on by sea; mine by land; and may*
> *God assist us to re-establish peace and harmony . . .*
>
> *Hamet Bashaw, son of Alli Bashaw Caramale*

Eaton was, of course, thrilled. "I cannot but congratulate you," he immediately wrote to Hull, "and felicitate myself after so much apprehension, doubt and solicitude, that we now calculate with certainty on the success of our expedition, we are sure of the Bashaw." Eaton noted that he would now dispatch the Bashaw's secretary to carry another copy of the viceroy's passport to him and would advise Hamet to meet him in Alexandria instead of Rosetta. (Like all things Hamet, setting up a rendezvous would prove surprisingly difficult.) Eaton didn't mention that he was sending money to Hamet as well.

It was indeed prescient that Eaton sent some cash. In a private letter that Hamet sent to his negotiator, the governor of police, Muhammed, he revealed his financial quandary. "You're well aware that when we left Tunis [in 1803], we had nothing and that which we acquired in Derne, all of it was lost, and therefore this mission will require much troops and money for camels and horses and other goods and the Bedouin are now like the Turks and want money. As for my own needs, I do not demand anything now but in due time, my needs will be around 15,000 'Tolari' [presumably, dollars]. You must advise the American general of that amount so that we will receive it when we arrive at the house of Abed Elearu Bagosi in Behira . . . I pray that you make an agreement with the General to prepare the 15,000 dollars, that you give him your solemn promise and take a similar promise from him."

Hamet knew that Eaton had once paid a fortune to ransom an Italian slave girl; he expected very deep pockets. Eaton had sent one-tenth of the desired amount, that is, 1,500 "pesos duros" (approximately equal to a dollar) to Hamet. And even to muster that sum, he had been constrained to take advantage of a line of credit granted to him by the Briggs Brothers of Alexandria; he promised to repay the loan "by drafts on Leghorn, Naples or Department of the Navy." Since Eaton had no established credit with any of those three entities, he was basically bluffing and gambling that he would be able to repay Briggs after a successful mission.

On Thursday, January 10, Eaton and his small cadre of American officers returned to the palace to take leave of the viceroy. (No Egyptians lined up to gawk this time, especially after Goldsborough's shenanigans.) More pipes were smoked, coffee drunk, and attar of roses misted about. Each man this time, though, received a superb saber, worth about $200, and Eaton collected one for Captain Hull in Alexandria. After having spent thirty-five days in Cairo, he made preparations to depart on the Nile to return to Alexandria.

Meanwhile, Captain Hull on the coast had not *yet* received the good news of the Hamet letter. He seriously weighed leaving but decided to wait for one more messenger from Cairo.

Now Hamet began his slow trek north from Minyeh. The Mameluke beys allowed him to leave, but to make sure that he did not lure any troops to him, they imprisoned thirty Arab sheiks who might have been loyal to Hamet. The Arab mercenaries were the wild card in the battle of Turk versus Mameluke. Each side craved sheiks.

On Saturday, January 12, Hamet, perennially broke, received the money from Eaton and made his way to a village called Ohu'isa. His bedraggled entourage headed north from the war zone into the desert on their way to the oases of Lake Fayyum. A recent influx of deserters added to the area's harshness. Fresh foods and sturdy beasts proved scarce. Hamet's newly found money barely paid for some wretched horses and camels . . . no doubt Hamet also had debts to pay. Now he drew up a list of supplies he wanted Eaton to deliver to a village called Abu Sir (a day trip south from Cairo): ample provisions for men, camels and horses, three or four large tents, clothing for his officers.

Hamet, on the same day that he petitioned Eaton, also wrote privately in the tone of a petulant prince to one of his Cairo negotiators, Minister Mahmud. "The money that was given me by the general was very little and this displeased me but at the moment I could say nothing. . . . So tell the general he must have courage with respect to expenditures . . . make him understand this is war and whoever wishes to make war must spend without thought and take no account of money." (Since copies of these letters wound up among Eaton's papers, it's safe to assume that through some guile he was reading Hamet's private communications.)

Hamet ended his note almost forlornly. His men are in rags, he has no saddles for horses or camels and is surrounded by mercenary Arabs. "We are in the desert and we do not know what to do. I hope God will do well for us." His courier mounted his camel and proceeded north to Cairo; the delivery fee of four dollars was to be paid on arrival.

While Hamet dawdled and Hull fretted, Eaton moved forward.

William Eaton left Cairo with his companions on Saturday at 3 P.M. aboard a *marche* and traveled downstream, reaching Rosetta on Monday at 11 A.M. The journey with the Nile current was typically uneventful, but as they arrived, they saw storm clouds. Eaton sought shelter at British House just as heavy winds and rain pounded the coast and made the Bogaz, the nearby bar of the Nile, too unpredictable to pass. Eaton wrote to Hull by foot messenger that he was especially eager that the three of them—Hull, Eaton, and Hamet—sit down and plot out military plans for the expedition against Derne and Bengazi.

On Saturday, January 19, Eaton finally reunited with Hull aboard the *Argus* in Alexandria harbor. Neither man recorded the conversation, but Hull had been cooling his heels in Alexandria for almost two months. He certainly conveyed his impatience to Eaton. The following day, Eaton received another message from Hamet; however, this one turned out to be a reply *to the first note Eaton had sent way back on November 28.* Communications in the early nineteenth century were haphazard at best. In war-torn places such as Egypt, and even in countries with established postal services, letters almost always began . . . "Having received yrs of such-and-such date, I now . . ."

This reply from Hamet, which predated the one Eaton had received in Cairo, stated that Hamet expected to meet Eaton at the house of "Bagosi" near Lake Fayyum on the border of the desert, about 180 miles south of Alexandria. Exasperated at this seeming change of plans, Eaton instantly decided that he could take no chances and prepared to depart for Fayyum.

Monday was spent looking for supplies and especially horses. They found a few decent steeds, but they wound up forced to rent two dozen mill horses. Freed from their endless circular drudgery, these broken-down mounts hardly cut a dashing figure. The Americans bought over-priced provisions, cleaned their pistols, and sharpened their cutlasses. On the morning of Tuesday, January 22, Eaton mounted up, along with two navy officers, Lieutenant Joshua Blake and Midshipman George Washington Mann, as well as a motley Christian force of twenty-three recruits and his interpreter, Selim Comb. They began the trek south.

The odd cavalcade—which included two officers in U.S. Navy uniforms but which did not fly the American flag—accomplished 75 miles through the rich delta in two days. On Thursday evening, they stumbled into a detachment of five hundred Turkish Albanian soldiers. These fierce-looking troops, wearing a kind of chain mail across their chests and knee-high buskins, stopped them. The commanding officer, the Kourchief, promptly arrested Eaton and company.

Eaton found himself a prisoner in Demanhour, an overgrown village that thrived on cotton manufacture. Beautiful cultivated fields stretched out in every direction, but despite this prosperity, most houses were built of earth or rough brick.

Since Eaton was a prisoner, he found plenty of time to write a long description of his ongoing adventure to his friend Commodore Preble.

(The account captures the personality of Eaton as much as his efforts to manipulate his Turkish adversary.)

> *No Argument I could advance could at all modify the severity of his first resolution <u>not to let me pass</u> his lines; though in every thing else he treated us with distinction and great hospitality. However mortifying the concession, I cannot but applaud the correct military conduct of this chief: for it was, in itself a suspicious circumstance that a body of armed unknown foreigners should be found shaping a course for his enemy's rendezvous with no other pretext than to search <u>for a refugee Bashaw</u>!*
>
> *Our situation here was somewhat perplexing and vastly unpleasant. I do not recollect ever having found myself on a ground more critical. To the natural suspicion of a Turk this General added a fierce and savage temper—of course proud and arrogant. I soon found my point of approach—I passed high compliments on the correctness of his military vigilance and conduct; said it was what I . . . certainly would have done myself in similar circumstances, but, knowing . . . the magnanimity of his soul, I was . . . in full confidence that he would aid a measure so purely humane & so manifestly to the Turkish interest in Egypt.*

Eaton showed to the officer the viceroy's passport for Hamet, and then added that he might be able to offer the man a "douceur," that is, a bribe. The Kourchief seemed to awaken at that moment. He said Eaton's "confidence should not be disappointed," and he called into his tent the sheik of the "Eu ed Alli" [Aulad Ali], a group of Bedouin tribes that had often been banished from their homelands in Tripoli since Yussef came to power.

"I asked [the sheik] if he could give any account of Hamet Bashaw? The young chief, in an extacy, exclaimed that he Knew <u>every thing</u>! He [said] that twenty thousand Barbary Arabs were ready to march with him from this border to recover their native country and inheritance; repeated that he knew our plan; and, now that he had seen me, he would plight his head to the Turkish General to bring me Hamet Bashaw in ten days—The Turk accordingly dispatched him with a companion on this [mission] the next morning."

Eaton, however, sensed that the Turkish officer was still suspicious, so he offered to send his armed troop and their mill horses back to Alexandria while he would remain "with only the gentlemen in company and our Servants" until the Bedouin returned with Hamet. The Turk seemed pleased and ordered a small feast for Eaton and his officers. The next morning he escorted Eaton and the handful of men to a house in Demanhour.

Eaton, a bit naïve, was now confident that he had properly analyzed his captor and that suspicion had been banished. *Au contraire*. The following morning, Sunday, January 27, once Eaton had sent off his small armed force, the Kourchief increased the guards surrounding Eaton, Blake, Mann, and their servants. Sentries now stood on the terrace next door, at the courtyard gate, and even inside the house. The guards explained they were placed there "to prevent intruders."

Over the next few days, Eaton learned more about the man holding them prisoner. The Kourchief was then trying to collect taxes in the rich region of Behira, but half the villages were refusing to pay, expecting some new conqueror to arrive soon.

"The Kourchief," wrote Eaton, "in a little excursion to gather <u>contributions</u> has cut off between fifty and sixty peasants' heads for no crime but <u>poverty</u>, and just without the eastern gate of the village a gallows is now erecting to hang a child of twelve years old, the only son of the chief of the village Rahonania, because the father cannot pay the contribution levied on him! God! I thank thee that my children are Americans."

The sight of Eaton's little band had apparently given hope to the peasants that he might be leading an advance force for the British. Although Eaton tried hard to dispel that notion, he found Frenchmen everywhere ready to confirm it. Two Frenchmen, dressed in full Turkish garb, were officers for the Kourchief. Indeed, hundreds of castaways from Napoleon's invading army of 1798 had stayed on as "renegades," serving as mercenaries for the Mamelukes and Turks. A visitor to Cairo around this time met a shoemaker from Toulouse, France, who had risen in the Turkish Army. "Nothing could be more amusing," wrote Vicomte Chateaubriand, "than to see Abdallah of Toulouse take the strings of his caftan, lay them about the faces of the Arabs and Albanians who annoyed him, and thus clear a wide passage for us through the most populous streets."

Eaton, for his part, was hardly amused when the Frenchmen at Demanhour spread rumors about him. The Kourchief confided to Eaton that the French consul in Alexandria, Drovetti, had sent a note denouncing them as "British spies." Eaton wrote Preble that he planned on punishing that "savage" for exposing them to being hanged for espionage.

(Drovetti was also making mischief for them in Alexandria. He sent the governor a tip that the Americans were secretly recruiting soldiers in his city and that Eaton's troop had raised the American flag at Demanhour. Captain Hull instantly disbanded the Christian troops who were doing nothing anyway and called on the governor to calm the man.)

Eaton—despite being a prisoner and not having rendezvoused with Hamet—sent a letter to Hull that they should start planning the expedition. "[Derne & Bengazi] will be . . . an easy conquest and will give an honorable and advantageous termination to our expedition . . . the recruits at Alexandria will be useful in the execution of the plan—Some small field Pieces should be sought for and conditionally be stipulated for."

Also Eaton denied raising the American flag, although he did concede that they enjoyed showing it in private. He advised Hull to expect that he and Hamet would reach the *Argus* on Wednesday or Thursday. "Everything is tranquil with us, it will be so with you when the truth of facts shall have expelled the mist of misrepresentation."

A messenger from Hamet arrived in Demanhour on Sunday, February 3, at 3 P.M. He reported that Hamet was traveling with an entourage of only forty people. To prove he truly represented Hamet, he carried with him Eaton's first letter to Hamet, which had an Arabic translation on the back. Eaton found that fortunate, because the note affirmed that Americans had great respect for the Grand Sultan of the Ottoman Empire and that Hamet should take no steps which might damage the relationship between the two countries. The Kourchief read the note and seemed to relax; he was also relieved that Hamet had no army.

The Kourchief then invited Eaton to ride out and dine with him at his camp. He also offered to send troops to escort Hamet into Demanhour and to provide soldiers to convoy him safely to Alexandria. Not so coincidentally, Eaton around this time dashed off a note to Hull that he needed $1,000 in small local currency in order "to clear out from this [place]." *Omnia vincit argent.* Money talks. Eaton promised the mounted courier a big tip if he could rush the message to Alexandria and race back with a reply within two days. The man arrived on the *Argus* at midnight, achieving 75 miles in about eight hours.

Hull wrote back that he distrusted the authorities in Alexandria, and he thought it too risky to send the $1,000. However, a miscommunication must have occurred, or perhaps O'Bannon stepped in, because another courier did indeed carry $500 in small coins to Eaton.

On Monday, February 4, at 4 P.M., Hamet and his weary entourage, who had tramped five days through mostly desert from Fayyum, reached the outskirts of Demanhour. The endless foreplay seemed at an end.

An escort of twenty Turkish cavalrymen rode out six miles to greet him and conducted him with fanfare to a grand tent. An infantry honor guard, commanded by the Kourchief himself, saluted him.

William Eaton, who had waited years for this moment, walked over to Hamet. The thirty-nine-year-old ex-Bashaw, with his long beard and colored turban, looked older than his age; a decade of exile had battered him. Of medium height, not thin, he was a prince without a kingdom, a walking acknowledgment of his own disgrace. But Hamet, whatever his faults, was an endearing and gracious man, and the two allies greeted each other warmly in broken Italian and snippets of Arabic. As soon as Eaton gained a moment alone with the prince, he swore to him by whatever Hamet held holy that he would place him back on his rightful throne or that he would die trying.

CHAPTER 12 *Preparing for War: Fresh Enemies and Money, Money, Money*

S HAMET AND EATON WASTED no time in leaving this armed Turkish camp. The host's hospitality might evaporate in a mood swing or a new *firman* received. And even though Eaton had already scattered $500 around to various officers and guards, he found himself forced to promise to the Kourchief a very expensive gold watch to accelerate their departure. Eaton swore to send the jeweled timepiece immediately upon arrival in Alexandria. With their partnership just beginning in earnest, full-bearded Hamet rode alongside clean-shaven William. Though both men had longed for this meeting, they couldn't chitchat or make plans easily because they both spoke bad Italian. Along with about forty of Hamet's men, basking in the afterglow of their first good meal in weeks, they headed through the rich delta fields to Alexandria.

Half a day had gone well, then at a place called "English Cut" they were stopped by a troop of Turkish guards. Hamet presented a copy in Turkish of the viceroy's *firman* allowing him to travel throughout Egypt. No discernible impact showed on the faces of the officers. By whose order were they stopped, Eaton demanded to know. He was told: the admiral of the Port of Alexandria.

Did not the viceroy rule all of Egypt? The question seemed legitimate. The admiral's men informed Eaton that the viceroy's jurisdiction ended at the low water mark, and that therefore the admiral considered it his responsibility to protect the coastline and all of Alexandria, since the town jutted out into the sea. The officers announced that the admiral refused to allow Hamet to embark at, disembark from, or enter Alexandria.

Now Hamet and Eaton had some quick choices to make. They were not arrested, but while Eaton could go to Alexandria, Hamet could not. So they decided that Hamet would circle to the south of Lake Mareotis and set up camp at an abandoned fortress, thirty miles from Alexandria, called Arab's Tower.

More important, the two men now finalized a major strategy decision. Since Hamet couldn't embark from Alexandria, he and Eaton would march across five hundred bleak miles of Libyan desert to attack Derne from the land side. If the U.S. Navy would not provide ships to carry troops . . . if the Turkish authorities closed the Mediterranean ports to them, then they would travel overland. As far as either man knew, no army in a thousand years had attacked Derne from the deserts of Egypt.

Their route, which would follow in the footsteps of Alexander the Great, would carry them into the northernmost Sahara, across the edge of the Great Libyan Desert. An avid reader, Eaton had not found one single detailed account by any travelers of this stretch of land; he knew it was a desert and not much else. He hoped to rely on Hamet, who had traveled the route once before, when fleeing his country. Eaton also knew they would have to rely on guides, camel caravan leaders, and local Bedouin tribes whose hospitality might determine whether they lived or died. All his hardships and exploits to this point would be nothing compared to the challenge of this desert.

Eaton and Hamet, together for all of forty-eight hours, now parted company. Eaton continued on horseback to Alexandria and to the *Argus* in the harbor. Hamet headed toward Arab's Tower but would make it only a dozen miles to a seaside town called Marabout before deciding to pitch camp.

When Eaton reached Alexandria, rumors of renewed French-English battles were sending jitters through the seaside metropolis. The British consul, Samuel Briggs, heard that the massive French fleet led by Villeneuve, long bottled up in Toulon by Nelson, had escaped and was heading to Egypt; the French could be expected any day to offload the Grand Army.

Despite the chaos in Alexandria, Eaton hoped to recruit troops, drill them, buy provisions for them, hire a camel caravan, and be off on his way within two weeks. All this in a war-torn city, with supplies scarce and with suspicious city officials. To speed the process, he chose the obvious candidate for quartermaster, Richard Farquhar, a veteran of Mediterranean trade who had been lobbying for this post for two years in letters to President Jefferson and to Hamet. The Briggs Brothers also vouched for him. Farquhar intended to hitch his nonexistent merchant business to the regime change in Tripoli. On February 7, Eaton handed him the not so princely sum of $500 to amass supplies and recruits. The two men would chafe each other raw.

Within days, Farquhar informed Eaton that he had run out of money, was buying on credit, and would need more cash. Eaton gave him $250 more but demanded to see the accounts.

To Eaton's military upbringing, Farquhar's early bookkeeping was singularly cavalier. Eaton found fault with him—loudly and publicly. He must have really tongue-lashed the Scot because on February 12, a mere five days into his long-coveted job, Farquhar threatened to quit. He had developed a relationship of sorts with Hamet over the years, and he informed Captain Hull that Hamet had told him several times that he would *never* go overland to Derne unless Farquhar came along. So, convinced of his strong bargaining position, Farquhar high-handedly made an offer to the Americans to return to work: "I will do [the expedition] on the following conditions—Viz. that Mr. Eaton shall be <u>more reserve</u> in his manner of speaking, and that my account shall be paid up till today, and that at least one hundred and fifty men shall go from this to join the Bashaw, with three or four small guns, and [I receive] an agreement stating the pay and time of service."

The Scotsman added that British consul Briggs would be pleased to settle the details. No record has survived of the string of curses with which Eaton greeted this offer. Farquhar sheepishly resumed his job as quartermaster.

Hull, beyond impatient and out of provisions and money, wanted to leave immediately to rejoin the squadron, which meant that Eaton must now plead his case in a letter to Commodore Barron for supplies and reinforcements. In brusque military fashion, Eaton noted his needs: three small navy vessels (to rendezvous with them at Bomba, a harbor east of Derne), two brass fieldpieces (capable of shooting four-pound balls) with balls and powder, and a hundred rifles with cartridges. He added that for the plan to be "beyond caprice," he would need a hundred marines with fixed bayonets to deliver a "coup de main" (a deathblow).

He noted that he had already disbursed $10,000 (borrowed from the Briggs Brothers) and expected to need $10,000 more.

Turned down for funds so many times, Eaton knew the ill commodore was fiscally tight, especially toward this mission. So during his brief hours with Hamet he had quickly roughed out an agreement that called for *complete repayment of expedition costs.* "The Bashaw assures me," Eaton wrote to Barron on February 14, "he will be able immediately to refund these sums when established in those provinces. And to indemnify the United States for all expenses arising out of a cooperation with him, he pledges the tribute of Denmark, Sweden and Batavian Republic in case of recovering his throne, which may be calculated upon as a certain event."

The latter was a staggering concept—it's unlikely that the irony was completely lost on Eaton. The United States, fighting to stop paying tribute to Barbary pirates, would receive the blood money of three European nations. Taking this gold would make the United States a beneficiary of Tripoli's piracy and extortion. (This kind of fuzzy thinking on Eaton's part infuriated lawyerly Jefferson.)

In addition, Eaton wrung a dazzling list of concessions from Hamet, which he now used to lure Barron into cooperating. Hamet promised to release all American slaves for free; he would stipulate a permanent peace with the United States; he would treat all future war captives as prisoners of war liable for exchange instead of as slaves; he would deliver Yussef, his family, as well as Murad Rais (Scotsman Peter Lyle) to American authorities; he would hand over any Tripolitan privateer vessels that had ever attacked a U.S. ship.

Eaton sweetened the entire request by painting a glowing picture of Barron's future role. "You will have the glory of carrying the usurper a prisoner in Your Squadron to the United States and of relieving our fellow citizens from the chains of slavery without the degrading conditions of a ransom."

Eaton folded the letter, applied wax, sealed it with his ring, and handed it to Captain Hull to give to Commodore Barron. Now all Eaton could do was to try to gather an army of mercenaries and then go traipse off into the desert, without enough supplies, food, or ammunition for a war or even to last them many days beyond the journey itself . . . *on the hope, the slender hope* that Commodore Barron would send the U.S. Navy to show up to save them at the far end of their 500-mile trek.

Would Barron's ailing liver allow him to make prompt decisions? Would he be willing to spare the ships, guns, and men? Would he regard it all as outrageous tomfoolery? Eaton was wagering his life that Barron would deliver.

Hull was ready to weigh anchor, but Eaton convinced him to let him borrow a handful of men: Lieutenant O'Bannon and seven U.S. Marines, as well as two midshipmen, George Washington Mann and Pascal Paoli Peck. He sent his stepson Eli back on board.

On February 19, Captain Hull and the *Argus* left Alexandria for the thousand-mile voyage to Malta. (He would soon run into a horrific winter storm, pushing him off course.) Within days, Eaton finished formalizing his agreement with Hamet into what Eaton called a "Convention between the United States of America and his Highness, Hamet, Caramanly, Bashaw of Tripoli." The document was signed by Hamet and Eaton, later witnessed by Lieutenant O'Bannon, Dr. Francesco Mendrici, and Pascal Paoli Peck, and a copy in English, Arabic, and Italian filed at the British consulate in Alexandria. The "Naval Agent" with imprecise responsibilities had just negotiated a fifteen-clause treaty.

While Alexandria braced for a French invasion, quartermaster Farquhar scrambled to find supplies. A desert trek required portable food that wouldn't spoil: Farquhar was able to locate only 25 bushels of rice and 18 barrels (100 pounds each) of biscuits. He bulked out the fodder with beans (68 bushels) and barley (90 bushels). But, without a head count, who knew whether that would be enough for a month-long trek? The sloppiness of the planning galled Eaton. In the meantime, the Scot sent fresh mutton and goat and beef to Hamet's camp and to the table at British House. Farquhar, who had spent time in Cairo with Eaton, made special effort to load in ample liquor both for current imbibing and for the trek, including 14 bottles of brandy, a bottle of rum for the doctor, and two 63-gallon hogsheads of wine. Military supplies almost seem to have been an afterthought: 100 flints, 48 stirrups, 5 saddles, a ramrod.

Farquhar submitted to Eaton a revised expense account. Prickly Eaton planted little *x*'s all over it, signifying denied charges. He singled out a huge sum of $622.83 and thickly underlined it and branded it: "Neither authorized, specified nor vouched—Inadmissable." William Eaton, whose own consular expense account from Tunis had been denied, was clamping down. If those charges were disallowed for items already purchased, then Farquhar would have to reimburse Briggs Brothers out of his own—empty—pockets.

One afternoon, a new threat to the mission arrived out of the deep blue sea. A ketch darted into the port of Alexandria carrying a messenger from brother Yussef in Tripoli, who promised great rewards to the governor of Alexandria and the admiral of the port if they would arrest Hamet. Through a bribe to the governor's translator, Eaton learned, however, that the messenger carried no gold or silver to back up his words and that in desperation he had started pleading for help, saying that Yussef might lose his throne. "If the [messenger] has not the means of touching a more sensible nerve than a turk's pity," observed Eaton, "[then] his case is forlorn."

Despite Eaton's plans inching forward, the New Englander still had one glaring missing item on his agenda: an army. He had persuaded Hull to let him borrow a handful of men. He still had some Cairo recruits, including a French musician and that eccentric Jean Eugene, but that was it. Anyone else would have to be hired from the human flotsam and jetsam stranded in Alexandria, the soldiers cast off by other armies or hiding from them.

Farquhar scoured for Christian mercenaries. Cripples were weeded out. He fortunately found an intact troop of thirty-eight Greeks—Spiro, Constantin, Cosmo, Giorgi, et al. under Captain Luca—and twenty-five artillery men of various nationalities, including French, Maltese, Italian,

Coptic. Eaton, in an offhand comment, once described them as "principally old soldiers." They might be cannon fodder for other armies, but they were Eaton's stalwarts. The muster roll, with rare exception for some officers, lists only first names. (Many of them were probably deserters.) Some are identified as merely "the cook" or "the drummer."

Farquhar still had to wrestle with the new recruits over their salaries and signing bounties. Back in Cairo, he had paid a $20 signing bonus, but now Eaton wanted him to be stingier, especially since an age-old trick among soldiers was to collect the bounty, then skip town. "I have endeavoured to perswead the men to take Eight Dollars telling them they would get Prize Money but they will not go for less than Ten Dollars. Therefore all is at a Stand which I am very Sorry for. They all want a Months advance. Their Officer will be Securety for them."

Ten dollars a month, while still a low-end wage for men about to march across the desert, was more than privates in the U.S. Marines earned at the time. Eaton, a man in a hurry, agreed to the ten-dollar price tag, but he still regarded Farquhar's inventories and expenses as all muddled. "You will immediately make out your account, supported by proper vouchers . . . The statement of your account will specify the dates, weights and measures . . . all articles will be reduced to English Standard."

Hull had already been gone a week; Eaton wanted to leave town. "The delay in your account have already caused a suspense in our operations . . . the expedition will move the day after tomorrow morning, after which all your unclosed accounts, must be submitted to the department of the treasury of the United States to be audited, and passed or rejected, according to vouchers you may produce."

Midshipman Pascal Paoli Peck delivered Eaton's letter to the Scot and demanded any cash still on hand. Farquhar denied having any, and teenager Peck, inspired by mentor Eaton, loudly berated the older quartermaster.

All this time, Hamet and his forty followers were camped at Marabout, the spot where Napoleon had landed his army in 1798. By now, Eaton had discovered that Hamet had a second wife in Alexandria who lived there with their child and a black slave woman. (Hamet's first wife and family were still hostages in Tripoli.) No doubt Hamet's wife visited him. Farquhar also continued to take care of his old friend, delivering by pack ass a steady supply of various fresh meats, and even of tobacco and pipes. The two men, who had corresponded on and off for years, grew more intimate.

As William Eaton cracked down on Farquhar's spending, Hamet made a *very curious* decision. He chose the Scot over the American. He wrote an unctuous note that implied that he wanted to abandon the Tripoli mission and instead sneak off with the Scot.

To our Friend and Son, Mister Fahr, English Merchant.

I inform you if God wills it, you are our friend, I swear by God if you will come to me it is no concern of anyone else. [Apparently Eaton had forbidden Farquhar from visiting Hamet.] You are like my son and not like the others, and when you come, you may do as you desire. If you come, you will be welcome, you are as one of my sons M'hamed and Omar and Ahosen.

I have need from you of a little money, and I will give you a letter written in my own hand; to you I owe much money, and you have spent much on me and I have much love and friendship for you.

The camels have arrived and we wish to depart with the money in safety. If you love me, you will get along with me better and better. Not to know all is to know nothing.

That last paragraph reeks of a getaway conspiracy. Hamet, with a life of setbacks, must have found Eaton's passion and temper daunting. Hamet sent the note on February 28 and received no reply. (Maybe Farquhar found it dangerous to take Eaton's money and saunter off with Hamet.)

Even British consul Briggs tried to help Farquhar, who was busy trying once again to deliver accounts acceptable to Eaton. He submitted them; the effort was doomed. At the very top of the muster roll from Cairo, Eaton found four phantom recruits; others listed as receiving $20 had been given $10, according to Eaton, who wrote in his notebook that

Farquhar had "chiefly embezzled or misapplied" the bulk of $1,350. Eaton fired him.

Eaton had yet again refused to compromise and had made an enemy, and this very vocal enemy, it so happened, would head in the next month to Syracuse and Malta, where he would meet with two of the most important men in Eaton's life: Commodore Barron and Tobias Lear. Upsetting Farquhar further was the fact that his own son George had decided to abandon his father and join Eaton's expedition across the desert.

Yet another sideshow feud was going to make a hard mission harder.

Eaton, taking over the quartermaster job himself, raced to finish buying supplies and landing recruits. Tough men were hard to come by. While he never admitted committing the following recruiting caper on the French, he never denied it either. French consular records indicate that a fellow identified as "Roc Maltais" helped two criminals, a couple of soldiers named Angelo Agravanni and Bernard Semerelli, escape from the prison at the French consulate. (Eaton had hired three Maltese as couriers, and he had an officer named "Rocco" on the muster roll.) The French guards lost the trail and Roc Maltais led the escapees—possibly thieves or murderers—to the Bashaw's camp at Marabout, where they enlisted in the American-Hamet expedition.

The French found out in a way that certainly seems like Eaton was taunting them. While running an errand at Colucci's Pharmacy, Eaton's personal servant told the druggist within earshot of the *dragoman of the French consulate* about the whereabouts of the escaped prisoners.

The French consul, Drovetti, found the insult totally unacceptable. He dashed off an angry protest to Samuel Briggs, British consul.

The world in 1805 was split into friends of Napoleon and his foes. The British diplomat wrote a carefully crafted reply stating that he could not contact Drovetti as a representative of the British government because of the state of war between the two nations; nor could he contact him as a representative of the U.S. government because he had no authority over American *public* officials. However, *as a private citizen,* he would relay the French consul's complaint to Eaton. Briggs, with faux politeness, added: "I am persuaded that a regular report directed to him will receive all the consideration that it merits."

Eaton's reply to Drovetti was more direct. "My reports . . . [will] require your explanations to our respective governments and to the world for the open indignity you have shown the flag of the United States in this port . . . [and for] the singular insult . . . [of] your order, 'French subjects in this city should have no intercourse with Americans.' " Finally, he expressed his "extraordinary outrage" that Drovetti had accused them of spying on the Turks.

Eaton had once again exacerbated a public dispute and transformed it into a personal quarrel. Antagonizing the French consul would quickly reap unpleasant consequences. The following week, Drovetti would hire a special courier to deliver to Bashaw Yussef in Tripoli a detailed report of the American-Hamet troop strength and of their plans to attack Derne. Eaton's surprise attack on Derne would be no surprise.

On March 2, 1805, William Eaton directed supplies to be loaded onto a lateen-sailed *djerm* to carry them from Alexandria to Marabout. The mission was finally nearing its start. Once the dockworkers had finished loading all the sacks and barrels, Turkish guards immediately seized the vessel and the American supplies. Simultaneously, a troop of Turkish soldiers began the ten-mile march to Marabout to arrest Hamet. French intrigue might have caused the crackdown, or maybe Yussef's emissary had borrowed some money for bribes.

Eaton sent a messenger racing to Marabout to warn Hamet. Never the warrior, Hamet decided to flee to the desert. Exact details haven't survived—because Eaton rarely wanted to memorialize Hamet's cowardice—but Lieutenant O'Bannon in command of seven marines changed the prince's mind. "The firm and decided conduct of Mr. O'Bannon prevented their movement," wrote Eaton tersely.

In Alexandria, Eaton applied to the British consul Samuel Briggs for help. Since Briggs, along with his two brothers at Briggs Brothers, had already lent Eaton $10,000, Samuel had a huge incentive to protect him from disaster. (Foreign consuls then could supplement their incomes; oftentimes, their schemes dovetailed with home office policy.)

Briggs investigated the problem. "We found . . . a supervisor of the revenue, who had not yet been bought," he told Eaton. Cash was delivered; the small vessel departed carrying supplies. The Turkish troop was recalled.

On Sunday, March 3, Eaton and Midshipman Peck arrived at Marabout, where they found an odd disjointed army camped by the Mediterranean. Hamet—to his credit—had succeeded in landing a troop of about two hundred Arab cavalry from a nearby tribe, who agreed to join the mission. Their encampment sprawled over an open field. In another spot was Hamet's Tripoli entourage, which had swelled to around ninety. Bivouacking in yet another area were Eaton's 75 Christian mercenaries, in various uniforms from earlier stints, including Greeks, Italians, Maltese, a Tyrolean, several French. Near them in U.S. Marine uniforms were stationed Lieutenant O'Bannon and his seven U.S. Marines. Dozens of Arab baggage and camel handlers filled out scene. The sound and smell of camels mixed with the sea breezes.

In theory, Eaton commanded this entire troop. His "Convention" with Hamet specified that Eaton "be recognized as General, and Commander in Chief of the land forces . . . and said Highness, Hamet Bashaw, engages that his own Subjects shall respect and obey him as such."

Bereft of a quartermaster, Eaton found himself forced to negotiate for camels. It seems extraordinary that this agreement should have been hammered out so near the day of departure. With Hamet helping translate, Eaton struck a deal, or so he supposed, that Sheik Tayyib would supply 190 camels at eleven dollars a head for the journey to Derne. It's unclear how much Eaton paid in advance, but in any case, the sheik quickly "raised fresh demands for cash," as Eaton wrote in his travel journal. "[He] seemed determined to retard the march until his pretentions were satisfied," complained Eaton. "Pacified him with promises." The following day, at the start of the march, Eaton counted 105 camels.

So begins yet another contentious relationship for Eaton, one that would jeopardize their lives.

The motley band set off on a desert path for Arab's Tower, a fortress that from the sea appears like a tower. The freestone fortress walls are five feet thick and thirty-two feet high.

The march was so disorganized that most of the camels and baggage straggled far behind and had to catch up. Just as their caravan began snaking along the dry road, a messenger on horseback raced to catch up with them. The Briggs Brothers—perhaps fearing that Eaton's own navy would abandon him—offered to send a shipload of food to Bomba. He declined.

Midshipman Peck in a letter captured the first day's events.

> *After marching near 40 miles in a burning sun, buoyed with the idea of finding water at the end of our march, we found on encamping, not the least sign of water nor was a green thing to be seen. All hands were employed in clearing out the well but were so thirsty and fatigued they could hardly move. For myself, not having taken the precaution to procure a small skin of water to carry on my horse, had it not been for a few oranges I had, I should hardly have been able to move next morning. I laid myself down on my bed to sleep but I could not, being for the first time in my life almost dead with thirst. Had I possessed thousands I would have given them for a gill of water.*

Five hundred more miles of desert stretched out before them. The Americans had no map; they didn't speak Arabic; Eaton didn't trust his guides, and they didn't trust him. The bleached bones of dead horses and camels were scattered in the area around this unexpectedly dry water hole.

Eaton quickly learned that the physical challenges of the trek would be made far worse by simmering religious hatreds between his Moslem and Christian troops, and by the conniving of the greedy camel drivers, who could halt the caravan. At many moments of life-and-death crisis ahead, he also would learn uncomfortable truths about his man Hamet.

WILLIAM EATON SLEPT in his homemade general's uniform. He later wrote that he didn't take the uniform off for the *next ninety-five days* except to change his "linen."

At Eaton's side that first morning and throughout much of the trek was Lieutenant O'Bannon in his blue coat with two long vertical rows of brass buttons. (He and Eaton would soon discover that the officers' bounty of brass buttons would prove enticing to the Bedouin women.) The seven U.S. Marines in their blue-with-scarlet-trim uniforms stood nearby, looking unnaturally tall in their high brimless hats.

These uniformed Americans—clustered together—seemed like an honor guard for this sea of irregular troops; they were a handful of men lost in a multitude of robes and turbans.

William Eaton, contrary to myth, did not ride a camel; he was mounted on a Barbary horse, as was Lieutenant O'Bannon and Midshipman Peck—and all three hundred or so Moslem troops. The Christian recruits marched on foot with the camel drivers. The baggage train of camels brought up the rear.

About an hour after dawn, one of the Arab guides found some fetid water within a mile of camp, and the men headed there for a drink. Eaton, meanwhile, was forced to wait for the camel caravan to catch up and reach Arab's Tower.

Besides a brief letter by Midshipman Pascal Peck, William Eaton's journal provides the only source for this extraordinary journey. His prejudices color the account; neither Hamet nor Sheik Tayyib would leave any words in their defense.

Eaton, unlike Lawrence of Arabia a century later, did not try to assimilate the ways of the Bedouins or any of the Moslems; Eaton tried to impose his American will upon them, to remold them. Mutual disenchantments would detonate deep hatreds. Mutual enchantments would spark brief exaltations. When World War I ended, T. E. Lawrence had written: "Pray God that men reading the story will not, for the love of the glamour of strangeness, go out to prostitute themselves and their talents in serving another race." Eaton was never seduced by strangeness but rather was irritated by it; his quest was to re-establish the *honor* of the United States, and to defy a *strange* time-honored custom of state-sponsored piracy and tribute.

Eaton's army was a deeply divided troop of distrustful mercenaries. The fault lines were obvious: hats and turbans, clean-shaven and beards; uncircumcised Christians and circumcised Moslems. Eaton at one point counted a dozen distinct nationalities: American, English, French, Maltese, Greek, Arab, Turk, Tyrolean, Neapolitan, Tripolitan, and others unspecified.

The merest glance at the encampment near the walls of the fortress on that morning of March 7, 1805, revealed the fissures. Europeans peacocked in tight pants and coats while town Moslems wore baggy pants and bright-colored vests and turbans. And desert Arabs wore the long-flowing *barracan*, a single brown or white wool garment, six yards long and two yards wide, fastened at the left shoulder and looped around the body. No shirt beneath, no underwear; it afforded both privacy and freedom; by night, it served as a blanket.

Eaton devoted the entire day to getting the various troops organized for the trek ahead. They were all about to embark together to cross a desert, but it wasn't the "sea of sands" of Lawrence of Arabia or the Sahara of the French Foreign Legion.

Geographers classify this coastal tract as the fringe of the deserts of Cyrenaica or as "desert steppe": consisting of parched ridges and gullies and vast dry plains. It is inhospitable terrain but not endless dunes. The distance between wells—each claimed by various Bedouin tribes—could be fifty miles or more, which might require two or three or even four days of travel. A dry well might mean death. All food must be carried, since the few animals that lived in the region were mostly hard-to-catch jerboa (desert rats) and lizards. Banditti, who would slit a throat for a saddlebag, also flourished in this no-man's-land between Egypt and the eastern region of Tripoli. Although hajj pilgrims and couriers from Morocco and Algiers used this route to head to Egypt, very few Christians for a thousand years since the conquest of Islam had ever passed this way.

One condition, however, aided the enterprise, and that was the time of year. The month of March meant that summer heat hadn't yet arrived; it also meant that the winter rains had given some of the valleys a baby's down of pale green, of grasswort or kali herbiage. Camels would eat even the thornier varieties, and maybe horses would also, if desperate enough.

Eaton expected the entire 520-mile run from Marabout (near Alexandria) to Derne to take approximately fifteen days. As quartermaster, Eaton had loaded more than enough food and animal fodder for a journey of that duration. He made his estimates based on the fact that a camel, carrying a thousand pounds, moves at three miles an hour and can walk from sunup to sundown.

On that Thursday, March 7, as the men prepared, Midshipman Peck learned from his mistake about not carrying water. Peck drank at the well, and this time he bartered for a couple of water skins and filled them. Bedouins over the centuries had perfected the art of skinning the entire goat to create a huge water sack. The goatskins were often greased inside and out with camel lard to prevent them from cracking in the heat. One Christian traveler found the taste of the water, after long marinating in these skins, exceptionally vile.

While Eaton continued to wait for the camel caravan, he used the day to try to strike some order in his troops, which he had not once drilled. The would-be conquerors barely knew one another.

In theory, according to a signed piece of paper, the Convention, Eaton ruled this disparate army. Eaton, perched atop the chain of command, gave orders to Lieutenant O'Bannon for his seven marines, to Selim Comb and Lieutenant Connant for the motley European artillery crew, and to Captain Luco Ulovix and Lieutenant Constantine for the

Greek company. To direct the Arab cavalry, he would relay his orders to Hamet and two sheiks: Tayyib and Muhammed; and for the camel caravan, wily Sheik Tayyib acted as intermediary. *That was on paper*.

Since the first day's march of forty miles had proven too ambitious, Eaton led the troops on a fifteen-mile march the next day to a place with good water on an elevated bluff by the sea. The Europeans drank wine and brandy under the stars. Each nationality cocooned into a distinct camp.

From his first taste of the dry coastal landscape, Eaton regarded the trek as hard but manageable if they kept moving forward at a steady pace. His years of military training made him accustomed to giving orders and seeing them obeyed. None of it prepared him for the tricks of the caravan leaders. (Their delay tactics would exhaust his food supply.) On March 9, only the fourth day of the trek, the camel drivers refused to work. The trick was as old as the Bible: Wait till the caravan is out on the desolate road, then demand more wages. Eaton figured if they received too much of the total amount promised them, they might vanish. "It was not safe to do it," he wrote. "They became mutinous."

Sheik Tayyib had riled up the camel drivers and footmen by telling them that once the march was over, the Christians would cheat them out of the balance of their wages. Eaton indignantly denied the charge and looked in vain to Hamet for help. "The Bashaw seemed irresolute and despondent," wrote Eaton.

The morning was spent bickering. "Money, more money was the only stimulus which could give motion to the camp." Eaton, whose Barbary mission was about stopping extortion, refused to give in. At noon, he ordered all the Christians to march *back* toward Alexandria. Obviously Sheik Tayyib could not get any more money if the mission was aborted.

The Christians began to retrace their steps; Eaton caught the glimpse he hoped for . . . an Arab messenger galloping to catch up with him. Sheik Tayyib agreed that the camel caravan would resume. The army—despite their afternoon start—accomplished twelve miles in the right direction that day, passing through low sand valleys and then twenty miles the next day through rocky desert plains. They glimpsed the ruins of a castle, an odd reminder that the region had once thrived under earlier rulers. No one knew the name of the castle. Eaton guessed by the architecture that it was ancient Greek.

In the middle of the following afternoon, a courier coming from the opposite direction, that is, from Derne, sought out the Bashaw to deliver startling news: The province was arming to join Hamet and to overthrow the government and, he added, the current governor had locked himself inside the walls of the palace. When word spread, some of the Arab riders at the head of the army performed feats of horsemanship and many of them fired off *feu de joie* into the sky. When the camel drivers at the back of the caravan heard the firing, they thought it meant that Bedouins were attacking. "[They] attempted to disarm and put to death the Christians who escorted the caravan," wrote Eaton. In a crisis, religion trumped all other loyalties.

As the two religions squared off, a Moslem leader intervened, shouting that the Arabs should not kill anyone until they found out the cause of the shots. Both groups waited in an uneasy truce with weapons pointed at one another until the good news arrived. After that incident, both Christian and Moslem continued the march, but their mutual animosities now lay out in the open. Four hundred heavily armed distrustful men must continue to coexist and someday fight together on the same side.

The divided army camped on a rocky ridge overlooking the Mediterranean, at a spot where a half dozen deep wells, cut centuries earlier through solid rock, provided good water. The men slung long ropes down into the hundred-foot-deep dark shafts and hauled up heavy full goatskins. At eight pounds a gallon, quenching an army's thirst worked up quite a thirst.

The next day, the three hundred horsemen and hundred or so on foot trekked onward around twenty-six miles across a "barren rocky plain" past more ancient ruins. Eaton reported that night they encamped "upon the dividing ridge between Egypt and Tripoli, near a cistern of excellent water." What is staggering is that Eaton was nowhere near the border between Egypt and Tripoli, which lies at least a hundred miles farther west at the edge of the fertile plain of Cyrenaica. The man on the now-not-so-secret mission clearly did not have a remotely accurate map of this region through which he was passing.

The army marched twenty-five miles off the ridge of Aqabet Ageiba and down into a ravine, with abundant rainwater stored in natural reservoirs carved by winter cascades into the solid rock. At evening the U.S. Marines gathered firewood and boiled water to cook rice in cauldrons balanced on stones. The meat had run out, and now their entire rations consisted of two biscuits handed out in the morning and a bowl of rice per man in the evening. That night of Friday, March 15, the tenth day, clouds gathered and a chill hung in the air. A sudden downpour filled the ravine and flooded the camp, soaking everyone.

During the chaos, someone stole from the marines' tent a musket, a bayonet, and cartridges in a cartouche box. Eaton immediately assumed "Arabs" did it. "We had heretofore experienced daily losses of provisions and barley, which they stole and concealed." The thefts drove yet another wedge between the camps.

On Saturday, the eleventh day, the sodden men huddled together in the ravine as the storm grew more intense and strong winds blew in from the northwest. Zigzags of lightning lit up dripping faces. The soggy army couldn't head out in the morning, and by 3 p.m. the entire camp was flooded again. Despite spooked horses, jittery camels, drenched hungry men, they had to tramp to higher ground. At the start of the mission, the men worried about dying of thirst; now they feared drowning, getting swept along this ravine by a flash flood.

Sunday morning, day twelve, the army marched a dozen miles, then set up camp in another deep ravine. Looking up the steep banks, everyone prayed for no more rain. They found enough small brush to make fires, to try to dry out. Hundreds of men skulked around near naked, trying to wring the last drops out of their sodden garments. The Bedouin tied *barracans* to tent poles.

On Monday, the army marched fifteen miles to a valley near the coast, which the Arabs called "Masrocah." High sand dunes blocked the view of the sea. Eaton saw the ruins of Roman mansions and garden walls. A stone castle, 150-foot square, still stood there, with 11-foot-high walls intact. Eaton marched up to the castle and found a sheik living there with a handful of Bedouins camped in tents. After almost two weeks on the road, this marked the first permanent dwelling they had encountered. He found for sale cattle, sheep, goats, fowls, butter, dates, and milk, but the prices—thanks to the sheik's lack of competition—were "very dear."

The camel drivers suddenly went on strike again. This time, however, no matter how much Eaton promised, threatened, cajoled, they adamantly refused to go another mile. "I now learned, *for the first time,* that our caravan was freighted by the Bashaw only to this place," wrote Eaton, "and that the owners had received no part of their pay." This was startling news. What had the Bashaw done with funds given him by Eaton? Why would he negotiate a trek of only two hundred miles of a five-hundred-mile journey and not tell his general? Eaton would never learn the answers.

The camel drivers began packing to return to their families in Egypt; Sheik Tayyib advanced their claims to Eaton.

The New Englander had spent years negotiating with the Bey of Tunis, and months with Jefferson; he had experienced long hard arguments full of feint and counterthrust. But he also knew when "no" meant "no."

Eaton offered to try to find some money to pay them if they would agree to march two more days to where Hamet and Eaton expected to find a very powerful Bedouin tribe, the Eu ed Alli, who in Egypt had vowed they wanted to join Hamet's revolution. (Since Eaton had misplaced the border by one hundred miles, it was anybody's guess whether he was identifying the correct location for this Bedouin tribe.)

The camel drivers, through Sheik Tayyib, agreed to the deal.

Eaton was carrying a little more than $540; he gave it *all except for three Venetian sequins.* (Since a Venetian sequin traded for about $2.25, Eaton's cash worth now totaled $6.75 to last him three hundred miles to Bomba.) Eaton, explaining the direness, convinced the Christian officers and men to chip in another $140 of their own money. Eaton, with a vast show of empty pockets, turned over $673 to the Bashaw, who supplemented it with an unspecified amount and handed it over on Tuesday, March 19, to the leaders of the camel drivers.

With many salaams, they thanked Hamet and Eaton for the payments. That same night, the drivers of about seventy camels sneaked off to return to Egypt, and the next morning the drivers of the remaining forty camels refused to budge. General Eaton, besides being furious, looked outmaneuvered. He described their situation as "perplexing and embarrassed" since it was "impossible to move without the caravan and uncertain whether we could procure them to start from this place."

Hamet suggested to Eaton that they leave their supplies with a small guard inside the castle and proceed ahead to look for the Eu ed Alli Bedouins. Eaton, with three sequins to his name, judged the risk too great.

That night, the remaining drivers disappeared with the rest of the camels. The following morning, Sheik Tayyib and the other sheiks controlling the Arab cavalry announced that they too refused to proceed. Tayyib claimed that a pilgrim on his way from Morocco to Mecca had told them that at least 800 enemy horsemen and even more foot soldiers, en route from Tripoli city, had already passed Bengazi, 175 miles from Derne. "I thought this an argument that urged acceleration rather than delay," wrote Eaton.

No camels, no money, now the report of a superior force advancing. The fodder of barley and beans for the horses was almost gone; the food supplies other than rice and biscuit were exhausted. All conspired to disjoint the factions further. Eaton was not allowed to attend the Moslem council as the bearded men in turbans and robes debated loudly. They invited Eaton into the tent at midnight and informed him that they would not budge until a "runner" had rushed the three hundred miles to Bomba and returned with news as to whether the American ships had arrived. That meant a ten-day wait, at minimum. Ten days in which the army would be consuming Eaton's precious supplies.

General Eaton stood in their tent, oil lamps transforming the faces into ghastly caricatures; the tired officer was surrounded by the sheiks and the Bashaw. Although his Christian forces were outnumbered by four to one, he announced that rice rations would be immediately stopped for anyone not planning on traveling forward. He made his announcement and abruptly left the tent.

After midnight, he vented some of his anger, railing in his journal against Islam. He referred to Mohammed as "one of the most hypocritical fanatics" who incited "wretched victims [on] a tedious pilgrimage to pay their devotion at his shrine." But he did find a saving grace to the fanaticism: that Moslem pilgrims had dug wells there in the desert that now gave water to soldiers fighting for "the liberation of three hundred Americans from the chains of Barbarism, and [for] a manly peace."

Eaton began that night to work out secret plans to try to take the castle so that his Christian troops could hole up there with the rice and the ammunition until a messenger could reach Bomba and bring back U.S. Marines.

At sunup, European soldiers guarded the food supply. No Moslems, including Hamet, had access to the food. Eaton waited; he banked on hunger in this showdown; the Moslem leaders blinked first.

The sheiks brought fifty camels back to the encampment and agreed to march two days farther. At 11 A.M., with the usual camel snorting and snuffling, the caravan recommenced. The bedraggled army proceeded thirteen miles, to "an elevated stony plain" with good cistern water. The following day at 3 P.M. Eaton along with Hamet in the fore led their horses up a ridge and at the top peeked over into a vast fertile plain stretching to the sea. There, Eaton saw a scene from the Bible: the tents of the wandering tribe of the Eu ed Alli Bedouin, almost 4,000 men, women, and children, along with their grazing horses, camels, sheep, goats. Midshipman Peck, perhaps no expert in counting live-stock, estimated about 10,000 camels and 50,000 sheep. After so many disappointments, Eaton had caught a break. These were Hamet's strongest allies, a tribe with deep animosity against Bashaw Yussef and his tax collectors.

Eaton allowed the men to rest and recuperate. The mission appeared again on solid footing. These Bedouin greeted Hamet like a hero and were surprisingly open and friendly to the foreigners.

"Bedouin ways were hard even for those brought up to them," wrote T. E. Lawrence, "and for strangers terrible: a death in life." He was *not* re-ferring to the Eu ed Alli tribe, who for much of the year lived a fairly pleasant nomadic existence on the verdant Cyrenaica Plateau. The men and women wore the long *barracan* draped over their shoulders; extended family groups pitched their tents in clusters, each ruled by a sheik. Their fiercest moments came in protecting their grazing lands or water holes.

Most of the tribe had never ventured farther than a couple hundred miles toward Egypt or south to the desert oases.

"We were the first Christians ever seen by these wild people," wrote Eaton. "We were viewed by them as curiosities. They laughed at the oddity of our dress; gazed at our polished arms with astonishment; at the same time they observed the greatest deference towards such of us as bore any distinctive marks of office." The brass buttons and gold epaulets dazzled them. The Bedouin women, though Moslem, did not veil their faces.

The downtrodden army had stumbled into paradise. "They brought us for sale everything their camps afforded, and as rarities offered us young gazelles and ostriches." Rather, they had stumbled into a *pay-as-you-go* paradise, and they had three Venetian sequins. Luckily for Eaton and company, these Bedouin adored rice and coveted brass buttons and other trinkets. The Christians bartered for succulent dates, recently delivered by caravan from Siwa, the oasis of Jupiter Ammon, visited by Alexander the Great.

The next morning, 80 mounted tribesmen, each carrying a long musket, a dagger, and a pair of pistols, offered to join Hamet. Eaton was thrilled until he realized they required money in advance. "Cash, we find, is the only deity of Arabs, as well as Turks," he sourly noted. The fiercely territorial Eu ed Alli allowed the camels and horses of the Hamet-Eaton army to graze, an especially important privilege, since the sacks of barley were empty. While the warriors wouldn't ride without money, Eaton succeeded in striking a bargain for Eu ed Alli to freight a camel caravan of 90 beasts at $11 a head to Bomba, *payable at Bomba*. And Eaton sent a courier ahead to look for Captain Hull's ships.

Sunday was a day of rest for all. On Monday, forty-seven Bedouin families moved to the Hamet camp and agreed to march forward with the army to Bomba. Included among the families were about 150 warriors on foot, willing to fight. Eaton's army was growing.

The Bedouin displayed a natural curiosity toward the foreigners. Being accustomed to fried flat bread, they had never seen ship biscuit. "They examined it carefully; and after breaking it with their shepherd's club or hatchet, tasted it with symptoms of hesitation; finding it palatable they sought every means to obtain it."

Eaton also discovered just how much the Bedouin appreciated the taste of rice. "A woman offered her daughter to my interpreter for a sack of it: and the girl consented to the traffic. She was a well proportioned, handsome brunette of about thirteen or fourteen years, with an expressive hazel eye . . . black, arched eyebrows, perfect teeth and lips formed for voluptuousness."

Eaton weighed the deal. "Prudence forbid it," he wrote. (It would turn out that that final sack of rice, a day's rations for 90 men, would help save their lives.)

On Tuesday, March 26, as the refreshed army prepared to resume its march, a courier on horseback suddenly arrived. He was bearing bad news, and he claimed his information was not hearsay but fact. He reported that Bashaw Yussef's army of at least 500 cavalrymen, along with a great number of Bedouins from various tribes, "were a few days march from [Derne] and would certainly arrive before . . . we could."

Yet again, the Moslem portion of the army lost hope. The camel caravan fled backward. Some of Hamet's closest advisers conspired with the cavalry tribes to return to the Fayyum region near Cairo. Eaton once again ordered all rice rations stopped until everyone returned and agreed to proceed.

The Moslem leaders held a council. At 11 A.M. Sheik Tayyib, his jeweled dagger bobbing at his hip, announced that he would not proceed with his horsemen until unimpeachable news arrived of the American ships waiting in Bomba.

Eaton snapped, unleashing the full hurricane of his temper. He accused Tayyib of being a liar and a coward. "You have promised much and fulfilled nothing," Eaton shouted, barely waiting for the translator to catch up. He said he regretted ever having met Tayyib, and that he would be delighted if Tayyib would execute his threat to return to Egypt.

Tayyib, the second most powerful leader on the mission, stormed out of the camp "in a rage, swearing by all the force of his religion to join us no more." Hamet suggested sending an officer after Tayyib, but Eaton refused.

Tayyib galloped straight to the tents of the tribe of the Eu ed Alli and convinced half the families who had decided to accompany Eaton to travel instead to Egypt with him. At dawn on the following day, Hamet asked Eaton yet again to send an officer to request *in Eaton's name* that Tayyib return. Eaton did indeed send a message to Tayyib, but it stated that if he now became their enemy, then Eaton would have the right to punish him and that only respect for Hamet had restrained him so far. "I have a rifle and a sabre true to their distance," Eaton threatened. The general had no doubt already demonstrated his prowess at fifty paces blowing the head off some desert rat.

When Tayyib received the note, he "swore vengeance against the Bashaw and his Christian sovereigns, as he styled us."

Eaton ordered the remaining men to march. Three hours later, a messenger arrived to tell them that Tayyib had begun leading his caravan back to Egypt. Eaton sent the courier back with a simple message to the sheik. "I have nothing further to do with you but to take steps for the recovery of the cash and property you have fraudulently drawn from me."

Two hours later, at noon, the messenger reappeared. Tayyib would rejoin the army if Eaton would halt the march. Hamet convinced Eaton to stop. At 1:30 P.M., Sheik Tayyib came to Eaton's tent. "You see the influence I have among these people," said Tayyib. "Yes, and I also see the disgraceful use you make of it," replied Eaton.

At dawn on the following day, the twenty-second of the expedition, Eaton, having temporarily outflanked Tayyib, gave orders to prepare for a good day's march. He saw no reason why twenty miles could not be achieved. He ordered his officers to go saddle up. They approached the area where the horses were grazing. Armed guards stopped them, telling them that Hamet, who had agreed to provide horses for the top foreign officers, had changed his mind. His minions informed Eaton that the horses for officers such as Lieutenant O'Bannon and Midshipman Peck would now be given to Hamet's footmen instead.

In addition, the Moslems were not ready to head out on the trail.

Eaton had the drummer beat for marching formation. The Christians lined up . . . the robed Moslems with Hamet in command stood off to one side. With no preamble or diplomacy, Eaton demanded the horses. Yet again, he snapped. In front of everyone, he accused Hamet of being weak and capricious. He spit out piles of angry words.

At some point Eaton abruptly stopped haranguing Hamet and ordered the march to proceed. Eaton's uniformed troops with fixed bayonets forced the camel drivers to lead the camels carrying the food and supplies to the forefront of the troops. Eaton had learned his lesson and would never again let the camels trail behind. Hamet's forces lingered off to the side, watching the sacks of rice disappear down the road.

About two hours later, Hamet and a few horsemen caught up with Eaton's marchers and camels. Hamet praised Eaton for his "firmness" and claimed that he had merely been pretending to stall, to pay lip service to the "wishes of his people" and "to render them more manageable."

The divided army achieved twelve and a half dusty miles and reached a beautiful castle at "Shemees" (modern-day Zawia el-Shammas), an "enchanting" spot set in a fertile plain, with excellent well water and some gardens of fig and palm trees. They rested there that afternoon, waiting for the Eu ed Alli foot warriors and families to catch up. They never arrived. Eaton learned that his nemesis Sheik Tayyib "had discouraged and dissuaded them," and they had once again set off for the borders of Egypt. Both Eaton and Hamet realized that the Eu ed Alli were key allies and would be a great help in rallying other Bedouin tribes. Hamet sent his right-hand man, Ahmet Gurgies, to try to lure them back with promises of plunder at Derne.

Eaton and his troops found themselves holed up in another little paradise, though once again without the cash to enjoy themselves. The cattle, sheep, butter, fowls, eggs, and dates were offered but at outrageous prices.

Sometime that afternoon, the local sheik of the castle at el-Shammas, as a special mark of respect, invited Eaton within the walls. "Curiosity brought every Arab about me who belonged to the tribe. They examined the lace of my hat, epaulettes, buttons, spurs, and mounting of my arms. These they took to be all gold and silver. They were astonished that God should permit people to possess such riches who followed the religion of the devil!"

Eaton through his interpreter explained that the religion of the United States was different "from that of all other nations who wore hats, that we made no distinction in our respect to people of different creeds . . . that all honest men were equally respected in America."

The Bedouin were skeptical that such a Christian nation really existed.

The interpreter pointed to Eaton and said that he was a good man and great friend to Moslems. "They lamented that so good a man should go to hell." They offered to save Eaton and gain him entrance to the paradise of Mohammed if he would repeat: "Allah Allah Muhammed Benallah." The tawny-skinned Bedouins gathered around him, again and again begging Eaton to repeat after them.

Eaton told them that Americans believe that all good men after death will be allowed "to make parties of pleasure" into the paradises of the Moslems and of the Catholics. The Bedouin smiled at his farfetched story but added they would be pleased to see him in their paradise, although they doubted Mohammed would let him in even for a visit.

Late that night, this New England Protestant, who rarely attended church, reiterated his bafflement over other people's *deep* faith. "How frail is human reason! How absurd is the pride of bigotry! Yet how happy are these ignorant Arabs in their faith and intolerance! A desert [is] their patrimony; a wretched hut their dwelling; a blanket their bed and wardrobe; a wooden bowl and spoon their furniture; and milk and roots their food. Like the patriarchs of old, 'They seek a country.' Their hope is in heaven. Of arriving there they have the faith of assurance. They are contented."

Apparently, that encounter with the friendly Moslem faithful and their confusion about America and its religion inspired Eaton to spend the following day working with his French aide-de-camp, composing a "Proclamation" in French to deliver to the people of Tripoli. The cadence makes it sound like the sermon of a prophet, explaining America.

To the inhabitants of the kingdom of Tripoli . . . Brothers, sons of Abraham, faithful believers of the faithful messengers of Truth . . .

At the uttermost limits of the West, beyond the great and deep Atlantic Ocean, we have for several centuries possessed a country larger than the whole [Ottoman] empire of the Grand Signior. . . . We put [our enemies] to flight . . . Soon, the United States of America became a sanctuary for all men who fled from oppression and sought asylum there, and a refuge for those who had no other country. People of every nation, every tongue and every faith could come to us and dwell in safety, because our religion teaches us to fear and worship God and be kind to all creatures.

. . . We cultivated our soil and we sent products to all nations. . . . but although we endeavored to maintain in good faith friendly relations with all the powers of the earth, Yussef, the traitor, the usurper of the throne of Tripoli, a bloodthirsty scoundrel, having learned of our success . . . sent out his armed pirate ships against our commerce and even brought some of our ships into the port of Tripoli, and without provocation had their crews put in chains and reduced to slavery.

He would not listen to our offers of peace, or at least only on such humiliating terms as paying him an enormous sum of money and making ourselves and even our posterity his tributaries; which we disdained to concede to him for we are not accustomed to humiliate ourselves before men, nations, nor the powers of the earth, much less before this base and perjured traitor, whose naval commander [Murad Rais] is a drunken renegade, and whose principal counselor is a grasping Jew.

. . . If you [a citizen of Tripoli] were to fall into the hands of his enemies, would he pay one piastre to ransom you? No . . . he scoffs at your sufferings, saying: Of what value are these Moors and these Arabs? They are just beasts which belong to me, worth a great deal less than my camels and my asses. . . . The voice of God and the voice of justice should inspire you with a desire for vengeance, even the blood of his father and of his brother . . . cries . . . to you for vengeance.

. . . Come on, Moors, Arabs, Americans, brothers, come along from every corner of Barbary where the truth of the prophet has been received. Be assured that the God of the Americans and of the Mahometans is the same; the one true and omnipotent God. Be assured, therefore, that there was no thought of any difference in religion which could have induced us to make war on the city of Tripoli and on its piratical ruler; on the contrary, we do not wish to harm any of the inhabitants of that city, unless it be those who stubbornly adhere to the party of Yussef; we are joined and united with Sidi Hamet Pasha, and thus with the loyal children of his country, and we are resolved to re-establish him in the realm of his ancestors, by this means being able to offer peace to his kingdom and to his city of Tripoli. . . . We shall furnish you with war supplies and with food supplies, with money and, in case of need, with regular soldiers to aid you in vanquishing . . . your oppressor. And I shall be always with you until the end of the war and even until you have achieved your glorious mission, in proof of our fidelity and our goodwill.

William Eaton signed his name, with a customary flourish of long loops and curlicues underneath. He datelined it "Desert de Lybia, 29.eme Mars 1805." At the time, he meant every word of his promise "to be always with you until the end of the war."

That signature, that covenant in the desert, that promise, would haunt Eaton to his grave. Eaton handed the document off to be translated into Arabic and distributed to influential Arabs.

The same afternoon, Ahmet Gurgies returned, bringing with him the Bedouin families and warriors back from the trail to Egypt.

The drummer beat reveille before dawn on Saturday, and by 6 A.M., Eaton had the Christians and the baggage on the march. As he exited the camp, he saw Hamet's forces mounted and apparently preparing to leave. By 2 P.M., with men on foot and plodding camels, Eaton's troops had gone twelve miles and were resting. Hamet and a small troop of men galloped up. And Hamet informed Eaton of yet another snafu. The influential cavalry leader Sheik Muhammed accused Sheik Tayyib of cheating him and the others by not equally dividing the $1,500 given to him by Hamet. The other sheiks including the Eu ed Alli agreed that Tayyib had cheated, and they once again set off to march toward Egypt.

Eaton, irritated beyond measure, decided it was best to march his caravan three miles back along the trail to the nearest water to await the outcome. Hamet and his dozen men, along with Eaton's interpreter, rode back to the castle at El-Shammas and from there would chase after the departing sheiks.

On the next day, Sunday, March 31, the twenty-fifth day of the adventure, the weather turned cold. Winds off the coast picked up. Chill rain fell, soaking the general and the tents; the precious rice was carefully protected. The army sat around, trying to stay dry, waiting for Hamet.

April 1 brought more miserable rainy weather. To the ping of raindrops on the sides of his tent, Eaton sat stewing over delays and lost opportunities. Writing in his journal, he tried to force himself to dwell on the Arab characteristics he admired: "a savage independence of soul, . . . discipline [of the body], a sacred adherence to the laws of hospitality." His tent flap opened suddenly and six Arab sheiks bustled in out of the rain. These men, with Tayyib as their leader, ran the camel caravan. Spokesman Tayyib, addressing the general, demanded an increase in the rice ration, which was set at a half pint (an eight-ounce cup) per day per man. (Midshipman Peck pegged it at a "handful" a day.) Eaton refused. Tayyib threatened.

The two men had squabbled from day one, with Hamet playing diplomat between them. Eaton, cloistered in the crowded tent, with wild-eyed angry men making demands and gesticulating at him, did what he often did when threatened.

He exploded with an in-your-face tirade. It didn't matter that he was outnumbered or that he had no map of the wells. He called Tayyib "the cause of all our delays" and a double-crosser in all agreements. He said

Tayyib had promised to take the army to Derne in fourteen days; after twenty-six days, they had reached only half the distance. Tayyib blamed Hamet and the other sheiks.

Eaton said the others were all better men than Tayyib. "I can place no reliance on anything you say or undertake," shouted Eaton. Tayyib claimed indifference to Eaton's opinion of him so long as he raised the rice ration. He warned that without more rice for the troops an insurrection might be brewing. He added that for his own meals, he would now expect biscuits in addition to rice. "Remember you are in a desert, and a country not your own," Tayyib said, with undisguised menace. "I am a greater man here than you or the Bashaw."

Eaton replied: "I have found you at the head of every commotion which has happened since we left Alexandria. You are the instigator of the present one among the chiefs. Leave my tent! But mark, if I find a mutiny in camp during the absence of the Bashaw, I will put you to instant death."

Tayyib left the tent, mounted his horse in the rain, and rode off. All Eaton could do was wait.

Four hours later, after weighing Eaton's threat, Tayyib returned and, instead of confronting Eaton, entered the tent of the foreign officers. He approached young Scot Farquhar and Midshipman Peck and informed them that he would follow the general anywhere. He asked them to relay the message to Eaton.

At 5 P.M., Tayyib entered Eaton's tent. He made a show of loyalty and swore that at the battles of Derne he would prove to Eaton that he was a great man. Eaton said all he wanted was that he stop trying to stir up trouble among the sheiks. Tayyib held out his hand, and Eaton grasped it. The rain kept coming down as the sky darkened. By nightfall, Hamet had still not returned with the other sheiks and it was feared they might have been captured or killed.

After a long anxious day cooped up in his tent, Eaton decided he needed some kind of diversion, something to take his mind off everything. He tramped over the slick terrain to the Bedouin camp. His first observation, as curious teenagers surrounded him, was how handsome and healthy so many of them were; he was even more impressed when they opened their mouths. "Never saw teeth so universally sound and white, even and well set."

One of the wives of the principal sheik greeted him, and invited him into the family tent, serving him dates out of a thatched basket. She seemed elated by his visit, and Eaton, in turn, complimented her "on her elegant proportion and symmetry." (Didn't he have enough troubles without flirting with a sheik's wife?)

The woman coquettishly replied that in the camp there were some young women far more beautiful than she. Eaton said he doubted that could be true. To prove her point, she escorted in more than a dozen "fine girls and young married women." Eaton noted in his journal that Bedouin women "have nothing of affected reserved and bigoted pride" of the city women.

Eaton, brass buttons glinting in the tent's firelight, admitted the women were "handsome" but he refused to give up his original opinion as to who was the tribe's most beautiful. As he walked back in the puddles to his tent, with a parade of kohl-eyed beauties lingering in his mind's eye, maybe he was freed for a few moments from his obsessive quest.

At 3 P.M. Tuesday, April 2, the missing Bashaw finally returned, and he brought with him the other sheiks and the missing Eu ed Alli. Hamet had ridden all night on March 31 and the following day through the rain, his party living on the charity of dates and milk given to them by Bedouins they happened to encounter. They had caught up to the departing sheiks almost sixty miles away and had convinced them to return. That night at 7 P.M. inside Eaton's large tent, by firelight, Eaton implored all the sheiks and Hamet for the umpteenth time to rally together; they yet again swore oaths of honor to the mission.

Querying each of the sheiks as to their numbers, Eaton discovered that their united force now totaled between 600 and 700 fighting men, not counting the Eu ed Alli families and some camp followers. Altogether, he estimated their entire horde at 1,200 people. General Eaton gave the order that the drummer would beat reveille before first light and they would be on the road by six o'clock.

That morning, along with the foreign soldiers on foot and camels carrying the rice, Eaton rode at the front, and they traveled ten miles.

Then word reached him that the Bedouin had pitched camp a ways back on an elevated plain with fine cistern water. General Eaton wheeled his horse and rode back to confront the laggards, but he found out that the tribes had a legitimate reason for stopping. (Why they didn't tell him the day before at the council is unclear.) They didn't have enough food to last them much beyond reaching Bomba, and they couldn't risk so many lives on the assumption of victories in battle. They needed more supplies and had sent a caravan south to Siwa to bring back dates from the oasis there.

Eaton blustered—he knew his own rice supply was running short, and he couldn't afford to wait for the caravan; finally the Bedouin agreed to go forward on the following morning, while their dispatched caravan would be told to bring the dates directly to Bomba.

Eaton was returning to the Christian encampment when he heard the sound of musket fire. He rushed back to the Bedouin tents and discovered that what he had heard was celebratory gunfire accompanying a wedding. The march's delay afforded the Bedouin the chance to hold festivities and gave Eaton the rare opportunity to witness a Bedouin wedding up close.

Within minutes, the Protestant New Englander seemed agog at the gaudy desert display, mesmerized by it. For once, his journal sounds more like Sir Richard Burton than Lawrence of Arabia.

A pair of festooned camels loped at the head of the procession; one carried the bride completely concealed amid swaths of swaying colored silks, the other toted the hidden groom.

"The women had their places near the camels, chanting a savage kind of epithalamium," wrote Eaton, "the men performing feats of horsemanship, and an incessant *feu de joie*. In this manner they took a circuit quite round their own encampment, and then proceeded to ours, and made the same circuit."

Eaton and several other officers followed the procession. "We were treated with marks of peculiar distinction; and great exertions were taken to give us a place near the carriages. During the procession the camels were frequently halted, and dances were performed by young men and girls, exhibiting the most lascivious gestures."

The cavalcade returned to two tents set apart, "where the camel which carried the bride was driven seven times round the tent assigned for her by the singing women."

The bride's camel was then made to kneel, and she was "precipitated head first" into the tent.

> After the ceremonies were over it was signified to me that a present would be expected on the occasion. I asked a chief who would be the proper person to receive it? He pointed out a middle aged woman: whom I observed to have been very officious during the ceremony of marriage, and whom I supposed to be the mother of the bride, [and] to whom I presented two half rupees of two dollars each. And [I] invited an old man of about fifty five, who . . . seemed deeply concerned in the affair, and whom I supposed to be the father of one of the married couple, to accompany me to my tent, and ordered him a small present of extra provisions. He was followed by sundry other Arabs of distinction. Being seated in the tent, conversation turned to the marriage ceremony, which led to questions of the parentage and ages of the married pair: when, what was my surprise to find the old man to whom we had exhibited our civilities to be himself the groom; his bride, a girl of thirteen years, and the officious middle aged woman, whom I took to be the mother, another wife of this newly married dotard. It appeared that the old man was a Sheik; his new bride a daughter of a family of the same rank whom he had bought of the parents, according to custom, before marriage. We were told that the bride must remain three days in the hands of matrons before consummation.

Eaton in his private journal revealed himself quite curious about certain Bedouin rituals. "[The older women] perform the office of examining [the bride's] abilities for this final ceremony [sexual intercourse], and in fact lay the ground for easy access by artificial operations. Meantime, the husband has three other wives for his amusement." Eaton never clarified what he meant by "artificial operations." In fact, at a later date, he drew a faint *X* over the entire paragraph.

The next day, Thursday, April 4, the drummer in his dusty uniform hammered out reveille predawn as usual, and surprisingly, the straggling horde of 1,200 accomplished a good day's march, achieving a foot pace of two miles per hour. They halted at 4 P.M. after eighteen miles. Somewhere along the route, Eaton's artillery captain, Selim Comb, saw the tracks of a "wild cat" and chased it down with his greyhound. Selim shot the animal, which Eaton described as mottled black in color, five feet long, two feet high. "It was cooked and it eat [sic] very well," noted Eaton. The men hadn't tasted meat in weeks. A Bedouin followed the animal's tracks and found the wildcat's brood. "They were too young to be raised," wrote Eaton regretfully. Raising exotic animals as pets (and future meals) was then considered a fine recreation.

The horde spent the night at what was likely Suani Samaluth, where Eaton was deeply impressed by wells drilled through one hundred feet of solid rock, imagining the sheer labor required. He noted ancient ruins scattered about and evidence of bygone cultivation. With his New England thrift-and-hard-work ethic, he always seemed shocked that any place could ever fall into such disrepair.

The days of rain were now long gone, and their sojourn on the Eu ed Alli's fertile plateau in the past. They were entering a much drier, sandier region. It takes only one entire thirsty day for water to begin to dominate everyone's thoughts. Each afternoon's march now formed a kind of pilgrimage to the next well or cistern or large puddle of water. The horde carried its drinking water and expected to replenish its supply each night. By evening, dry tongues ran over parched lips.

The cavalcade and foot soldiers proceeded twelve miles on Friday to a "remarkable ancient castle of hewn stone" with massive walls—eighteen feet high and five feet thick and 180 feet long; at the corners, V-shaped bastions jutted out. One of Eaton's officers found two ancient Greek coins lying among the ruins and presented them to Eaton.

The Bedouin guides expected to find water there, but instead, the castle's huge rainwater cistern was dry, and a nearby deep well offered only vile water, extremely sulphurous and salty. Inside the walls were numerous graves of hajjis who had died there, presumably of thirst, with markers in simple Arabic and Turkish. Barren desert surrounded the walls.

The thirstiest men dropped goatskins down the 150-foot well outside the walls and hoisted up this stinking liquid. They tried to hold their noses to gulp it, but Eaton said it made most of them feel nauseous. Eaton and the guides decided to press on at daybreak to the next well and hopefully there find water to give to the horses and camels and the troops. That night a roving band of Bedouin stole nine of the Bashaw's horses.

On Saturday, up at sunrise, the thirsty horde moved on. At noon, with the sun directly overhead, a servant's horse died of thirst and exhaustion. A six-hour march brought them to another well. A goatskin splashed down 70 feet into the well—the sound echoing—and the water pulled up was . . . "fetid and saline." Men thirsty enough will drink anything that might revive them; a Bedouin will pierce a vein in his camel's thigh and drink. This well water, though brackish, was more drinkable than the last, and the horses had not drunk in forty-two hours. Most of the men and women and children were down to doling precious sips from their last reserves. One thousand thirsty people converged on the small opening in the rocks. Men and beasts crushed into the area; the surging crowd pushed. Something spooked Eaton's servant's horse, and the beast slipped and cracked its head. Everyone drank as much as their bodies could tolerate.

The army lurched forward along this coastal ridge near the Bay of Sollum, with glimpses of the sea; it's cruel to see so much undrinkable saltwater. An army kicks up dust, which dries out the mouth, eyes, and nostrils. Moslems pulled their head scarves across their faces; Christian mercenaries raised their neckerchiefs. At 3 P.M., Eaton mercifully halted the march. The general, still muscular and fit at forty-one, walked four miles with young George Farquhar down to the deserted port of Sollum. Eaton's map, a French maritime chart, showed the spot as Cape Luco, and it appeared to be 90 miles from Bomba. On paper, he was five or six days' march from the first goal. That night at their encampment, they had no fresh water.

The following morning, Sunday, April 7, Eaton and officers on horse led the way, followed by rice-laden baggage camels guarded by foreign soldiers along with a handful of U.S. Marines on foot. They commenced forward at 6 A.M. and by switchbacks ascended a mountain. The Moslems began their staggered start. They all then marched along the summit, achieving eighteen miles total before camping at 4 P.M. in a valley. Again there was no water. Men tossed their packs on the ground and slumped down with fatigue. The U.S. Marines, the lowliest service, were earning six dollars a month to trudge through this hell. Dust billowed everywhere. Men rationed their sips from their goat sacks; lips cracked; bodies ached with exhaustion worsened by dehydration.

The situation was so dire that no one—not even the camel drivers—bickered. They knew better than Eaton what kind of trouble this situation posed. Another day without water and more of the horses would die. Another day after that, fatigued men would want to lie down instead of marching forward.

April 8. Monday, on day thirty-eight of the expedition, the drummer roused the camp. Eaton led the tired troops down the switchbacks on the western side of the mountain. At 9 A.M., they trudged down into a deep ravine, and there at the bottom was a natural cistern of excellent rainwater. Men splashed the precious stuff on their faces, dabbed it on the backs of their necks, and drank like beasts till their bellies ached. "This was a precious repast to our thirsty pilgrims," wrote Eaton, grandly.

While everyone crowded in to drink before the horses and camels would have their turn, Eaton rode off with a handful of officers to scout the surrounding region. He returned an hour later, the time of day still being late morning, ready to resume the march, only to discover that the Moslems had pitched camp. Eaton sought out the Bashaw to demand an explanation. Hamet blamed exhaustion, but Eaton's translator, who had become friends with some members of the Bashaw's suite, discovered the true reason: Hamet once again wanted to send a courier to Bomba to make certain that the American ships had arrived.

Not surprisingly, this cautious man feared turning up in Bomba or Derne without food or naval support; he thought he would be mere prey for his brother's army. His jitters defined him. Unlike Eaton, Hamet churned his options into perpetual quicksand.

Eaton sought out Hamet and told him that the army had six days' rations of rice left, and they must hurry, not delay. All other food—

biscuits, flour, dried meat, everything—was gone. Hamet blamed the sheiks and other tribal leaders and said they all demanded a chance to rest. "If they prefer famine to fatigue, they might have their choice," Eaton told Hamet. General Eaton, on the verge of the worst crisis yet, again ordered a stop to the rations of the Moslem troops.

For hours, Hamet and the sheiks and the Moslem cavalry argued among themselves. At 3 P.M., Hamet announced the Moslems would return to Egypt by way of the Oasis of Siwa. Servants began to dismantle tents; cooking pots were loaded on camels. He and other Moslems prepared to head back along the trail up the ravine.

The hats would remain; the turbans would depart, but not before one last parting betrayal.

As Eaton observed the tent poles pulled and the tents flopping to earth, he feigned indifference. He wanted to convey the message loud and clear that his army of one hundred men advancing on foot, without Eu ed Alli's camels or Hamet's horses, would reach Bomba. As he watched the servants scatter about their tasks, he noticed some of the Moslems clustering in suspicious groups between the camps. Eaton sent his interpreter to investigate; the man reported back that the Arabs— before heading out—*planned to try to steal the rice.*

Eaton instantly ordered the drummer to beat to arms. The ominous drumroll filled the ravine. The American and European soldiers grabbed their weapons and rushed to join their companies. Eaton ordered his officers to form their men into lines in front of the supply tent. The six U.S. Marine privates, in blue-and-scarlet coats and high brimless hats, blocked the tent's entrance. The 60 or so other men—Greeks and European castoffs—half-ringed the tent in front of them.

With the sun still high in the west, Eaton's men stood at attention, guarding the precious sacks of rice. Not a word was said, but the mere aligning of guard troops in the lonely desert ravine acted like an accusation. The men in turbans milled around threateningly as servants packed up tents and other belongings.

The departing Moslems now knew that they would have almost no food to tide them over on the first leg of their journey. The Arab sheiks rode out first, with their men; Hamet mounted and followed. The Christian soldiers remained in formation, sweating in the heat. Eaton waited; he was gambling that yet again the prospect of hunger would bring them back.

In less than an hour, Hamet re-entered the ravine, with the primary sheiks in tow. He said he had convinced them to persevere with the Americans. After dismounting, Hamet ordered his tent pitched off to one side. The sheiks began to do likewise.

Eaton then made a horrible mistake, one that almost scuttled the entire mission. He thought the rebellion over and that the camp would now settle into the late afternoon routine of gathering wood for making fires and boiling water for cooking rice. Wanting to take advantage of the lull, he decided to drill his Christian troops. So he ordered "manual exercize," that is, drills with presenting arms, shouldering arms. The three troops—the Greeks, the mixed mercenaries, and the U.S. Marines—stood at attention; their officers began calling out orders.

The instant the soldiers began to twirl their rifles, the Arabs, encamped a few hundred feet away, thought they were being attacked. They raced to remount their horses, shouting in Arabic: "The Christians are preparing to fire on us." The Bashaw climbed on his horse, at the head of the cavalry, and ordered a charge. Two hundred Arab horsemen, most of them expert riders, armed with muskets and scimitars, thundered forward at full gallop toward the eighty or so Christian soldiers, now standing at attention, arms at their sides. No order was given to raise their weapons and none of the men moved, except Eaton's aide-de-camp, named Davies, and an unnamed troop doctor, who both scurried away to their tents. The others stood still as the dust of two hundred horses enveloped them in a cloud and the sound of pounding hooves mixed with guttural shouts.

The only sound missing was gunfire.

The Arab cavalry wheeled to a halt just in front of the Christian formation—no one had fired on either side. Commands in Arabic apparently directed them to aim at the American officers. Dozens of men swiveled their muskets toward Eaton and Lieutenant O'Bannon and Midshipman Peck. With slow deliberation, they steadied their guns. Someone shouted: "Fire!"

In the stunned silence, the instant before anyone squeezed off a shot, the Bashaw's officers shrieked a counter order: "W'allahi . . . In the name of Allah, do not fire! The Christians are our friends."

General Eaton, who had been standing next to Farquhar and O'Bannon and Peck, now strode forward, moving directly toward Hamet. Only a man willing to die very soon steps out between two armies. As he walked, he was yelling to Hamet in broken Italian: Do not allow this stupidity, this act of desperation. At once, "a column of muskets" was pointed at his chest. One flinch and the ground might be spattered with blood, and Eaton's quest might quickly end in an unmarked grave in a nameless ravine.

Eaton shouted up to the Bashaw in Italian, speaking fast, but the prince looked dazed, paralyzed with indecision. Hamet said nothing, did nothing. Each instant increased the risk of some jittery forefinger pulling a trigger.

The Moslems began shouting commands and counter-commands in Arabic. A turbaned rider danced his mount forward and leaned down and pointed his pistol at the breast of young George Farquhar, the son of the Scottish quartermaster. The man pulled the trigger, but the gun misfired.

Eaton abruptly raised his hand, waving it, demanding silence. The Arabic shouts only grew louder. Another group of horsemen surged forward.

Hamet looked dumbfounded. The officers around him, seeing no hint of an upcoming command, took it upon themselves to rush ahead, sabers drawn, and surround Eaton and separate him from the attackers.

In the brief lull, Eaton barked words of reproach at Hamet. At that moment, Hamet's *casnadar*, his treasurer, asked Hamet, "Have you lost your mind?" Hamet snapped out of his stupor and struck the *casnadar* hard with the flat of his sword. The Arab horsemen, seeing the glint of a blade in the sunlight, began shouting again and closing in to rescue him.

A firefight lurked one trigger-pull away.

Throughout it all, the European soldiers and the U.S. Marines held their ground, fighting their nerves to remain statues of discipline.

Eaton grabbed the reins of Hamet's horse and guided it to one side a little ways from the crowd; he convinced the prince to dismount. "Do you know your own interests?" Eaton asked. "Do you know who your friends are?"

Like a man awaking from a bad dream, Hamet admitted he had panicked. He called Eaton his "friend and protector." Heading with Eaton toward the American's tent, Hamet gave orders for the Arab cavalry to disperse.

Inside the tent, Hamet suggested that Eaton order a ration of rice to calm the situation. The American general replied that he would agree only on the condition that the march would begin promptly the next morning at reveille beating. Hamet consented. Arab chiefs filed in and swore yet more oaths of loyalty.

Lieutenant O'Bannon, a warm Kentucky man who had amused them all with his fiddle, stood nearby. Throughout the armed confrontation, O'Bannon had maintained his cool, smiling, trying to calm everyone. Eaton had been deeply impressed by the courage of both Farquhar and O'Bannon to stand still and dignified in the face of attack. A dozen muskets aimed at their hearts hadn't spooked them. Hamet now walked over to O'Bannon, and with a surge of emotion, called him "My Brave American" and embraced him. The long beard pressed against the marine's dusty blue uniform.

That night in the ravine, the "turbans" and "hats" sat around campfires, hundreds of yards apart, eating their small bowls of rice, deeply distrustful of one another.

Writing later in his notebook, William Eaton, still angry, gleaned one overshadowing lesson from this near-death incident: "We find it almost impossible to inspire these wild bigots with confidence in us or to persuade them that, being Christians, we can be otherwise than enemies to Mussulmen," he wrote.

On Tuesday, April 9, day thirty-nine, Eaton took full advantage of the march-at-reveille agreement. The drummer cut short the men's dreams at 5 A.M. and the first riders hit the trail at 5:30 A.M. The horde marched ten miles before halting at a water cistern near fine fields for grazing. They approached the cistern; finally a day with an early start had led to fresh water before noon. The ugliness of yesterday was fading. The first man walked over, wanting to drink before the horses and camels.

Kneeling down, he tossed his goatskin into the cut-out reservoir. He looked over the clear expanse shining in the high sun; something lurked near the edge beneath the surface. The man jumped into the water and reached down and pulled up an arm, then a leg. "In this cistern, we found two dead men; probably pilgrims murdered by the Arabs," wrote Eaton, who added matter-of-factly: "We were obliged nevertheless to use the water."

The next day, the straggly army marched ten miles and at noon camped in a "beautiful valley" with grazing for the horses. On top of one side of the valley was a stone ridge with a good cistern of water. With food running out, Eaton cut the rice rations in half, presumably to four ounces per man a day. The courier had not yet returned from Bomba.

Eaton learned from his Arabic-speaking spies that Hamet's fears of betrayal had been growing, that he suspected that the Americans were merely using him to strike a better peace with his brother. He told colleagues that "he has been twice deceived by Christian powers, and that the English deceived mameluke leader, Elfi Bey." Unsettled by these fears, Hamet worried that one day the Americans would hand him over to his brother Yussef.

At 3 P.M. that Wednesday afternoon of April 10, Eaton was invited into a general council of war. Hamet and the sheiks again refused to proceed until word of the American ships arrived. Eaton pressed for two more days' marching before halting, which would bring them nearer and shorten the messenger's distance.

Bomba lay fifty to sixty miles away, and Eaton queried the men working supply duty and found that three days of half rations of rice remained. At the pace they were moving, the army had little or no chance of reaching Bomba with any food left. With more delays, hunger, possibly even starvation, threatened, especially if the Christian troops were ever abandoned en route.

The Bashaw and the sheiks refused to proceed. "Our situation is truly alarming," Eaton wrote. It instantly got worse.

Some of the European mercenaries were overheard plotting a mutiny to demand full rations of rice. The men whispered about gathering their weapons and confronting Eaton or else storming the supply tent. Walking ten miles in the dusty heat on a handful of nourishment had taken its toll.

Eaton told Lieutenant Rocco to try to *quietly* explain to the men about the extreme shortages and what was required for survival. If that approach failed, he was to tell them that any man who approached Eaton in arms to make demands risked being shot.

Eaton re-counted the exact number of bags of rice remaining; his diary doesn't reveal the number, but the tally was grim; he informed only Lieutenant O'Bannon. Men clustered around campfires, very quiet.

At 7:30 P.M., in the tense camp, the courier who had been sent to Bomba rode in amid the fires. He yanked the reins and swung off his horse. He shouted his news: The American ships were seen off the coast of Bomba. As Eaton phrased it, the army was transformed "from pensive gloom to enthusiastic gladness." The news promised food: salt beef, biscuits, and butter. Hamet and the sheiks now agreed (again) to persevere to Bomba.

That night, with the battle looming perhaps less than a week away, Hamet suffered an attack, perhaps of panic; with "spasms and vomiting" through most of the night. The sight of a retching commander hardly inspires confidence. Very quickly, the whole camp knew of their leader's illness.

The next day, Thursday, day forty-one, a sunrise start produced five miles, but Hamet fell direly ill. Eaton, fearing he might die, decided it best to halt, although no water happened to be at that spot. The army waited for Hamet to recover. The next-to-last half ration of rice was issued.

Around sundown, Hamet started to feel better. Eaton, per usual, scheduled an early start. On Friday, they continued down along the valley. Knowing the food shortage, Eaton pushed them to trek as far as possible. The straggling army, reinvigorated by hope, achieved twenty-five miles on growling stomachs. That evening, they camped on a ridge that had neither water nor firewood. Eaton gave orders for the last of the rice to be distributed. The men, unable to boil it, were forced to gnaw at their half handful of raw rice. Uncooked rice in dry mouths tasted little better than gravel. The Bedouin families, exhausted from hunger and marching, camped five miles back.

On Saturday, April 13, "Marched seven and a half miles. Hunger and fatigue rendered the foot soldiers and Bedouin families unable to pursue the march." Hamet ordered one of his camels killed, and he exchanged another camel with the Bedouin for a sheep. (The Bedouin were very reluctant ever to slaughter any animals that provided them with milk or transportation or wool.) The two beasts were slaughtered, and since a camel often weighs as much as 1,500 pounds, there was a lot of meat. Eaton reported enough to feed the entire army, perhaps seven hundred men. Camel meat is considered a delicacy, although Europeans tend to find the meat tough. Obviously, with men starving, nothing was wasted, but many travelers report that whenever the Bedouin slaughter a camel, they utilize every last sinew. "No part of the animal capable of being gnawed by human tooth is suffered to be lost," wrote Frederick Horneman, who traveled in Northern Africa in 1797. "The very bones pass through various hands and mouths, before they are thrown away . . . they makes sandals of the skins and they weave the hair into twine."

April 14, day forty-three. "Marched fifteen miles. Camped in a pleasant valley of rich strong land, but totally uncultivated. Good and abundance of feed for our horses, and sundry cisterns excavated in the ridges on the borders of the valley contained excellent rain water; but we were totally destitute of provisions." Eaton spent the hungry hours looking at the nearby ancient ruins . . . "visible marks of former cultivation but now all is waste."

Everyone knew that the ships had been sighted and everyone knew that Bomba could be reached sometime the following day. The men scratched at the ground, looking for edible roots, and waited for dawn and the hike to Bomba.

On the forty-fifth day on the road, Eaton—making an uncharacteristic accommodation for human frailty—allowed the exhausted troops a bit more sleep. He ordered the day's march to begin at 7 A.M. The men fanned out through the plain, scavenging for anything edible to staunch the hunger pangs. Wandering in small ravines nearby, they found some wild fennel and sorrel. During the day's march, the army ran into three Bedouin coming from Bomba, who reported seeing two vessels at sea; the tribesmen even described a ship that resembled the *Argus*. At 4 P.M., on a day without water, Hamet, Eaton, and their army reached Bomba, a port city of antiquity, long since abandoned. Eaton, at the forefront, cantered ahead and scanned the horizon, out across the Bay of Bomba. And there he saw . . . not a single ship, not a sail, nothing but the blue waves of the Mediterranean.

He scanned again for the hint of a sail, a paleness on the blue, but nothing. The Arab sheiks rode up and looked, as did Hamet; the marines looked and the mercenaries. Nothing. The straggling army gradually arrived en masse on the crest of the hill. After the recent reports from trustworthy witnesses, this completely unexpected reversal—going from the prospect of food to the prospect of nothing—bewildered them all.

As word spread, the shouts and curses of the five hundred Moslem soldiers resounded louder and louder. "Nothing could prevail on our Arabs to believe that any [ships] had been there," wrote Eaton. "They abused us as imposters and infidels." The sheiks and others accused the Christians of luring them into some kind of trap.

With no food and no water and no money, the various groups started to scramble for their own survival. Hamet and the sheiks held a council and decided to leave the next morning, in a direction that would not include the Americans or Christians. Eaton, finding his entire mission crumbling, pushed his way into the council tent and said the army should now try to attack Derne. His plan was quickly dismissed as "impracticable."

It was all falling apart.

Eaton went off with his 9 Americans and his 75 Europeans; they marched back up the mountain overlooking the harbor. Eaton ordered the men to find anything combustible . . . from a twig, to a stick, to a log, to a sack. They tossed it all in heaps to create as many bonfires as they could. All night, they fed the fires. No wine or whiskey to pass the time, just flames roaring into the night sky. Maybe O'Bannon played the fiddle.

At dawn, Eaton scanned the horizon: nothing.

The Arabs down below began packing up.

Hamet's *casnadar* (treasurer), a reasonable man who trusted the Americans, climbed the hillside for a last look and a farewell. The time was 8 A.M., and the sound of camels grunting to stand could be heard.

Zaid, the *casnadar*, squinted hard, methodically inching his line of sight along the horizon. He saw a fleck of white, he thought. Others looked; it might be a sail approaching. As the speck slowly grew in size over the next three long hours, they came to realize that this was the *Argus*. "Language is too poor to paint the joy and exultation which this messenger of life excited in every breast," wrote Eaton.

Midshipman Peck attempted to put his feelings on paper. "When I think on our situation in the desert, where no other Christian ever sat his foot and consider what thieves the arabs are, who would shoot a man for the buttons on his coat, and their religious prejudices, which would have been sufficient to warrant our deaths, as christians and enemies to their religion, I frequently wonder how it was possible for us to succeed in reaching Bomba. Certainly it was one of the most extraordinary expeditions ever set on foot. We were very frequently 24 hours without water, and once 47 hours without a drop. Our horses were sometimes three days without, and for the last 20 days had nothing to eat, except what they picked out of the sand."

The "hats" and the "turbans," who had come so close to killing one another, would now prepare for a combined attack on Derne, which would be a mere prelude to conquering Bengazi. From there, they hoped to march to Tripoli city itself to plant Hamet on the throne.

CHAPTER 14 *Tobias Lear:*

Peace at Any Cost

WHILE JEFFERSON'S SECRET AGENT, Eaton, starved in the desert, Jefferson's diplomat Tobias Lear lounged in the perfumed gardens of Malta and decided that the time was ripe to reopen peace negotiations with Tripoli. Lear—eager to settle the peace himself—chose to ignore Eaton's covert mission. If Lear's advice had been taken, those supply ships would have never gone to Bomba. To Lear's thinking, tough diplomatic conversations would end the four-year war and bring home the hostages, not some half-baked, dim-witted, far-fetched plot to overthrow Yussef.

The two prongs of American foreign policy—diplomacy and military force—were operating in denial of the other's existence. Such blinders could lead only to collision or even betrayal. Though neither man expressed it so baldly, their efforts amounted to a race for results. Would Lear negotiate peace before Eaton could place Hamet on the throne? The Bashaw brothers were rivals, and so were the two Americans.

On March 28, a scant two weeks before Eaton reached Bomba, Tobias Lear took time off from the round of diplomatic balls and garden parties to dash off a half-page reply to the Spanish consul, Don Gerando Joseph de Souza, who in the name of the Bashaw had invited Lear to come to Tripoli under a white flag of truce. De Souza's vague Christmastime message had stated: An honorable peace can now be had.

Lear sealed his answer to De Souza and handed it to the captain of a British ketch, *Eliza*, which had an American passport to pass through the ongoing American blockade of Tripoli. By replying to De Souza, Lear—in the circuitous way of diplomats—was cracking open the door for peace. "We should not refuse to negotiate . . . upon honourable grounds . . . compatible with the rising character of our nation." He was hinting that negotiations could perhaps be concluded *before* the American Navy ships unleashed the huge bombardment that everyone knew was scheduled for the summer. Lear didn't even deign to mention Eaton-Hamet as a threat to Yussef.

Tobias Lear, whose schedule frequently brought him to dine at the governor's palace in Malta, sometimes with poet Samuel Coleridge, remained on the British-controlled island to await a reply. Two weeks slipped by pleasantly for Lear and his slender young wife as he awaited an answer from Tripoli.

Around the same time, Captain John Rodgers aboard the USS *Constitution* off Tripoli received a strange stack of letters. A man in a small boat in the vicinity of the island of Djerba—a place often used for coastal smuggling—had waved down the massive frigate. Two of the letters came from imprisoned Captain Bainbridge, dated March 16 and 22, and one was from the Danish consul, Nicholas Nissen, dated March 18. All three were addressed to Commodore Samuel Barron. For Rodgers, they posed a dilemma. The letters were a month old and might contain vital *timely* information. Rumors abounded about an escape plot by the American prisoners; maybe they wanted Rodgers to slip a boat shoreward on a given night.

"I hope I have not acted incorrectly in opening [them]," Rodgers later wrote. In the privacy of his captain's cabin on the rocking vessel, Rodgers read the letter from the Danish consul to Barron. Nissen relayed an impassioned plea from the foreign minister of Tripoli, Sidi Mohammed Dghies, to restart peace negotiations. The elderly minister apologized that a long illness of the eyes had sidetracked him from public affairs; he now claimed that he wanted to help the United States solve its problems. He recommended that the commodore send a fully authorized negotiator who would be willing to come ashore under "perfect inviolability."

The previous summer the U.S. fleet under Commodore Preble had tried to negotiate by means of the French consul ferrying verbal messages under a white flag between Preble on ship and the Bashaw onshore. The whole process had stumbled in confusion, with each side misconstruing the other's demands. (Negotiations in Barbary were often as convoluted as a comic opera as foreign consuls vied to meddle, sometimes helping, sometimes garbling messages to suit their own agendas.)

Consul Nissen in his letter now vouched for the sincerity of Dghies's offer to mediate. The Dane, a pacifist who had become close friends with Bainbridge, added: "A sincere & lasting peace is at any time preferable even to a successful war."

Rodgers then opened the two missives from Bainbridge. The first appeared to be a brief polite note, asking Commodore Barron to give serious thought to Nissen's suggestions and to consider—as a goodwill gesture—sending a navy surgeon to come treat the eyes of the "friendly" minister, Mohammed Dghies.

Bainbridge had used a standard-size sheet of heavy paper. Most of it appeared blank, but Rodgers knew better. He lit a candle and carefully held the letter high over the flame. In the heat, handwritten script—etched out by quill dipped in lime juice—began to appear.

In this hidden message, Bainbridge implored Barron to trust Dghies, who "has great influence over the Bashaw." Bainbridge also downplayed the effects of possible naval bombardment, since "the Houses here [are made] of stone and mud and badly furnished."

Bainbridge also allowed himself to give an unsolicited suggestion to a superior officer. "Permit me, my dear Barron," he began, "I suppose . . . the object of our government and your expectation is to release us from captivity without paying; [that] is in my opinion impossible" without landing an army. He also argued that the United States' honor would remain intact if it paid for "the liberty of its unfortunate citizens" because a ransom payment wouldn't mean this country was paying "one farthing" for peace. (This is the same distinction that Eaton rejected and Jefferson was reluctantly willing to accept.)

Rodgers opened the second Bainbridge letter, dated March 22, which was even briefer. He held the paper over the flame, and the secret information that emerged seemed far more important: a tentative price for peace. Bainbridge stated that Dghies had told Nissen that the

Bashaw might accept a ransom payment as low as $150,000, about one-third of what he had demanded from Preble.

Rodgers continued reading in the lime juice and the ransom dropped further: "I have no doubt that if a Person was to come here to negotiate before an attack was made, that Peace could be effected for $120,000." Bainbridge counseled that *the fear of the attack* might be more stimulus to peace than the *actual attack*. "I think it a most favourable moment," he enthused.

Rodgers digested the information: Bainbridge was advocating negotiations *before* the U.S. Navy could crush the corsairs. Jefferson's orders to Tobias Lear and Commodore Barron had clearly stated: "We hope [peace with Tripoli] may be effected under the operation and auspices of the force in the hands of [Barron] without any price or pecuniary concession whatever." Rodgers knew about those orders; all navy officers did.

He rushed off a note to Commodore Barron to accompany the letters that he would send immediately by the USS *Vixen*. He did not allow himself to offer any suggestions to his superior officer. The following day, he penned a more candid note to his longtime friend Tobias Lear. (Rodgers had met Lear a few years earlier in the Caribbean during the bloody slave uprisings of Haiti's independence movement, and the men had survived several battles together.)

Captain Rodgers opened by expressing his amazement that these letters from Tripoli dealt with the "subject of peace!" But he cautioned Lear that he didn't expect the enemy would agree to what "you will consider equal terms" until the navy showed its warships and opened fire. Rodgers reported that his scouting missions into the harbor hadn't revealed that Tripoli had bulked up its defenses or its fleet. "I feel more than ever Confident, our present force, with an addition of two Mortars & two Gun Boats will enable us to give you the opportunity of negotiating a Peace perfectly to your Wishes."

Rodgers, who had witnessed the Barbary corsairs close up, could not resist imploring Lear to let the navy have a crack at it. "If the attack is made within Six Weeks, under proper regulations, I will pledge all that's sacred and dear to me in this World! That we succeed in the most perfect handsome & honorable manner." (Rodgers's passion to fight was no idle boast; he would back up his words with a lifetime of hard-won victories at sea during a long career.) He had recently written to his fiancée, Minerva: "I am only afraid that the Tripoline dogs . . . will barely afford me an opportunity of gaining a trophy worthy of laying at the feet of my little goddess."

This war against Yussef would most likely end in one of three scenarios: either by the U.S. Navy crushing Tripoli into submission, or by Eaton placing Hamet on the throne, or, lastly, by the diplomatic maneuvers of Tobias Lear. So now, Rodgers joined Eaton and Lear, jockeying for a share of the glory.

Rodgers sent off the USS *Vixen* with these important messages.

At that same moment, yet more peace-for-a-payment letters, addressed to Tobias Lear and Commodore Barron, were about to leave Tripoli on the *Eliza*, which had completed its errand of delivering a $4,000 tribute payment for England. Tucked among the outbound letters was a thick packet addressed from the Spanish consul De Souza to Tobias Lear; also in there were three more missives to Lear and one more to Barron from that prolific letter writer William Bainbridge. Yussef, a shrewd manipulator, was clearly using surrogates to lure the Americans back to the bargaining table.

It's easy to see why the Bashaw was making peace overtures. One glance around Tripoli revealed empty shelves in the stores, bread shortages, trade drying up. Several diplomats noted that the Moslem populace, blaming all Christians for the American blockade, were throwing more stones than usual and had made the streets more dangerous. Yussef—vulnerable to attack from within his borders—had taken hostages from the leading Arab tribes living to the south to ensure their loyalty. In addition, hard up for cash, the Bashaw was also demanding tribute payments earlier than scheduled from Denmark and Sweden. Repeated rumors of Hamet's attack added to the unrest.

The *Eliza* returned to Malta on April 21, and a crewman immediately delivered the letters to Lear. The letter from De Souza relayed a firm offer from Yussef that he would accept $200,000 from the United States for peace and ransom, but the United States must hand over all Tripolitan prisoners for free. Included in the folded and sealed paper was

a *tiskara* (a passport) guaranteeing safety for any person coming to negotiate in Tripoli. Yussef was trying once again to tempt the American
diplomat.

Although the Spaniard called the proposal a starting point, Lear privately called the offer "totally inadmissible." He then went to visit ailing
Commodore Barron at his home to discuss the matter. When he arrived,
a secretary asked him to read a letter sent by Captain Bainbridge. That
letter opened a whole new tack in the negotiations, adding blood to what
had been mere haggling over dollars. Yussef chose not to threaten the
hostages through official diplomatic channels, but he instead opted to
leak a report to his near-blind foreign minister, Mohammed Dghies,
who, in turn, leaked it to Nissen and on to the imprisoned Captain
Bainbridge.

The letter stated that the Bashaw had reacted with fury when he
had received reliable report that his brother Hamet was teaming up
with the American squadron. He now drew a sharp contrast between
the ongoing payment squabble and this new attempt to overthrow his
government. "Now, it is a war over my personal safety," Bainbridge
quoted the Bashaw as saying. "I w.d therefore act in a manner that the
feelings of the U. States sh.d be hurt in the most tender part it is in my
power to hurt." Bainbridge said the Bashaw meant the American prisoners and added that aiding Hamet would endanger them and complicate any negotiations.

Yussef's threat, however veiled, was deeply disturbing. Slaves were
captured, worked awhile, then were ransomed. Rarely, if ever, in the history of Barbary did anyone threaten the mass execution of slave-
prisoners. The logic was simple: Slaves, alive, had enormous value; slaves,
dead, roused the enemy.

How real was this threat? The letters of Antoine Zuchet, the Dutch
consul, provide a veteran Barbary observer's viewpoint on Yussef's threats
of mass execution. On April 16, 1805, Zuchet reported home to his foreign ministry: "The American prisoners—at the moment that Bashaw
Yussef is forced to leave the city—are to be sacrificed. Captain Bainbridge is very often greeted by the same threats, and the Danish consul is
invited by Minister Dghies to transmit these *pantomimes* to Commodore

Barron so that the commodore will attack in a manner that is *amiable* and then request peace." Those two words in italics are dripping with sarcasm.

Zuchet was calling the threats "pantomimes," that is, "empty gestures," and he perceived that the purpose of the threats was that the Bashaw wanted the upcoming American attack to be waged not with full fury but rather in an "amiable" way, that is, a symbolic bombardment or two to save face, followed by a polite adjournment to the negotiating table.

Lear's reaction to these various letters from Tripoli (of course, he wouldn't see Zuchet's report) would go a long way toward determining whether this war would end by sword or by word, with payment or without payment, with or without honor.

* * *

Tobias Lear was born in 1762 in the bustling seaport of Portsmouth, New Hampshire, the fifth generation of his family in America and actually the fifth Tobias Lear. Though he passed his late teens during the patriotic fervor of Revolution, he—unlike William Eaton—didn't run away to serve in the Continental Army. Scrawny and bookish, he attended Harvard College, graduating with the thirty-member class of 1783. He would indeed become a historical figure in the early years of the nation but one of decidedly mixed record.

Lear taught school for a while but then caught an astounding break. Lear's uncle, Major General Benjamin Lincoln, recommended him to George Washington for the job of tutoring Washington's grandchildren and, more important, the post of personal secretary, handling reams of correspondence. Washington's letter welcoming Lear reveals just how intimately Lear would be living with America's foremost family, beyond even eating at table with them. "He will have his washing done in the family," wrote Washington, "and may have his socks darned by the maids."

Very quickly, Lear's post evolved beyond mere clerk. Washington treated Lear as his right-hand man, jack-of-all-trades. One day, he tutored grandchildren, the next, he visited properties, the third, he carefully filled out expense reports. Lear wrote stacks of letters in his immaculate hand, and he showed himself adept at assigned tasks.

Lear accompanied his patron to the nation's capital, New York, when Washington began his term as first president, and often lived closer to the Founding Father than even Martha. President Washington—realizing he couldn't open his doors all the time to would-be callers—frequently dined alone with Lear. Tobias mentioned in a letter to Martha that the presidential chef, "Black Sam," routinely set up such "a number of fine dishes," especially oysters and lobsters, that he and the president often held "long consultation" before making a selection.

Lear also learned bookkeeping. He kept Washington's infamous expense account—the president had shrewdly turned down a hefty $25,000-a-year salary, offering instead to work for expenses (which wound up totaling much more). During a swing through New England, Lear enjoyed the prestige of bringing the president to his mother's house in Portsmouth.

Despite all these experiences and advantages, Lear, apparently full of ambition, chafed at remaining in the shadow of the great man. At the start of Washington's second administration in 1793, Lear decided to venture out on his own, with a little help from his patron. He founded T. Lear & Company and focused on two initiatives: working with Washington's Potomack Company to develop river traffic to the nation's future capital and joining the speculators in the Federal City/District of Columbia land rush.

Lear—armed with glowing recommendations from Washington and others—traveled to Europe to try to broker tracts of land in the District but failed to close any deals. Lear's Potomac project also ran into difficulties, specifically, the nightmare of undertaking engineering projects to allow navigation past two waterfalls on the river.

Lear—despite partnering with wealthy investors—lost money. Meantime, his personal life was also troubled. He married Mary Long in 1790, but she died in 1793; then in 1795 he married Frances Basset Washington, a Washington niece, known as Fanny, the widow of Augustine Washington, but she died the following year.

In the late 1790s, Lear's financial woes continued to mount. He still moved in highly respectable circles but with a little less panache. Then Lear did the unthinkable: He stole from George Washington, or he at least diverted some rent money into his own pocket. (Lear still sometimes ran unpaid errands for Washington.) George Washington, no longer president, found out when he approached a tenant about nonpayment of rent, only to be informed that the man had already paid it to Lear. "I must therefore request in explicit terms," Washington wrote to Lear, "that you will receive no more monies due to me. I have not the slightest doubt of my being credited for every farthing you receive on my A/c; but that does not remedy the evil." Washington, still furious the next day, added: "I have not approved, nor cannot approve, of having my money received and applied to uses not my own, without my consent."

Lear apparently apologized profusely, and Washington quickly forgave him. The following year when Congress, fearing attack from France, appointed the former president once again to command the troops, he tapped Tobias Lear to be his chief aide, with the rank of colonel. Although the French never attacked by land and the army never garrisoned, Lear for the rest of his life retained the title and preferred to be addressed as *Colonel* Lear.

Lear, still deeply in debt, was caught again in financial shenanigans, this time by his business partner. He had pocketed the ample proceeds from the other man's land sale. Lear ducked meeting the partner for months, pleading illness, but then finally tearfully apologized and agreed to repay him.

George Washington suddenly died at the age of sixty-seven, after a two-day illness that started as a mere sore throat and cold. Lear happened to be visiting Mount Vernon at the time; it was his heartfelt and detail-filled diary entry that captured the bedside scene for posterity. "About ten o'clock [Saturday, December 14, 1799], [Washington] made several attempts to speak to me before he could effect it—at length he said, 'I am just going. Have me decently buried, and do not let my body be put into the Vault in less than two days after I am dead.' I bowed assent. He looked at me again and said, 'Do you understand me?' I replied Yes Sir. 'Tis well,' said he."

Lear helped oversee funeral arrangements, even measuring the corpse the next day (an astounding 6'3½", with 1 foot 9 inches across the shoulders); Washington bequeathed to Lear a lifetime interest in Walnut Tree farm. Eventually nephew Bushrod Washington approached Lear about organizing Washington's papers, and the two talked about collaborating on a biography.

Now came Lear's *least* finest hour: the missing Washington papers. The case plays out like a whodunit. Instead of nephew Bushrod, Supreme Court Justice John Marshall wound up volunteering to write a biography of George Washington. He received the papers from Lear, who had kept them for a year. Marshall, who didn't examine the whole trunk of papers right away, was quite upset when he discovered swaths of Washington's diary were missing, especially sections during the war and presidency, and that a handful of key letters had also vanished. Lear, in a long rambling letter to Marshall, denied destroying any of Washington's papers, but Lear's own correspondence would later surface to refute his own denial.

A letter has survived that Lear had written Alexander Hamilton to offer to suppress Washington documents.

"There are, as you well know," Lear had written, "among the several letters and papers, many which every public and private consideration should withhold from further inspection." He specifically asked in the letter if Hamilton wanted any military papers removed. (Interestingly, while almost all the presidential diary is gone, Washington's entries for his New England trip to *Lear's* family home have survived.)

Beyond the missing diary, six key letters—that might have added a chapter to American history—were gone. Many sources claimed that Thomas Jefferson and George Washington had suffered a huge falling-out over a letter that Jefferson sent to a friend in Italy. In it, Jefferson had characterized Washington's administration as being "Anglican monarchial & aristocratical," and stated that Washington had appointed officers, "all timid men who prefer the calm of despotism to the boisterous sea of liberty."

The Jefferson letter, sent to one Philip Mazzei, was eventually published abroad and then translated by Noah Webster back into English and republished in America. Its appearance in print allegedly sparked a nasty private fight, a three-round exchange of letters between Washington and Jefferson. Lear, in a conversation with friends over bottles of wine, had once admitted the existence of the letters but then later denied that he had ever said that.

A fellow named Albin Rawlins, an overseer at Mount Vernon, informed one of Washington's nephews that he personally had seen the letters and that the second exchange of replies was so harsh that it made the "hair rise on his head" and "that he felt that it must produce a duel." Those letters, which would have been extraordinary weapons in the hands of Jefferson's enemies, disappeared sometime during the year that Tobias Lear safeguarded Washington's papers and have never been seen since. (Lear's only biographer, Ray Brighton, is convinced—despite no smoking-gun evidence—that Lear destroyed the letters at Jefferson's request and that Jefferson rewarded him for the rest of his life.)

Thomas Jefferson, when he became president, gave debt-ridden Lear the potentially lucrative job of American commercial agent in Saint Domingue (future Haiti). Lear, in turn, hired Albin Rawlins to be an overseer at Walnut Tree farm during his absence.

Tobias Lear departed for the Caribbean, pleased that his post included the right to conduct private commerce. Unfortunately for Lear, he arrived just as France was secretly preparing to crack down on the slave rebellion there.

On January 17, 1802, in a grateful twelve-page letter to Jefferson, Lear predicted the long-rumored French invading force wouldn't arrive for at least six months. A week later, a French armada with 20,000 troops appeared off Cape Francois. General LeClerc attacked and captured the main port from Toussaint L'Ouverture, but only after a horrific night of pillage and arson by the fleeing former slaves. Lear spent his time along with merchant captain John Rodgers trying hard to help the American citizens and merchants stranded inside this now embargoed port.

Unfortunately for Lear, this wasn't the stance that the American government wanted at the time. The Jefferson administration, salivating over the prospect of the Louisiana Purchase, quickly informed him *not* to irritate the French commanders. Secretary of State Madison wrote to

Lear that if his presence might "hazard the goodwill of the French," he should leave.

Lear had definitely been an irritant, so he made plans to leave.

This was when he became especially close to Captain John Rodgers, who had been thrown in prison by General LeClerc for disrespecting a French officer and other petty crimes. Rodgers was first incarcerated in a large oven, then cast into an almost pitch-black dungeon "full of lizards, spiders and many noxious insects." He used a toothpick and his own blood to write a note to smuggle out to Lear. Rodgers was moved to more tolerable quarters. That week, Lear departed for the United States. (Rodgers held no grudge for the departure, since he himself was freed about ten days later.)

Lear returned home, his mission a disaster. American cargoes had been confiscated, ships held, and the French had refused to recognize him as "Commercial Agent." Lear had the gall to file a claim for personal losses of $6,586. Considering that he was in debt at the time of his appointment and he had no receipts for new borrowing or new expenditures, his expenses seemed suspect. Congress ruled there was no precedent for reimbursing a "Commercial Agent" but they did offer cold comfort by praising his conduct as "highly patriotic."

Jefferson once again took care of Tobias Lear; he appointed Lear as consul general to the Barbary States, another potentially lucrative post. In addition to the ample $4,000-a-year salary, he was again granted the right to conduct private trade. It was common knowledge that the rulers in Barbary offered get-rich opportunities to sympathetic consuls. Zealot Eaton, after Tunis, had recommended that consulate officials be prohibited from engaging in trade.

Before departing, Lear married yet again, and once again to a Washington niece, this time a much younger one, twenty-three-year-old pouty-lipped Frances Henley; Lear was then forty-one. From lines in his letters, it's clear Lear doted on his "Fanny," as he called her. "I will fly on wings of love to your arms," he wrote in one typical passage during a brief separation. He and his bride honeymooned on the USS *Constitution*, gliding to the Mediterranean with Preble. Lear was personally in charge of doling out $43,000 in consular presents for Algiers and Tunis, stowed for safekeeping in Preble's cabin.

Tobias Lear, who had embezzled from George Washington, who had burned the president's letters, who had bollixed every business opportunity, was heading to the Mediterranean to handle the extremely delicate peace negotiations with Tripoli.

CHAPTER 15

*An American Flag
on Foreign Soil*

WILLIAM EATON ROLLED UP the pants leg of his homemade general's uniform and walked out into the surf off Bomba beach. With the sun glinting off his epaulets, he waited for the American boat coming ashore.

"All was now rejoicing and mutual congratulation," wrote Midshipman Peck. The sight of the two-masted *Argus* brought elation that morning to the weary Americans, lifting them from the prospect of starvation or massacre to granting them yet another chance to pursue their unlikely mission.

Eaton and the midshipman stepped aboard the longboat; a dozen sailors rowed them out to the USS *Argus*, anchored safely offshore. "I enjoyed the pleasure of embracing my messmates," later recalled Peck, "and sitting down to a comfortable meal which I had not enjoyed for near 40 days."

Eaton was thrilled to see Hull again, who throughout had remained his steadfast advocate. Hull, like Eaton, hailed from the Massachusetts/Connecticut region with family members residing in both states. At fourteen, he had gone to sea as a cabin boy, and when shipwrecked at sixteen, he had saved his captain's life. Now thirty-two years old, Hull was known as an adept seaman, with an uncanny knack of squeezing every ounce of speed out of any vessel. "He was a rough boisterous captain of the sea," noted a contemporary, adding, "his manners were plain, bluff and hearty." Hull, like Eaton, did not suffer fools gladly. He could be "ruffled on sufficient occasion," added the observer.

Beyond Hull's welcome, Eaton was greeted by a long letter from Commodore Barron. Given Barron's lukewarm support of his mission, Eaton no doubt unfolded the document with trepidation. Within moments, he was calmed. "I cannot but applaud the energy and perseverance that has characterized your progress through a series of perplexing and discouraging difficulties," Barron had written on March 22. (Actually, too ill to write, he had dictated the words to his secretary.)

Barron noted that he had instantly ordered military supplies and food to be loaded onto the *Hornet* and *Argus* to be rushed to Eaton, as well as the ample sum of 7,000 Spanish dollars. But Barron, in this note, was not uniformly supportive. He wrote that he deeply opposed the Convention that Eaton planned to sign with Hamet. (Barron didn't know that Eaton had already signed it.)

"I reiterate to you . . . my dissent from any guarantee . . . [that] the United States may stand committed to place the exiled prince on the throne." By way of clarification, Barron stressed that the United States was helping Hamet to help himself . . . and that if Yussef offered honorable terms of peace, the United States must be free to accept them and "then our support of Hamet must necessarily be withdrawn." In stark terms, he described Hamet "as an instrument to an attainment."

Obsessive Eaton weighed the mixed message, and he decided not to waver. He planned to capture Derne, Bengazi, then Tripoli. Though it's clear from later letters that Eaton understood Barron's calculated use of Hamet, he deeply opposed that approach. Eaton's world featured Good and Evil; and Yussef by enslaving American sailors was Evil.

At 6 P.M., the crew of the *Argus* rowed a feast ashore for the weary troops. Eaton remained on board that night, eating well and drinking well and no doubt regaling his messmates with the tales of faithless Tayyib and the Bedouin women's love of brass buttons. In the morning the sailors in the *Argus* longboat rowed him ashore.

That afternoon, the *Hornet* sloop arrived, carrying the bulk of the supplies. Over the course of the next two days, the sailors rolled and hoisted 30 hogsheads of bread, 20 barrels of peas, 10 tierces of rice (approximately 3,000 pounds total), 10 boxes of oil, 100 sacks of rice, one bale of cloth, and 7,000 Spanish dollars into longboats and rowed it all ashore. The army's thirst requirements were not ignored. The *Hornet* off-loaded one hogshead (63 gallons) of brandy and two hogsheads of wine. Since, in theory, only the Christian troops drank liquor, and since that contingent totaled 75 men, each soldier—in a fair apportionment—could look forward to about two and a half gallons.

The troops, having survived the long march, spent three days lolling about, recuperating, eating, drinking. O'Bannon played his fiddle; the drummer avoided anything martial. Eaton, in his tent, finalized attack plans as best he could from his perch in Bomba about forty miles from the battle site in Derne.

A turbaned messenger arrived from the Moslem camp with yet an-other rumor that Yussef's army had reached Derne with 500 men. Eaton complained in notes to Hull that this fact—if true—made his need for field artillery even more acute, and that he was disappointed the *Congress* hadn't arrived with the promised fieldpieces. "Besides the terror that Cannon impress on the undisciplined Savages we have to dispute with, they will be our best resort against the Walls of Derne," he wrote.

Eaton then requested that he be allowed to borrow two of the *Argus*'s 24-pound carronades. (Carronades were short-barreled guns that launched a heavy shot for a short distance.) He also asked for four barrels of musket gunpowder, balls and flints, and as many muskets as could be spared. Eaton warned the carronades might have to be aban-doned in case of retreat.

As to the specific plan of attack, he wanted his forces to reach the eastern hills overlooking Derne and then attack from there; he hoped that the navy would come close enough to shore to blast out the town's batteries. Eaton waxed optimistic, especially if he could afford to buy the loyalty of the local Arabs. "I find them like the rest of mankind, moved by the present good . . . Cash will carry them . . . with this the Gates of Tripoli may be opened."

On the days leading up to battle, many soldiers cannot avoid thoughts of mortality. Eaton confronted his own possible death. "Of the effects I leave on board, in case I see you no more," he wrote to Hull, "I beg you will accept my cloak, and small sword, as marks of my attach-ment; the Damascus Sabre, which you will find in my chest, please give to

Capt. James Barron, it is due to his goodness and valor, I owe it to the Independent integrity of his heart; my Gold watch chain give to [my stepson Eli] Danielson; every thing else please deliver over to Mr. Charles Wadsworth my Executor." (Conspicuously absent is any sentimental mention of his wife.)

Two other men also sent letters to Captain Hull, both requesting permission to fight alongside Eaton. Lieutenant Presley O'Bannon wrote that he was "unwilling to abandon an Expedition this far conducted." Midshipman George Washington Mann asked to go onshore and replace Midshipman Peck. Mann labored to avoid insulting his commander. "I am actuated by . . . a wish to contribute generally by my services to the Interest of my Country." Captain Hull granted both requests, and allowed Eaton in addition to keep his six U.S. Marine privates and one sergeant.

All this while, Hamet and his followers, and the hired sheiks and the Bedouin, camped away from the Christians. Swarthy teenage boys hut-hutted their camels to fertile pastures to graze. The more devout prayed five times a day. So close to open enmity but a week earlier, the two allies kept a safe distance.

Before Hull gave any reply to Eaton's tactical letter, the *Argus* suddenly disappeared from port. Eaton could only assume—and hope—that Hull had seen a sail and taken off in pursuit. Then the next day, heavy clouds darkened the sky, and a storm hit the coast. Eaton in the rain was left wondering whether Hull would be able to rendezvous with him for the upcoming combined attack at Derne. But he had more pressing matters: moving an army the final leg to the battlefield.

The Gulf of Bomba sits ringed by mountains. The army, which had marched down along the coast to relax, now had to hike back up to head west to Derne. High cold winds mixed with rain soaked the troops as they marched ten miserable miles on Tuesday, April 23, up over rocky terrain. They camped in a ravine, within a mile of natural fresh water "springing from the top of a mountain of freestone, near Cape Ras el-Tin," as Eaton recorded in his diary. In the distance could be seen cultivated fields. Hamet sent a herald throughout the various camps to announce: "He who fears God and feels attachment to Hamet Bashaw will be careful to destroy nothing. Let no one touch the growing harvest. He who transgresses this injunction shall lose his right hand." By forbidding plundering, Hamet was trying not to alienate the local peasants who might rally to his cause.

The Americans, after so long in the desert, had finally reached a cultivated region. In antiquity, these lands bloomed with diverse crops; wealthy Romans squabbled over vacation homes. "Marched fifteen miles over mountainous and broken ground, covered with herbage and very large and beautiful red cedars—the first resemblance of a forest tree we have seen during a march of nearly six hundred miles." The mixed troop camped in a valley along a stream. Eaton estimated them to be "about five hours march from Derne."

A messenger arrived with news that the governor of Derne had fortified the city to repel any attack and that Yussef's army would probably reach Derne before them. Another messenger reported that no American ships could be seen off the coast, since that harsh storm of the previous day. Eaton, with his typical bullheadedness, recommended haste, a quick march double time to Derne. The turbaned allies reacted differently. "Alarm and consternation seized the Arab chiefs, and despondency the Bashaw," recorded Eaton. "The night was passed in consultations among them at which I was not admitted."

At 6 A.M., before dawn, the drummer pounded out a general wake-up call; everyone hustled about, striking their tents; Eaton promptly gave orders to prepare to march. The European mercenaries and the American Marines in uniform lined up. The followers of Hamet also lined up but in the opposite direction. Sheik Tayyib and Sheik Muhammed guided the 300 cavalry slowly back toward Bomba. The Bedouin merely refused to move and remained in camp.

Eaton's babysitting duties had commenced again. By now, he realized that the sheiks felt no overarching loyalty to Hamet or to the overthrow of Yussef. They were Moslem mercenaries on a sliding pay scale, which slid upward as the dangers increased. Eaton began with encouragement, shifted to reproach, and ended up promising $2,000 to the sheiks. They agreed. At 2 P.M. the Hamet-Eaton horde reached a hill overlooking Derne. The general was finally looking at his first target.

The easternmost town of any importance in the kingdom of Tripoli, Derne had a population of around five thousand. Nestled in a *wadi* (valley) of incredible fertility, the local crops included fig, pear, peach, orange, peas, tomatoes, cucumbers, pumpkins, jasmine, and sugarcane. Derne was famed for its honey and its unusual butter, concocted of butter and mutton fat and prized for Middle Eastern stews. The town's limestone buildings piggybacked on much older dwellings, with most of them having entrances on the second floor, reached by grapevine-trellis-covered staircases. In the summer, the local inhabitants liked to sit on their stoops under the shade of the grape bunches. Unfortunately for a place with so much to export, the harbor was miserable, shallow, pocked with reefs and exposed to high winds from the north and east. One traveler reported it unusable for seven months of the year, from February to August.

Eaton, along with Hamet, surveyed the target. From his hilltop, through his spyglass, he observed that a battery of eight cannons, probably nine-pounders, pointed seaward, guarding the harbor. To the northeast of the town, he saw residents building up some temporary breastworks, while to the southeast, the walls of old buildings blocked access. Eaton also noted a "ten inch howitzer" mounted on the terrace of the governor's palace. Spies told him that in town the inhabitants had fortified their terraces and knocked loopholes in their walls for shooting. They also said that because the governor of Derne "could bring 800 men into battle, and he possessed all the batteries, breastworks and seaboard, we should find it difficult to dislodge him . . . besides Yussef's army was just at hand." In addition, no American ships had arrived.

Eaton looked at Hamet. "I thought the Bashaw wished himself back to Egypt."

The following morning, at 8 A.M., Eaton ordered the Christian soldiers to build big bonfires in hopes the smoke signals would alert the American ships to their location. Without field artillery or ships, the attack would be foolhardy, even by Eaton's standards. In the meantime, he sent a letter under white flag of truce to the governor of Derne.

Sir, I want no territory. With me is advancing the legitimate
Sovereign of your country—Give me a passage through your city; and

for the supplies of which we shall have need you shall receive fair
compensation—Let no differences of religion induce us to shed the
blood of harmless men who think little and know nothing.—If you are
a man of liberal mind you will not balance on the propositions I
offer.—Hamet Bashaw pledges himself to me that you shall be
established in your government.—I shall see you tomorrow in a way
of your choice.

The governor's response arrived quickly:

My head or yours.—Mustifa

At 2 P.M. a distant sail was spotted. At 6 P.M. Lieutenant John Dent, captain of the *Nautilus*, sent a boat ashore, rowed by U.S. Navy sailors in crisp blue and white. "You will please send a large party down early in the Morning for the field pieces & ammunition, which I am afraid you will have some difficulty getting up the hill." Dent added he was ready to send over any supplies that Eaton might want. "Make my respects to O'Bannon & all your Brave followers & wishing you all the Success you so fully deserve."

After so many months at a slow pace, events were coming quickly to a head. General Eaton decided that, with Yussef's army on the march toward Derne, he must order an immediate full-scale attack for the following day, Saturday, April 27.

The next morning, at 5:30 A.M., the Americans spotted three more ships hovering near the 14-gun *Nautilus*. Hull had arrived in the 18-gun brig *Argus* towing a lateen-sailed prize, while Lieutenant Samuel Evans showed up in the pip-squeak 10-gun sloop *Hornet,* which had formerly been a Massachusetts merchantman named *Traveller.*

The *Argus,* days earlier, had indeed spotted a ship and captured it. The vessel was flying Ottoman colors but carried mostly Tripolitan passengers on board, including a gunboat captain and several leading citizens of Bengazi. The cargo included gunpowder bound for Tripoli. Though Hull admitted he didn't know whether Barron considered the whole coast under blockade, he decided he would keep the vessel as a prize.

The *Argus* carried long guns capable of firing 24-pound shot; the *Nautilus* sported stubby carronades hoisting 12-pound balls, and the *Hornet* carried brass cannons throwing 6-pound balls.

At 10:30 A.M. a longboat began ferrying the brass fieldpieces ashore to a spot east of Derne. The men rowed in close to the shore, only to discover that cliffs lined that whole section of the coast and that even the best place would require hauling the heavy gun up an almost twenty-foot-sheer cliff. While another boat looked for an alternative, the men hoisted up nine barrels of gunpowder, 200 bags of musket balls for grape filler, and 150 rounds for the fieldpiece as well as the rammer and wadding. (A bag of musket balls is a cannon's equivalent of bird shot, delivering a lethal spray at the enemy.)

The fieldpiece was a problem. The weight is not listed, but a good guess might be 1,500 pounds, to be hoisted from a rocking boat up a cliff and over the edge. The men, using ropes and horses and struggling for several hours, finally lugged up one fieldpiece. Eaton decided that it would take too long to haul up the other, so he left it to be carried back to the *Nautilus*.

The three U.S. Navy ships began to sail to take their positions outside Derne harbor.

Eaton readied the army. The Christians and Moslems would have separate missions. Eaton with his small force would tackle the governor's main defense. Hamet and his hundreds of robed riders would circle around back of the town to try to capture an old castle to the southwest of town. They hoped to meet at the governor's mansion. The navy would try to take out the shore battery, then plunk balls into the town.

At 2 P.M. General Eaton along with Lieutenant O'Bannon, leading an attack force of 7 U.S. Marines and 26 Greek recruits as well as 24 European mercenaries to handle the fieldpiece, advanced on the southeast corner of Derne. Hundreds of men opposed them, shooting up from a fortified ravine, protected by earthworks. The fieldpiece rained big balls and sprays of musket balls down upon the enemy.

Upon the start of gunfire, the brave little *Hornet* sailed to within one hundred yards of Governor Mustifa's battery of nine-pounders and spit out a relentless barrage of grape and balls from its brass six-pounders. The *Nautilus* stood about a half mile from shore and lobbed its 12-pound balls over the *Hornet* and toward the battery and the town. Anchored a bit farther out was the *Argus*, at the right distance to shoot its 24-pound shot.

Hamet's troops—more than 1,000 men—galloped downward, green Moslem flags streaming, and quickly took the largely undefended old castle on the hill at the back of the town, but then they remained there, stock still in that safe zone.

Eaton's French Maltese-Sicilian artillery team learned the niceties of their new weapon on the run; they mastered it quickly, but their speed of reloading was diminished when the crew accidentally fired away the only rammer.

The three ships kept up constant fire on the enemy's shore battery on the ramparts above the harbor. The *Hornet,* located within pistol shot, repeatedly tacking, braved especially heavy fire. At one point, a shot from the Derne battery snapped the halliards that held aloft the large American flag in the stern. From war immemorial, there has been an almost mystical disgrace to losing one's national flag, to having it captured or seeing it lowered. It is the symbolic embodiment of the will to fight. Lieutenant Blodget scooped up the immense flag, fifteen feet long, and climbed the ratlines amid a torrent of musket fire. Just as he nailed it to the main masthead, he was hit with a musket ball near his hip, which miraculously "lodged in his watch while in his fob," according to an eyewitness account. He escaped injury as did the flag, which now caught the breezes.

The *Hornet* sprayed jagged grapeshot on the shore battery. The navy men kept up such a constant barrage that the brass six-pounders pulled the planks out of the deck. The turbaned gunners tried to remain brave as ball after heavy ball from the *Nautilus* or *Argus* plowed up the earth nearby. After three-quarters of an hour, the governor's gunners abandoned the battery and rushed to join the governor's troops defending the southeast section of town.

Eaton and O'Bannon had approximately one hundred soldiers,

including seven U.S. Marines perched on the hill to the southeast of town. The total enemy force was estimated at close to one thousand, well entrenched, firing their muskets from behind bulwarks.

At around 3:30 P.M., Eaton came to a grim conclusion. "The fire of the enemy's Musketry became too warm and continually augmenting. Our troops were thrown into confusion and undisciplined as they were, it was impossible to reduce them to order." The British infantry, fighting against Napoleon, was famous for its unflappable lines of muskets. This hodgepodge European-American unit was verging on chaos and retreat.

Eaton made a desperate decision: a charge. His hundred against their thousand. The men attached bayonets. He gave the signal. The drummers pounded the skins.

Eaton and O'Bannon in full uniform led the charge down the hill into the teeth of the enemy. A polyglot war cry rose from the throats of the attacking men: English, French, Italian, Greek. Young Scot Farquhar raced near the front, as did the U.S. Marines. The men poured downward toward the earthworks, completely exposed during this rumble down the hillside. The enemy could squeeze off target-practice shots at them, but only one round or possibly two before the attackers would reach them. Eaton's goal was to descend quickly enough to fluster the enemy. He had had little choice; the firefight had been going badly.

The Americans and Europeans poured forward. U.S. Marine Private John Wilton was instantly killed by a shot to the heart. Another marine, Edward Steward, crumpled, as did several of the Greeks. A pair of marines—David Thomas and Bernard O'Brian—were also hit. Maniacal Eaton, at the very front, suddenly spun to the ground. He grasped his left wrist; a musket ball had torn through the wrist and exited the other side. Blood poured out, staining his general's coat, splattering in the dust of the dry *wadi*. O'Bannon and Mann kept on charging with the 75 men, and Eaton quickly gathered himself, somehow wrapped the wound, and continued forward.

With this determined force coming at them, the men of Derne fired off another round, but then most of them didn't dare to try to reload; they scattered from the earthworks to the safety of the nearby houses. A bayonet can skewer a man before a scimitar can do any harm.

Twenty-nine-year-old O'Bannon, along with twenty-one-year-old Mann, as well as the few U.S. Marines and Greeks zigzagged through the shower of musket fire from the loopholes in the buildings. They fought and raced to the abandoned battery and fort in the harbor.

Captain Hull observed the action through his spyglass on the *Argus,* a half mile offshore. "At about half past 3, we had the satisfaction to see Lt. O'Bannon and Mr. Mann, midshipman of the *Argus,* with a few brave fellows with them, enter the fort, haul down the Enemy's flag, and plant the American ensign on the walls of the Battery."

This marked the first time the American flag—then fifteen stars and fifteen stripes—had ever been planted in battle on foreign soil outside of North America. Eaton and the Marines never explained their rationale, but it's *unlikely* that Thomas Jefferson ever envisioned that his reluctant permission to allow Eaton to aid Hamet would lead to an American flag flapping in conquest over a city in Tripoli. Whatever Jefferson might have thought, the sight greatly stirred the emotions of the handful of hardened men who witnessed the accomplishment.

The soldiers who captured the fort labored hard to turn the heavy guns and point them upon the town. They discovered that the enemy in its haste to retreat had left a round loaded, primed, and ready to go. Around this time, Hamet Bashaw and his cavalrymen advanced into the southwestern end of town. And now the allied forces pinned the defenders between two streams of gunfire as the navy ships kept lobbing balls into the town, creating chaos.

With the tide of battle turning, the Bashaw and his men cantered through the narrow streets, harassing the enemy. They took possession of the governor's palace, and the cavalry chased the fleeing enemy. As Eaton later described it: "They held safe positions to catch fugitives until the doors of the Enemy were open'd for plunder, when they became at once brave & impetuous." The governor of Derne first took refuge in a mosque then somehow slipped into the harem of one of the town's leading citizens and claimed the ancient rights of sanctuary. Most of the defenders of Derne tried to hide their weapons and slip back into civilian life.

By 4 P.M. Eaton claimed the town as captured. Hull sent a boat ashore to bring more ammunition and carry off the thirteen Christians wounded, including U.S. Marine Bernard O'Brian. At 5:30 P.M. Eaton went aboard the *Argus* to have his wound dressed; it was described as "musket ball through the left wrist," in other words, a metal ball of at least three-quarter inch in diameter had passed through just below the wrist joint. (Eaton would never regain full use of the arm.)

The time for recuperation for Eaton and the other Christian wounded, however, would be brief. A spy reported that Yussef's troops were within fourteen hours' march of the town. The doctor bandaged Eaton's arm and made the general put it in a sling, which was draped next to his shiny epaulet. Eaton later complained he could no longer wield his rifle. (In this era, the rifle, with its longer range and accuracy, was replacing the cumbersome musket.)

Eaton allowed himself one night aboard the *Argus*. The next day bright and early, the New Englander began orchestrating the town's defenses. He set up his own headquarters under the American flag in the small fort by the harbor battery. Someone, probably Eaton, dubbed it "Fort Enterprise"—a telling name that brings to mind hard work and boldness. Eaton, with help from his engineer, colorful Jean Eugene, repaired the ramparts and the fort and set about permanently pointing the cannons into the city. He placed barricades in various spots in the city to create ambush points. The guns were cleaned and repaired. Nine-pound cannonballs were neatly stacked nearby. Local reports estimated that about one-third of the quite perturbed populace remained secretly loyal to Governor Mustifa Bey, then holed up in the sheik's harem.

After consulting with Eaton, Hull decided that he would send off the *Hornet* to Malta, both for repairs to its sheered planks and, equally important, to inform Commodore Barron of their victory. In four years of war against Tripoli, this easily ranked as the United States' greatest victory.

Eaton, still weak from his wound, set about the pleasant task of relaying their good news. "We are in possession of the most valuable province of Tripoli," he announced. Eaton recounted the battle in vivid blow-by-blow detail and begged the liberty to praise O'Bannon, Mann, and the commanders of all three navy vessels for their courage and competence. He recommended them all for reward or promotion.

Eaton signed it, sealed it with wax, and handed it to go by the *Hornet*. But the winds were not favorable, and the small vessel was forced to return to port the next day. This gave Eaton the chance—a mischance really—to write a long May 1 postscript to Barron. Maybe the wound made him edgier than usual, or maybe he'd had more than one glass of brandy to soothe the pain, but in this missive, Eaton shows himself too honest, too blunt. He starkly stated that Hamet lacked the "military talent and firmness" to conquer Bengazi and Tripoli City. And that for Eaton to help him do it, he would need detachments of U.S. Marines and more money.

Eaton also testily analyzed the commodore's last letter, which had placed nuanced limits on American support of Hamet. Eaton argued that if Hamet was "to be used solely as an instrument . . . to the advantage of the United States, without any consideration of his future well-being, I cannot persuade myself that any bonds of patriotism dictate to me [that] duty." The issue of honor and betrayal was clearly starting to weigh on him. He baldly pointed out the conflict of interest: that the mission's own success would spell its doom; that is, if he and Hamet succeed in threatening Yussef, then Yussef would propose peace "to rid him of so dangerous a rival." That built-in disloyalty to an ally disturbed Eaton.

"At all events," he wrote, "I am deeply impressed with the opinion that the post we have secured here [Derne] should not be abandoned, nor the terms of peace precipitately embraced." Eaton regarded Derne as America's strongest bargaining chip. And in this rambling letter, he couldn't resist taking one last crack at gaining backing for pursuing his original mission to overthrow Yussef. "It would probably be a death blow to the Barbary System." Eaton's wound finally induced him to close.

"It is with much pain that I keep a sedentary position to write . . . I have not language to express my sense of gratitude and obligation for your exertions in forwarding us supplies; without them we must have perished."

The *Hornet* departed with his letters, but stormy weather would slow its path to Malta.

Over the next week, Eaton, ensconced in Derne, prepared for the inevitable battle against Yussef's army that must arrive on the scene very soon. Its whole existence couldn't be a phantom of the rumor mill.

While Hamet was lording it inside the governor's mansion, Eaton wanted to capture the ousted governor of Derne, the third-ranking minister in all of Tripoli. With his usual short temper, he found it infuriating that the man, Mustifa, who had written "My Head or Yours," could be basking in a harem in town. Eaton noted in his diary for May 2: "Used exertions to draw the Governor from his sanctuary. The Hiram [Harem] in which he had taken asylum appertained to a Sheik of Mesreat, one of the departments [loyal to Hamet]. Neither persuasion, bribes nor menace could prevail on this venerable aged chief to permit the hospitality of his house to be violated. He urged that whatever may be the weakness or even the crimes of the Arabs there was never an instance known among them of giving up a fugitive to whom they had once accorded their protection." The sheik added if he violated the laws of hospitality, Allah would avenge the crime on him and on his children.

Over the next couple days, the enemy army finally arrived on the outskirts of town and shrewdly chose for their encampment the same high ground to the southeast that Eaton had chosen back on April 26. The attacking force appeared to number about 1,000, but its total shifted almost daily with recruits and defections from among the Bedouin tribes and from among the townspeople. From Eaton's perspective, the people of Derne seemed to care only about aligning themselves with the eventual winner. Unfortunately for them, no one was yet sure who that would be. To lure supporters, the enemy spread the word that their attacking army would slaughter and plunder anyone loyal to Hamet. The governor from his luxurious prison in the harem helped relay the threat through the streets via messengers. (While Eaton accepted the validity of a foreign embassy as a sanctuary, he couldn't wrap his Christian mind around the inviolability of a Moslem harem.)

Day followed day, and by May 12, Eaton had had enough of comfortable Mustifa. Eaton marched to the sheik's house at the head of a force of fifty Christians with fixed bayonets. Through his interpreter, he loudly declared his intention to bring out the governor. Word in Arabic of the general's arrival spread quickly throughout the quarter. Someone shouted: "The Christians no longer respect the customs of our fathers and our laws of hospitality." Eaton through an interpreter retorted to the crowd that the Bey was an outlaw, had insulted him, had been defeated, was in a conquered town, and by all rules of war, was Eaton's prisoner. Worse, the man was carrying on a secret war from his sanctuary. Eaton—in his typical hardheaded way—then said he would now have the governor "dead or alive."

The murmur in the street rose; the townspeople began massing to attack the Christians. The bayonets glinting in the sun apparently gave pause. Hamet arrived and became deeply upset. He pleaded with Eaton to delay his attack until the following day, promising to try to negotiate the governor out of the harem. Reluctantly, Eaton led his fifty bayonets back to Fort Enterprise. That night, the old sheik smuggled the governor out of town and allowed him to slip over to the enemy camp. The governor, with his knowledge of goings-on inside Derne, wasted no time; he immediately organized an attack.

Just before dawn, five flags, Moslem standards, flapped in the breeze on the hill behind the town. The cavalry of Bashaw Yussef, about 700 horsemen with muskets and scimitars, stood ready to attack, along with about 300 men on foot. These enemy troops remained poised on the hill, a menacing silhouette.

According to Captain Hull's account, Hamet was informed of the enemy's position and he ordered about 300 men to ride out to meet the enemy. "At 1/2 past 9 the parties met and began a brisk fire, which lasted about fifteen minutes." The brief battle ended when Hamet's troops, outnumbered, dissolved back into Derne. About 300 enemy horsemen pursued them in the winding streets of the town. From out of the limestone houses, from gaps in the garden walls, some of the locals fired upon the attackers, picking off one here and one there. Hull credited the townspeople as well as Hamet's troops in ambush with killing enough of the enemy that they decided to retreat. As the enemy poured out of the eastern side of town, Hull stated, this gave the guns of the *Argus* and *Nautilus* a clear target, and they peppered them with shot. Eaton's harbor battery chimed in as well. (To aim at the town itself from a rocking vessel a half mile offshore was far too risky to the lives of allies.) By 11 A.M., the enemy marched back up the hill to their original starting point, "defeated." So stated Hull.

Interestingly, William Eaton left a different account of the same battle. His is much more dramatic and features a stunning turning point. Eaton stated that Hamet sent only one hundred horsemen out to meet the enemy, and that they fought bravely but, far outnumbered, were forced to retreat. The enemy advanced through irregular ambuscades right to the edge of the governor's palace in the heart of town. "The attackers seemed resolute in capturing [Hamet]," wrote Eaton.

Eaton and O'Bannon judged an infantry sortie from Fort Enterprise, which would leave the guns unguarded, too risky. Over the next hour, Eaton listened as the pop-pop of musket and pistol fire began to slow, and he feared that the enemy had captured most of the town and would surround the governor's palace. In his telling, he then made a bold decision. He decided to fire the battery guns upon the town; the risk of course was that they might accidentally kill loyal citizens or some of Hamet's forces. "Very fortunately, a shot from one of our nine pounders killed two of the enemy from their horses in the courtyard of the palace," wrote Eaton. A pair of horsemen gored by a cannonball is not a pretty sight. "They instantly sounded a retreat, and abandoning the town at all quarters, were everywhere pursued by Hamet's cavalry until they were chased under the shot of our vessels, which galled them sorely in their flight."

In a grim aside later to Hull (perhaps not meant for posterity), he added: "The Enemy are shamefully flogged, we have collected twenty of their heads besides those you have killed, which are said to be an equal or greater number."

Eaton hoped that Hull would now allow a troop of U.S. sailors and marines to parade in downtown Derne to overawe the inhabitants into believing that the Hamet-American forces would win. He also requested more gunpowder, musket balls, flints, and cartridge paper. Equally as important, he added: "We are destitute of Spirits and Wine—The cask sent off was something more than two thirds gone, either by leakage or theft." No self-respecting Christian soldier in 1805 wanted to celebrate a victory . . . sober.

That night, with everyone calling it a victory, the local sheik who had sheltered the governor in his harem sanctuary came to the palace. All that day, he and his men had fought for Hamet. He kissed Hamet's hand and squatted down in front of him. He told him that he had shown his unwavering loyalty all day, but he added, looking Hamet in the eye, that perhaps the prince did not deserve his support. "You would have yielded to the Christian General in violating the hospitality of my house, and of degrading the honor of my name. You should have recollected that, not quite two years ago, you were saved in this same asylum, and secured in your escape by the same hospitality from the vengeance of this very same Bey." The sheik then renewed his oath of loyalty to Hamet.

The following day, an Italian slave escaped from Yussef's army. He reported the enemy dead totaled 39, with 45 wounded.

Eaton and Hamet were both also completely penniless, and Eaton was at wit's end trying to buy some more loyalty. Eaton convinced Captain Hull to put up for auction some of the prize goods he had seized off the small vessel a week earlier. He convinced him that he and O'Bannon would sign bona fide receipts for the sale and then give the money to Hamet, and that Hull and crew would later be reimbursed by the U.S. government. The scheme made sense, except for the fact the vessel had not yet been judged a legitimate prize by any admiralty court. Eaton was desperate.

An auction was held on the morning of May 15. Expensive cloths— striped and glazed, blue linen, as well as 31 silk turbans and more cloth and 100 handkerchiefs and more turbans . . . generated $331.50. Eaton handed the cash over to Hamet and a receipt over to Hull.

The enemy forces grouped again on the hill overlooking Derne, about 1,000 men. A spy reported they were readying to unleash a huge attack on the following morning. The only possible hitch: The Bedouin tribes were balking at using their camels as moving breastworks.

Since the *Hornet* hadn't returned from Malta, Hull regarded it as his duty to send the *Nautilus* to update the commodore. Now only one U.S. Navy ship remained offshore. As for onshore: five healthy U.S. Marines, Eaton, Mann, and O'Bannon remained with the fifty ragtag Christian mercenaries. Eaton worried about diminishing food supplies, especially if the *Argus* had to leave.

On Monday, May 20, on a beautiful spring day, the entire opposing army massed on the hill overlooking the town. Standards fluttered in the breeze. Joy shots filled the air. It was abundantly clear that they planned to attack.

On that day, the men serving under Eaton signed an amazing document, a testament to Eaton's fortitude. Very few officers ever receive such spontaneous support. It was written in French.

Monsieur,

Vu le desir et le courage qui nous anime . . .

Sir,

In view of the desire and the courage which animates us all to participate in the glory of an expedition which is worthy of such a warlike nation, we are coming today to state to you again the zeal which we have to take part in it. We could not serve a better chief. The heroic ardor and the talents with which you are endowed can only ensure the happiness of your men. We offer our services in the campaign, to strictly carry out your orders, to exact respect for the honorable flag of the United States of America, and to encounter the enemy wherever he may be.

Everything assures us of a complete victory under your command. We are only waiting for the moment to win this glory, and to fall on the enemy.

We believe you are assured in advance of the sentiments which we are proclaiming. Yes! We swear that we shall follow you and that we shall fight unto death.

It was signed in varying degrees of legibility by:

Chevalier Davies, Major
PN O'Bannon, Lt. Marines
George Mann
George Farquhar
Geny Inspectore [Jean Eugene]
Filippo Galea
Selim Capt.
Count Lieut.—for the entire company of artillery
Rocco Lieut.
Cap.no Luca—for the entire Greek company

To William Eaton, Agent of the United States of America for all the Barbary Regencies and General Commander in Chief of the allied land forces against Tripoli.

At the camp of Derne 20 May 1805

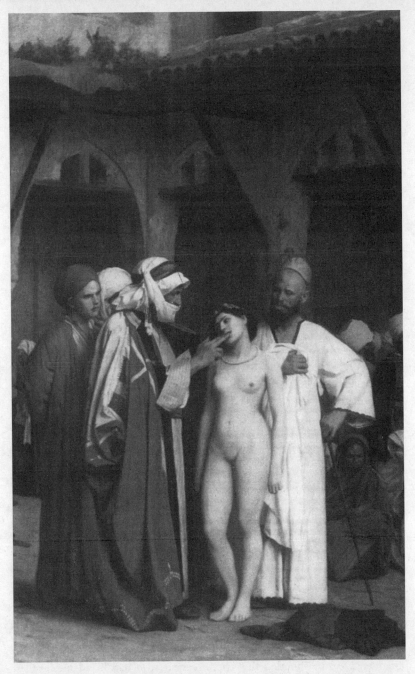

A prospective buyer on the Barbary Coast of North Africa carefully examines a female slave before bidding. ("The Slave Market" by Jean-Leon Gerome.)

Battle fought in Tripoli harbor, August 1804. This stylized scene shows Stephen Decatur shooting the Tripoli corsair who had killed his brother; meanwhile, an American sailor, often identified as Reuben James, sacrifices his head to save Decatur's life. (Anonymous engraving. Naval Historical Foundation.)

William Bainbridge, as a twenty-four-year-old lieutenant in 1798, around the time of his first surrender. (Miniature—owned by Mrs. Theodore Frothingham—released to the Naval Historical Foundation.)

William Eaton, a former U.S. Army captain, was sent on a secret mission to North Africa by Thomas Jefferson in 1804. (This portrait, painted by Rembrandt Peale, is owned by great-great-great grandson Thomas Eaton Root, and is currently on loan to the Mint Museum in Charlotte, N.C.)

Thomas Jefferson at age fifty-six, about a decade before the outbreak of the Barbary War. (Portrait, painted in 1791–1792, by Charles Willson Peale. Credit: Independence National Historical Park.)

Typical garb of a prince in Tripoli. Bey Hassan Karamanli (shown here) was murdered in 1790 by his younger brother, Yussef, who later became the first foreign ruler to declare war on the United States.

(Source: Frontispiece of *Narrative of a Ten Years' Residence in Tripoli* by Miss Tully. London, 1817.)

His Excellency the Governor of Derne —

Environs of Derne
april 26

Sir,

I want no territory with me in advancing the legitimate Sovereign of your country. Give me a passage through your city; and for the supplies of which we shall need, you shall receive a fair compensation. Let no differences of religion induce us to shed the blood of harmless men who think little & know nothing. — If you are a man of liberal mind you will not balance on the disposition I offer. — Hamet Bashaw pledges himself to me that you shall be established in your government. — I shall see you tomorrow in a way of your choice —

— Eaton

answer —

Same Date

My head or yours

Mustifa

Request for surrender sent by William Eaton to the governor of Derne, April 26, 1804. Eaton also jotted down the governor's reply: "My head or yours—Mustifa."

(William Eaton Papers. By permission of the Huntington Library, San Marino, California.)

Harvard graduate,
one-time secretary to
George Washington,
U.S. consul general
in Barbary,
Tobias Lear
(1762–1816)
and his young wife,
Frances Henley Lear
(1779-1856).

(Current location of these
two portraits is unknown.)

Article Sixteen on Captives. June 4, 1805.
A mistranslation in the Arabic version
of the treaty signed by Lear appears to
allow the continued enslaving of
American sailors and passengers.

(Source: *Treaties and Other International
Acts of the United States of America*,
ed. Hunter Miller. Washington, D.C., 1931.)

A citizen of Tripoli,
early twentieth
century, sitting on
a pile of thirteen
cannons salvaged
from the wreck of
the USS *Philadelphia*.

(Naval Historical
Foundation.)

CHAPTER 16 *Malta: Diseased Liver and Cold Feet*

FOUR DAYS EARLIER, on May 16, the damaged USS *Hornet*, after battling headwinds and heavy gales, arrived in Malta, carrying the victory dispatches of Eaton and Hull. Commodore Samuel Barron, still quite ill, was staying at a country house outside of the main port of La Valetta. A boat was rowed out to the quarantined *Hornet* and a messenger took the letters, which, in turn, were rushed by horseback to Barron.

The commodore immediately ordered his secretary, Robert Denison, to scrawl out copies and have them galloped over to Tobias Lear.

The news of victory at Derne—along with Eaton's analysis of the situation—seemed to snap Barron out of his lethargy and bring him to several momentous conclusions. He decided on the spot that it was time to cut off aid to Hamet. He decided it was time to begin negotiations in earnest for peace with Yussef, time to do anything to accelerate the freeing of the hostages, and time for him to step down as commodore of the fleet. From his sickbed, he made these key calculations, even though less than a week later he would admit: "I have never disguised from myself that my powers of attention have been weakened by the effects of my long and distressful Indisposition."

Barron first outlined his newfound clarity in a letter on May 18 to Tobias Lear. He framed the decisions as hinging on several factors. He complained that the U.S. Navy lacked gunboats and bomb ships needed to attack Tripoli City, and mentioned how both Venice and Naples had refused to loan him any. He also groused that three of his frigates weren't up to braving another winter's weather off Tripoli. The Virginia native also considered the moment opportune for peace because he found very little upside in pursuing any cooperation with Hamet. He parroted Eaton in pointing out to Lear the prince's "want of energy and military talents, his total deprivation of means and resources." Barron also noted that even though we had placed Hamet in command of the second largest province in Tripoli, one that had once been loyal to him, he was nonetheless unable to proceed on his own. Hamet is "no longer a fit subject for our support." Barron was sounding a death knell for Jefferson's ambivalent secret mission; all that remained in doubt was how many would die if U.S. aid was abruptly withdrawn.

But Barron refused to consider Eaton's accomplishment a total waste. "Whatever may be the final result of this Cooperation, I cannot reject the belief that it has had a powerful effect upon the reigning Bashaw, and it may be fairly presumed that the gallant conduct of our friends in the affair at Derne, and the capture of that place will have its influence and dispose him to moderate his pretensions and to think seriously of Peace."

Barron concluded that it was now indeed the right time for Tobias Lear to go negotiate a favorable peace and ransom. He couldn't help but mention a sentimental motive. "I know the value of such a man as Captain Bainbridge and of his Officers . . . no reasonable & honorable occasion should be neglected which affords the prospect of releasing them from the bondage of a bigoted and unfeeling Tyrant." The USS *Essex* frigate would stand ready to carry Lear to Tripoli.

Peace was apparently at hand.

Lear, well trained from his long stint as Washington's personal secretary, noted that he received Barron's letter at 9 P.M., May 18. By noon the following day, he had drafted his reply.

Lear interpreted his diplomatic instructions to mean that Barron, as commander of the navy forces, was entitled to choose the fittest moment to negotiate, and Lear answered that he would indeed comply with Barron's wishes. (Lear would later be accused of manipulating the ill commodore; if anything, it appears that Barron's decision catapulted

Malta-garden-party Lear into action.) Lear stated he would be ready to leave "in a few days."

The consul general, however, could not end his brief letter without taking a swipe at Eaton's mission. "Altho' I cannot, Sir, agree with your Opinion that any impression favourable to us has been made on the mind of the Bashaw from our co-operation with his brother thus far, excepting what may arise from the undaunted Bravery and perseverance of the few of our Countrymen at Derne, which will be to him a further proof of what we can do alone against him." This awkward-sounding sentence has the ring of a man about to say something really nasty, then swerving off into niceties.

Lear compacted his mission: "Yet as I am of opinion, that, as he [Yussef] has discovered a disposition to Open a negociation, we should embrace it, in order to see if such terms can be made as are admissible on our part, and to relieve our unfortunate Countrymen out of his power, whose fate ought not to depend on small punctilios."

A "punctilio"—originally a teeny line on the face of a clock—is a trifle. Apparently, Lear considered the U.S. cooperation with Hamet as a trifle.

Having received this endorsement from Lear, Barron now drafted letters to Hull and Eaton. He blamed his health and haste for the brevity to Hull. He did not offer a syllable of congratulations for Derne. He raced to the point. "The letter I have written to Mr. Eaton by this conveyance [the USS *Hornet*] . . . will no doubt determine him and the Officers to leave the Coast as a measure rendered necessary by existing circumstances, and especially by the intention of the Consul General to open a negociation with Joussef, reigning Bashaw of Tripoli." Barron then ordered that Hull, "as soon as the requisite arrangements are made," make sail to return with all navy ships to Syracuse.

Barron directed the navy agent in Malta to supply food to be carried to Derne, but he specified that it be "for the use of the crews of the United States vessels and the Christians under the command of Mr. Eaton." (Eaton would find this religious distinction, denying food to Hamet and his men, offensive.)

Barron thoughtfully included private supplies for Eaton and the officers: 72 bottles of Porter, a quarter cask of Marsala, coffee, brown sugar, and tea. He didn't specify his intention, but maybe he thought that the luxuries would dull their pain at abandonment.

Barron's letter to Eaton was several pages long and did include grudging praise for the capture of Derne, saying that Eaton's conduct "would not discredit the character which our countrymen have established among the Nations of Barbary." (*"Not discredit"* . . . Eaton no doubt had been expecting more of a parade.)

Barron immediately zeroed in on Eaton's descriptions of Hamet that Eaton had written in that blunt impolitic postscript of May 1. For a man in a sickbed, dictating to a secretary with serious inflammation of the eyes, Barron's letter is surprisingly thorough and well reasoned. He stated: "If the Ex-Bashaw, after being put in possession of Derne, his former Government & the District where his Interest is said to be the most powerful, has not in himself energy & talent, & is so destitute of means & resources, as not to be able to move on with successful progress, seconded by our Naval force acting on the coast, he must be held as unworthy of further Support, and the Co-operation as a measure too expensive and burthensome." The erstwhile commodore pointed out that he had used every penny of the discretionary money set aside by Washington ($20,000) and he didn't have unlimited funds.

Barron did not expressly order Eaton to abandon the coast immediately. Nonetheless, he clearly believed he had shaped the situation so that Eaton would find departure as the only reasonable choice. Barron informed him that the U.S. Navy would no longer supply any food, ammunition, or money to Hamet and that "Colonel Lear" was heading to Tripoli to begin peace negotiations. Since Barron wanted Eaton and the navy to have a smooth departure off the coast, he did send $2,000 to allow Eaton to clean up any "little engagements" and he did concede that the navy gunners could aid Hamet while the ships remained in the vicinity. Barron's leeway was designed to avoid a massacre; his overriding message, however, was clear: Leave Derne.

"The interests of Sidi Hamet will not be overlooked," Barron added, stating that Lear would "endeavor at stipulating some Conditions for the unfortunate Exile, provided this can be done without giving up points that are essential, & without any considerable sacrifice of National advantage on our part." Caveat climbed upon caveat.

The half-blind secretary carried the letters to the ailing commodore for his signature. They were sealed and rushed to Lieutenant Evans of the *Hornet*, who immediately made sail toward Derne. The winds would determine when these doom-the-mission orders would arrive.

Tobias Lear now had to prepare to leave the sheltered nest of Malta. His life as suave diplomat with beautiful bride would be briefly interrupted. His calendar succinctly reveals his lifestyle and his priorities.

> Tuesday May 21, 1805—Employ'd as yesterday & in making visits to my acquaintances &c. Rode out with Mrs Lear to St. Julian to see D^r & Mrs Stoddert.
>
> Wednesday—May 22, 1805—I rec^d a letter from Commodore Barron informing me that he had resigned the command of the U.S. Navy to Capt. Jn. Rodgers, now off Tripoli, and that the frigate ESSEX wd. be ready to sail immediately for that place. I answered I wd. be ready to embark onboard her tomorrow.
>
> In the afternoon I rode with Mrs Lear to St. Antonio, and from thence, we went with Sir Alex^r & Lady Ball to St. Julian and drank tea . . .
>
> Thursday May 23d 1805—Preparing to embark on board the ESSEX, Capt. [James] Barron dined with us and promised to get his ship out of the harbour early in the morn^g and then come on shore for me.
>
> Friday May 24, 1805—I waited until 12 O'clk expecting Capt. B. on shore. At one, he sent the gig on shore for me. I embark'd abt 2 P.M. where I found Mr. Pulisse our consul in Malta, <u>who is going</u> to Tripoli with me. . . .

The choice of Joseph Pulis to accompany Lear was an unfortunate one. Captain Preble, before departing the previous year, was convinced that Pulis, a former consul to Malta *for Tripoli*, was acting as something of a double agent. Preble had found bags of mail intended for the American prisoners hidden in Pulis's office, marked for return to the United States. "He has no respectability attached to his character—cannot speak a word of English, and is by no means a proper representative," Preble had written to the secretary of the navy. Eaton in early 1805 complained that Pulis was the only one in Malta in whom he had confided part of his Hamet plans and that he later learned that his words had reached Tripoli almost immediately via a ship from Malta.

The hardest part of Tobias Lear's preparation for departure was clearly the prospect of leaving his young Fanny. The silver lining for historians is that he would write a prompter and more detailed account of the upcoming negotiations to Fanny than he ever would convey to Secretary of State Madison or to Jefferson.

The *Essex*, carrying Lear and Pulis, sailed out of La Valetta harbor of Malta on May 25, bound for Tripoli. Both Lear and Barron had high hopes for a speedy end to the four-year-old war.

* * *

The following day, *about thirty hours* after Lear's departure, the deeply laden *Ceres* arrived in Malta from Baltimore, carrying an enormous quantity of military supplies and, more important, updated navy orders that crystallized the aggressive plans for the attack on Tripoli. Navy Secretary Smith described the impending delivery by another navy cargo ship of 300 barrels of gunpowder and a huge supply of cannonballs, from 32-pounders to 24s, 18s, 12s, and 6s. (Even the dimmest officer knew this was not all intended for salutes and target practice.) Secretary Smith also mentioned that ten gunboats, each bearing a 32-pound short-barreled gun at each end, should be arriving soon with crews of fifteen, as would the *John Adams,* with 500 new recruits aboard.

The navy secretary was describing an enormous buildup in firepower that would facilitate an attack on Tripoli. The men in Washington clearly wanted to attack first, negotiate later.

Barron, recognizing the gravitas of this new information, realized he must quickly tell the new commodore. He had no U.S. Navy ships in La Valetta harbor, so he commissioned a *speronara,* an express sailboat, to head immediately for Tripoli. But first, his half-blind secretary, the brother of Captain Rodgers's fiancée, had to copy the orders in case the boat capsized. Since Barron was no longer in command, and since he couldn't know how far negotiations had proceeded in a couple of days, his accompanying note to Rodgers mentioned "the importance of the Intelligence" but left any decisions up to Rodgers. While the documents were being copied, the winds shifted and began a relentless blow into La Valetta harbor.

CHAPTER 17 *Tripoli: Fear*

TOBIAS LEAR HAD BEEN dead wrong. The news of the victory in Derne by Eaton and Hamet had deeply disturbed the powers and populace at Tripoli. The Dutch diplomat Zuchet recorded in his diary for Thursday, May 23:

> Yesterday there arrived here from Derne, after 18 days passage by camel, dispatches that brought the devastating news to the Bashaw that his brother, Sidi Ahmed, with around 1,000 men, Infantry and Cavalry and 300 Americans commanded by "Colonel Aiton," former U.S. consul at Tunis, have captured a city in the province of Derne, and that a tribe of Arabs have joined them.
>
> This news has produced alarm in this Regency and in the whole country, although the Bashaw deludes himself that his enemies will be soon destroyed by his troop of 5,000 soldiers, which is only a little ways from Derne. Many of the inhabitants of the city who, trying to avoid the bombardment, rented at great expense villas in the countryside were ordered to return to the city. The Bashaw lavished money and clothes on the Arab tribes camped around the city walls to keep them loyal.

This news compounded the fears already caused by an earlier report from Malta that the U.S. Navy was ready to bring 60 ships to attack Tripoli (a fivefold inflation over the truth).

William Wormley, a second lieutenant in the U.S. Marines, was a prisoner in Tripoli. He later recalled: "It was apparent to the most indif-ferent observer that on the arrival of the second courier announcing the defeat of the reigning bashaw's army by General Eaton and Hamet Bashaw that the greatest terror and consternation reigned throughout the whole town."

Tension mounted in Tripoli. The day of May 23 was unseasonably hot. A work crew of twenty-four American sailor-slaves was sent with a cart to gather wood. Their route took them on a march through the desert. The hot winds picked up, and the sand whirled. "They stopped through fatigue, and asked their driver, who was a Turk, for liberty to drink at a well which was near there," recorded Dr. Cowdery in his diary. "The Turk replied that they were *Romo kelbs* (Christian dogs) and said they should have no water. He gave them all a severe beating with a club . . . and made them go on with the cart, which the poor fellows had to drag, loaded with timber, through the burning sand. They re-turned towards night, almost perished." William Ray, the diminutive and learned marine, later read Cowdery's account and vouched for it, only adding: "This is true but no more than what occurred almost every day."

On May 24, the day that Lear boarded the *Essex* in Malta, Yussef sent a boat loaded with gunpowder, musket balls, and money to his troops near Derne. This expense so straitened him that he could barely keep the palace running. His steward bought food on credit, and Yussef ordered his bodyguards and his servants to eat but one meal per day. Wealthy citizens were forced to volunteer to feed the city troops. Yussef locked up Hamet's eldest son in a room near his own in the castle as a lifesaving hostage.

Dr. Cowdery recorded in his diary: "The Bashaw was so much agi-tated at the news of the approach of his brother that he this day declared that if it were in his power to make peace and give up the American pris-oners, he would gladly do it without the consideration of money."

CHAPTER 18 *Tripoli Harbor:*
Lear to the Rescue

I shall, my dearest love, give you a detail of my situation &c.
from day to day as far as my time admit, knowing how deeply
interesting to you everything is which relate to me.

—TOBIAS LEAR TO HIS WIFE, FANNY, MAY 25, 1805

THE WINDS AIDED HIS PURPOSE. A strong steady breeze filled the dozen sails of the USS *Essex,* propelling the ship and Lear rapidly toward Tripoli. Within a scant thirty-six hours they reached the destination, and on the morning of Sunday, May 26, spotted two American warships on blockade duty about five miles outside Tripoli harbor.

The captain of the *Essex* and Tobias Lear were rowed over to the USS *Constitution.* Lear had the pleasant task of informing his friend Captain John Rodgers that Barron was stepping down and that Rodgers would now be commodore, the highest position in the squadron. From all evidence from his letters, Rodgers for months had been eagerly awaiting the summer season to attack Tripoli; he envisioned days of naval glory for his country and himself. He even joked about winning medals and freeing the ladies in the Bashaw's harem.

In his letter of resignation, Barron informed Rodgers that he was sending Tobias Lear to negotiate peace. To Rodgers, the good news of his promotion was dampened, if not doused, by the likelihood of aborting plans to shower Tripoli with cannonballs and to sink their ships. All winter, Rodgers and fellow officers and crews had slogged their way through the dullness of blockade duty by daydreaming of summer glory. He was a commodore with his hands tied behind his back, at least for now.

Formality ruled in all things diplomatic. Newly minted Commodore Rodgers donned his dress uniform: a long blue waistcoat with a standing white collar, trimmed in half-inch-wide gold lace that swirled down the long lapels; the gold lace also ringed the cuffs and pocket flaps. Gold epaulets adorned each shoulder. The phalanx of more than a dozen brass buttons were stamped with an anchor, an eagle, and fifteen stars. Tobias Lear was also formally attired in waistcoat and high collar.

Rodgers and Lear then boarded the smaller frigate *Essex* and stood in to Tripoli harbor. Lear informed Rodgers of the prearranged signal for peace negotiations. The sailors hoisted a white flag of truce at the foremast, and a Spanish merchant flag at the mizzenmast. As the ship glided toward the inner harbor, the *Essex* gunner fired off two salutes. The officers, also in uniform, stood upon the deck. Crewmen, in clean outfits, performed their duties. A U.S. Navy ship did not slouch into port; it paraded in.

Lear could see the Bashaw's castle rising over the harbor with minarets peeking out behind. No response came from the land.

The prisoner Dr. Cowdery happened to be onshore with Bashaw Yussef that morning. When word came of three U.S. frigates in the outer harbor, the Bashaw went to his castle's large balcony that overlooked the port, the same viewing stand from which he had gloated over the mangled corpses of American sailors washed ashore the previous summer. "At about 11 A.M., the smallest [frigate] came near in and hoisted the banners of peace," wrote Dr. Cowdery. "The Bashaw asked his head men of the town, who were with him in his gallery, whether it was best to hoist his white flag. All except one, the chargé d'affaires for Algiers, declared in favour of it, and of making peace if possible. They expressed great contempt towards the Algerine consul for his advice, and said that whoever would advise the Bashaw not to hoist the white flag at such a critical moment must be his foe."

The Bashaw ordered that two shots of salute be fired by way of equal respect and that the white flag be raised over the ramparts of the castle.

Photographic view of Tripoli in 1905 from the roof of the French consulate looking seaward. The cityscape changed little from the Barbary Wars era, with one notable exception: the stout minaret of the Gurgi mosque.

About a half an hour later, at about 2 P.M., the Bashaw sent out to the frigate his negotiating team: the Spanish consul, Don Gerando de Souza; Jewish moneylender Leon Farfara; and Shoush Hammad, the rais of the marine (harbormaster).

With all due ceremony of piping and drums, the men boarded the *Essex* to confer with Lear. The Spanish consul repeated the Bashaw's previous demand of $200,000, and Lear rejected it immediately as absolutely unthinkable. The elegant Spaniard implored Lear to come ashore to conduct direct talks with the Bashaw. After fruitless conversations throughout the afternoon, Lear agreed that he would come ashore the next day, if the Spanish consul would guarantee that the Bashaw "would put aside in toto" his current offer. The Spaniard said he would go ashore and return the following morning with the Bashaw's answer. (Since negotiations in Barbary always involved great jockeying back and forth, bluff and counterbluff followed by steady price reductions, there appeared little doubt that the Spaniard could deliver a yes to that very modest demand by Lear.)

Dr. Cowdery's diary entry for that Sunday concludes with a clear interpretation of how Yussef's negotiators perceived the talks. "They returned at evening with the joyful news of a prospect of peace. There was a visible change from gloominess to joy, in the countenance of all the Turks." Marine private William Ray also wrote that there were "paroxysms of joy" among the prisoners.

Yussef had gone to sleep on Saturday night—fearful of rebellion, financial ruin, and impending American bombardment—and had woken up to see a U.S. frigate with a white flag at the foremast and a diplomat eager to negotiate.

A storm suddenly hit Tripoli. High winds angled toward the coast on Monday. Commodore Rodgers deemed it too dangerous to linger so close to shore. The last thing he wanted on his first days as commodore was to beach another U.S. frigate on Kaliusa Reef. The three American ships, exchanging signals, headed out to sea, meandering in curtains of the rain, completely out of sight of Tripoli. The gale winds tossed the ships all day. Once safely far offshore, the ships reefed sails to ride it out. Around 5 P.M., the winds diminished enough that Commodore Rodgers had himself rowed back from the *Essex* to his flagship, *Constitution*.

All that day Monday, the people of Tripoli gazed seaward. Sunday's hopes were seeming like a tantalizing dream. Did the Spaniard misunderstand? Was it all a ruse? "Both Turks and Christians were all anxiously looking out for the frigates," wrote Dr. Cowdery. "It was said that Col. Lear had promised to come on shore this morning and that the Spanish consul was preparing a dinner for the gentlemen who were expected to come with him. We were all agitated alternately by hope and despair. The terraces and every eminence in town were covered with people of all classes and ages who were looking for the wished for peacemaker. But not a frigate nor a sail hove in sight during the day."

On Tuesday, midmorning, a fleck of white appeared on the gray horizon; over the hours, the blur crystallized into a vessel flying American colors, but it turned out to be a brig that merely hovered far offshore. (The ship was the USS *Vixen*, come from Malta, with dispatches, looking for the American blockade vessels.)

"The Turks began to think the frigate had gone to fetch the whole fleet, which they had heard consisted of 60 sail, of different sizes," wrote Dr. Cowdery. "They thought that the flag of truce was only a [ploy] of the Americans to find out the force of Tripoli."

The long day slipped away; the sun began to dip down. Then silhouetted against the rose red horizon were the sails of three American frigates and a brig. "[That sight] revived our hopes," wrote Dr. Cowdery. "The Bashaw showed the greatest anxiety for peace. He was sensible of the danger he was in from the lowness of his funds and the disaffection of his people."

Meanwhile, at sea, Lear had no idea of the desperation of his adversary. No communication from inside Tripoli had reached any American official since Eaton and Hamet had captured Derne, and Lear made little effort to explore the situation in the capital. He had predetermined his major conditions, and except for the so-called punctilios, he intended to stick to them.

At 8:15 A.M. on Wednesday morning, the *Essex* glided into the harbor with a billowing white flag at its foremast. The Americans fired a two-gun salute; the Tripolitans answered in kind. Turbaned men in a fine little pleasure boat rowed the Spanish consul out to the *Essex*. Instead of demanding that Lear come ashore, the Bashaw had granted De Souza a *tiskara*, that is, a commission to negotiate in his name. Lear eyed the Arabic document and Spanish translation and around 11 A.M. he invited De Souza to join him on the flagship *Constitution* to continue the discussions.

All day they jockeyed. Given Lear's manners, the whole procedure was probably slow and courteous, perhaps even embellished with patriotic speeches about amity and commercial prosperity. However, as for the sticking points, the Spaniard relayed that the Bashaw would relinquish his demand for annual tribute payments, but his ransom demand would not dip below $130,000. (One wonders whether Yussef's spies, perhaps through Joseph Pulis, had learned that Lear's secret orders allowed him to go as high as $500 per prisoner.)

All eyes in Tripoli were fixed upon the Bashaw's boat bobbing at the side of the massive frigate. Lear and De Souza fell into a rutted circle. "I told the Sp Consul, to prevent unnecessary delay and altercation, I would give him my <u>ultimatum</u> which must be decided on," Lear wrote. This haste, after four years of war, must have seemed odd to the Bashaw. Lear's terms called for the delivery *within two days* of all the American prisoners; in exchange for which, Lear, acting for the United States, would deliver all Tripolitan prisoners and would pay $60,000 ransom. Both sides would agree to enter into a "mutually beneficial" treaty.

That evening, Lear on the *Constitution,* amid the mealtime hubbub of more than 350 sailors, recapped the day's events to his beloved Fanny. "Thus stands the business at present, and I hope and believe it will terminate favourably and honourably for us. The great object on our part is to get our unfortunate fellow citizens, and on his, a wish & necessity for making peace."

Lear had been separated five days from his young bride and he couldn't help adding: "My dearest Fanny, I have not much time for my own amusement, which would be to write much more to you, and [you] will therefore receive my letters, long or short, as the effusion of my heart."

The following morning, the Spanish consul reached the *Constitution* around 10 A.M., was piped aboard with due ceremony, and descended into the captain's cabin to conduct negotiations in private. The Bashaw sent along a huge gift of fresh fruit—dates, oranges, lemons, limes—for the commodore and consul general.

With customary politesse, the Spaniard informed Lear that the Bashaw had not accepted his ultimatum. Lear remained adamant. He relayed his heroism to his wife. "I have declared that I will not recede one inch from it and that it is unnecessary for us to exchange another word on the subject." The Spaniard requested permission to send a letter ashore to ask the Bashaw's opinion.

Rodgers, hearing this and no doubt still hoping for war, wrote: "How things will turn out is yet uncertain." At that moment, he sent the USS *President* to Malta and Syracuse to refit and try to find the other five U.S. Navy ships and order them to prepare for a ten-week cruise. (Barron's various errands had scattered the fleet.)

The harbor boat returned hours later with an answer to the Spaniard's question. The Bashaw stated simply that he requested that Lear come ashore to negotiate. Lear refused, and while the Spaniard attempted to sway him, the winds started beating toward shore. Commodore Rodgers ordered the ship to tack away from Tripoli. The Spaniard spent the night as the guest of the U.S. Navy.

The following morning, Friday, May 31, Rodgers timed his efforts to bring the *Constitution* into the harbor as early as possible. At 7 A.M. he ordered the reefs out of the topsails. A quarter hour later, he had the Spanish consul rowed over to the *Vixen*, which set sail and gingerly steered around Kaliusa and brought the Spaniard shoreward. Around 1 P.M., the *Vixen* towed the Spaniard in his boat back to the *Constitution*. The consul informed Lear that the Bashaw would agree to the $60,000 but that he could not possibly allow the American prisoners to leave immediately. And he could not complete the ransom negotiations without first settling on a new peace treaty. (The implication was clear: The Bashaw, without the hostages, would have no leverage on setting the treaty.)

Lear was once again adamant. "I told him the business had already been protracted beyond what I conceived to be a reasonable time but as the weather yesterday would not admit of our countrymen being sent on board, I would allow the Bashaw 24 hours from this time to agree to my proposition in toto or reject them." Lear put those conditions in writing.

De Souza begged for further time, but Lear refused. As the Spaniard was leaving the *Constitution* around 5 P.M., Lear gave him a large American flag. If the Bashaw agreed to Lear's conditions, De Souza was to fly the flag over the old American consulate the following morning.

The morning of Saturday, June 1, broke clear and warm. A sail appeared on the horizon; it turned out to be the USS *Nautilus*, arriving from Derne by way of Malta with copies of the latest orders from Washington. (Barron, knowing their importance, had not only sent them by *speronara* but also by the *Nautilus*.) Rodgers now learned firsthand of Eaton's victory at Derne and of the arrival of the heavily laden store ship *Ceres*, and more important of plans for a massive naval buildup. Within a month, barring storms, the new commodore would have in total a dozen ships and ten gunboats, five hundred new recruits, and plenty of ammunition for the cannons and food for the men. He could pound Tripoli from afar with his frigates and come in close for the kill with his gunboats.

The logistics of an attack on Tripoli were solved . . . and the administration's appetite for war was clearly revealed. But his friend Lear was already handling peace negotiations and had made an offer.

The men aboard the *Constitution*, and the *Nautilus* and the *Essex*, stared into the harbor at the site of the old American consulate. Tobias Lear and Commodore Rodgers traded the spyglass. No American flag, no sign of a treaty, could be seen flying from the old building. The Bashaw was turning down Lear's proposal.

CHAPTER 19 *Derne: Defiance*

THE COMMANDER OF Bashaw Yussef's forces at Derne put a price tag on William Eaton's head, offering $6,000 for the trophy detached from his body and double that amount for the general delivered alive as a prisoner. "Why don't he come and take it?" Eaton snarled in a rhetorical flourish in his diary. For the other Christians, commander Hassan Bey dangled a mere $30 per head.

The ten Americans and fifty Christian mercenaries hunkered down in the small fort in the harbor under the American flag, and the troops loyal to Hamet spread out across the city. The remaining U.S. Navy ship, *Argus*, pointed its cannons shoreward.

Meanwhile, Yussef's cavalry and the tribes on his payroll encircled the city. The situation was turning into a kind of a stalemate, with the Bedouin's loyalty the key to tipping the balance to victory. "We want nothing but cash to break up our enemy's camp without firing another shot!" wrote Eaton in large passionate letters in his diary.

Daily spy reports, mostly from Bedouin women able to move freely between the camps, revealed that Yussef's forces planned numerous attacks but that the Bedouin refused to join in. The freewheeling tribes, with their slow-loading muskets, apparently didn't like American-style warfare: the whoosh of sudden cannonballs and the relentless charging of men with bayonets.

Each day brought a fresh rumor of an impending attack. All Eaton could do was try to retain control of Derne until he heard back from

Commodore Barron. Any future plans depended on reinforcements and supplies. At the moment, he was surrounded on the land side, and to make the situation more challenging, he was penniless. To feed his troops, Eaton convinced Hull to let him barter more prize goods from the *Argus*, trading with the Bedouin for mutton, milk, and eggs.

To shore up defenses, Eaton and his engineer, Jean Eugene, directed the digging of a long trench along one side of town to repel a cavalry charge. Captain Hull allowed sixteen men from the *Argus* to come ashore to help, including Eaton's stepson Eli E. Danielson and Pascal Peck, the midshipman who had made the trek across the Libyan desert. And while the men were coming ashore, Eaton thought up a ruse. To delude the enemy into thinking more American soldiers had arrived, Eaton and Hull kept the shore boat coming and going all day from the *Argus*. The same marines took the little boat ride back and forth. No additional marines actually remained ashore, but to a watcher on a nearby hill, it appeared that a steady stream of marines was pouring into Fort Enterprise. The bluff might buy time.

Tired of conflicting spy reports about troop strengths and locations, Eaton, despite having his arm in a sling, decided to go on a scouting mission; he also opted to take along the two teenage midshipmen, his stepson and Peck; they sneaked out of town on foot and slipped as close as they dared to the enemy's main camp. They discovered the main force to be bivouacked three miles in back of the hill on the southeast approach to town. When Captain Hull later learned that his young midshipmen had accompanied Eaton, he immediately ordered the crew of the shore boat to find them and instantly bring them back to the *Argus*. Hull's implication was clear: Risk your own life in a reckless mission but don't take my boys along.

Throughout the wait for Barron's response, Eaton dwelled on questions he couldn't answer. Would Barron surprise him with reinforcements? Would caution prevail? Would the commodore abandon Hamet in the midst of his enemies? His ruminations were rudely interrupted.

A sandstorm suddenly hit Derne. "Five o'clock, P.M. Overwhelmed with the Scyroc [sirocco] or hot wind of the desert," wrote Eaton in his diary. "It come in as a hurricane and brought with it a column of heated dust, which resembled the smoke of conflagration, and turned the sun in appearance to melted copper and swept everything to the ground that had life and filled everything with a hot subtile sand, or rather powder. We were distressed for breath—the lungs contracted: blood heated like a fever and a perspiration covered the surface of the body. It lasted ¾ of an hour."

Another traveler described the onset of a sirocco in the same region. He said the air almost seemed to tremble and then the upper part of the sky turned an odd yellow, while the lower sky grew a darkening red. The heat felt like an oven door was suddenly opened. The whirling sand intruded everywhere.

On Saturday, May 25, the sirocco renewed its attack on Derne and blew in from the southwest. "So piercing was the heat," wrote Eaton, "that the white pine boards of our folding table and book coverings in our tents warped as if before a close fire. The heated dust penetrated everything through our garments;—and indeed seemed to choak the pores of the skin. It had a singular effect on my wound, giving it the painful sensations of a fresh burn. The skin, after perspiration, became dry and parched, and the lungs compressed and inflamed. Water standing in tumblers in a few minutes became heated to such a degree as not to be borne in the hand and even stones, naturally cold, were so hot that the soldiers were obliged to suspend labor at the trenches."

The men wrapped layers of cloth around their heads and faces, and tried desperately to breathe. They curled up, tried to cocoon themselves. This biblical misery lasted hour after hour, throughout the day. The relentless whooshing sounds deafened them. The wind blew so hard at the *Argus* in the harbor that Hull was afraid the anchor cable would snap; so he ordered the men to veer out the entire hundred fathoms of cable, letting the ship waggle out to sea. It was tossed and pounded like a toy boat on a long string. About 2:30 A.M., the storm finally broke.

Now began the cleanup. Men stripped off all clothes and shook them out. They washed themselves in the Mediterranean to banish the dust. The soldiers had to clean and oil all their weapons, especially the firing locks of their guns. They performed endless shoveling and sweeping to clear the streets. The digging out was apparently all-consuming because the normally prolix Eaton wrote nothing in his diary for May 26 or May 27. Perhaps the wound was hurting much more, in the wake of being coated in sand and roasted.

On May 28, Eaton was tired of waiting, of shoring up defenses. He had sent his letter of victory in Derne to Barron on May 1. The journey to Malta can take as little as three days, and four weeks had passed. His nature was to attack.

In the morning, the enemy sent out a raiding party of 60 men on foot and a small cavalry troop, and they attacked an encampment of Bedouin loyal to Hamet, living at the edge of Derne. In the chaos, the attackers drove off cattle and camels. Hamet's troops galloped out of the city after the raiders, and caught up with them before the mountain southeast of town. They shot several of them and recovered the animals.

Eaton, the instant he heard of the raid and the pursuit, decided on a bold move to rush to try to cut off their retreat. His officers, who had sworn passionate loyalty a week earlier, now followed him as he led the march on foot. Lieutenant O'Bannon, in blue uniform jacket and cocked hat, and Midshipman Mann, and eager Farquhar, and a handful of marines and two dozen Greeks marched double time out from the harbor fort and up along a ravine parallel to the one taken by the enemy. Just past the crest of the mountain, Eaton's marchers caught up with the raiders. They exchanged a round of gunshots; then while the enemy was reloading, Eaton ordered a charge of bayonets. Simple geometry favored the Americans. The sharp blades, mounted on the end of long muskets, can impale man or horse. The enemy fled.

The American force pursued and shot and killed their captain and five men, wounded several others, and captured two prisoners. Not one of Eaton's men was injured.

The enemy "beat to arms," in Eaton's words. It's unclear if they used a drum like European armies or if some other sound rallied them. In any case, several hundred men mounted up and advanced in a body toward the small American force, but then halted and remained outside musket shot. They lined up their ranks, hovering, their leaders debating.

A charge would probably wipe out the American-European platoon.

While the enemy hesitated, Eaton led a retreat back toward Derne. The enemy did not attack or follow. The former army captain later surmised: "They [perhaps feared] that we were an advanced party aiming to draw them into an ambush on disadvantageous ground."

Spies reported the enemy planned swift retribution.

The following morning, May 29 (as Lear made his written offer for peace in Tripoli), the enemy gathered in formation of more than a thousand men on the hill behind Derne, ready to attack. "About nine in the morning they advanced their whole force and posted themselves on an eminence in fair view—Proper stations were taken on our part to receive them."

The cannons in the harbor battery were aimed toward the hill, as were the fieldpieces. The men climbed into the trenches; Hamet scattered troops around the city.

The enemy commander, Hassan Bey, ordered the attack, but the Bedouin at the last moment refused to advance. They marched away from the hill, and the attack was canceled.

Hassan Bey knew that he would probably be executed if he failed on this mission for Bashaw Yussef, so he opted for a new strategy: assassination.

Eaton's journal: "A Mirabout (saint) who has experienced some charities from me . . . states that two women, one at camp, and the other in town, have engaged to take me off by poison—and that the commander in chief of the enemy has already made them large presents, among other things, a diamond ring, brilliant solitaire, in anticipation of this Service. The Saint cautioned me against accepting any presents of pastry cooking, preserves or fruit from any persons of the town."

Finally, on May 31, the USS *Hornet* reached Derne from Malta. Contrary winds had bedeviled the journey. The Arabs onshore, seeing the return of this U.S. Navy ship, celebrated, firing off their guns and performing feats of horsemanship. They had no idea about the contents of Commodore Barron's orders.

Eaton dodged his way amid the joy-shooting Arabs on the beach, and then pigtailed sailors rowed him out to the *Hornet*. On the shifting deck, Eaton read the blunt discouraging words about Hamet. "He must be held as unworthy of further support and the Co-operation as a measure too expensive and burdensome." No more supplies would be given to Hamet, no more ammunition, no more money. Barron was sending food, but only for the Christian troops. Tobias Lear, peace negotiator, had already been dispatched to Tripoli.

Each bit of bad news was a body blow to Eaton. He struggled hard to control his temper, and he knew that for now no one but Captain Hull must know about this abrupt change of plans.

To Hull, who also received orders, the decision was now simple: a matter of orchestrating a safe evacuation. To Eaton, who had found Hamet in Upper Egypt and prodded him across five hundred miles of Libyan desert, it was anything but simple.

"You would weep, Sir," he wrote to Barron, "were you on the spot, to witness the unbounded confidence placed in the American character here, and to reflect that this confidence must shortly sink into contempt and immortal hatred; you would feel that this confidence at any price, should be carried through the Barbary regencies, at least to Tripoli, by the same means that it has been inspired here—But if no further aids come to our assistance and we are compelled to leave the place under its actual circumstances, humanity itself must weep: The whole city of Derne, together with numerous families of Arabs who attached themselves to Hamet Bashaw and who resisted Yussef's troops in expectation of succour from us, must be abandoned to their fate—havoc & slaughter will be the inevitable consequence—not a soul of them can escape the savage vengeance of the enemy."

Eaton expected many would be massacred; he knew the town would be looted. Eaton was outraged at the prospect of using Hamet as a tool to achieve a cheaper ransom and peace. "Could I have apprehended this result of my exertions, certainly no consideration would have prevailed on me to have taken an agency in a tragedy so manifestly fraught with intrigue, so wounding to humane feelings, and, as I must view it, so degrading to our national honor."

Eaton calmed himself long enough to point out some practical considerations. If negotiations failed in Tripoli, then Derne, a valuable city, will have been needlessly abandoned to the enemy; he also noted that even if the treaty carried some protections for Hamet and his allies, by the time those details reached Derne after U.S. forces leave, it would be too late to help them: They would be dead, wounded, or robbed. Eaton said he would prefer a "manly defeat" over this "mode of safety."

After much soul-searching, the naval agent for the Barbary Regencies came to a remarkable conclusion. "I consider it due to the confidence of [the U.S.] Government and a bond imposed by all the injunctions of humanity to endeavor to hold this port till the last moment in hopes that some happy occurrence may take place to secure our own and at the same time to assist the interests of our friends. And I most devoutly pray Heaven that the blood of innocence may not stain the footsteps of us who have aimed only to fight the enemies of our Country."

On June 1, as Tobias Lear awaited word on his latest peace proposal, Eaton decided to remain steadfast in Derne. Each morning, a drumroll would accompany the raising of the American flag, which would then flap in defiance of the enemies ringed in the hills above.

CHAPTER 20

Tripoli: Peace?
Freedom? Honor?

ON THE MORNING OF JUNE 1, in the nervous city of Tripoli, the Bashaw refused to accept Tobias Lear's written demand; the thirty-eight-year-old ruler did not fly the American flag that would have announced he was willing to free the American prisoners by sunset. As the sun rose in the sky, Yussef, with much anxiety, moved ever closer to flouting the deadline of the ultimatum. But Bashaw Yussef Karamanli, ever a shrewd negotiator, did not yet know the measure of Tobias Lear; he had no way of knowing whether breaking Lear's ultimatum would result in an immediate attack, and Yussef did not want to find out. He had until sunset to work something out. Emboldened by daylight, he was playing a dangerous game to gain a better treaty and ransom.

Yussef's first minister, Mohammed Dghies, stepped in to help. The aging, almost blind merchant-statesman was angry that the Bashaw had entrusted these critical negotiations to De Souza, consul of Spain. He claimed that the Spaniard had bungled matters by even discussing that the prisoners might be freed *before* a treaty was finalized. And the Bashaw instantly voiced his agreement, saying to Dghies that if he gave up the hostages without first securing peace, what would stop the Americans from immediately attacking? from never paying?

Dghies came up with a plan. He sent a messenger over to the home of Danish consul Nicholas Nissen, the longtime friend of the Americans, who had sheltered the American officers, giving them books and food, and helping in many ways. Nissen had negotiated with the outside world for them; he even wrote imploring letters to the American commodore for them.

The messenger reached the Danish consulate. He was informed that the consul had left earlier in the morning. The messenger told the servant that it was urgent to find his master. Servants fanned out to the marketplace, to the gardens. Nissen was found, the search made easier by the dearth of pants-wearing, waistcoated foreigners in Tripoli. He rushed through the narrow streets to the castle and was conducted past the scimitar-wielding guards into the presence of Dghies and the Bashaw. The turbaned minister, speaking in French, told Nissen that even though everyone was saying that peace was at hand, actually the negotiations were "*embrouillees*" (all jumbled up).

Dghies told Nissen that the Bashaw couldn't possibly let the hostages go without a treaty first being in place. Nissen agreed that Lear's demand appeared "unreasonable" and wondered whether it might be the result of a misunderstanding. With the sunset deadline looming, Dghies suggested that the single most effective negotiator, the person most likely to sway this apparently inflexible Lear, would be the prisoner Captain Bainbridge. The mere sight of him would play on Lear's emotions. At that moment, guards ushered in Bainbridge, haggard but clearly buoyed by all the talk of ransom.

Dghies and Nissen worked hard to convince the Bashaw that his wisest move would be to voluntarily send Bainbridge, his most valuable hostage, to the American warship to reason with Lear. The American officer, with freedom within sniffing distance, instantly agreed to give his word of honor as an officer that he would return within hours. He also stated that all his officers would also give their *paroles*, and agree to suffer any punishment if he did not return.

The Bashaw decided to take this important decision to his *divan*, or governing council. (As with most advisory boards, its main function was to take the blame for any wrong decisions.) The leading men of the government—bearded, turbaned, in colored vests—assembled quickly in the nearby room. The discussion raced forward. Members of the *divan*, such as Murad Rais, the Scot-turned-Turk admiral of the fleet, and Salah, aga of the *divan*, questioned whether the word of a Christian could be trusted. They leaned toward denying the request. Nissen then jumped in to offer his personal guarantee as well. They still leaned toward rejection when Mohammed Dghies, a foresightful man, gestured to a guard, and Dghies's son was brought into the ornate chamber. Dghies said the Bashaw could hold his son hostage and that he could cut off the boy's head if Bainbridge did not return. The *divan* was swayed.

The sun now stood almost directly overhead. The minaret sundial, soon shadowless, would announce it was noon and the full-throated muezzin would call the faithful to prayer. The weather was pleasant with light winds. The brig USS *Vixen*, of shallower draft than the frigates, had performed its usual duty of entering the harbor, under a white flag, staying ready to bring any negotiator out to the *Constitution*.

"We stood in under the batteries and lay to for the boat which we momentarily expected," wrote Hezekiah Loomis, *Vixen* steward, in his journal. "At 12 o'clock the boat came off, and to our joy Captain Bainbridge was in it. He came on board and exhibited a spirit of joy and gladness, mixed with humiliation which I never before saw in all my life time. His first entrance on board was truly a specimen of joy to excess, but his pale meagre countenance showed how the confines of the Barbary fiends would dilate [sic] the whole system of a Christian."

Bainbridge, his first time at sea in 576 days, sailed on this beautiful day through the tricky harbor, past the site of the grounding of the *Philadelphia*, out to the *Constitution*. John Rodgers greeted him as did near 400 American sailors and marines. No account has survived, but the men must have cheered him long and loudly and the fellow officers must have prepared a spontaneous feast for him.

Lear and Bainbridge met in private in the captain's cabin. And Bainbridge, long-suffering, informed Lear that the Bashaw had told him that "it was more for the sake of peace than anything else that he consented to give the [prisoners] up" and that he wouldn't do so without a treaty. "As it is our intention to conclude a treaty," Bainbridge told Lear, "it would be cruel to let our Countrymen languish in Captivity merely on the punctilio of negotiating the treaty before or after their delivery."

Lear wrote Fanny that he promptly consented to the changes "as it makes no difference to us in the terms of peace whether it was made before or after the people were delivered up." (Veteran diplomats might find it fairly astounding that the order of negotiations was a trifle to Lear, but, then again, this is the same man who advised Barron to abandon Derne *before* the negotiations began.)

The red disk of the sun was now sinking toward the horizon and the Bashaw was waiting very anxiously onshore for an answer. Dghies's boy sat nervously in the castle.

Bainbridge had one other request for Lear: ask for a new onshore negotiator, someone other than the Spanish consul, who, beneath his mask of politeness, seemed to be sowing confusion. Lear drafted a note in English for Bainbridge to carry to Dghies; he basically stated that he would abandon his ultimatum of the prisoners being delivered by sunset today and that he would negotiate a peace treaty first if the Bashaw would send out a new fully accredited negotiator. This was hardly a hardball request. Bainbridge was thrilled. He stayed aboard the American frigate past sunset, talking to fellow officers. The *Constitution*, according to its log, drifted to about four miles northwest of Tripoli. At 6:45 P.M. rail-thin Bainbridge, in a tattered captain's uniform, climbed over the side and down into the boat, and then reboarded the *Vixen*. His four-mile trip probably took close to an hour.

When Bainbridge had not yet appeared at sunset, the tense Bashaw was overheard yelling at Mohammed Dghies for taking the word of a "Christian dog." But around 8 P.M., the captain was escorted into the lamp-lit chamber, and he presented Lear's note to Dghies. Relief spread through the room: no bombardment and no beheading. Evaluating the simplicity of Lear's new request, Yussef now had the measure of his adversary. The minister and the Bashaw immediately decided that Nicholas Nissen would be the best choice to negotiate.

Nissen was reluctant to embroil himself in such a powder keg situation. "I did not much desire this commission," Nissen wrote in a report to his government. "[But] the Pacha assured me that he would consider it as a token of friendship and declared that if, the occasion should arise, when I might have matters to settle concerning my own nation, he would show his appreciation."

The following morning, Sunday, the Bashaw and Dghies briefed Nissen on the Bashaw's positions on four key points. They handed him a *tiskara*, fully empowering him to represent Tripoli. Very early, the *Vixen* glided into the harbor, picked up the Dane, and delivered him to the towering frigate *Constitution* at 10 A.M. Nissen later summarized his speedy negotiations with Lear.

The American consul general remained immovable on the amount of $60,000 ransom, and the Bashaw accepted the figure. Both men agreed that officially "nothing has really been paid for peace." (Lear needed to stress the Jeffersonian distinction between ransom and peace.) The Bashaw, emboldened by Lear's easy abandonment of the ultimatum, now through Nissen demanded two gunboats as "articles of peace"; Lear refused but said the United States might possibly one day restore two captured Tripolitan vessels to him.

Now came two very important issues for the Bashaw: Hamet and Derne. The Bashaw wanted Lear to agree that the United States would withdraw support from Hamet and would leave Derne. "The Bashaw seemed very anxious about this point," Nissen later wrote, and added the Bashaw was particularly enraged that the U.S. flag had been raised alongside Hamet's on one of the Bashaw's fortresses. Lear was quite willing to cede this point (especially since he figured that Barron's orders might have already prompted Eaton to leave Derne.) However, Lear demanded that, in exchange for exiting Derne, the Bashaw should liberate Hamet's wife and children, held hostage for almost ten years.

By noon, the efficient Dane climbed into the longboat and returned to shore to consult with the Bashaw.

Around this time, Captain Bainbridge, fresh from his triumphant voyage the day before, sent a note to Dr. Cowdery that peace was imminent. The Bashaw's family physician had the kindness to read it to the prisoners "who were so overjoyed that many of them shed tears." The taskmasters, however, still forced them to labor on this Sunday, and many, daring to balk, were beaten. The men, once gathered back in their prison in the late afternoon, voted to fulfill a promise they had made. They sent a letter to Captain Bainbridge asking if their wages could be docked to the amount of $300 to buy the freedom of a slave from

Naples, the personal servant to the chief warden. He had been repeatedly kind to them. (The man was, in fact, freed, then enlisted immediately in the U.S. Navy; marine private Ray—perhaps relaying his own prejudices—wrote that navy discipline later caused the former slave to yearn to return to Tripoli.)

Lear waited on board for an answer and we know exactly what he was thinking because he found time to write to Fanny. He was quite optimistic about peace and optimistic they would be reunited within a week. "[Nissen] will be on board again this evening when I trust the business will be brought to a conclusion."

About 4:30 P.M. the *Vixen* ferried its passenger to the frigate. Nissen reported that the Bashaw was quite pleased with the progress of negotiations but that he wanted the parts about Derne put into writing. He wanted the United States to add that it would try to persuade Hamet to leave the country. Lear acquiesced, but he demanded once again that Hamet's family be restored to him.

Nissen relayed Lear's stance. "This demand seemed severe to the Pacha," wrote Nissen, "as he thought that he would in this way lose the hostages which he held as security against further hostile attempts on the part of his brother; he even distrusted the North Americans and feared that they, when they had their prisoners of war, as well as Sidi Hamet's family, in their power, would perhaps again engage in hostile acts to the advantage of his brother."

Nonetheless, Lear refused to budge. He handed Nissen preliminary written articles that summed up the $60,000 prisoner exchange and the Derne evacuation, but still included the restoration of Hamet's family. After sunset around 7:15 P.M., Nissen climbed over the rail of the frigate and departed for his five-mile ride to town.

That Sunday night, everyone anticipated peace. The new commodore dashed off a "Private" note to the ailing ex-commodore. "Our business is so far finished as not to leave me a hope of receiving a Button for my services much more a Medal. . . . Nothing on the score of Peace remains to be done, farther than the discussion of some trivial matters." (From Rodgers's perch, Hamet's family was "trivial.") Rodgers was clearly nettled by not being able to attack or to force a better treaty, which he later called "quite honorable but not corresponding to my own ideas."

The sun rose, breaking the plane of the Mediterranean. A handful of officers ate breakfast with Tobias Lear. And Rodgers, always known for his seaman's directness, made a gallant offer—ostensibly said in jest but perhaps not. "If the Bashaw would consent to deliver up our Countrymen, without making peace, I will engage to give him $200,000 instead of $60,000 and raise the difference between the sums from the officers of the Navy." He added: "I am perfectly assured that they will contribute with the highest satisfaction."

Lear, not surprisingly, did not relay Rodgers's offer.

Onshore, now even the Bashaw expected peace. That Monday morning, the five American prisoners who turned Turk were brought to the palace: Quartermaster John Wilson (whom Bainbridge wanted hanged), Peter West, Thomas Smith (who had a wife and four children in Boston), Lewis Heximer, and young Thomas Prince. These men had all been circumcised and now wore the turban. The Bashaw informed them that peace was coming and he asked them whether they would prefer to remain as Moslems in Tripoli or whether they would prefer to return to America. Four of them responded that they wished to rejoin the American fleet. Only Wilson, the most hardened of the group, thanked the Bashaw but said he chose to remain a Moslem in Tripoli in the service of the great Bashaw. Marine private Ray reported that Wilson was rewarded for his choice, while the others were marched under guard out of the gates of Tripoli and onto a road leading to the hinterlands. "We had a glance at them as they passed our prison," wrote Ray, "and could see the horror and despair in their countenances."

At 9 A.M., on Monday, the Danish consul boarded the *Constitution*. He reported to Lear that the Bashaw would agree to all conditions except for one: He would not return his brother's family. Lear again gave his most detailed account to Fanny, painting himself in heroic colors. "[Nissen] said the Bashaw would never agree to the article. . . . I told him I would not yield it, and when he went on shore again, if it was not acceded to, the white flag would be taken down." This was a major threat. With the flag down, Rodgers could bombard.

Light breezes blew on a fine cloudless day as Nissen returned ashore to inform the Bashaw that Lear wouldn't agree. The Dane convinced the Bashaw that the Americans had no intention of aiding Hamet any further once their hostages and Hamet's family were restored.

Captain Bainbridge was given the honor of attending the *divan* at which the preliminary articles were voted on. The eight ministers sat at a dais arranged in a crescent; the Bashaw sat in the middle, with Mohammed Dghies at his right hand. The first vote was six to two against accepting the treaty, with only Dghies and the Rais of the Marine (harbormaster) in favor. Dghies rose to speak, and with an eloquent speech the nearly blind old man swayed two more to join his side. The vote now stood at four to four, and Dghies pointed out that the decision now rested with the Bashaw. The Bashaw pulled out his signet and pressed it upon the preliminary articles. "It is peace," he said.

At 4 P.M., Nissen once again made the harbor voyage out to the *Constitution*. "He came onb.d again with the article signed by the Bashaw," Lear wrote triumphantly to Fanny. Nissen later corroborated that he had delivered the preliminary articles with the clause intact about restoring Hamet's family.

Peace had officially arrived. The war that had begun over tribute payments and escalated when Bainbridge grounded the *Philadelphia* was over. All that remained was hashing out treaty language, and a few niggling details, "punctilios."

The afternoon sun illuminated the white canvas sails. A magnificent cloudless spring day on the Mediterranean reverberated with huzzahs and mutual congratulation. Smiles broke out everywhere (except perhaps on warlike Rodgers).

Consul General Lear, resplendent in waistcoat and high collar, joined the gentlemanly Dane, Nissen, aboard the *Vixen* for a pleasant glide into the harbor. The two-masted brig, with a hundred men aboard its cramped 80-foot deck, meandered around the end of the reefs. A large white flag flapped at the stern. The harbor pilot helped guide the *Vixen* under the battery by the castle. At that moment, sailors hauled down the white flag and hoisted the American flag with fifteen stars and fifteen stripes, an immense seventeen feet by thirty-two feet. The *Vixen* punctuated its change of flag by firing off a celebratory gun. The castle answered with a twenty-one-gun salute, that repetitive hollowed boom of an explosion racing out of a long gun barrel. The *Constitution* answered with twenty-one respectful guns, each time the men placing a flannel cartridge of measured gunpowder down the barrel. No need for wadding and cannonball, no need to aim. Smoke lingered in the air of the harbor.

With peace proclaimed, Colonel Lear now ventured to go ashore. Lear and Nissen climbed into the *Constitution's* large boat, with an American flag flapping on a short pole; they were rowed ashore into a loud happy celebration. "I was met by thousands of people on the landing and amongst them our American officers who had been liberated from their prison the day before," Lear wrote to young Fanny. "The sight of them so near their freedom was grateful to my soul and you must form an idea of their feelings for I cannot describe them."

The people of Tripoli, from the *barracan*-covered women to turbaned men and boys, filled the streets in a joyful mob. More than any other man that day, Tobias Lear was the liberator.

Nissen shepherded Lear to the Danish consulate; from there he paid a visit to aged Mohammed Dghies and was very impressed. "I found [him] a sensible, liberal and well-informed man." That Monday night, a handful of prisoners were allowed to spend the night in the officers' quarters, but most returned to their large arched barracks and were locked in for the night, apparently with copious amounts of liquor smuggled in.

Dawn broke on Tuesday, June 4, the 579th day of their enslavement. The taskmasters now usually arrived to roust the prisoners for work . . . Abdallah, nicknamed Captain Blackbeard, and Soliman, whom they called "Scamping Jack," and the bandy-legged Greek, and the arrogant French *rinigado,* and the meanest one, Red-Jacket of Tripoli. None of those rod-wielding overseers showed up for work, rightly fearing a beating from the newly freed Americans. Instead, the slaves remained locked in until 10 A.M. As soon as the gates opened, the men poured into the local shops to buy more liquor, from date-palm to wine, to toast their freedom. The men drank and sang and danced around. Many of them tore at the filthy prison rags they had been forced to wear.

Lear dashed off a note to Rodgers warning him about the high spirits of the 280 freed crewmen and advising Rodgers not to send boats until the afternoon. "The intoxication of Liberty & Liquor has deranged the faculties of as well as dress of many of the Sailors and Captⁿ B. wishes them all on board quite clean and in Order."

The shore boat or barge of the *Constitution* had also carried in a new flagpole to install at the United States consulate. (Lear had been forewarned about the timber scarcity.) At 10:15 A.M. Rodgers through the spyglass observed the large American flag raised on the consulate; the castle pounded out another twenty-one-gun salute and the *Constitution* responded.

Lear in his finest clothes, along with two naval officers, was conducted by ornate armed guard to the castle. A nine-gun salute heralded his arrival in the courtyard. The *Constitution* again answered. While Jefferson had walked to his own inauguration, eschewing all trappings of monarchy, Lear enjoyed the pomp. In fact, he later agreed to reimburse the Tripolitans for all the gunpowder used in marking the peace.

Lear was also quite impressed with Bashaw Yussef Karamanli. (His note to Fanny has an awed schoolgirl tone.) The American diplomat showed no outrage at this ruler who had enslaved Americans. "He paid me many compliments and expressed himself on the peace with much manliness," Lear wrote. "He is a man of very good presence, manly & dignified and has not in his appearance so much of the tyrant as he has been represented to be. His court was much more superb than that of Algiers—We spoke but little on the subject of the treaty etc. He observed that he had given stronger evidences of his confidence in us than he had ever before given to any nation. He had delivered our people before he had received his own, and as to the money he was to receive, it was merely nominal—the sum was nothing, but it was impossible to deliver them without something."

Gracious Lear showed none of the hotheadedness of Eaton when consul in Tunis, nor the hard bargaining of Cathcart, which helped start the war. His polite amicable meeting lasted a half an hour. By this point, Lear had set preliminary articles (favored nation status, $60,000, prisoner exchange, Derne abandonment, Hamet family return) and the Bashaw had agreed. Many issues remained, from annual tribute and consular presents to procedures regarding prisoners in the event of another war.

The Bashaw gave every sign of allowing Lear much latitude, saying he was convinced that Lear "would not insert anything that was not just." Lear, who had achieved his own goals for price and timing of prisoner delivery, would now be challenged over the fine print.

After his meeting, Lear scribbled another note to Rodgers, alerting him that the Bashaw would be sending a gift of bullocks, sheep, vegetables, and fruit. (Lear would later wind up agreeing to pay for this so-called gift.) The Rhode Islander, so long in the service of George Washington, was a stickler for protocol, however arcane. He informed Rodgers that he should fire off a three-gun salute on receiving the present, give the Tripolitan officer four cartridges of gunpowder, and not forget to offer them the customary cup of coffee. The consul knew that American sailors would now be rowing boat after boat to and from the shore to ferry prisoners away from Tripoli. He added a postscript: "The sailors who go off sh.d not be permitted to come on shore in the boats, as they have bad places." These "bad places" must have been bordellos, packed with Christian slave girls, as well as dozens of liquor houses.

Over the course of the spring afternoon, the freed Americans changed into newly issued clothes and walked (or staggered) to the harbor to catch a boat to the various American vessels: the *Constitution*, *Constellation*, *Vixen*, and *Essex*. The *Essex* brig had room to welcome only thirty sailors and marines, a midshipman, and Lieutenant David Porter. Marine private William Ray, for one, boarded the *Essex*. Lear witnessed the joyous transit of the former slaves. He was especially pleased that the Americans were departing prior to the formal signing of a complete treaty. "The manner in which [peace] has been made," he wrote to his wife, "and the terms exceed the calculations of every one, but I must not boast."

One matter, though, required immediate attention: Derne. In that era of slow communication via sail or camelback, the Bashaw's latest report, three weeks old, still had the American flag flying over the country's second largest city and Hamet firmly entrenched at the governor's palace.

Commodore Rodgers, experienced in war, realized that battles could be occurring at Derne at the very moment that American sailors in Tripoli were reveling over peace. (Treaties in that era often included clauses pardoning acts committed during the lag time needed for word to reach a particular region.)

Rodgers wanted to dispatch a ship for Derne immediately. He knew that Barron had withdrawn supplies, but Rodgers had heard an offhand remark over dinner that had disturbed him. Lieutenant Dent, whose *Nautilus* had departed Derne on May 18, mentioned that Eaton had vowed: "I will not evacuate Derne until I receive an answer from Commodore Barron to my last communications."

Amid all the festivities on the June 4 liberation day, Rodgers found time to write a quick note to Lear on the subject. "To be sure, after [Eaton] has received Commodore Barron's directions *to evacuate Derne,* a non compliance will make the responsibility his own: nevertheless the consequence will be his Country's."

Rodgers counseled Lear to ready dispatches for Derne so that a ship "shall proceed without delay—her early arrival there may prevent impending mischief."

The American ships were now severely overcrowded, and Rodgers wanted to send them out of Tripoli as soon as possible. He also needed to deliver from Syracuse $60,000 in ransom money and the one hundred Tripolitan prisoners.

Lear politely requested that Rodgers keep one of the two large frigates in port—the *Constitution* or *Constellation*—as befitting the honor of a diplomat, but Rodgers ultimately deemed it unfeasible because of disease aboard the *Essex* and damage aboard the *Vixen*. He decided on June 5 to rush the *Constellation* to Derne with news of the formal peace. (He left Lear the brig *Vixen*.)

Lear had been working to draft the formal twenty-point treaty in English so it could be delivered to a translator for rendering into Arabic. Lear asked Rodgers if the *Constellation* could wait until the following day (June 6) to leave for Derne, and Lear also mentioned that the Bashaw had asked a favor. Could he send a *choux* (an officer) to Derne merely to observe and perhaps to send a few letters ashore, now that the United States and Tripoli were on friendly terms?

Lear said that he had seen no harm in the request and had already agreed. (Lear apparently did not consider the possibility that the *choux* could be delivering a death sentence to all residents who had aided Hamet and had trusted the United States.)

As Tobias Lear drafted his letter to William Eaton, he apparently worried that the hardheaded patriot might ignore his words. So Lear requested Commodore Rodgers also send a strong letter to Eaton. Rodgers bristled at the thought of Eaton disobeying Barron's directive. He abruptly opened his note to Eaton by saying that he didn't expect to find him still at Derne but if he still was there . . . He informed him that peace had been concluded on June 3 and "[I] have to desire that no farther hostilities by the forces of U. States be committed against the said Joseph Bashaw, his subjects or dominions, and that you evacuate and withdraw our forces from Derne." The message contained no mention whatsoever of praise for Eaton's conquest.

On Thursday, June 6, the sailors aboard three U.S. Navy ships prepared to leave Tripoli. Captain William Bainbridge, safely aboard the *Constitution,* wrote a jaunty note of thanks to Lear, his mood so fine that he joked that if the Bashaw imprisoned Lear, he would return and take the diplomat's place. (Perhaps the navy men sensed a certain nervousness on Lear's part to be left in Tripoli, with only Dr. Ridgely for American company onshore and the wobbly *Vixen* at sea.)

Lear labored over his letter to Eaton, trying hard to strike the right tone. As he arrived at the ticklish subject of Hamet and Derne, all his skills in diplomacy and circumlocution would be required.

"I found the heroic bravery of our few countrymen at Derne, and the idea that we had a large force and immense supplies at that place, had made a deep impression on the Bashaw—I kept up that idea, and endeavored, from thence, to make an arrangement favorable to his brother, who, altho' not found to be the man whom many had supposed, was yet entitled to some consideration from us. But I found that this was impracticable, and that if persisted in, would drive him to measures which might prove fatal to our countrymen in his power."

The word *fatal* is no random dire adjective. Although Lear might have believed what he wrote, very few others in the region believed that the captives' lives were at stake. Dutch consul Zuchet had dismissed the threat as a "pantomime." Yussef was nearly out of funds, missing a third of his kingdom, with his troops on the verge of mutiny and his navy in tatters, and a revitalized U.S. fleet soon to arrive. Commodore Rodgers also didn't share this belief of his friend. Two days later, he wrote to the secretary of the navy: "I never thought myself that the Lives of the American Prisoners were in any danger."

Lear tiptoed onward in his letter to Eaton: "I therefore engaged, of course, that on the conclusion of peace, we should withdraw all our forces and supplies from Derne, and other parts of his dominions, and the Bashaw engages, that if his brother withdraws himself quietly from his dominions, his wife and family should be restored to him.—This is all that could be done, and I have no doubt but the U. States will, if deserving, place him in a situation as eligible as that in which he was found."

Lear closed his letter: "I pray you will accept yourself and present to Mr. OBannon and our brave countrymen with you, my sincere congratulations on an event which your and their heroic bravery has tended to render so honorable to our country."

Lear sealed the letter and had it rowed out to Captain Hugh Campbell on the *Constellation;* Campbell instantly made ready to sail eastward to Derne.

Tobias Lear, amid his flurry of hollow compliments, had failed to mention that he had crafted a secret agreement with the Bashaw postponing the return of Hamet's family. Lear would never write home a single word about the "Secret Article." That duplicitous document would remain hidden from Eaton, Jefferson, and the world for two years.

CHAPTER 21 *Derne: From a Kingdom to Beggary?*

ON MONDAY, JUNE 3, to the east in Derne, unaware of the impending peace treaty, William Eaton remained steadfast, refusing to leave the town or abandon Hamet. Eaton—when not shoring up the town's defenses—began writing an open-ended letter to Commodore Barron, a kind of bombastic rant of a very frustrated soldier. He said he thought his mission was "to chastise a perfidious foe rather than to sacrifice a credulous friend." He balked at the indignity of lowering the American flag "in the presence of an enemy who have not merited the triumph." He lamented losing an opportunity to remake the entire Barbary Coast by standing up to the extortion in Tripoli and then doing likewise in Tunis and Algiers, and then watching the rest of the victimized nations follow our fine example. And if we do leave Derne, how can we reconcile "honor" and "justice" with our treatment of Hamet? He might not have been a great general, wrote Eaton, but the people welcomed him as a peaceful alternative to that madman, Yussef.

Eaton, of course, at that moment had no way of knowing how Lear's peace negotiations were proceeding. (Camel-back messengers took about two weeks; a ship with favorable winds could make it in four days.) These first days of June were hard for him. The inevitability of abandoning Hamet grew every minute. Evening after evening after receiving Barron's letter, Eaton had himself rowed out to the *Argus*. He could look back shoreward and see the harbor battery and rickety fort that he and his men were trying so hard to repair.

Apparently Eaton, Hull, and Lieutenant Evans of the *Hornet* enjoyed supper together and then drank down some of the 72 bottles of Porter and quarter cask of Marsala sent by Barron. Eaton—with his usual bullheadedness—was trying to shake off the sense of impending doom.

On June 3, the enemy feinted an attack on the back of Derne to discover how the townspeople would react. Eaton was thrilled when the locals manned the defenses. "During the alarm, a detachment from the garrison, under the command of Lieut. O'Bannon passed through town. Everybody, [old and young], even women from their recluse, shouted: 'Live the Americans! Long Live our friends and protectors!'"

That night Eaton could not avoid bitter thoughts on the fate of the "hapless" families of Derne. If they could see the reversal in their near future, their "acclamations of confidence" would turn to curses.

The rhythmic pull of the sailors brought him to the convivial table of Hull, Peck, Evans, and Mann. It gradually dawned on Isaac Hull that, despite the words of Barron, his New England friend here, with his "unquiet" eyes and ramrod bearing, had no intention of leaving Derne. Hull faced a quandary. His orders called for him to leave Derne with Eaton's forces, but Barron—accepting the vagaries of war—had not specifically ordered Eaton to leave immediately.

To cover himself from censure (even though he saw Eaton daily), he wrote him a note: "I have . . . to inform you that the *Argus* & *Hornet* are ready for sea, and in readiness to receive you and the men under your command on board, at any moment that you inform me of your intention to abandon your post, and a favourable opportunity offers to take you off."

Eaton replied that he intended to wait for fresh "Advices" that he expected to arrive any day from the commander in chief in Malta.

For his part, Captain Hull could order his marines and his midshipmen back on board, and then depart the coast, leaving Eaton, Hamet, and the mercenaries to their fate. *He could do that.* Hull mulled his options and weighed what waiting a few more days might do to his promising career in the navy.

The following day, June 5, events took a sudden turn, at least in the eyes of Eaton and Hull. It was a temperate breezy morning, and a crew of sailors rowed in from the *Argus* to help shovel dirt and pile stones at the old harbor fort. The sailors in white pants and blue shirts and neckerchiefs joined the Greek and Sicilian mercenaries and the half dozen U.S. Marines living in tents nearby.

Eaton had bribed a Moslem holy man to spy for him. That morning, the man returned from the enemy camp with some remarkable news. A messenger had arrived from Tripoli. The man, traveling on camel, had taken eleven days to make the 650-mile journey, so this was eleven-day-old news. (In that era—or any era for that matter—a letter provided a still life of a past moment . . . that situation, that mind-set might now no longer exist.)

The messenger had left Bashaw Yussef in Tripoli on May 25, the day *before* Tobias Lear arrived in the *Essex*. The Bashaw was ordering his commander at Derne, Hassan Bey, to hold his army together at all costs because the Bashaw planned on hurrying to negotiate peace with the United States, *even if he had to sell his royal wardrobe*. In other words, the Bashaw said he was willing to pawn his clothes to buy peace. According to the spy, the short note concluded: Then, once there was peace with the United States, he intended to dispose of his enemies. He implored the officer to hold on until peace could be finalized.

The spy added that he had overheard that several Bedouin allies in the enemy's camp were pondering switching allegiance over to Hamet because, they said, America's cannonballs and bayonets were taking the joy out of cavalry campaigns.

A couple hours later, two Moslem officers deserted to Hamet's side, and they confirmed the spy's report. They added that in Tripoli City, Bashaw Yussef was so unloved that he could count on only about 200 loyal troops.

Late that afternoon, yet another overture came from a Yussef ally willing to switch sides. Abd-el-Selim came over with a few other riders and said that another bey would bring over 150 cavalrymen if he can have guarantees that the Americans would never abandon him to Yussef, "who would devour his family and lands."

Captain Hull, who happened to be ashore that day to check the progress of bolstering the fort, heard all the spy reports and defections. Eaton and Hull deemed it imperative to rush this news of Yussef's weakness to Commodore Barron . . . perhaps Barron could pull back Lear or at least instruct Lear to drive the hardest peace bargain imaginable, and certainly not pay a penny. Hull ordered the *Hornet* to prepare to carry messages to Malta. Eaton took the opportunity to put in writing to Barron his refusal to depart, pending definitive news of a treaty or fresh orders.

Eaton added, "Be assured, Sir, we only want cash and a few marines to proceed to Tripoli & to meet you in the citadel of that piratical kennel for the liberation of our captives."

That night, Eaton and Hull drank together on ship; Eaton wasn't rowed ashore until midnight. Eaton's latest message to Barron, his last hope, was tucked aboard the *Hornet,* which was ready to sail in the morning. But on Thursday, June 6, as the men rowed in to work at the fort, everyone noticed winds out of the west picking up force. Since Tripoli lay due west into the teeth of the breezes, Hull decided to wait to look for a shift; maybe he hoped the *Nautilus* would arrive in the meantime with clear-cut orders.

Another desertion struck the enemy. The second in command, Hadji Ismain Bey, leader of the cavalry, sneaked off for Upper Egypt with a handful of followers and a chest of money.

The winds out of the west blew harder. Hull thought it politic to enter into his ship's log for June 8: "Had some conversation with [Eaton] concerning his abandoning his post which he consented to do after waiting a reasonable time for the arrival of the *Nautilus*—if she did not come." Neither man defined "reasonable." On Sunday, June 9, Hull pushed Eaton again on the topic: "Had some conversation with him about abandoning the fort, which he agreed to do at first good opportunity."

Steady winds blew in from the north and west. Eaton could look out and see the brig *Hornet* anchored offshore. Had it disappeared, carrying his messages, he would have some hope. Soured, Eaton wrote nothing in his journal, nothing in his open-ended letter to Barron.

The bleakness was hitting home; Eaton couldn't stand to dupe Hamet any longer. He decided he must tell him that there was a strong possibility that the United States would sign a peace treaty with his brother. That Eaton told Hamet took courage because Eaton and his 70 men were ringed onshore by about 2,000 of Hamet's followers.

Eaton in his homemade general's uniform looked squarely at Hamet in his colorful finery. The men had shared an extraordinary four months together. With typical directness, Eaton relayed Barron's motives for withdrawing support, stating that the commodore claimed Hamet lacked "energy & talent" and "means & resources" to be worthy of further aid. Eaton told the ousted Bashaw that he completely disagreed and would continue to lobby to change Barron's mind. Hamet's hopes had been betrayed before; his reaction was swift and bitter, according to Eaton.

"He answers that, even with supplies it would be fruitless for him to attempt to prosecute the war with his brother after you shall have withdrawn your squadron from the coast; but without supplies, he must be left in a most forlorn situation; for he can command no resources here, nor can he place any faith in provisions which may be stipulated with his brother in his favor, unless guaranteed by the United States. He emphatically says that to abandon him here is not to have cooperated with him, but with his rival! He wishes us to take him off in case of a peace."

On the morning of June 10, Eaton was able to banish the dark thoughts for a while. The enemy—after weeks of hesitation—attacked.

Hassan Bey finally rallied a formidable force of near 3,000 men, including a large cavalry, to swoop down on Derne. The day had begun innocuously enough. Just after dawn, the shore party from the *Argus,* fresh from rowing a mile, had arrived to help with the digging and wall building. The men were hard at work in the cool morning when a scout reported enemy movements on the nearby mountain.

The local terrain would dictate many aspects of the conflict. A short-stack mountain looms over the eastern side of Derne, the closest edge about two and a half miles away. All morning Eaton, through his spyglass, observed the enemy troops on horseback gathering in clusters, with advance parties trying various paths down the steep craggy mountainside. They were looking for an alternative to the one widely used path that funneled them downward onto a rough plain along the rocky edge of the seashore. This constricted route and seaside angle of approach would make them vulnerable to cannonfire from both the ships at sea and from Eaton's advance battery along the shore.

At 10 A.M. the enemy noticed Hamet's lookouts scouting along the plain by the shore. The enemy sent a troop down to try to cut them off. Hamet's men signaled for reinforcements, and enough arrived to beat back the attackers. This skirmish pitted Arab cavalry armed with muskets, pistols, and swords against one another, mostly from a safe distance. A shot here and a shot there and then the fine slow art of reloading on horseback. The enemy regrouped up the mountain, and by the darkening numbers blotting the pale landscape, they seemed poised for an all-out attack.

Eaton fired off a signal of "battle" to the ships at sea, and the favorable breeze allowed the *Argus* to glide in closer. At noon, the enemy filed down through the narrow pass to attack. Hamet's troops ranged at a spot on the seacoast plain about three-quarters of a mile from Derne. Captain Hull, who had a clear spyglass view of the enemy descending behind a half dozen green Arabic-script banners, guided the *Argus* to a spot "about half a gunshot" from the fort, and he dropped anchor. He used "springs" (thick ropes) attached to the anchor cable to help maneuver the ship. The sailors also had to haul one heavy gun from the starboard bow to the port side in the aft of the ship. By 1:15 P.M. his gun crews began to light up the long guns, sending twelve-pound cannonballs hurtling half a mile up into the attacking enemy. Each time a troop emerged from a gully or a ridge, the *Argus* let fire. The gunners timed their lighting the fuse to the uproll of the sea swells; they couldn't swivel right or left but relied on the captain to align the entire ship. This bombardment was certainly hit-or-more-often-miss. But even when it missed, the whistling balls, the flying clods of pounded earth, struck terror.

The shallow-draft brig *Hornet,* closer to the beach, also opened up on the enemy, but Lieutenant Evans found himself a bit too far under the cliff to have enough loft to hit the plain. Eaton's gunners in town also opened fire.

Hamet dug in; he knew that American support might be withdrawn very soon; given Eaton's bluntness, Hamet knew the American commodore's criticism. Hamet flourished this day. His two thousand men held their ground against the three thousand men attacking. Hull through the spyglass had a fine vantage point to observe Hamet's forces "warmly" engaging, "keeping up a brisqu fire." This battle was fought Arab-style with horsemen charging and firing a musket or pistol shot and wheeling back to safety. Foot soldiers scattered and picked off targets. Rarely, some clusters of men crossed scimitars. (There was none of Europe's disciplined lines of reloading muskets or relentless bayonet charges.)

By 2 P.M., the fighting spread out across the plain. (Eaton later learned from a deserter that the enemy had 945 men on horses recruited from eight regions of the country and 2,000 soldiers on foot.)

Eaton was forced into the unusual role of spectator and the more unusual role of having to *restrain* someone from fighting. "Lt. O'Bannon was impatient to lead his marines and the Greeks (about 38 in number) to the scene of the action," Eaton later wrote. "This could not be done without leaving our post too defenseless in case of a reverse; besides, I confess, I had doubts whether the measures lately adopted by our commissioner of peace [Lear] would justify me in acting offensively any longer in this quarter."

The engagement lasted four hours, and "though frequently charged, the Bashaw lost not an inch of ground." Around 4:30 P.M., the enemy retreated, desperately trying to squeeze back through the mountain pass. Hamet's men pursued. Frantic to escape, many were knocked off their horses in the jam up at the pass. Hamet's men captured dozens of mounts.

Eaton soon discovered that the Bashaw sustained casualties of about 50 people killed or wounded, including four high-ranking officers, while the enemy had 50 fighters killed and another 70 or more wounded.

From his vantage point at sea, Hull was impressed that Hamet's army rebuffed repeated cavalry charges. In the very late afternoon, after the battle, Eaton traveled out to the *Argus*, and the two Americans compared notes on Hamet's great victory. Eaton requested the ship's surgeon follow him ashore to treat Hamet's wounded. The *Argus* also supplied Eaton with three casks of gunpowder to replace what they had used from their advanced battery.

Hamet, at long last, had shown himself in battle.

With contrary winds still anchoring the *Hornet* in Derne, Eaton now added more lines in his open letter to Barron. In addition to relaying reports of Yussef's desperation for peace, Eaton now scratched out a long detailed account of Hamet's victory.

The winds finally did shift . . . but violently and to the north, not west. At midnight, Captain Hull recorded that the waves were rising and breaking hard on the shore. The *Argus* stood at risk of being smashed on nearby rocks. According to his ship's log, Hull turned out all hands at 4 A.M.; the hundred men rolled out of their hammocks on the hard-tossing ship. The sailors had to prepare the ship for slipping anchor. That meant they had to attach buoys onto the anchor cable, so when they cut it loose, they could later come back and retrieve the anchors. They lashed everything fast.

At 4:30 A.M. in the dark, with the winds howling and the waves slapping amid a "very heavy sea," Captain Hull decided it was too risky to remain anchored this close to shore. The men slipped the anchor cable, and the ship plunged off into the storm to the east.

About an hour later, as Hull was buffeted out to sea, he had the misfortune to see that the *Hornet* was having trouble fighting its way offshore. At 6:30 A.M., he noted that the *Hornet* was dangling with only one anchor cable holding fast. "I was under very great apprehension for her safety but could not go to her assistance without indangering the brig."

Hull rode out the storm, heading to the east, the hundred-foot-long, two-masted brig diving and climbing the waves. In the darkness and haste, Hull had left the launch towing behind on a long rope, but the storm threatened to smash the small boat into the brig; the men fought on the slippery rainy deck to hoist the launch into the *Argus*.

By 7 A.M. on Tuesday morning, Hull found himself five leagues to the north-northwest of Cape Ras-et-Tin, heading back toward Bomba. Hull experimented with various sails, trying the mainsail reefed, both fore and aft; at 11.A.M., heavy seas forced him to send the men aloft to haul up the fore topsail. (This brutal June storm showed why navies waited for summer to attack off the coast of Africa.) The nautical day begins at noon, and Hull noted, "Commences with Fresh Gales from the North.d and a very heavy sea under Close Reef.d Topsails and storm stay sails."

In late afternoon, fresh gales and a heavy sea were cartwheeling the men and the ship. The timber groaned and creaked. Hull was appalled to discover that a brutally strong current heading to the east made him lose ground in his efforts to return westward back to Derne. He worried about the *Hornet* and about Eaton and the unprotected troops on the ground, surrounded by a more numerous enemy. As he was struggling in this nautical quicksand, he noticed a large sail upwind of him, closer to Derne. He put spyglass to eye but couldn't puzzle out the ship's identity.

Day by day onshore from the eve of Hamet's victory, William Eaton had looked out to sea to scan for the return of the *Argus*, which would bring back its firepower and the bottles of brandy. He had also continued looking seaward for the return of the *Nautilus* from Malta.

Around 6:30 P.M. on Tuesday, June 11, he spied a sail. The more he squinted, the larger the sail appeared. It was a very large sail. Not a brig or schooner. The ship was clearly not the *Argus*, but in the evening gloom, Eaton could not be certain. It appeared to be a frigate. Would it bring fresh orders from Barron? A reprieve for Hamet?

Eaton saw a boat lowered from the large ship. The sailors pulled at the oars and the launch lurched forward. Eaton watched it take more than an hour to reach the shore.

After the storm, the air was clean and clear. At the water's edge, Eaton greeted the U.S. Navy officer identifying himself as arriving from the USS *Constellation*. Lieutenant Wederstrandt, no doubt all smiles, began to announce to Eaton that the American prisoners were free and that peace had been declared, but Eaton shouted at the man to hold his tongue. Any word of that treaty escaping into the streets of Derne could spell a death sentence for all of them.

Lieutenant Wederstrandt handed Eaton letters from Commodore John Rodgers and Consul General Tobias Lear. Eaton retreated somewhere private to read these two letters that he knew would formalize the end of his mission. Anticipation didn't soften the blow.

Commodore Rodgers not only offered no congratulations but instead began by berating Eaton for still even being at Derne, in defiance of Commodore Barron's directive. Rodgers informed Eaton that peace had been concluded on June 3. "[I] have to desire that no farther hostilities by the forces of U. States be committed against the said Joseph Bashaw, his subjects or dominions, and that you evacuate and withdraw our forces from Derne." Rodgers enclosed the three preliminary articles of peace. Eaton discovered for the first time that the United States had agreed to pay $60,000 ransom. History has failed to record the stream of expletives that flowed from his lips.

And in the third article, he found his covert mission turned on its head. After bringing Hamet to the eastern province of Tripoli, he must now try to make the legitimate ruler disappear. "The Americans will use all means in their power to persuade the Brother of the said Bashaw, who has co-operated with them at Derne &c to withdraw from the Territory of the said Bashaw of Tripoli; but they will not use any force or improper means to effect that object; and in case he should withdraw himself, the Bashaw engages to deliver up to him, his Wife and Children now in his power."

To Eaton's mind, it was a piddling offer to the conqueror of Derne—not even a governorship or a fat bribe—but at least it was something.

Eaton unsealed the letter from Lear and unfolded it.

Over the course of the rest of his life, Eaton would at various times chronicle his reaction to Lear's words. Appalled, dumbfounded, disgusted, disgraced, outraged, furious, start to paint the picture. He would eventually accuse Lear of being ignorant, cowardly, and devious and would one day call him "Aunt Lear."

Eaton read along as Lear vaunted of chopping Yussef's price down from $200,000 to $60,000. Eaton was incredulous. He later wrote that indeed Yussef had 200 more prisoners than the U.S. Navy had, but that Eaton and Hamet had 12,000 residents of the eastern province under their control. "Could this not have been exchanged for 200 prisoners of war? Was the attempt made?" Eaton brusquely reassessed Lear's bargain: "We gave a kingdom for peace."

Eaton bristled at Lear's statement that Yussef was the better choice to preserve the treaty with the United States and rule Tripoli. "If parricide, fratricide, treason, perfidy . . . and systematic piracy [give guarantee] of good faith, Mr. Lear has chosen the fittest of the two brothers."

His anger surged when he read Lear's account that the diplomat had been forced to stop bargaining for Hamet out of fear that his efforts might "prove fatal to our countrymen." Eaton later wondered aloud about Lear's ignorance. Anyone who ever dealt with Yussef knew that the Bashaw blustered but never risked his own skin to bite. The previous summer Yussef had threatened to kill all the prisoners if Commodore Preble fired one shot. Instead of hurting anyone, Yussef had retreated to a bomb-proof room. "Was Mr. Lear sent out to co-operate with Joseph Bashaw?"

Finally, Eaton found Lear's words of praise almost as irritating as the treaty itself, which he regarded as a "wound on the national dignity." He stated he would never ever consider it an honor to receive a compliment from the provisional colonel Lear, "who never set a squadron in the field nor the division of battle knows."

The night of Tuesday, June 11, in his tent at the small fort in Derne harbor, Eaton, though shell-shocked, had pressing problems to confront: what to do with Hamet and how to evacuate Derne without a massacre. Eaton summoned Hamet to his tent and informed him *in deepest secrecy* of the peace treaty just concluded between the United States and Tripoli. And Eaton explained that a clause had been negotiated, that if Hamet left Derne quietly, his family would be restored to him.

Hamet has left no memoirs, but Eaton reported Hamet decided quickly that, given his lack of money and supplies, he must leave Derne with the Americans. And he warned Eaton: If word of their plans to evacuate leaked out, their betrayed allies would certainly try to kill them. Eaton probably slept very little that night, not out of fear but out of guilt. It was too late for a miraculous reprieve from the U.S. Navy. Maybe he weighed becoming a kingmaker and staying on in Tripoli to march westward with Hamet.

At dawn on June 12, Captain Hugh Campbell sent Lieutenant Wederstrandt ashore again with another message for Eaton, this one from Campbell himself "requiring of you to withdraw the American forces from Derne with all possible dispatch." Campbell added that the *Constellation* would remain at the ready. "It rests with you to say in what manner and when her services will be required—and when the white flag is to be hoisted on shore—I need not say what pleasure it will give me to see you on board the *Constellation,* where a cot is provided for you by your very respectful & Obedient Servt."

Upon receipt, Eaton in haste replied: "I doubt the propriety of showing a white flag until after this post shall be evacuated—Shall have the honor to wait on you on board immediately to consult on certain measures too complicated to be comprised in this note."

Campbell wasted no time; after receiving the note, he came ashore with several officers. (By now, word had reached the enemy that a large 36-gun three-masted frigate—much bigger than either brig—had reached Derne harbor.)

Hull in the *Argus* still fought the eastward currents, still trying to claw his way back to Derne. With absolute secrecy, Eaton and Hamet plotted their escape.

In a lifetime filled with many setbacks and some stunning victories, this day, June 12, 1805, must have ranked as the worst in Eaton's life. This hater of duplicity spent the day deceiving his Moslem and Christian allies. He gave orders that the troops should prepare to attack the enemy. Considering that reinforcements had seemingly just arrived in the heavily armed *Constellation,* the idea was more than plausible. He sent ammunition and extra rations to his Arab allies and Derne militiamen; he dispatched spies to ferret out the enemy's whereabouts. At sunset, Eaton inspected the troops: his 6 remaining U.S. Marines, his 38 Greeks, his artillerymen. He ordered them to divest themselves of any heavy baggage and to be ready to advance at a moment's notice.

The edginess that precedes a battle was everywhere. Men cleaned muskets, sharpened swords, and prepared to fight and possibly to die. The bad jokes fell flat; the melodramatic last words were waved off. The flags of Hamet and the United States flapped side by side on the little fort in Derne.

At 8 P.M. Eaton sent out small patrols to block off any access to the fort. Since this was nominally the rule—though honored more in the breach—no one suspected anything. By now, all the *Constellation*'s launch boats were huddled by the wharf. Eaton ordered officers, Rocco and Selim, to escort their men into the boats and to load the howitzer they had captured. Then the Greek company filled the other boats.

These riffraff mercenaries recruited at Alexandria did as commanded, quickly and silently, but Eaton noted that the men were filled with "astonishment." The attack was actually a retreat; the general had lied all day. The American, who never tired of talking about his country's commitment to honor and fairness, was sneaking out of town under the cover of darkness.

The U.S. Marines remained at their posts. The transit of the boats to the *Constellation* took almost two hours each way. The pigtailed sailors pulled at the oars of the longboats. The only sound: the rhythmic plash of oars.

A little before midnight, Eaton puzzled out in the dim light that the boats were returning to shore, and he sent a messenger on foot to Hamet to request a brief meeting. This was the signal for Hamet to ride over with his retinue of about forty to the fort. They dismounted and climbed straight into the waiting boats. The marines followed, along with Lieutenant Presley O'Bannon, George Washington Mann, George Farquhar, and Jean Eugene. When every single other person in the garrison was safely aboard the longboats, William Eaton, arm in a sling, stepped aboard. The rowers, calloused hands gripping the oars, pulled the men away from the coast of Derne, and out to the waiting American getaway vessel.

The boats were just beyond pistol shot when the wharf suddenly filled with angry soldiers and citizens of Derne. *The United States and Hamet had betrayed them. The Christians had again betrayed the Moslems.*

Some shouted for the Bashaw, others shouted at Eaton, some uttered shrieks of rage; others cursed them. The people onshore fell to plundering the tents and horses left in the fort. In the darkness, the rowers pulled them to the *Constellation*; they reached it at 2 A.M. and boarded. The 160-foot-long ship, with 300 crewmen, now had more than a hundred extra people aboard. Deck space was precious. In a few hours, Moslem jostled Moslem to kneel and pray at dawn.

As the sun's first rays peeked over the calm sea, Eaton, using a spy-glass, could see the townspeople of Derne trying to flee the city, driving every animal before them. They expected a massive attack as soon as Yussef's forces discovered the flight of the Americans. He also saw the *Argus*, which had finally wrestled its way back to Derne and was skittering closer.

In midmorning, with Hamet and Eaton safely aboard, Captain Campbell allowed Yussef's *choux* to go ashore with his messages. He was rowed in a boat under a white flag of truce and delivered letters of amnesty for anyone now willing to swear allegiance to Yussef.

On the man's return later in the day, Eaton asked his Arabic translator to query the *choux* on the state of Derne and the residents' reaction. He said despair was etched on their faces. He said that almost no one accepted the pardon; they distrusted Yussef and planned instead to defend themselves.

At high noon, Eaton watched for a massacre.

A spy sailed out to the ship and told him that the enemy had been so troubled by the arrival of the *Constellation* that they had retreated helter-skelter in panic to a spot fifteen miles away from Derne. Eaton could only muse bitterly about what money and naval support might have done for Hamet's efforts. In the late afternoon aboard the crowded frigate, he wrote a letter to the new commodore, John Rodgers, an officer he sincerely believed to be courageous and patriotic. He had once heard Rodgers at Washington say: "My name shall be written in blood on the walls of Tripoli before I will consent to pay one cent for ransom or tribute." Eaton closed this note to Rodgers as the foretopmen climbed to unfurl the sails to depart.

> *In a few minutes more, we shall loose sight of this devoted city,*
> *which has experienced as strange a reverse in so short a time as ever*
> *was recorded in the disasters of war; thrown from proud success and*
> *elated prospects into an abyss of hopeless wretchedness.—Six hours ago*
> *the enemy were seeking safety from them by flight—this moment we*
> *drop them from ours into the hands of this enemy for no other crime*
> *but too much confidence in us! The man whose fortune we have*

accompanied thus far experiences a reverse as striking—He falls from the most flattering prospects of a Kingdom to beggary.

Our peace with Tripoli is certainly more favorable—and separately considered, more honorable than any peace obtained by any Christian nation with a Barbary Regency at any period within a hundred years; but it might have been more favorable and more honorable. It now remains however to dispose of the instrument [Hamet] we have used in obtaining this peace in such a manner as to acquit our conscience and honor—this will require some diplomatic skill.

Eaton concluded: "The duties . . . annexed to my appointment in the Navy Department having ceased with the war, I have no reasons for remaining any longer in this sea. I request therefore you will have the goodness to allow me a passage in the first ship of war . . . which you may dispatch to the United States."

CHAPTER 22 *Tripoli: Lear Days*

Finding that the translation of two copies of the Treaty into
Arabic will require more time than I expected, I have thought it best
for the Constitution *to go over to Malta & Syracuse with our late*
captives, and return here again for me, which will deprive me of
that happiness of seeing my dearest Fanny for 8 or 10 days more
than I expected.

—TOBIAS LEAR (TRIPOLI) TO HIS WIFE, JUNE 6, 1805

LEAR WANTED TO REMAIN as short a time as possible in Tripoli.
The shore breezes ruffling the palm trees, the smell of exotic
spices in the marketplace, the sounds of half a dozen languages
echoing in narrow alleys did nothing for him. Not only did the twice-
widowed diplomat miss his young bride but he suffered from chronic
pain in his ankles (probably gout) and the lotion and cotton cloths that
he had brought were not working as well as the flannel bandages he had
left behind in Malta.

Helping Lear cope with his absence from Fanny was the man's near
glee at the outcome of his negotiations. In every piece of correspondence, he referred to the "favourable" and "honorable" peace. "Within
twenty four hours after I landed," he wrote to William Higgins, naval
agent at Syracuse, "every officer & seamen belonging to the late U. States
frigate Philadelphia were sent on board our ships and the settlement of
the whole left to my arrangement."

In that decorous age, no one said anything critical directly to Tobias Lear. The Bashaw was full of smiles, as was Danish consul Nissen and Jewish financier Leon Farfara, who both gave him the ultimate compliment, informing him that the conditions he had imposed were indeed harsh. A four-year war was over; hostages were freed. No one *said* anything to man-of-the-hour Lear. However, around this time in early June Dutch diplomat Zuchet gave his government an insider's perspective on the treaty. The veteran diplomat sent a report home recounting the conditions and then stated: "What misery has this Bashaw caused by his behavior! He personally should have suffered more than everyone else. He was held by the throat by the United States but, out of pity—that's the only way to put it—he was accorded $60,000, which is still half of what Commodore Preble offered him last year." Zuchet was baffled by the American diplomat's largesse, and he was irritated that the impoverished beleaguered Yussef had yet again dodged disaster. Zuchet noted that with peace came a return to piracy, or in more precise terms, to state-sponsored attacks against nations without peace treaties. The instant the American blockade was lifted, Yussef sent out four Barbary cruisers to try to capture Neapolitan vessels and refill the treasury. Zuchet also observed that Murad Rais, the renegade Scot Peter Lyle, had completed refitting a 12-cannon xebec and was expected daily to go chase ships of the Hanseatic League.

Lear settled in as a guest at the Danish consulate, and he showed little curiosity about touring the city. Leather-bound books lined the walls of the study, and noontime brought ample meals and discussions of the ancient classics. Life without Fanny was made a tad more bearable by the cask of Madeira Lear had sent ashore as a present for consul Nissen. From the roof deck on the Danish consulate on June 6, Lear had watched the sails of three U.S. Navy vessels disappear carrying the prisoners to safety. Now Lear was left in Tripoli with Dr. Ridgely, a genial navy man emerging from eighteen months captivity, and with the convivial Dane Nissen, and with constant visitor Leon Farfara, the unofficial (and well-reimbursed) liaison between foreign diplomats and the Bashaw.

On the evening of June 6, when Lear found himself sleeping ashore, no *full* version of U.S.-Tripoli treaty yet existed. Rodgers had departed with the prisoners, but he carried only the preliminary articles. Although Lear would date the final treaty as signed on June 4 (thus confusing historians), that date was a finesse, a diplomatic connivance, to fulfill the Bashaw's demand that peace be struck before the hostages departed.

Back on June 4 in the august salon of the *divan,* the Bashaw had signed *the preliminary articles* and rather airily told Lear to draft the rest of the treaty himself. Yussef had added that he foresaw no problems in the fine print.

Perhaps the reason the Bashaw anticipated no difficulties was that, as a perceptive judge of character, he already had sensed the accommodating nature of Lear and, more importantly, he knew that two very shrewd men would be helping Lear: Nissen and Farfara.

Lear sat down to draft the treaty. His task was made easier by the fact that he carried with him a draft of a peace treaty with Tripoli written in spring of 1803 by James Leander Cathcart, the meddlesome former U.S. consul to Tripoli. Lear borrowed thirteen of the seventeen articles verbatim and took the gist of two others.

The treaty—aimed at preventing abuses by one country against another—gives a fascinating glimpse into daily life on the Mediterranean circa 1805. Almost half the treaty concerns the arcane game of capturing ships and holding cargoes and passengers hostage. Many of these conditions might seem niggling to a modern reader, but they were the fine print that determined whether a vessel disappeared or returned home intact, whether cargoes survived, whether passengers slipped into slavery. In many respects, this treaty drafted by Cathcart (who was then furious at Tripoli's actions) and copied by Lear was indeed among the most favorable ever written on the Barbary Coast. It stated, for instance, that American goods being carried on a ship of a nation at war with Tripoli shall not be confiscated.

But, and it is a very large caveat, Tobias Lear did not choose to copy one immensely important clause from Cathcart's draft. Cathcart wrote in Article 16: "No pretence of any periodical tribute or further payment of any denomination is ever to be made by either party." This cessation of tribute goes to the heart of the war, and to the essence of the principles of the United States.

Lear never revealed why he dropped this demand for no tribute. The Jefferson administration had clearly stated its preference to stop paying tribute, but it had also allowed Lear in its April 9, 1803, Department of State instructions to agree to tribute but *preferably in secret*, in "no part of the public treaty."

That is, apparently, what Tobias Lear did. In his only later account of the peace process, he wrote: "No Consular present is mentioned in the Treaty; but that it is understood will be given as is usual with *all* nations when a Consul shall be sent, it does not exceed 6,000 Dollars, and the particulars I shall send in my next." Either Lear never sent the "particulars" or those particulars were so embarrassing as to be conveniently lost.

The U.S. prisoners had already departed from Tripoli, so Lear's generosity is a bit baffling. One clue might be that Nissen and Farfara hammered the fact that all nations paid this. Also, Farfara, who often supplied the jewels or lent the money, at great profit to himself, had a huge incentive for the practice to continue. Lear demonstrated over and over that he had difficulty rejecting requests for traditional payments, "customary fees" or what European diplomats called *usanza*.

One aspect of *usanza*, however, the United States dearly wanted to stop was the enslaving of prisoners in times of war. The greatest outrage in the United States centered on Americans being forced into slavery, popularly pictured as being forced to wield palm-frond fans to keep flies off turbaned noblemen and their veiled harem girls.

Cathcart had written a clause which stated that—in the event of war—any prisoners captured by either side shall not be made slaves but shall be exchanged rank for rank. However, Cathcart—who had been imprisoned in Algiers for eleven years—had added a formula for redemption in case one side had more prisoners: $500 for a captain, $300 for a mate or a supercargo (owner's agent), and $100 for each seaman. (This clause would have pleased Farfara, who often handled these transactions.) Cathcart also stipulated that no longer than a year should elapse before a prisoner is redeemed. This pragmatic approach would keep ransom timely and affordable. (Lear had paid $300 per each of 200 sailors while 100 prisoners were exchanged man for man at no cost.)

Lear adopted Cathcart's language word for word, even though it seems staggering that the United States would codify a ransom system that could place a monetary value on American prisoners and could encourage Tripoli corsairs to capture U.S. ships. (Neither Jefferson nor Madison would ever comment directly on this humiliating clause in the treaty.)

Eaton favored a much tougher approach, as did Commodore Rodgers, who vowed never again to pay a ransom. When Eaton struck his Convention with Hamet Karamanli back in February near Alexandria, he specified in Article 10: "In case of future war . . . , captives on each side shall be treated as prisoners of war, and not as slaves, and shall be entitled to reciprocal and equal exchange, man for man, and grade for grade and in no case shall a ransom be demanded for prisoners of war, nor a tribute required. . . . All prisoners shall be given up on the conclusion of peace."

Eaton was modeling his agreement on the gentlemanly rules of European warfare, in which French officers sometimes dined with their English adversaries as each side waited for appropriate prisoner exchanges.

Tobias Lear finished drawing up the treaty, and he handed it to Leon Farfara to have it translated into Arabic. According to Arabic scholars, the text sports at least a dozen mistranslations, most of which appear minor. However, one slip stands out as perhaps an intentional "dirty trick."

The English for Lear's Article 16 stated: "The Prisoners captured by either party shall not be made *slaves*." The Arabic asserted the exact opposite: "The men captured by either party shall not be made *prisoners of war*." The Arabic langauge boasts many words for *slaves*, but the translator chose to use none of them. Since both the Arabic and the English versions were considered "originals," this misconstruction was also binding.

The American consuls before Lear were not devotees of Leon Farfara. Cathcart had written a half decade earlier: "On my arrival here [Farfara] like a pusillanimous scoundrel wrote me a letter imploring me for the love of God not to mention his name to the Bashaw, as it would be ruinous to him and detrimental to our affairs. I never saw him until I had delivered the Consular presents, when all the difficulty was surmounted he came like a Jerry Sneak and offered his services. And yet this fellow expects $1,000." And with more than a whiff of anti-Semitism, he had added: "I have had this Christ-killing puppy and all his family in my house."

Cathcart also recounted that Farfara had once purposely mangled the translation of Sweden's treaty with Tripoli by omitting the clause that specified *four* years between payments instead of *three*.

Lear had failed on two key points of the treaty: no tribute and no slaves, and now he would botch the agreement regarding the treatment of Hamet.

From day one, Bashaw Yussef deeply regretted agreeing to restore his brother's family, and he badgered Consul Nissen to try to convince Lear to change his mind. Nissen, for his part, worried that he had perhaps pressed too hard a bargain on Yussef, and that it might one day come to haunt Danish interests. So Nissen asked Lear to soften on this demand. Lear remained firm at first.

Then, sometime in early June, this generous scholarly Dane, perhaps over a fine glass of Madeira or a collegial chat about Sophocles, swayed Lear into making a breathtaking concession: The United States would grant the Bashaw *four years to return Hamet's family*. And the agreement would remain absolutely secret.

This marks an extraordinary change: Hamet was induced to leave Derne on the promise of regaining his wife and sons and daughters. Now, unbeknownst to him, he would be on probation for four years, and then he would have to hope that the United States would still be interested enough to force the Bashaw's hand into fulfilling the bargain. From any angle, this was subterfuge. (Eaton, when he first heard of it in late 1807, called it far worse: a "national disgrace," a "dishonor.")

Lear, in a Secret Article, which he dated June 5, agreed to the following: "Whereas his Excellency the Bashaw of Tripoli has well grounded reasons to believe, if the wife and children of his brother (Hamet) should be delivered up to him immediately . . . the said brother would engage in new operations of hostility against him. . . . And the said United States willing to evince their good disposition . . . do hereby agree to a modification of the said article . . . so that the term of four years shall be fixed for the execution . . . during which time the said brother is to give evident proofs of his peaceful disposition towards the Bashaw."

Lear signed it and put the U.S. diplomatic seal on the document. Lear, Nissen, Farfara, and Dr. Ridgely knew of this document, but it was a tightly held secret. Dutch consul Zuchet, who ferreted out the darkest plots and relayed much gossip, never found out about it, and Lear made no official report about it to Commodore Rodgers, the Department of State, or to Jefferson. If Lear ever wrote a syllable about his motives or rationale, those documents have since been lost or destroyed. After safe-keeping the letters he wrote daily to his wife from May 25 to June 6, he preserved no letters that cover events from June 7 to June 21. Perhaps, just as during the Washington incident years earlier, Lear was once again demonstrating he was not above destroying embarrassing letters.

With utmost secrecy, Tobias Lear had chopped away the only favor-able consideration that Hamet had won from his dangerous five-month expedition with Eaton.

Nissen later wrote to his foreign ministry to explain why he had swayed Lear. "Although this matter might seem of very little importance to our affairs or to me, both as consul and as a private individual, I never-theless desired this modification, in order to show the Pasha and his Di-van that I had not tried to deceive them, and the Pasha will regard it as a great service on my part, which he will perhaps repay to my successor, when the opportunity offers." Nissen had sold out the United States, or really Hamet, for a vague promise of future gain. (Ironically, two years later, the Bashaw would demand an unusually hefty gift of $30,000 and 33,000 pounds of gunpowder from Denmark to renew its $5,000-tribute-a-year treaty.)

That second week of June, Lear had time on his hands waiting for Rodgers to return with the ransom and the Tripolitan prisoners. So he went shopping. He tried to find some Barbary horses worthy of sending to Washington City but found none fine enough. He did purchase two ostriches and several unusual breeds of sheep to take with him, as well as many unspecified presents for Fanny and his friends in Malta.

On June 10, one dozen officials signed and sealed the treaty, includ-ing Yussef's son, first minister Mohammed Dghies, and Murad Rais, the admiral. At this point, Lear handed out tokens of the United States' pleasure at this august signing. Lear made no mention of it in his official reports, but Dutch consul Zuchet stated: "They carried a present to the Bashaw and to his sons and to all the ministers who put their signature on the treaty, of jewelry in diamonds, cloths and watches, to the value of about $6,000."

Tobias Lear was slavishly indulging the men who had enslaved Americans. James Madison and Thomas Jefferson assumed that Lear would avoid unnecessary tribute, but they assumed wrong. His orders allowed him to make payments in secret, and apparently he did just that.

A week later, on Monday, June 17, the sails of the *Constitution* hove into view. Choppy seas prevented the frigate from approaching the shore, but the battery on the castle volunteered a twenty-one-gun salute, and Commodore Rodgers answered boom for boom. Lear in his consular report never mentioned agreeing to reimburse Tripoli for gunpowder, but his expense account much later listed $250 paid for the general salute at the conclusion of the peace and then $152 for the first and second salute to the *Constitution*. (That $402 would buy enough gunpowder for ten times that many salutes.) A later American diplomat once disgustedly summed it up: "Mr. Lear never opposed a single demand; never evaded a threat."

On Tuesday, June 18, at 9 A.M. the *Constitution* lowered two cutters and ferried 48 Tripolitan citizens and 41 black slaves ashore, who had been made prisoners by the U.S. Navy. Huge joyous crowds greeted them at the wharf. Lear, however, was extremely apprehensive on two counts. First, he had promised 100 prisoners (not 89), and second, he worried about the Bashaw's reception of slaves, who were not natives of Tripoli. "I was therefore obliged to make it appear that the blacks were his subjects, and were to be included in the exchange. I found no difficulty in the case, tho' I am sure he was not <u>convinced</u> of the propriety of it."

The Barbary nations were notorious for not ever redeeming their own captured citizens—the Dey of Algiers once said that he wouldn't give an orange peel for one of his countrymen. The Bashaw was no doubt thrilled to receive 41 slaves worth as much as $500 each, or $20,000.

Lear had requested that Commodore Rodgers bring $65,000—that is, $60,000 for ransom and $5,000 to establish a consulate. Rodgers ordered the ransom carried ashore and sailors, two at each end, carried eight wooden chests of money into the castle and laid them at the Bashaw's feet. He duly signed a receipt, dated June 19, which Lear attached to the treaty.

Lear was not done handing out money. Again, his official report makes no mention of this, but his expense account lists it. Nissen advised Lear to pay Leon Farfara $1,555 for his services, and Lear agreed. He put a note in the margin that he had paid the sum to Nissen, who gave him a receipt and promised to deliver it to Farfara, who apparently was unable to give him a receipt. (This secret payment would help lead the following year to Farfara's murder by the Bashaw.)

Lear was also informed that for generations countries had paid a $10-per-head tax on all freed slaves who were allowed to leave Tripoli. Lear's expense account chronicles $2,950 paid "to be divided among marine captains, first and second *kasnadars*, Bashaw's secretary and the guardiano bashaw." The 295 figure represents the 307 men and officers of the *Philadelphia* minus the five who turned Turk, five who died in captivity, and two who sought refuge at the French consulate.

In case Lear ran the risk of leaving Tripoli with any taxpayer dollars jangling in his pocket, he found it appropriate to tip very generously. He gave the astounding sum of $150 to servants and slaves of the Bashaw and prime minister, while taking coffee and refreshment. (To put it in perspective, the highest-paid Tripolitan servant at the United States consulate, the dragoman, received $4 a month.)

To cover his two-week stay, Lear also handed out $75 in tips to Nissen's servants and to the former American dragoman. For a man representing the world's only democracy, Lear assumed a magisterial pose.

Commodore John Rodgers remained briefly in Tripoli, long enough to come ashore to meet the Bashaw, an event he hardly mentions in his reports, and long enough to get into a fight. The consul for France, with Napoleon then riding high, had sent Lear and Rodgers a note demanding back pay for two freed American prisoners who claimed to be French citizens. Lear shilly-shallied over the legalistics, but Rodgers wrote Beaussier that he couldn't respond at length because the "dark features of the subject preclude the admissibility of even decent language." In other words, if I answer you, I will curse you. "I charge you, Sir, with having afforded protection to two Deserters from the U. States service." Rodgers added, to save them from the noose, the French diplomat should keep the pair, but he shouldn't even think of asking again for their wages. "I hope for both the regard I have for your Country and my own feelings, that you will not oblige me to say more." Thus, with force, the matter ended.

On the afternoon of June 21, at 2 P.M., Lear boarded a cutter along with his friends, Danish consul Nissen, Spanish consul De Souza, and that clever observer Zuchet. The sailors rowed the diplomats about two miles out in the harbor, and a half hour later, the four men boarded the massive frigate *Constitution*. The masts, with sails furled, tilted this way and that. The frigate fired a seven-gun salute to these diplomats, and the men stayed aboard for three and a half hours, talking and drinking.

From the vantage point of the frigate, the diplomats could see the seven little corsair vessels and two other larger ships that the Bashaw was preparing to carry troops to Derne to take vengeance on the people who had supported his brother Hamet.

At 6 P.M., the foreign consuls climbed overboard into the second cutter and were rowed back to shore. The sailors aboard the *Constitution* in their white summer uniforms began hauling up the anchors. At 8 P.M. the cutter returned and was hoisted aboard.

The ship tacked, and the town of Tripoli faded in the darkness to the southeast. After a mere weekend of sailing, they reached Malta but were forced to remain in the quarantine area in the harbor.

Tobias Lear, feted as a hero, immensely pleased, wrote instantly to Fanny to come meet him aboard the ship and to bring his lotion for his ankles and his flannel bandages. He hoped that she felt well enough to proceed with him to Syracuse and maybe after that they could take a vacation together in Palermo, perhaps with another American couple, Dr. and Mrs. Sewell. He was confident that he had earned a vacation: "I have finished all our affairs [in Tripoli] much to my satisfaction and to the honor of our country."

CHAPTER 23

Wounded and Restless

WILLIAM EATON AND HIS victorious mercenaries headed sullenly to Syracuse, underappreciated and eager to drown their sorrow in whatever spirits the navy would spare. The evacuation of Derne had soured Eaton and his officers, as did the lack of congratulations for their role in imposing peace. The crowded ship *Constellation* fought contrary winds and tacked its way northward. One hundred men—Eaton's 35 Greek mercenaries, 25 artillerymen, and Hamet's 40-person entourage—camped out on the deck or curled up in whatever uncluttered space they could find. A navy frigate was serving as a ferryboat.

No one has left an account of daily shipboard life, but letters written later imply the weeklong voyage was no celebration. The sense of betraying Hamet hung in the air like a foul odor. No one rejoiced at handing Yussef $60,000; no one toasted Tobias Lear, commissioner of peace.

Eaton arrived in Syracuse, the unofficial headquarters for the U.S. Navy in the Mediterranean, on June 23, 1805, two days before Mr. and Mrs. Lear would arrive with Rodgers from Malta on the *Constitution*. Eaton's mercenaries still called him "General," but to Captain Campbell and the other officers of the U.S. Navy, he was now politely addressed as "Mr. Eaton."

Syracuse, population 12,000, was an impoverished, intensely Catholic backwater on the island of Sicily, just outside the French Napoleonic domination of mainland Italy. Church and opera dominated the place. Midshipman Ralph Izard Jr. called Syracuse "detestable" and once said that despite having liberty, he hadn't bothered to set foot onshore for six weeks.

The *Constellation* anchored in the harbor near the *Vixen* and *President*; Captain Hull in the *Argus* arrived soon after and then came the *Essex*. The scattershot American fleet was finally gathering in one place.

Eaton had absolutely no money except what he could borrow from navy officers. His main concerns were to get his mercenaries paid by the navy and fed as well—no small feat in a bureaucracy. He convinced local navy agent George Dyson to provide 95 rations a day on the promise that Eaton would soon clear it with Commodore Rodgers. Of greater urgency, Eaton wanted to provide for Hamet, now and for the future, and then to get out of the Mediterranean and go home. While undertaking these tasks, Eaton complained to anyone about the rushed peace.

Mr. and Mrs. Lear arrived in port on June 26, but Mrs. Lear said she found the heat oppressive onshore (or maybe she found the town dull or Eaton threatening), but in any case she chose to remain day after day aboard the American flagship and Tobias hovered at her side. The only documented face-to-face meeting in Syracuse between Lear and Eaton would take place in a week, and it would be harsh.

On Saturday, June 29, Eaton, restless and irritable, found himself drafted for an unusual task. He was asked to serve as judge advocate for a U.S. Navy Court of Inquiry. The case was the conduct of William Bainbridge during the grounding of the *Philadelphia* on October 31, 1803. Eaton, normally impassioned, seems to have performed his duty in a singularly lethargic fashion.

The extremely formal proceedings lasted a few hours aboard the *President* in Syracuse harbor; clearly, by the tenor of the questions, little appetite existed among the three captains on the panel—James Barron, Stephen Decatur, Hugh Campbell—or Eaton to probe too deeply into the matter. Bainbridge, the most gaunt of all the prisoners, had suffered for eighteen months.

The most aggressive question was the first: "Had you any boats sufficient to carry out an anchor?" The answer of no by Lieutenant Porter, accompanied by the statement that the enemy had command of the waters where the anchor needed to go, seemed to defuse the probe immediately. Eaton asked only one perfunctory question: "Did you notice anything of remissness or neglect in her commander which would tend to the loss of the *Philadelphia*?"

The court of inquiry ruled that Bainbridge had acted "with fortitude and conduct" and "no degree of censure should attach itself to him from that event." Case closed. The thirty-one-year-old New Jersey native would be free to resume his career.

Eaton now tried to rally support for Hamet. The prince, anticipating that Eaton would leave soon, had just sent him a farewell letter that was both poignant and pathetic. It reeked of a Moslem man eager not to be abandoned in a Christian land, of a royal heir in need of a new meal ticket, but it also showed Hamet graciously refusing to blame his misfortunes on Eaton. (A copy would be sent to President Jefferson.)

"I cannot forbear expressing to you, at this moment of our final separation, the deep sense of gratitude I feel for your generous and manly exertions in my behalf. . . . It is true my own means were small. I know indeed they did not answer your reasonable expectations. And this I am ready to admit is a good reason why you should not chuse to persevere in an enterprise hazardous in itself and perhaps doubtful in its issue. I ought therefore to say that I am satisfied with all your nation has done concerning me—I submit to the will of God and thank the King of America and all his servants for their kind dispositions towards me."

Hamet then asked Eaton for a monthly stipend and for a U.S. Navy ship to go pick up his family.

On July 1, Eaton gained a brief meeting with Rodgers. He apparently had little opportunity to recount his victory at Derne or his march across the desert, but Eaton did lobby for Hamet and did inform Rodgers that he would need $6,000 to pay off his troops. Eaton said he would give receipts for the sum, and he also offered to "hold [himself] responsible" for the amount. Once again, Eaton was putting his personal credit on the line to make sure his government acted honorably.

Eaton also repeated his request that he wanted to return home. His first choice of transport was not a frigate but a U.S. supply ship because he had learned that the *Ann* of Baltimore intended to take in salt at

Cagliari in Sardinia. Eaton had no hankering to lie on the beach; he told Rodgers he hoped to recover a debt owed to him by Count Porcile. (Relentless Eaton was still chasing that down-at-the-heels nobleman.)

Commodore Rodgers, weighing Eaton's request to pay off his mercenaries, resented the New Englander's abrupt tone. Rodgers demanded "a pay roll, with a statement of contingent expenses." Rodgers had been the junior officer back in Tunis when Commodore Morris' bailed Eaton out of his $32,000 debt. As for food for Eaton's mercenaries: "It is totally out of my power to order subsistence for Men that have not been reported to me, agreeable to the regulations prescribed by our Service. The Governor has this Ins.t made a complaint to me of some of the Greeks, landed here by the Vessels from Derne, having committed various outrages on the Inhabitants of the Town—I can only say on this subject that these people are accountable to the laws of the Land . . . and no interference of mine shall rescue them."

Yet another commodore was mucking with Eaton. Navy agent Dyson stopped feeding the European soldiers on the Fourth of July.

Sometime during that day of national celebration, it appears that Eaton finally got a chance to tell his tale of adventure to Commodore Rodgers. Maybe it was during the endless rounds of toasts that evening aboard the *Constitution*. The ship, fitted out with patriotic bunting and banners, was the site of a gala ball for navy officers and for the town's leading citizens and local aristocracy. (Several silver spoons would later be found missing.) A half dozen U.S. Navy ships bobbed proudly nearby, flags flapping. Eaton, at some point in the festivities, mesmerized the officers with his extraordinary tale of finding Hamet in Upper Egypt, coaxing him down the Nile, and shepherding him on that desperate desert march.

Two days later, gruff Rodgers performed a complete about-face in his approach to Eaton and Hamet. In a letter to the secretary of the navy, Rodgers called Eaton's mission "that Singular expedition." (For Rodgers, that adjective denoted high praise; he called the pint-size U.S. gunboats crossing the Atlantic Ocean "a singular phenomenon [which] will greatly astonish all Europe.")

Rodgers stated that he would immediately order the $6,000 paid to the Greeks and the rest of the mercenaries. "If it was double the Sum, policy dictates that it should be paid, and this you will no doubt be convinced of after reading the accompanying correspondence."

Rodgers also committed to paying $200 per month to support Hamet and his entourage in Malta or Messina and said he hoped one day to send him to the United States, if Hamet would agree. "He is a helpless unfortunate being and humanity dictates that something ought to be done for him."

Eaton was informed of all this good financial news. His loyal troops were paid off and dismissed; Hamet could survive on his allowance, but one matter still rankled him: Hamet's family held hostage in Tripoli. *Our three hundred prisoners were free; Hamet deserved his wife and five children.*

So, Eaton in his typical direct manner, arranged a meeting in Commodore Rodgers's cabin aboard the *Constitution.* He was rowed out through the harbor to the tall frigate, its sails furled, the American flag flapping. Eaton climbed over the side. He was no longer in a homemade general's uniform but in civilian clothes.

When he entered the cabin, he saw Tobias Lear standing alongside Commodore Rodgers. Eaton repeated to Rodgers his request for a small naval vessel, a brig perhaps, to go pick up Hamet's family "agreeable to the treaty." Aboard the gently rocking ship, Eaton continued to press his point. He later recalled of the meeting: "I urged the measure as a just claim on our national honour and our humanity, till at length Mr Lear observed, that it would be useless at present to send for Hamet's family; for that it was expected by the reigning bashaw, that they were not to be claimed until Hamet should be so withdrawn and so situated as to remove all apprehensions of his ever further attempting to regain his kingdom."

Eaton was flabbergasted. No one recorded his angry words to Lear. Perhaps he restrained himself in the presence of the commodore. From this moment on, he began to suspect "a secret engagement on the part of the commissioner of peace." Eaton soon queried other officers and heard rumors that the United States had no plans to compel Bashaw Yussef to return Hamet's family. Commodore Rodgers, a friend of Tobias Lear's, accepted the commissioner's advice and refused to send a brig.

This refusal, which Eaton blamed on Lear, infuriated him, and he started drinking a bit more and changing and rechanging his plans for leaving the region. He didn't sail on the *Congress*, *President*, or *Ann*. He lingered.

* * *

Over in Tripoli, mercurial Bashaw Yussef began to alter his perception of his peace treaty. While the $60,000 had saved him from disaster, nonetheless the sum was a far cry from the $1,000,000 he had once expected for his hostages. Also, his corsair fleet was in shambles, his finances still dire, and he feared the tough U.S. peace accord would embolden other countries to reduce their payments. Diplomat Zuchet reported that Yussef was acting even "more ferocious and barbarous" than usual. Yussef began to view the most trivial errors by his subjects as major crimes and started personally inflicting the punishments. "Recently, the Bashaw tired himself to the point of exhaustion beating a miserable wretch, who had tried to use the royal name to buy wheat . . . and then, to fully assuage all his rage, he poked the man seven or eight times in the genitals with the point of his dagger."

The Bashaw's rage was also felt at Derne. Eaton had written that Barron would have wept to see how the Americans were loved and respected for helping the townspeople. Now those same townspeople were being hunted down by Yussef's henchmen. Many of Derne's leading citizens were kidnapped and never reappeared. "This has the look of a ruined country," wrote Zuchet.

It was an odd, unpleasant summer on the Mediterranean for some officers of the U.S. Navy as well. The precipitous end to the war with Tripoli seemed to throw the navy into a kind of malaise. Bickering and backbiting abounded. Rodgers made some remark about Commodore Barron dallying and preferring not to fight. (The exact remark hasn't survived.)

Captain Bainbridge soon boarded the *Constitution* and informed Rodgers that Captain James Barron had heard that Rodgers had spoken disrespectfully about his brother Samuel, "for which aspersion he would call on him to answer in a proper place and a proper time and that Commodore Barron's illness prevented him from doing it immediately."

Rodgers wasn't the least bit cowed by this threat, especially since the Barron brothers and Bainbridge were sailing later that same day for the United States aboard the *President*. Rodgers said he fully expected to hear from Barron in America. As Bainbridge made ready to exit, Rodgers added: "Tell him if I do not hear from him, I shall impute it to a want of . . . what no Gentleman who wears a uniform should be deficient in." Bainbridge later wrote about his reaction to that insult. "Presuming he alluded to 'courage,' I replied I would not deliver such a message." (Some might have presumed Rodgers referred to "testicles.")

A couple of weeks later, by mid-July, seven gunboats arrived from America (too late to fight against Tripoli), and Jefferson's armada of six frigates, four brigs, two schooners, one sloop, and numerous gunboats were now all dressed up in the Mediterranean with nowhere to go. Rodgers took many of the ships to Tunis and rattled his saber, and wrote about wanting to make the Bey "call for mercy on bended knees." Ultimately, however, Tobias Lear, who handled the negotiations for Rodgers, allowed the Bey of Tunis to wriggle off the hook. Lear agreed to delay the final settlement until after a Tunisian minister, Soliman Melli-Melli, went on an all-expenses-paid diplomatic trip to the United States. (Secretary Madison, acting as a good host, would later approve the cost of hiring a Greek prostitute for Melli-Melli, and would expense the item under "appropriations to foreign intercourse.")

After Tunis, Tobias Lear arranged for a vacation with his wife in Catania on Sicily, a town famed for its ancient buildings built of volcanic stone. When headwinds prevented a small boat from getting them there, Rodgers assigned the navy schooner *Enterprize* to carry the consul general and his wife to the historic locale. After that, they took a leisurely two months to return to Lear's post as consul in Algiers.

By then, William Eaton was homeward bound, stewing in his bitterness, inexpressibly eager to recount his version of the events that had ended the U.S. war with Tripoli and to criticize the administration for caving in just when the United States could have set an example for the world by defying the Barbary pirates. He was convinced that no ransom

needed to have been paid, that the consular present should have been officially abolished, and that no dollar figure should ever again be attached
to freeing an American. The squandered opportunity galled him, and he
intended to place the blame squarely and loudly on Tobias Lear and
Thomas Jefferson.

CHAPTER 24 *Homecoming*

EATON DECIDED TO BRING four horses home from the Barbary
Coast. Accommodating the thoroughbreds had limited his options in selecting a ship, so he was forced to miss Sardinia and
again failed to collar Count Porcile about getting his money back. In
Eaton's hostile mind-set, perhaps he might have taken beautiful Anna
hostage again and stowed her next to the horses.

The U.S. transport ship *Franklin* left Gibraltar on September 24, in
company with two American merchant sloops, the *Harmony* and the
Mary Maryland. Eaton, traveling with his four horses and a fourteen-
year-old Egyptian serving boy, passed forty days in crossing the Atlantic.
This did nothing to improve his mood.

As the *Franklin* entered Chesapeake Bay the first week of November
of 1805, Eaton wrote a long letter to his fifteen-year-old stepdaughter,
Sarah. (He was still too angry to communicate directly with his wife.)
This letter captures the bleakness in his soul and his mounting irritation
at finding himself underappreciated not only by the U.S. government but
also by his own family.

> *I am yet at sea but a pilot boat just raises to our sight . . . —and
> will soon be alongside to receive this note—possibly I may enter the
> Chesapeake with him; most certainly I shall if I find any person on
> board who can answer me a thousand interesting questions. Where are
> all my relations and friends in Brimfield? Or have I none there? Not a*

*syllable have I received from anyone of them since the date of the third
day after my leaving this coast [in July 1804]—Am I forgotten by the
children of my love? Where is Eliza [now age ten]? I once thought her
like an angel, good—If she has ceased to love her Pa, still should fillial
duty prevail on her once in a year to pay him the respect of one
seeming friendly line—My amiable Charlotte [age eight], have not
her fingers been taught the art of communicating with those she loves?
I think she is old enough to write a letter to a friend who will make no
unkind criticisms upon it—And my dear little too sensible Almira [age
five]?*

*Sarah, you would have done kindly to have occasionally mentioned
her in a letter. But no person has mentioned either of them to me since
I left them. If my daughters knew how sincerely I love them, certainly
they would be solicitous to let me know their welfare . . . —Not a day
nor an hour has passed these last long eighteen months that they have
not occupied my affections—and, on serious occasions, when the shafts
of death flew thick about me; if a thought could act which was not
altogether employed in the scene, it was a prayer to Heaven for their
felicity—Is there no sympathy of soul that should sometimes make
them think of p-a? Or has he imparted nothing of the natural
sensibility of his own soul to his daughters? I have indeed thought it
cruel that nobody should write me from home. M-a, you tell me,
cannot write often as she has many family engagements. Can it be
true, My Sarah, that the family engagements of your Mama are such
as not to enable her to redeem one half hour annually to address the
guardian of her children? Then must they be singularly pressing!
Ought she not to believe that I take an interest in most of the
family concerns and should always be happy to know how they
succeed? But I still hope that you have not any engagements which
you will permit so much to occupy your attention as not to allow
you a winter's evening after the receipt of this to write me
everything which has happened since my departure which you
may imagine will be interesting to me—And tell Eliza to send me
also at least a sample of her improvement—Address me at Washington
City.*

The sailboat carrying the local pilot reached alongside the *Franklin*, and the man from the Virginia coast climbed aboard.

Within minutes, William Eaton discovered—to his immense surprise—that he was a national hero, and not just a minor celebrity but a front-page-of-every-newspaper-in-America military hero. For more than two months, unbeknownst to him, the nation had been applauding his exploits.

The news of the victory and treaty had reached the United States two months back, on August 28, first arriving in Salem, Massachusetts. The newspaper editor had written: "With heartfelt joy, I announce to you the fortunate and honorable TERMINATION OF THE WAR WITH TRIPOLI. A vessel (*Belle-Isle*, Captain Leach) is now entering our port from the Mediterranean and brings the important news that Genl Eaton gained a great victory, on the 10th June, over the Bashaw's army, slaughtering a large part of his forces—he is wounded but it is hoped not badly. He dictated the terms of peace on the spot. Our prisoners are all to be released without ransom, of course no tribute in future."

This glorious bit of misinformation was reprinted down along the coast, until it reached Washington and appeared in the Jefferson-friendly *National Intelligencer* on September 4. Every day, more skewed updates popped up from various letters and verbal accounts from the likes of Captain Leach and others aboard the *Belle-Isle*, which had sailed from Naples on June 25. The *Salem Register* reported everyone in the small but ferocious American Army killed except Eaton. The *Boston Gazette* had the ex-Bashaw conquering Tripoli city, directed "by the intrepid spirit of our countryman, Gen. Eaton." The *New Hampshire Gazette*, a newspaper in Tobias Lear's home state, trumpeted Eaton's success: "This event [the peace treaty] is said to have been accelerated by the success of an expedition projected and executed by William Eaton, Esq., late consul of the United States at Tunis . . . His genius is said to have stimulated the ex-Bashaw to raise a force to recover the throne of Tripoli; of which Mr. Eaton was appointed Generalissimo."

In Philadelphia, *Poulson's Daily Advertiser* breathlessly confessed: "The Public are anxious to learn some particulars of their countryman, who has recently acquired so much fame in Africa."

News traveled haphazardly in those days. A private letter was as good a source as any. The *National Intelligencer* on September 6 quoted a letter received on September 1 in New York from Boston, which stated that Eaton had gained a great victory one hundred leagues from Tripoli, then marched on the main city and dethroned the Bashaw. "And Mr. Eaton then formed a treaty, the first article of which provides for the immediate release of the American captives."

Journalists were so eager for details that it led one paper to rant about the fact that no government officials happened to be in Washington in early September to open the newly arrived Tripoli dispatches. "Our servants, Tom, Bob, Jim, Albert [Jefferson, Smith, Madison, Gallatin] and god knows who else are out of the way, we are not allowed to taste till they have fully feasted."

Back on September 10, the USS *President* had reached Hampton Roads, delivering Captain Bainbridge and other freed officers. Would Bainbridge try to burst the Eaton bubble? Apparently not right away.

Although caviling began over various aspects of the treaty, one central fact of the coverage remained, and it ranked as fairly astounding. The Republican press (manipulated by Jefferson and his stalwarts) and the Federalist press (controlled by Jefferson's enemies), newspapers that couldn't agree on anything, both decided to elevate William Eaton as a bona fide flag-waving, enemy-crushing American military hero. Not since the public had enshrined Stephen Decatur for burning the *Philadelphia* in Tripoli harbor had anyone been raised this high.

The United States, less than thirty years from the Declaration of Independence, was clearly starved for heroes to replace the British ones, who had been spoon-fed to colonial schoolchildren for generations. Washington, general and statesman, was already a demigod. Many empty pedestals awaited statues in the American pantheon.

In Richmond, Virginia, in September, the leading citizens had hosted a dinner to honor Captain Bainbridge. After a fine meal, tradition held that guests would remain to deliver as many as two dozen decorous toasts, while downing more than a few glasses. (Drunken excess sometimes marred these events.) The toasts were arranged in order of importance, usually the "American people" ranked first, then the president, and so on. The seventh toast that night had gone to William Eaton: "Cambyses and Alexander traversed deserts to enslave nations; the American chief to liberate his brave countrymen." (No record has survived of the look at that moment on the face of Bainbridge, who had relentlessly opposed Eaton's mission.) Tobias Lear had received the fourteenth toast, just ahead of the Bashaw of Tripoli, who was encouraged "to profit by the lectures he has received on the laws of nations."

Jefferson, Republicans, Federalists—everyone in September and October embraced this unembraceable (and not yet arrived) man named Eaton. So starved were the public for information about him that even anecdotes about his courtship of widow Eliza were published in the Republican-backed *Richmond Enquirer*. This one ran: After being asked to marry him, Eliza had demanded that Eaton quit the military, to which our hero had replied: "Madam, I love you much but I love glory more." The hero machine was beginning to churn. The *Albany Register* called him "William Eaton IV or Modern Africanus." Newspapers around this time in October printed Midshipman Pascal Paoli Peck's highly dramatic letter of July 4, ensuring Eaton's heroism.

On Sunday, November 10, William Eaton, the hero, came ashore at Hampton, Virginia. Jefferson's newspaper, *National Inquirer*, called him "a distinguished officer and patriot."

Eaton was hardly off the boat when one hundred of the leading citizens of Virginia threw him a banquet on November 14 at the Eagle Tavern in Richmond. Etiquette and humility forbade any toasts to the guest of honor while he remained in the room. So when Eaton departed, one Alexander Stuart rose and said: "General Eaton—May each American when required, shew fortitude equal to his, in the cause of his country."

The following day, the pro-Jefferson *Richmond Enquirer* published a worshipful piece about Eaton. (One can only imagine the feelings of Eaton, after years of bitterness, reading this kind of idolatry; his close friend Charles Prentiss once observed that Eaton never shied away from receiving "a bare-faced prodigality of praise.")

GENERAL WILLIAM EATON. This brave and meritorious American has been among us. . . . He reached this city on Tuesday evening (Nov. 12th) on his way to the North. . . . His arrival was soon and rapidly spread; his countenance, the dimensions of his person, the wound in his wrist, the spirit of his conversation, became the topics of remark, and almost everyone was anxious to see or to tell of the appearance of Eaton. . . . The interest which he excited and that attention which he received from our most respected citizens are at least sufficient demonstrations that his countrymen are neither ignorant of his services, nor indifferent to his merits.

Let no man pretend to chaunt forth the ingratitude of republics! . . . If General Eaton is indeed contented with possessing the respect of his countrymen, his largest ambition must be satisfied. Though he has not received that enthusiastic respect which is due to the man who penned the declaration of American independence, or to him who gave it its last seal at the siege of York, he has at least received the gratitude which is due to the man of enterprise, who put to sleep the Turkish jealousy in Egypt, passed over the Lybian Desert, mastered the fortifications at Derne with an inconsiderable army, overthrew the troops of the Bashaw of Tripoli and contributed to give freedom to 300 American prisoners. Gen. Eaton has thus been received among us, and there can be no doubt that he will meet with the same reception throughout the union, without any distinction of principles or parties.

The appearance of Gen. Eaton is considerably in his favour. His person is of the middling order, but erect and dignified. His countenance is animated, good-humoured, expressive more of enterprising project than deep research. His eye is brilliant and full of fire. In conversation, his conceptions are quick, his style eloquent and laconic. Those who knew him in the army are surprised at the intellectual energy he now displays . . .

. . . Had Col. Lear waived the negotiation until the gallant Eaton had ransomed our prisoners with the sword, our triumph would have been much more glorious: but it would have been an indelible disgrace upon the annals of our nation, had the lives of so many men been sacrificed through a misguided oeconomy.

The debate over the treaty was just starting, but no one *yet* wanted it to interfere with the hero worship. Disgruntled, but at least not this minute, Eaton embraced his stardom.

Accompanied by a fourteen-year-old Egyptian and four Arabian horses, Eaton headed north from Richmond toward Washington by stagecoach. The carriage lurching over the rutted roads no doubt reminded him of his worst days at sea. At Fredericksburg, Virginia, on Sunday, November 17, the town's elite waylaid Eaton and begged the military hero to remain a few days so they could organize a banquet in his honor. At 3 P.M. on Tuesday afternoon, the well-dressed citizens gathered at Farish's Tavern. The first toast smacks of Eaton: "The United States—Tho' peace is its policy, yet war is preferable to dishonorable tribute."

On November 22, Eaton reached the sprawling odd enclave of Washington City. His timing was exquisite because this bureaucratic headquarters was just roaring back to life, with Congress about to resume session.

Almost immediately upon arrival, Eaton, riding high, sent an aggressive letter to Secretary of State Madison requesting that his expense accounts from Tunis finally be settled. "I believe it will be no difficult task to show that I have consumed eight years of my life, and embarked all the property I possessed or have acquired in establishing the point that our relations with Barbary may be maintained without the humilitation of tribute." He added that he also now would be asking compensation for the ransoming of the slave girl, Anna Porcile, because Count Porcile had sent him a letter stating that President Jefferson had forgiven the debt. He hoped for as little delay as possible. "My finances are low, and I am extremely desirous of returning to domestic life."

Just as William Eaton entered the nation's capital, so did William Plumer, a senator from New Hampshire. This was fortuitous for history, because Plumer's diary recounts the shooting-star arc of Eaton's reception, and provides an eyewitness account of Eaton and Jefferson as the two men jostled for the high ground over Tripoli.

From Plumer we learn that as soon as Eaton reached town, Jefferson invited the hero to dine at the President's House. No details have survived of that meeting.

The leading citizens of Washington City voted to host a public dinner at Stelle's Hotel on Thanksgiving, Thursday, November 28, to canonize Eaton. Plumer had arrived the night before after a ten-day journey south from Epping, New Hampshire; he had covered the last 150 miles from Philadelphia in what he regarded as an impressive 34 hours of mailstage riding.

The festive dinner at Stelle's lasted more than five hours. Man after important man elbowed his way to shake the hand of General Eaton. He often fixed listeners with a deep stare of those blue eyes. His voice full of command, he plunged into telling military exploits. While the previous banquet had led off with the possibility of war for the sake of honor, this feast in the heart of Jeffersonland took a different tack. "The people of the United States: honest, intelligent and brave; too happy themselves to disturb the happiness of others." Two bands—the Marine Band and Jefferson's Italian ensemble—stood off to one side to follow each toast with an appropriate splash of music.

Though back in the United States only two weeks, Eaton was stunned by the increased divisiveness poisoning American politics. Each party tried to attach Eaton—an independent-minded Federalist—to their causes. That night Eaton was allowed what was called a "Volunteer Toast." He boomed: "The FEDERAL UNION—Let political dissension and individual rancour be absorbed in that love of country which shall teach violence and rapacity that we are one!" (Few listeners at the time realized that Eaton actually meant those high-sounding words, and that he would not toe the line of either political party.)

The following day, Senator Plumer paid a call on President Jefferson. Arriving at 11 A.M., he spent an hour with him. "The President was in an undress—Blue coat, red vest, cloth coloured small cloths—white hose, ragged slippers with his toes out—clean linen—but hair disheveled." Jefferson's rebellion from British formality was reaching new extremes.

Plumer took advantage of the president being "social & very communicative" to pepper him with questions about Barbary Coast affairs, among other topics. Jefferson said that the United States should not pay tribute, and that while we were locked in a long-term tributary treaty with Algiers, Jefferson stated emphatically that the United States would not pay tribute to Tunis. He didn't mention Tripoli.

A few days later, on Tuesday, December 3, Thomas Jefferson, at a dangerous period in the history of the young country, delivered his "state of the nation" remarks to Congress. Plumer called the message more "energetic & warlike than any [Jefferson] ever sent to Congress."

The United States at that moment faced crises on two foreign fronts: Spain and England. After complaining about the borders set for the Louisiana Purchase, Spain had begun to harass American frontiersmen and Mississippi cargo boats. Many Federalists and even some Republicans lobbied for war to snatch away the Floridas and silence the lumbering giant. And, equally ominously, Great Britain—in a fierce fight with Napoleon—had started to stop American ships in the Atlantic, denying the rights of American vessels to carry goods under the flag of neutrality.

Jefferson in his speech did not call for war or for expanding the small U.S. Army. He did, however, suggest a new concept for the state militias that men aged 18 to 26 be parceled off to a separate force that would be more ready to fight than older family men. (This tidbit hardly thrilled the military men.)

Jefferson then delivered his first official words on Eaton and the Tripoli treaty. As with all of Jefferson's speeches, his words were carefully chosen and precise and perhaps subtly misleading. He elevated Eaton, took little credit for himself, and omitted the $60,000 ransom payment.

> I congratulate you on the liberation of our fellow citizens who were stranded on the coast of Tripoli & made prisoners of war. In a government bottomed on the will of all, the life & liberty of every individual citizen becomes interesting to all. In the treaty therefore which has concluded our warfare with that state an article for the ransom of our citizens has been agreed to. An operation by land, by a small band of our countrymen & others for the occasion in conjunction with the troops of the ex-basha of that country, gallantly conducted by our late consul Eaton and their successful enterprise

on the city of Derne, which contributed doubtless to the impression which produced peace: and the conclusion of this prevented opportunities of which the officers and men of our squadron destined for Tripoli would have availed themselves, to emulate the acts of valour exhibited by their brethren in the attack of the last year.

Jefferson had clearly weighed how to characterize Eaton. He chose a former title, "late consul," rather than identify his post as "our naval agent." A handwritten draft of his speech shows that Jefferson crossed out the word *important* before the city of Derne. Eaton's efforts, to Jefferson's mind, "contributed to the impression which produced peace." In an age that favored platitude and hyperbolic praise, Jefferson was holding back. One can only speculate that the president worried about elevating Eaton too high.

The Federalist press was beginning to complain about Tobias Lear, the mistreatment of Hamet, and, by implication, the administration's overall handling of the peace at Tripoli. Word was also spreading that Eaton, when not downing congratulatory toasts, was the source of those complaints. So Jefferson directed the secretary of the navy to ask Eaton point-blank to clarify the U.S. commitment to Hamet.

Eaton stood yet again at a strategic crossroad in his life. He could back the president by downplaying his disappointment over the treaty and the handling of Hamet. By doing so, he would be ensured a long status as a national hero, and might be short-listed for an appointment as a U.S. Army general. He also still owed the government the huge sum of $40,000 for his unsettled expenses in Tunis and could expect favorable treatment. Or he could stand honest to what he perceived as the administration's failings.

On December 4, Eaton spent the evening at Captain Coyle's boardinghouse as the guest of William Plumer and a handful of congressmen and senators. "His company was gratifying," wrote Plumer. "The accounts he gave of Egypt & his travel over the deserts with an armed force & the attack & capture of Derne were interesting. He is a man of information & great enterprize." Plumer, a very critical and sober-minded man, was impressed.

The following day, Eaton wrote his reply to Jefferson's question, in a letter to the secretary of the navy. He wrote that he had reviewed all the written correspondence between Commodore Barron and himself, reread his Convention with Hamet, and pored over Hamet's subsequent letters from Syracuse.

He concluded: "It is impossible for me to undertake to say that the bashaw has not been deceived." Eaton was as stubborn as ever. His death wish took no vacations. "Nor can I by any shape in which the subject can be viewed reconcile the manner of his being abandoned with those principles of national Justice and honor which has hitherto marked our character."

This very harsh letter almost marks a declaration of war against Jefferson. Eaton refused to be drawn into Jeffersonian niceties over language. He wrote that he always considered "co-operation" nearly synonymous with "alliance." He assumed that the engagement to cooperate excluded using Hamet as an "instrument" . . . especially since the president and the secretary of the navy always said we would "chastise the enemy."

Then Eaton added an anecdote that clearly revealed both his passion and his recklessness. "On entering the ground of war with Hamet Bashaw, Mr. O'Bannon and myself united in a resolution to perish with him before the walls of Tripoli or to triumph with him within those walls."

With those words, with that letter, Eaton had transformed the president into an enemy. To Jefferson's precise way of thinking, this sort of oath far exceeded Eaton's commission. It is quite clear that this military bravado infuriated Jefferson. The president would bide his time before striking back, but he would pick a shrewd moment to respond and even shrewder words.

Jefferson was then preoccupied with foreign affair issues. The disputes with England and Spain were not esoteric matters of principle; British ships impeded American nautical commerce, then the lifeblood of New England; Spanish hostility hampered American pioneering expansion. Jefferson, an isolationist who dreaded entanglements, was being dragged into European conflicts.

The Senate began to debate whether to ratify the Tripoli treaty. The

House began considering whether to honor William Eaton with a commemorative sword; some Federalists pushed for a gold medal as well. A great many speeches tried to evaluate Eaton's unusual achievement. Can a man without high military rank win such an award? Was he a private citizen when he acted? Nothing happened at this time in Washington City without the blessing of the powerful president. The debate over Eaton's reward grew heated and was shunted off to a committee, never to re-emerge intact.

Since Eaton's defiant letter of December 5 to the administration remained unpublished, Eaton was still the toast of Jefferson's town. Senator Plumer, who detested crowds, sought out Eaton on the morning of December 14 and found him eating breakfast alone in his hotel room. The pair spent a few hours together, and Eaton unburdened himself of all his complaints. He unloaded double barrels of bile; he had the naïveté to believe that he could criticize Tobias Lear and Samuel Barron without being seen as attacking Jefferson. Eaton told Plumer that he actually thought highly of the U.S. government but attributed the Tripoli failure to the "mean pusillanimous selfish conduct of Lear."

This would become Eaton's rant, a diatribe that he would launch into in taprooms, in stagecoaches, in council chambers. While he would refine it, Plumer witnessed it in early form: Lear was "a man of little mind—jealous—cowardly and, what was worse, *false*." No ransom needed to have been paid. Hamet is "a sober man—of talents, courage & enterprize." Lear withheld supplies from the mission, but Eaton and other officers bought them on credit. If we had marched on Tripoli, we would have taught all the Barbary regencies to fear and venerate the United States. Hamet, by slinking off, is ruined among the Arabs. It is "confidently asserted" that Lear secretly agreed that Yussef need not bother to return Hamet's family.

Eaton could not let go of the lost opportunities; he couldn't bask; he wanted, in effect, to finish his mission.

Politics rumbled along on Capitol Hill, with the usual horse-trading. Congress debated a bill that would forbid the *importation* of slaves after 1808; Lewis and Clark continued to send letters home from America's new backyard.

Around Christmas, Eaton decided to head home to Brimfield. Being so popular, Eaton's plans preceded him. The citizens of Philadelphia sent him a letter that he received en route inviting him to a banquet in his honor on January 3. Eaton climbed aboard the stage, operated by the United States Mail from Baltimore to Philadelphia. This federal outfit, which plied the round-trip daily, consisted of 14 drivers, 65 horses, and 11 carriages. Taking a mail stage meant not stopping at night.

On December 30, America's most popular military hero, a man with no official title, found himself comfortably ensconced in a fine room in a Philadelphia hotel. Eaton, at ease, wrote a joking letter to Preble about his upcoming banquet circuit. "I am arrested here and put under keepers for trial next Thursday [January 3]—arrangements are making, I am informed, at Elizabethstown [N.J. ferry stop], New York, New Haven, Hartford and Springfield to stop me on the road."

On that same day when Eaton wrote Preble, the U.S. Senate in an openly antagonistic manner passed a resolution requesting that President Jefferson lay before it all documents relating to Tripoli and the treaty, especially regarding Lear, Hamet, and Eaton. This was no pro forma request.

Thomas Jefferson took time out that same day to continue investigating the Tripoli discord. On a scrap of paper, he wrote himself a little note about the State Department's instructions regarding Hamet. "The cooperation of the exile was to cost no more than 20,000 dollars at the utmost, but it was referred to as little important." The whittling down of Eaton was beginning. Jefferson wanted to be well armed with facts.

The man whose mission was deemed "little important" was being feted all along the northeast coast. Eaton's name was even being mentioned for Congress, or as an army general in case of war. Some speculated he might replace Tobias Lear as consul general in Barbary.

Thomas Jefferson—losing control of Congress—had other plans for him.

CHAPTER 25 *Jefferson vs. Eaton*

I do not however insinuate that Mr. Jefferson is a model of
goodness. He has too much cunning.

—SENATOR WILLIAM PLUMER ON THOMAS JEFFERSON, 1806

JEFFERSON WAITED UNTIL Eaton had departed from Washington City before replying to any of Eaton's charges. Although Eaton had claimed to be lobbing shots at Lear and Barron, the president clearly regarded himself as in the line of fire. Around that time, it had become open season for both parties to attack the president. Even though Jefferson's Republican party had decimated the Federalists in the recent elections, Jefferson was facing an internal revolt led by vitriolic John Randolph of Jefferson's own Virginia.

Thomas Jefferson was no longer the shy young man who had sneaked away to write the Declaration of Independence; he had grown to become a masterful politician, but his style of governing often baffled his contemporaries. He rarely confronted the opposition head-on in a bull rush, but rather pursued several secret strategies at once. In a diary entry one Sunday early in 1806, Plumer tried to evaluate this soft-spoken, brilliant philosopher-writer.

The result of my investigation is that Mr. Jefferson has as much honesty as men in the higher grades of society usually have—& indeed I think more. He is a man of science. But he is very credulous—

he knows little of the nature of man—very little indeed. He has traveled the tour of Europe—he has been Minister at Versailles. He has had great opportunities to know man—but he has neglected them. He is not a practical man. He has much knowledge of books—of insects—of shells & of all that charms a virtuoso but he knows not the human heart. He is a closet politician—but not a practical statesman. He has much fine sense but little of that plain common sense so requisite to business & which in fact governs the world.

An infidel in religion—but in every thing else credulous to a fault! Alas [the] man is himself a contradiction!

On Monday, January 13, 1806, the president, standing in the Executive Mansion's drawing room, handed his final draft of a speech on the Tripoli war to his secretary, Mr. Coles, who then walked through the muddy streets to deliver it to the one-winged Capitol building. There, in the chill, it was read aloud into the record. Jefferson, with lawyerly precision, aimed to justify the treaty and to knock Eaton off his pedestal.

The president began by defending "concerted operations by those who have a common enemy" but stated that neither side was bound to guarantee the ultimate goals of the other. This precise philosophy was so Jeffersonian in its otherworldliness. He moved quickly to an examination of how events had played out.

"We authorized Commodore Barron, then proceeding with his squadron, to enter into an understanding with Hamet. . . . In order to avail him of the advantages of Mr. Eaton's knowledge of circumstances, an occasional employment was provided for the latter as an agent for the navy in that sea." (Jefferson was downgrading Eaton from the rank of "general" to a part-time employee.)

After explaining that the plan called for the U.S. Navy to attack by sea and Hamet by land, the president then laid the blame for the abandonment of Hamet squarely on . . . Hamet. The prince at Derne failed to command any resources or local support. "This hope was then at an end, and we certainly had never contemplated nor were we prepared to land an army of our own, or to raise, pay or subsist an army of Arabs to march from Derne to Tripoli."

Jefferson lauded Barron for his timing in aborting Eaton's mission and Lear for his in seeking peace.

Instead of casting a few crumbs of praise to Eaton for capturing Derne, Jefferson hammered him, implying that the former army captain had far exceeded his orders from Washington City. Jefferson argued that Eaton was supposed to take sides in a civil war, not create one from scratch.

"In operations at such a distance, it becomes necessary to leave much to the discretion of the agents employed; but events may still turn up beyond the limits of that discretion. Unable in such a case to consult his Government, a zealous citizen will act as he believes that would direct him, were it apprised of the circumstances, and will take on himself responsibility. In all these cases, the purity and patriotism of the motives should shield the agent from blame, and even secure a sanction, where the error is not too injurious."

Jefferson had further downgraded Eaton from part-timer to "zealous citizen" and now also insinuated that his actions fell into some category of "error."

Jefferson—in a long convoluted sentence—added that if Hamet, through misperceptions caused by Eaton, thought himself promised more than this administration intended, then the United States "establishing a character of liberality and magnanimity" should help him.

While ready to toss a few coins to Hamet, Jefferson had not yet finished skewering Eaton. He ended by accusing him of contradicting himself: "The ground he has taken being different, not only from our views, but from those expressed by himself on former occasions."

The speech seemed well crafted and apt to crush Eaton. Fair-minded, Senator Plumer heard the speech, perused the two dozen documents sitting on the Senate table, and came to a stunning conclusion: "The [documents] clearly show the imprudence & folly of Lear in opening at that time a negociation & making a treaty with the reigning bashaw. There is no doubt had Eaton been supported a few weeks more,

Tripoli by the joint attack of our fleet & army must have surrendered at discretion. The documents clearly show that we basely & ungenerously deserted the ex-Bashaw—that the moment his measures operated in our favor & secured to us a peace we abandoned him & his friends to wretchedness & ruin! I cannot but despise & detest that vile wretch of a *Lear!*"

Indeed, all Federalists and a surprising number of Jefferson's own Republicans were not swayed by the president. An anti-administration groundswell on Tripoli and other issues was mounting. The Federalists rushed to harness Eaton's charisma to defy the administration.

A few days later, Senator Stephen Bradley (Federalist, Vermont) dashed off a letter to Eaton, who hadn't even reached home yet, and implored him to return immediately to obtain that "justice which you have so richly merited from your country and the world." The Senate had appointed a committee to review Hamet Karamanli's application for aid, and the point man for research was none other than Bradley, who happened to be Eaton's first patron.

Bradley gleefully wrote to Eaton: "The Tripoline treaty is not agreed to as yet, its fate is doubtful, the probability is, it will not be ratified." The senator grew giddy with Jefferson-bashing. "You have no conception of the indignation with which [Lear's negotiating] is viewed and unless the President should immediately recall Lear I doubt whether the Senate will not express their opinion freely on the subject."

Eaton—the newly minted hero who had left Washington after Christmas—was at that moment detouring to Boston for more banquets and a private dinner with his friend Commodore Preble.

Then on a day in late January, he finally reached home in Brimfield, Massachusetts, and found waiting for him this enthusiastic letter from Bradley. Eaton hugged his wife, Eliza; and for the first time, he held his son, one-year-old William Sykes Eaton. Then, with little hesitation, he announced he would retrace his steps to Washington City. He was apparently still peeved at his wife and family for their spotty letter writing. After eighteen months gone, duty called again. Two years earlier he had written to Eliza: "In the bonds of wedlock, you have been ten years a widow." Now, that was even more true.

The hero did stay home another week, long enough to be feted by neighbors and to be treated well in the Federalist heart of the nation. The governor of Massachusetts appointed him a justice of the peace for a seven-year term.

On February 3, 1806, during a break from southbound stagecoaches, he wrote in a jaunty tone to his cohort-in-arms, Preble, that he was heading back to the nation's capital "with a view of helping Aunt Lear and her Lieutenants Barron and Rodgers out of some difficulty."

Preble, upon receiving Eaton's buoyant note, replied in kind: "If government do you the justice they ought and which your Gallant and meritorious service deserve, they will order you a medal, a sword, a Brigadier Gen.l Commission, a pay until promoted, recall Lear and appoint you Consul General in his stead."

Days later, with Eaton still catching ferries and carriages, the Massachusetts Senate voted to reward Eaton with 10,000 acres in Maine, then still part of Massachusetts. He could choose from state-owned tracts anywhere but in ten townships along the Penobscot River. This marked a plum grant. (Eaton, in a pinch, could sell the land for about half a dollar an acre, thus valuing the gift at a minimum of $5,000, at a time when manual laborers earned about $1 a day.) The Senate and House of Representatives of this Commonwealth praised Eaton for "undaunted courage and brilliant services so eminently contributed to release a large number of his fellow citizens, late prisoners in Tripoili from the chains of slavery." He was being showered with honors in the Federalist northeast.

Eaton arrived in Washington amid some of the strangest weather to hit the nation's capital. While the temperature hovered around 58 degrees at one point on Monday, three inches of snow fell later that same day. The mantle of white temporarily dignified the muddy expanses, but warm weather melted the snow the next morning.

Senator Bradley wasted no time in contacting Eaton about testifying before the Hamet Committee, and the two teamed up to track down more witnesses. William Wormley, lieutenant of the U.S. Marines and one of the *Philadelphia* prisoners, happened to be in Washington City. Wormley, as did most marines, lionized Eaton, and he said he thought he'd still be a prisoner without the capture of Derne. "I moreover believe that general Eaton could have marched from Derne to Tripoli, almost without firing a shot," he said, citing the country's instability.

Over these winter days, Eaton was in effect stalking Jefferson. He wanted to force the president to change his mind and begin pushing for relief for Hamet, punishment for Lear, reward for Eaton, and a settlement of his accounts. Jefferson, meanwhile, was occupied elsewhere, trying desperately to avoid getting entangled with England, Spain, and France in the endless Napoleonic wars. His job wasn't made easier by snide warmongering comments from his own *Republican* Congressmen: "We have a bold and enterprising sergeant-at-arms, who is ambitious to execute our orders," observed John Randolph. "Shall we send him with [a club] in a canoe to Admiral Collingwood to order him to surrender the royal fleet of Great Britain?"

* * *

Amid all this turmoil, a Machiavellian figure suddenly appeared in Washington City and began to try to entice both Jefferson and Eaton to help him. The man's disruptive force, his utter deviousness, would cause miracles. It would one day reunite Jefferson and Eaton in a common cause; it would solve Eaton's financial woes; and it would almost split the United States in half.

Aaron Burr hit town in late February. Discarded from Jefferson's 1804 presidential ticket after he killed Alexander Hamilton in a duel, Burr was ever conniving to resurrect himself, on a grand scale. The former vice president was then *secretly* plotting to raise a private army to conquer parts of the Louisiana Purchase and Spanish Mexico and create an empire that would rival the United States. In some whispered tellings, he confessed that he hoped even to overthrow the administration. "Nothing will satisfy that man but the throne of God," sniped Senator Rufus King.

Unaware of the man's empire plans, Jefferson on February 22, 1806, invited Burr to dine with him. Burr tried to cajole his way to a plum diplomatic post but Jefferson turned him down. Charming and self-confident, Burr smilingly hinted that he might reveal secrets about Jefferson. "Perhaps no man's language was ever so apparently explicit and at the same time so covert and indefinite," observed one senator.

Burr then sought out Eaton. The two men began drinking together, sometimes in Washington taverns, often in private. Burr began to probe the open wound of Eaton's anger at the administration over Tripoli and over Jefferson's recent attempt to humiliate him. The 50-year-old former Revolutionary War colonel, dubbed "Little Burr" behind his back, gradually revealed his conspiracy plans to Eaton and eventually offered him the post of third in command of the new army, behind Burr himself and U.S. Army general James Wilkinson. "I listened to the exposition of Col. Burr's views with seeming acquiescence," Eaton later wrote.

Though maybe a bit sympathetic at first, Eaton grew deeply disturbed by Burr's plot. Around this time, Eaton did a strange thing, an act quintessentially Eaton, which in its own odd way, revealed his patriotism. Since Eaton had no written evidence against Burr, he decided he would try to avert the crisis by asking Jefferson to appoint Burr as an ambassador in Europe, somewhere far away from Mexico or Louisiana.

Succeeding in gaining a few minutes alone with the president, Eaton proposed that Burr go on a special mission to Spain or even England. Jefferson balked at the idea. Then Eaton warned Jefferson that within eighteen months Burr might incite a rebellion in the West. The president dismissed that possibility, saying he counted on the "integrity and the attachment to the Union" of American citizens. With historical hindsight, it's easy to see that Jefferson probably perceived Eaton as a messenger for Burr, delivering a veiled threat in order to land Burr a diplomatic post. This exchange did nothing to endear Eaton to the president.

That unpleasant impression was cemented days later when Burr again approached Jefferson for a diplomatic post and again threatened to embarrass the president. Jefferson later recalled saying to Burr: "I never have done a single act or been concerned in any transaction which I fear to have fully laid open." That kind of sanctimoniousness irritated Jefferson's opponents.

While Burr's plot simmered in secret meetings nationwide, Eaton was still trying to finish the more mundane task of settling his accounts from Tunis. His letter to Madison in November had gone unanswered. He now wrote again, and this time Madison replied almost immediately with some very *un*helpful news. Madison informed him that he considered Eaton's expenses so far beyond standard State Department items such as house rental, stable fees, and transportation that Congress must intervene. Eaton, whose family was living on credit in Brimfield, was hurled back into limbo.

Eaton and Bradley accelerated their anti-Jefferson and anti-treaty lobbying. The opposition forces had gathered enough momentum that Jefferson felt compelled to bring up Tripoli contingency plans at a meeting of his five-man Cabinet. Jefferson posed the question: If Hamet's family has not been restored, should the United States renew the blockade of Tripoli? The answer: a unanimous no. However, they did decide that the new American consul to Tripoli should press for the family's return, and if it was not granted, the administration would then lay the issue of a blockade before Congress.

On Monday, March 17, in the drafty hall of the Senate, General Bradley delivered his committee's report on Hamet's request for aid. It was a complete exoneration of Eaton and a blistering critique of Lear and, by implication, Jefferson. The committee charged that Lear "dictated every measure, paralyzed every military operation by land and sea, and finally without displaying the fleet or squadron before Tripoli . . . against the opinion of all officers of the fleet, entered into a convention with the reigning bashaw." The committee reeled in disgust at the impropriety of ordering Eaton to evacuate Derne five days *prior* to Lear's sailing and dismissed Lear's excuse that American lives were at stake as "hav[ing] no foundation in fact." The report concluded: "The committee are confident that the legislature [Congress] of a free and christian country can never leave it in the power of a mahometan to say they have violated their faith, or withheld the operations of justice from one who has fallen a victim to his unbounded confidence in their integrity and honor."

The committee then proposed a bill for the relief of Hamet, with a space left blank for Congress to decide how many thousands of dollars

Hamet should be given. This brutal, partisan lambasting of the administration delighted Eaton.

The following day, Senator Bradley proposed that Congress set aside six square miles of federal public land to become a township called "Derne," and that it give 1,000 acres each to William Eaton, Presley O'Bannon, and George Washington Mann, and 320 acres each to the four surviving marines, Arthur Campbell, Bernard O'Brian, David Thomas, and James Owen. (Three had died, two of them at Derne.)

With praise resounding in his ears, Eaton directed a letter to the Speaker of the House, requesting his expense claims be finally settled.

That same day, Eaton, stubborn patriot, became convinced that the balance of power had shifted in his favor in his undeclared tiff with President Jefferson. Eaton wrote Preble extolling the Senate in higher-than-high-flown language. "The sense of honor, justice and indignation against baseness which has heretofore and always ought to mark the character of the nation is not wholly absorbed in the pusillanimity of the Executive; these virtues still exist in the representation of the States."

Eaton made a prediction: "The Executive has been probed to the core, every . . . document drawn from him which could throw light on the subject and you have the result—Lear will be impeached." Also, he saw financial daylight for himself. "My consular accounts are with the Committee of Claims—I shall be indemnified." Longtime friend John Cotton Smith (Federalist, Connecticut) chaired the committee.

Although the Tripoli treaty ranked in importance far below, say, war with England, Jefferson didn't want to add one single defeat or embarrassment when he needed every ounce of political credibility. All his life, he complained about the dirty infighting of politics, yet Jefferson over the years learned well how to sharpen his nails.

Senator Plumer visited Jefferson at 9 A.M. on April 2. The embattled president welcomed him. If someone wanted to stop rumors and shape "spin," Plumer was a fine choice for a confidant, trusted by Federalists and well liked by Jefferson's party.

Plumer informed the president that a "report was circulating with much industry" that Lear had signed a secret agreement to delay the return of Hamet's family.

> [Jefferson] assured me the report was not only utterly false—but that there was in fact no foundation for any suspicion of the kind. You must, said he, as a senator know that in fact no such secret article exists, for you have the treaty before you—And nothing can make a part of the treaty but what is agreed to by two thirds of the Senators present. And you may rest assured that Mr. Lear neither gave any written assurances to the Bashaw—or ever intimated to him, that the United States would not insist on Hamet's family being delivered up. So, far from it, that the reigning Bashaw has been uniformly told that this article must be literally & fully performed. He added, I have since I received the treaty issued new orders & given explicit directions to Mr. Lear to demand the fulfilment of that article from Joseph Bashaw.

Jefferson could count on Plumer to spread the word that the president had emphatically denied the existence of any secret article. It is beyond doubt that Lear never *officially* informed the administration about the secret clause, but did he tell Jefferson in a private or confidential letter? If he did, no such evidence still exists. Thomas Jefferson, however, was willing to partake in this kind of gamesmanship: Remember the administration's orders to Lear to try to keep any annual tribute payment as "no part of the Public Treaty."

After discussing ratification of the treaty, Plumer brought up the topic of the Bradley Report, which Plumer called "very extraordinary," questioning its fairness. "The president replied, the principles contained in that report are unsound, and the facts are false. The documents will not support the statements—They cannot be supported by testimony. The Senate ought to pass a vote to disapprove & reject the report. It appears Mr. Eaton wishes to blast the reputation of & destroy the character of Commodore Barron & Mr. Lear to raise his own importance. I presume there is an intimacy—a connection between Bradley & Eaton—& this connection has led Mr. Bradley into errors.

"The government of the United States," Jefferson continued, "never authorized any man to co-operate with Hamet in any way agt. the reigning Bashaw, [f]or any longer, than the United States should find it for their interest so to do." Jefferson was clearly irate.

"The character of Mr. Lear is good, fair and unblemished. We thought & still believe, it was a very fortunate circumstance for the United States that we could prevail upon him to accept the office of Consul-General upon the Barbary Coast. And I hope in his absence the Senate will not approve of a report calculated to wound his fame."

Jefferson then, unbidden, brought up the most troubling rumor of all. "A story has been circulated, & I was yesterday requested to explain it, that Mr. Lear while private Secretary to President Washington, was induced to a breach of trust. That he clandestinely procured & forwarded me the correspondence that passed between the General & myself. This story is false in every part & has been raised and circulated to injure Mr. Lear. The last letter I ever wrote to Genl Washington was in July 1796. In August following I received a partial answer—& not until May 1798 I recd a full one—& this was the last letter I had from him. I yesterday examined my files & read the letters."

This Plumer diary entry marks Jefferson's staunchest denial of the falling-out with Washington and the suppression of the letters. Despite this denial, it strains credulity that a lifelong correspondence should peter to nothing for *the final three years* of Washington's life.

Plumer, quite gregarious, would now tell many senators and congressmen about Jefferson's denials and opinions.

The president orchestrated other behind-the-scenes politicking to sway more congressmen. Secretary of War Henry Dearborn made the rounds of the senators, praising Lear and scorning Eaton as "uncandid." Secretary of State Madison buttonholed John Quincy Adams, a Federalist, to push for ratification of the Tripoli treaty. The atmosphere was growing testier. Smelling blood, some Federalist senators were talking about steering the next presidential election away from Jefferson's handpicked successor, James Madison.

Nonetheless, Jefferson's discreet lobbying worked. The Bradley Report was sent back to a committee with two new senators aboard, John Quincy Adams (Federalist, Massachusetts) and Thomas Sumter (Republican, South Carolina). The spin wars intensified. Eaton succeeded in convincing several newspapers to run his angry August shipboard letter lampooning Lear and Barron. It appeared April 8, the same day that Bradley introduced a resolution to postpone ratification of the Tripoli treaty till next session of Congress. The senators debated the issue most of the day. Again, Eaton and Bradley lost. The vote came down 10 in favor of delaying, 20 opposed. The tally is significant, because treaty ratification would require a two-thirds majority, that is, 20 to 10 or more.

Senator Bradley had also worked hard to sway his fellow senators to give generous aid to Hamet, to fill in the blank with quite a few thousand dollars. Again, Bradley failed. On April 9, the Senate voted to postpone the issue of Relief of Hamet "to the first Monday in December next."

That Wednesday turned even bleaker for Eaton. John Cotton Smith, chairman of the Committee of Claims, issued its report to the House. The members proposed a resolution that Eaton's settlement be returned *yet again* to the Department of State because "the [committee is] neither qualified nor disposed to become a board of auditors." Eaton was moved from one limbo to another.

The following day, Eaton, who had lost battle after battle, was invited to dine at a Federalist boardinghouse run by one Captain Coyle. These early senators and congressmen, at times behaving like frat boys, were thrown together far away from their families. "There is too many— We have too much noise," wrote Senator Plumer. "For [Samuel] Dana is as rude as a boy—very talkative—a voice harsh & loud as Stentor . . . — In each chamber there are two lodgers—This is very inconvenient. Tis difficult to obtain an hour's quiet—all is noise."

The evening of April 10 the disappointed Federalists brought Eaton home with them. Plumer, influenced by Jefferson, now referred to him disparagingly as "William Eaton Esq (alias the Arab Genl)." With liquor flowing freely, Eaton, preaching to the choir of Jefferson bashers, made an acid comment regarding the lack of aid to Hamet-the-betrayed. He said, with his typical bluntness: "A majority of the Senate have sold the honor of the country."

Duels were fought over far less wounding statements. Since Plumer was the only senator in attendance who had voted in favor of postponing

Hamet's relief, he didn't take the charge well. "I then observed he had assumed great liberties—but that I trusted the Senate would act agreeable to the conviction of their own minds—uninfluenced by the opinions of others." Plumer—who had been an Eaton disciple—was now turning. He vowed never to dine with Eaton again.

Eaton in his frustration began to drink more. It was gossiped by the likes of Plumer that Eaton started his day by downing a couple glasses of whiskey and that he had threatened to horsewhip a servant at Stelle's Tavern if he wasn't served his breakfast before all other guests.

A couple of days later, on Saturday, April 12, the Senate, with thirty senators in the chamber, remained in session to debate the Tripoli treaty. Eaton, believing truth on his side, desperately wanted the peace pact defeated. At least eight senators opposed the treaty. If they could find three more votes, they could defeat ratification.

In the chilly Senate chamber, many senators rose to deliver harangues on Eaton, Hamet, Lear, and Barron. The Senate, in those years, according to Plumer, offered a far less desirable stage than the House of Representatives for speechifying. The House had two stenographers and a gallery often packed with people yearning to hear John Randolph. The Senate had no stenographers, and any senator who wanted his words recorded for posterity needed "to submit to the drudgery" of writing them out in longhand and giving them to a sympathetic newspaper.

Senator Robert Wright (Republican, Maryland) proposed an amendment that the treaty would be ratified only on the condition that Bashaw Yussef delivered up Hamet's wife and children. Nine votes yea, twenty votes nay. It was defeated.

Senator John Smith (Republican, Ohio) proposed a postponement of the treaty to the next session, in December. Only eight votes in favor. Defeated.

"After 4 O'Clock," according to Plumer, "Wright & Pickering exercized the patience of the Senate with long dry & tedious speeches." The Capitol building leaked during rains and was perpetually damp, but one cozy nook tempted them all. "We withdrew to the fireside & spent our time cheerfully & left them to talk & read documents . . . to the empty chairs. At sometime, for ten minutes, there was not but four senators within the bar. Six several [sic] times they moved the President [of the Senate] to adjourn for want of a quorum. As soon as the motion was made, we took our chairs, negatived it & then immediately withdrew."

Finally, sometime long after 5 P.M., the Tripoli treaty came up for a vote. The main Federalists stuck together, but both Adams and Plumer defected. The vote came down 21 to 8 to ratify, topping the two-thirds needed. The Senate therefore did "advise & consent" the president to ratify the treaty. Lear had escaped official censure. This marked one more slap in the face for Eaton.

From that Saturday, a mad scramble ensued to finish business to escape the Potomac region. On the final day of the session, Monday, April 21, the House and Senate rushed to push through almost twenty bills for Jefferson to sign. Chaos reigned; tempers flared.

Among the motions, the House and Senate took up a bill brought by John Quincy Adams to offer "temporary relief" for Hamet, and the House took up its Claims Committee's recommendation regarding Eaton's accounts. Some of Eaton's paperwork was spread on the table in the House and some in the Senate for perusal.

The expense account was immensely complicated; Eaton regarded his patriotic motives as an all-encompassing defense for the unfortunate business setbacks and swindles that had resulted in him owing the government the gargantuan sum of $40,000.

Plumer sifted through the paperwork and came to a very different conclusion. "The money paid for the redemption of an Italian girl had no connection with his consulship—& the US. ought not to pay it." As for the bribe, "Tis a principle too vile & too dangerous to admit of moments consideration."

The House decided to postpone even voting on Eaton's account; the resolution was ordered to lie on the table. The Senate reached a third reading of its own bill, but it too never voted on it. Eaton's finances were firmly cemented in limbo.

Hamet fared slightly better. The House approved a bill for his temporary relief by an overwhelming 71 to 6, and the Senate did likewise. Hamet would receive a payment of $2,400 from a U.S. Navy agent in the Mediterranean.

Congress late that night adjourned. Many of the politicians were eager to leave town and get a head start out of the swamp. The next morning's stage to Baltimore was packed.

Thomas Jefferson had won most of his battles with Congress. He had dodged the revolt of Virginian John Randolph and avoided the warmongers. Beyond that, Jefferson had won *all* of his skirmishes with Eaton over Tripoli: The treaty was ratified; Lear was safe; Eaton was teetering on his hero's pedestal; Eaton's expenses were still embroiled.

Jefferson wrote a note to a friend, Judge John Tyler, summing up his thoughts, as the elected officials emptied out of the boardinghouses. "Congress has just closed a long and uneasy session, in which they had great difficulties external and internal to encounter. With respect to the ex-basha of Tripoli & many other more important matters, such a spirit of dissension existed, and such misrepresentation of fact that it will be difficult for the public to come at truth." The lanky Virginia lawyer was certain that he knew the truth; the stocky New England military man felt the same way.

Angry over his many defeats, William Eaton headed north in May of 1806 to return to his family in Brimfield, a Federalist stronghold. As he was still a hero to many, his journey north was punctuated by stopovers for huzzas in various taverns.

No amount of praise, however, could dispel his anger over Tripoli and over his shabby treatment in Washington City. His disappointment was eating at him like some cancer. General Eaton believed that the United States with him at the fore had once had the chance to stop the Barbary pirates and to inspire the world. That opportunity was lost; it galled him, and he refilled his glass, again and again.

CHAPTER 26 *Burr, Bottle, and Six Feet Under*

I am Eaton no more.

—WILLIAM EATON TO AN OLD FRIEND IN TUNIS, M. HUMBERT, 1810

WILLIAM EATON'S HORSE trudged up Breakneck Hill, the final three hundred yards into Brimfield. Eaton was yet again returning home from Washington City with no money.

Within days, he would be dunned for his wife's debts racked up in his absence. A country store, Munger & Wales, sent him a note on May 28, 1806. "You will not take it unkind if we state to you that we are now making a settlement of all our old matters." The family's trifles over three years tallied about $20 and then a stove, recently bought, had added another $15. To Eaton, this kind of nuisance was like being nibbled to death by minnows.

He tried to reconcile with his family, enjoy his children, and slow down to the pace of small-town life, but for a man who had led a charge down the *wadi* in Derne, it wasn't easy. "Tea parties, turkey suppers, apple bees, husking bees, spinning bees, quilting bees furnished almost the only amusement," wrote a local minister.

Perhaps William and Eliza weren't at complete loggerheads during this six-month stay because by late fall, Eliza became pregnant again (for her fifth time via William and eighth overall); and that signals at least moments, or a moment, of matrimonial bliss.

In Brimfield, with a population of 1,324, he was the town's greatest military hero since Eliza's previous husband, General Danielson. He bestrode the burgh like a colossus, so much so that some locals called him "The Great I" behind his back.

One Joseph Williams of nearby Springfield, Massachusetts, pitched him to run for Congress. Eaton declined. "I have already refused to be named as a party candidate," he wrote. "The names Fed. & Demo, which at this moment, split the affections of our countrymen ought to be lost in the proud name of American."

Thomas Jefferson, his Founding Father status notwithstanding, was despised throughout large swaths of New England for a pro-South bias. And in Brimfield, General Eaton made certain that everyone knew that he remained unrewarded and that his accounts remained unsettled because of Jefferson. He was the war hero, wronged.

Since Eaton was land rich, but cash poor, most merchants gave the hero the benefit of the doubt. However, to satisfy his most pressing creditors, he tried to mortgage or sell some properties. Eaton owned land in the western wilderness of Ohio from his army days, and his wife had inherited extensive Danielson acreage in the Brimfield area.

While sorting through various real estate transactions, some with the aid of his stepson Timothy, a remarkable letter fell into Eaton's hands around early October, one that would have enormous implications for the United States and for Jefferson.

A prospective buyer, Morris Belknap, mentioned in passing that he had personally witnessed Aaron Burr beginning to put his vast conspiracy into action. He reported that Burr was secretly building boats on the Ohio River and signing up mercenaries to join his Spanish Expedition, and that American men were pledging allegiance to Burr. Eaton suddenly faced a huge dilemma. He had already vaguely warned the president in person about Burr, with negative results to show.

Roaming about his unpaid mansion, with his toddler son squalling and his daughters running here and there, Eaton pondered his options. Jefferson was surely the puppeteer who had manipulated Congress not to pay him, not to grant him a sword or a medal. Eaton's name was never bandied about by the Cabinet for a command in the U.S. Army.

What should he do with this information about Burr's actions to split the union and create a Jefferson-free western America?

Eaton, a patriot first, decided to send Belknap's letter to the Department of State, and he contacted the postmaster general, Gideon Granger, to rush all information directly to the president about Burr's activities. Granger's letter, dated October 16, 1806, with Eaton's signature on it, provided "the first formal intelligence received by the Executive on the subject of the conspirator being in motion." (A decade later, Jefferson confirmed that fact in a letter to Granger.)

Eaton's patriotism had trumped his personal animosity.

Jefferson received the news and authorized additional troops to go to Louisiana. He also sent confidential letters about Burr to the governors of Ohio, Indiana, and Mississippi, as well as to the district attorneys in Kentucky, Tennessee, and Louisiana "to have him strictly watched and on committing any overt act unequivocally, to have him arrested and tried for treason, misdemeanor or whatever other offense."

Around Thanksgiving, word leaked to the newspapers about Eaton's role in exposing Burr. The Boston *Repertory* printed a long account of what Eaton told the president. William Eaton, hero of the Mediterranean, was now point man for thwarting Burr. His name, in certain circles, rose higher and, among Jefferson Republicans, regained some luster.

Fame was one thing: Eaton was still broke, Hamet was still unrewarded, Lear was still unpunished; Eaton was still unemployed; liquor still helped start the day. Sip by sip, he dulled the pain, and nothing went unobserved in tattletale New England. When he made a business trip to Boston, the wife of John Quincy Adams wrote to her senator husband: "Wm Eaton . . . was frequently in a state of intoxication—that the better sort of people avoided him—& he was going out of fashion there." That story spread in the rooming houses of the nation's capital.

Meanwhile Eaton tried to settle into small-town life at Brimfield and bury the Tripoli war, but he just couldn't do it. Projects such as building a new meetinghouse and picking the route for a state road occupied his time, but he was still very restless. He wrote to Senator Bradley that once he sorted out "the deranged state" of his affairs at home, he planned to head back down to Washington City to tend to unfinished business.

So, after Christmas, the forty-two-year-old ex-general departed Brimfield, and two weeks of slow travel later he moved into the Frost & Quinn, an elegant new boardinghouse in Washington City. Overstuffed chairs by the fireside welcomed the guests; the host placed a complimentary half pint of gin and of brandy *every morning* in the center of the dining room table. (New resident Senator Plumer was *not* happy to see Eaton arrive at the door.)

On February 6, 1807, a couple of inches of snow fell on Washington City, and around noon the storm gathered such force that one senator described it as a "hurricane" and "the strongest wind I ever witnessed." The gale plucked the roofs off buildings, tipped carriages, and flung several elderly politicians to the ground.

That weather matched Eaton's mood as he drafted yet another letter to Congress to demand a settlement of his claims.

"You cannot bring back to me nine years of active life—you cannot restore to me the strength of an arm but for actual disbursements for the benefit of our common country, whether voluntary or extorted, I have a right again to resort to your justice, and to believe that this justice will be no longer delayed."

He summed up his misery: "The heavy expenses incident to an appeal to this Chancery for such a length of time . . . and at so great a distance from my home . . . have necessarily laid me under pecuniary responsibility to my friends. The suspense of another year must lodge me in prison." With his penchant for drama, he asked the committee to pay him the money so that he could "ransom" himself.

Around this same time, Jefferson was trying to tighten the noose around Aaron Burr. A post messenger riding breakneck, exchanging horse after horse, reached Washington City and informed the president that the acting governor of Mississippi territory, with just thirty militiamen, had captured Burr near Natchez. Jefferson was extremely anxious to convict his former vice president of treason, because if Burr shook free and attacked Spanish territories, he might provoke a war.

With Burr alive and in custody, Jefferson now needed witnesses to help gain a conviction, and very few men had more firsthand knowledge of Burr's schemes than William Eaton. Jefferson also feared that the courts—with their Federalist leanings—would probably slip every benefit of the doubt to Burr. Jefferson needed Eaton.

On the very same day—February 18—that news of Burr's capture arrived, a congressman introduced a resolution to have the secretary of state settle William Eaton's accounts "on principles of equity." The timing of the resolution, after four fruitless years, certainly *seems* to confirm some kind of nod from Jefferson. It was a stunning turnaround. Also, that ornate phrase, "on principles of equity," might very well represent a windfall for Eaton. A judge, or an auditor, usually evaluates a case on the grounds of justice, that is, on his interpretation of legal precedent or of laws enacted by government. "Equity" is a much vaguer concept, something akin to fairness and common sense, and offers great leeway for selective interpretation. An old legalism is that "Equity is in the eye of the beholder."

A week later, the House passed the Eaton bill; now all that remained was for the Senate to vote on a similar resolution. Around this time, Jefferson was shocked to learn that a jury in Mississippi territory, showing frontier tolerance and a hatred of Spain, had refused to charge Burr and had released the man. The president, quite agitated, now hoped that a party of federal soldiers would capture Burr and bring him to Washington. With Burr slipping through the justice system, the president needed Eaton even more.

The Senate waited until the last day of the session, Tuesday, March 3, to bring up the Eaton settlement bill for a vote. That frantic afternoon, two dozen bills clogged the lectern, from compensation for Lewis and Clark to salt taxes.

Sometime toward evening, Eaton's settlement bill came to a vote. The vote was close, with New England Federalist senators Plumer and John Quincy Adams both voting against Eaton. However, Jefferson's Republicans pushed the final tally to 16 to 12 in Eaton's favor. Thomas Jefferson signed the bill about an hour before Congress adjourned at midnight.

Eaton had finally won a round in Washington City. While congressmen rushed to board stages in the snow, Eaton was quite pleased to linger to await his final settlement. The following week the federal auditor shaved every number and tilted every calculation in Eaton's favor. The justified expenses based on "principles of equity" added up to the weighty sum of $51,019; to which was added $2,420 of interest, dating back to April 9, 1803. Included in the figures approved by the auditor was $4,837 for the "Acco! of the Chev. Porcilla for the redemption of his daughter." In effect, the United States under Thomas Jefferson had agreed to pay for the purchase of the beautiful Italian slave girl, Anna.

This $53,439 of newly approved expenses was offset against Eaton's last balance sheet, in which he owed $40,803, leaving the U.S. government to pay William Eaton $12,636. That was a princely sum, a lifetime of wages for many Americans.

Would the money make him whole? Would he accept it as a vindication of his actions in Tripoli?

He boarded stagecoaches and hired carriages and returned home. A coachman asked him for a tip. Eaton tossed him an American Eagle ten-dollar gold piece, and told him to keep the change.

He returned to Brimfield in April 1807, and Eliza soon after gave birth to Nathaniel Sykes Eaton. Now he was a *moneyed* war hero. Brimfield voted him to represent the district in the state legislature, placing him instead of his friend Stephen Pynchon.

However, before Eaton could attend the Massachusetts Legislature in Boston, with its five-hundred-plus delegates, he was summoned to testify at the Aaron Burr trial in Richmond, Virginia.

Eaton arrived in Richmond during the summer of 1807 ranking as one of the nation's leading—and most controversial—citizens. The elite of the United States were converging there for this extraordinary trial in which the president was aiming to convict his former running mate of treason. Richmond's population doubled to more than 10,000 as frontiersmen tipped their beaver hats to New York society dames, and farmers rubbed elbows with swells. A man could easily find a drink and a card game; man-to-man bets abounded on the outcome of the trial.

William Eaton fell right into this thrum of conviviality; he played cards and drank while lawyerly motions delayed the start of the trial for weeks. Eaton believed Burr, with whom he had spent many hours, guilty of treason. Never shy, he laid wagers, some perhaps as high as $500, on the outcome of the trial.

And Burr's lawyers and friends—to bolster the defense and discredit a witness—attacked Eaton's character, even planting articles in the local newspapers. They accused him of wanting to join Burr on his expedition, and then betraying Burr to save himself. They also bad-mouthed Eaton's exploits in Barbary as an overrated tale.

Eaton could have ignored the taunts; he could have thrived in Richmond, buttonholing wealthy influential men for higher office, but something happened to him that summer in Virginia, something that had been building since the shameful midnight exit from Derne. During the month waiting for the trial to begin, his inner demons from the Tripoli war overwhelmed him. The $12,000 payout had clearly not made him whole. The war was clearly not over. He tossed around the government's money in card games; he drank whiskey, lots of it. He still craved praise from Jefferson and justice for Hamet.

Some days, he looked worse than others. "The once redoubted Eaton has dwindled down in the eyes of this sarcastic town into a ridiculous mountebank strutting about the streets under a tremendous hat, with a Turkish sash over coloured clothes," wrote one of Burr's coconspirators, Harman Blennerhassett. "When . . . tippling in the taverns . . . [Eaton] offers up with his libations the bitter effusions of his sorrows."

That was Blennerhassett's opinion and, with his life on the line, he clearly had an incentive to portray Eaton in the worst light.

After numerous preliminaries, the trial finally opened on August 3, with Chief Justice John Marshall presiding.

The prosecution—with Jefferson calling the shots—chose Eaton to be its first witness. Months of anticipation had built to this moment.

To Eaton and to Burr, this was a duel without bullets. Both men's reputations were at stake. The two former Army officers were both well dressed in high white collars and long dark jackets befitting the occasion; Burr of Manhattan, though shorter and balder, cut a more elegant figure than Eaton of Brimfield.

In the packed courtroom, held in the Virginia House of Delegates to accommodate the overflow, Eaton began dramatically by preempting the lawyers and making a statement.

"Concerning any fact which may go to prove treason against Colonel Burr, I know <u>nothing</u>. Concerning certain transactions which are said to have happened at Blennerhasset's island, I know <u>nothing</u>; but concerning Colonel Burr's expressions and his treasonable intentions, I know much; and it is to those my evidence relates."

With this large prestigious crowd, Eaton couldn't resist the temptation to speak about his own issues, to justify his conduct in Tripoli. Eaton would exonerate Eaton. He explained how Burr had approached him and why he would have *seemed* a ripe candidate for this treasonous expedition.

EATON: I had but a short time before been compelled ingloriously to strike the flag of my country from the ramparts of a defeated enemy, where it had flown for forty-five days. I had been compelled to abandon my comrades in war on the fields where they had fought our battles. I had seen cash offered to the half-vanquished chief of Tripoli as the price of pacification.

The Prosecutor interjected: By whom?

EATON: By our negotiator when as yet no exertion had been made by our naval squadron to coerce the enemy. I had seen the conduct of the author of these blemishes on our then proud national character, if not commended, not censured; whilst my own inadequate efforts to support that character were attempted to be thrown into shade. . . . Here I beg leave to observe in justice to myself, that however strong those expressions, however harsh the language I employed, they could not justify the inference that I was prepared to dip my sabre in the blood of my countrymen, much less of their children, which I believe would have been the case had this conspiracy been carried into effect.

Burr's attorney, Mr. Luther Martin, leaped up to object to Eaton's lurid language regarding Burr's expedition. Justice Marshall sustained the objection.

Eaton was clearly becoming more animated with every sentence, and the defense waited eagerly to needle Eaton into embarrassing himself. When Burr and his lawyers began to cross-examine the government's star witness, it's clear they wanted to show him up as a befuddled drunk and *a purchased witness.*

Defense lawyer Martin cleverly used the word *drunk* several times in his opening questions in various contexts before moving on to the issue of Eaton's recent settlement with the federal government.

> MR. MARTIN: What balance did you receive?
> MR. EATON: That is <u>my</u> concern, sir.

Aaron Burr, famous for his slippery geniality, followed up his lawyer's attack.

> MR. BURR: What was the balance against you?
> MR. EATON (to the court): Is that a proper question?
> MR. BURR: My object is manifest; I wish to show the bias
> which has existed on the mind of the witness.

Burr's wit drew snickers from the crowd.
The chief justice saw no objections to the question.

> MR. EATON: I cannot say to a cent or a dollar, but I have
> received about 10,000 dollars.

Burr now shifted to a new topic, one designed to show blustery Eaton as fantasizing about having an important role in Burr's enterprise. But the strategy would backfire.

> MR. BURR: You spoke of a command?

MR. EATON: You stated . . . that you were assured . . . that an
army would be ready to appear when you went
to the waters of the western country. . . . You
spoke of your riflemen, your infantry, your
cavalry. It was with the same view you
mentioned to me that that man [pointing to
General Wilkinson] was to have been the first
to aid you, and from the same views you have
perhaps mentioned me.

Mr. Martin objected to the witness interposing his own opinions in
this manner.

MR. HAY (government prosecutor): Some allowance is to be
made for the feelings of a man of honor.

Mr. Eaton, bowing, apologized to the court for the warmth of his
manner.

MR. BURR: You spoke of my revolutionizing the western
states. How did you understand that the Union
was to be separated?

MR. EATON: Your principal line was to be drawn by the
Allegheny mountains. You were persuaded that
you had secured to you the most considerable
citizens of Kentucky and Tennessee, but
expressed some doubts about Ohio; I well
recollect that on account of the reason which
you gave: that they were too much of a
plodding, industrious people to engage in your
enterprise.

Now, Eaton was playing to the crowd.

MR. BURR: How was the business to be effected?

MR. EATON: I understood that your agents were in the
western country; that the army and the
commander-in-chief were ready to act at your
signal; and that these, with the adventurers that
would join you, would compel the states to
agree to a separation. Indeed, you seemed to
consider New Orleans as already yours, and that
from this point you would send expeditions into
the other provinces, make conquests, and
consolidate your empire.

MR. BURR: Was it *after* all this that you recommended me
to the president for an embassy?

That was a snide question.

MR. EATON: Yes; to remove you, as you were a dangerous
man, because I thought it the only way to avert a
civil war.

Burr then asked Eaton if he had ever rejected Burr's offer of a command in the army.

MR. EATON: No . . . I determined to use you until I got everything out of you; and on the principle that,
"when innocence is in danger, to break faith
with a bad man is not fraud, but virtue."

The supposed drunk had come prepared. In this public clash of the titanic egos, Eaton had been bloodied but had survived Burr's fire.

After Eaton, the prosecution's case staggered as Chief Justice Marshall, a longtime foe of Jefferson, ruled repeatedly in favor of the defense, signaling that he would probably demand proof of physical actions of treason, not merely evidence of Burr's pipe dreams shared over drinks.

As the lawyers haggled, Eaton drank and played poker and wagered on the outcome of the trial. He seems to have wagered in favor of a treason conviction simply because he believed that to be the *correct* verdict. A scrap of paper reveals just how much Eaton was risking. On August 21, he sent a rush letter to moneylenders Theodore & Herman Eli in New York City; he requested permission to draw $500 on account and promised to pay them back on his next trip north. He cited as his reason for this somewhat odd request the favorable loan rates in New York. The implication, however, was that his credit was tapped out in Richmond. Eaton had received $12,000 in March in Washington City; he had paid off some of his debts; how was it possible that he needed $500 in Richmond in August?

The inescapable conclusion is that hard liquor, a deck of cards, and a bitter heart make a very dangerous combination. His love of risk and his bullheadedness doomed him as a gambler.

On August 31, Chief Justice Marshall—as expected—delivered his narrow opinion that the government must restrict itself to showing overt actions by Burr; the prosecution reluctantly abandoned its case the following day.

Jefferson was appalled, and so was Eaton, who lost considerable sums and prestige on the verdict. Eaton left no record of his gambling losses, but another clue is that on September 3, 1807, he sold property in Ohio to Morris Belknap, the man who had sent the letter that had tipped him off to Burr's movements.

The president, outraged that Burr might remain a "rallying point" for the "disaffected and worthless of the U.S.," wrote to prosecutor George Hay to pursue misdemeanor charges. Jefferson's decision to chase lesser charges meant that the handful of government witnesses must remain marooned in Richmond for the indefinite future. Eaton, with time to kill, continued to frequent inns such as the famed Eagle Tavern, where just two years prior a dinner had been held in his honor. He lost more money; liquor was his constant anodyne.

The misdemeanor cases against Burr also suffered a long slow death. On October 19, when it became clear to the prosecutor that General Wilkinson would not make a credible witness, George Hay abandoned those cases as well. Burr walked free; Eaton piled more bitterness onto his plate. His imbibing had never been light, but during the summer of

1807 he passed from excessive carouser (in an age of drinking) to border-line drunk. The false accusations by Burr's stalwarts at the beginning of the trial were coming true.

In late autumn in Washington City when Congress returned to session, Burr and Tripoli and everything else were suddenly pushed aside by the *very real* threat of war. Everyone wondered how the United States would respond to England's latest insult at sea. The HMS *Leopard* had laid a broadside into the USS *Chesapeake* when the latter refused to allow the British to search for deserters. Most everyone expected war. Mono-maniacal William Eaton, however, was still stuck fighting his battles in the Mediterranean.

On November 3, Eaton relayed an unctuous eight-month-old letter from Hamet to Congress. "In the depth of my miseries," Hamet had written from Syracuse, "my only consolation has been the reliance I placed on the powerful support of a republic so distinguished throughout the world for that justice which protects and sustains whoever confides himself to her patronage."

And Eaton wrote yet another plea to the Committee of Claims, imploring them on the grounds of "honor, justice and humanity" to give Hamet more than $200 a month.

The Mediterranean was last year's war. Eaton could not rouse even his Federalist friends to Hamet's side. These nights, in his boardinghouse room in Washington City, Eaton filled his notebooks with bile against the administration and especially against Lear and that man's empty excuses for negotiating peace.

"The danger of the American prisoners in Tripoli? What! A soldier in danger! such an apprehension . . . from a lovesick girl or a doting mother . . . might not have excited contempt but when it is made the subterfuge . . . by an ambassador. Who can restrain that nation's indignation?"

Then Eaton took aim at Jefferson's interpretation of a "co-operation" between allies. "Supposing I had said to [Hamet] that it was our object & intention to co-operate with him till a favorable occasion should offer and then dispose of him? Where is the wretch abject enough not to have considered [that] undignified and insulting?"

Around this time in mid-November Eaton made a discovery that roused him to even greater fury. He found out that President Jefferson had known for at least several months of the existence of Lear's secret article abandoning Hamet's family. *Jefferson had known!* The American consul, Dr. George Davis, had sent Jefferson a letter on June 2, 1807, from Tripoli and had included with it a verbatim copy of the secret article. Dispatched in duplicate via two vessels, that letter had arrived sometime in August.

On the evening of November 17, Senator Bradley, Eaton's first patron, told Eaton in deepest secrecy that President Jefferson had sent a "Confidential" message the preceding week to the Senate about the secret article. ("Confidential" meant that for national security reasons no senator could reveal it to anyone.) Eaton was so exasperated that in his personal notebook he sarcastically referred to Lear as an emperor. "Have we then an Emperor . . . who while he amuses our republican President and Senate with the apparition of an honourable treaty, cedes at discretion and in conclave with the enemy, the honor of the Government and the people of the nation by making them ignorantly accessory to fraud?"

He added a new charge: "Was it not enough that this diplomatic swindler for the consideration of a wheat speculation bartered away the proud claim we had established in that sea to military honor?"

Eaton had learned Lear was in the middle of a major wheat deal at the outset of the Tripoli negotiations. He had found out that Lear had shipped $37,000 worth of grain from Malta to Algiers just before he left to negotiate. Eaton was accusing Lear of rushing to a peace deal with Tripoli so as to protect his shipment from the risk of capture by Tripoli corsairs.

Eaton concluded: "Are we so bankrupt in talents and so bedased [sic, or perhaps hiccup, for "debased"] of soul as to be compelled to employ such agents and to countenance such duplicity? It is treason against the character of the nation: and he who gives it his countenance is an accomplice in the crime."

That "he" was clearly Jefferson, and Eaton now expected apologies and reparations. He was in for a shock. Amid the war fever and the

Chesapeake outrage, very few politicians or ordinary people cared about Hamet Karamanli or the secret article.

In the coming days, Eaton—waiting for an apology—somehow learned the text of Jefferson's "Confidential" message to the Senate, which the president had delivered on November 11.

Jefferson had explained to the senators that when the new consul, Dr. Davis, had arrived in Tripoli and demanded the release of Hamet's family, he was instead presented with the secret article.

The president then strung together a long convoluted sentence, *vaguely* intimating a mistake had been made. "How it has happened that the declaration of June 5 [secret article] has never before come to our knowledge, cannot with certainty be said; but whether there has been a miscarriage of it, or a failure of the ordinary attention and correctness of that officer [Lear] in making his communications, I have thought it due to the Senate, as well as to myself, to explain to them the circumstances which have withheld from their knowledge, as they did from my own, a modification, which, had it been placed in the public treaty, would have been relieved [removed], from objections which candor and good faith cannot but feel in its present form."

Eaton's hopes for a Jeffersonian mea culpa or a Lear lambaste were disappointed. The president, who had drafted an inspiringly clear Declaration of Independence, had chosen to obfuscate his meaning on Tripoli and Lear.

Lear's act of betrayal, in any case, was soon overshadowed by fresh crises in foreign affairs. News arrived that England had drafted an order-in-council that *all U.S. transatlantic commerce must receive British licenses and pass through British ports*; this outrageous insult seemed to guarantee that the United States would declare war on Great Britain.

Instead, Jefferson—completely in his visionary character—decided to try out his theory of Commercial Exclusion in the form of a nonviolent trade measure, an embargo on all foreign commerce. It was an otherworldly solution, worthy of the Sage of Monticello, and deeply frustrating to the Federalist military men of America.

At this very troubled time, on December 18, the newly reconstituted

Committee of Claims in the House issued its report on Hamet; their verdict in no way resembled the earlier Bradley report. The new team stated definitively that none of the American promises about return-of-family or stipend had led Hamet to leave Derne but rather "his influence and resources . . . were so small . . . that he, himself, considered it necessary to his own safety that he should withdraw." The report concluded that the United States was "not under any obligation to support the ex-Bashaw or to have given him what had already been bestowed." However, since Hamet "may have rendered . . . services and his expectations may have been improperly raised"—(read between the lines . . . by William Eaton)—therefore, "as an act of generosity," a gift of unspecified dollars might "be paid *under the direction of the president.*" That resolution would still have to pass both House and Senate.

On December 22, 1807, Congress passed the Embargo Act. No U.S. merchant ships could carry any goods whatsoever to any foreign ports and no foreign ships could carry American goods out of the United States. Jefferson intended to hurt England and France and Spain, to slow trade until the pain made the belligerents behave fairly toward the United States. Instead, it would turn out, the Embargo Act would strangle the commerce of New England and endanger the union; port business would dry up. New Haven, Connecticut, and Newburyport, Massachusetts, for instance, would never recover; American sailors would volunteer on British ships. Napoleon—tongue in cheek—soon said he would comply with Jefferson's wishes and capture all American merchant ships trying to enter French ports. British merchants were delighted at the reduced competition.

Impoverished by heavy gambling losses and disappointed by congressional indifference over Tripoli, William Eaton—still the Federalist hero—returned to New England to attend the Massachusetts Legislature.

Although the fervor of anti-Embargo and anti-Jeffersonism echoed in the chill corridors, Eaton—deaf to it all—delivered a long harangue against Chief Justice Marshall and the Burr verdict. He denounced Federalism as helping to free a traitor. And he sounded his new favorite theme: End your loyalty to political parties and start thinking first about the needs of the United States.

His speech won him no friends, especially since hometown Brimfield was overwhelmingly Federalist. Eaton stayed in Boston to attend the raucous session, spending much time drinking. He failed to "govern his glass," wrote a longtime friend, and "at such times, his wit was out."

In his cups, he tended to return over and over to his military triumphs, which led inevitably to Lear's betrayal of Hamet and of the United States. He repeated that this young idealistic nation had within its grasp the chance to stop the piracies. Eaton, the obsessive, could not move beyond that dark night when he had slipped out of Derne, or the ensuing dark years when he had failed to correct the mistake.

Almost two months had gone by since Jefferson's Confidential Message on Tripoli, and no newspaper had printed anything about Lear's betrayal. On January 26, 1808, sitting at a desk in a boardinghouse in Boston, Eaton wrote a letter that—in effect—threatened the president of the United States.

His Excellency Thomas Jefferson Pres: UStates.

Sir,

> *. . . I am assured that Tobias Lear did privately stipulate with Joseph Bashaw of Tripoli an article which he signed, that the family of Hamet Bashaw should not be surrendered, as by public treaty engaged, until after the expiration of four years—It is impossible to suppose that information of this dishonourable duplicity and fraud against the dignity of the government of these United States can have been reported to the Chief Magistrate; though Doctor Davis, our Consul at Tripoli, is said to be in possession of the document.*
>
> *Lest events should occur which may give sufferings to your feelings and fame from a concealment of these facts, I use the freedom, indeed I feel it a duty, to make this private communication—I shall make it public if Hamet Bashaw should not be provided for and our promises*

fulfilled—It is just that the world should know the iniquity from
which he suffers; and that infamy should fix on treachery and fraud—
I have the honor to be most respectfully, Sir,
your very obedient servant,

William Eaton

Eaton waited for a reply; he hoisted tankards in the taverns. The Chief Executive did not respond. On February 12, 1808, Eaton tried again; he relayed to Jefferson a misery-laden note from Hamet in Syracuse. "Having lost the hope of the restitution of my family . . . and seeing myself abandoned like a prisoner . . . now that there are no longer American ships in this sea and the Consul being about to depart without making provisions for payment of the monthly pittance . . ." And on and on. Hamet asked Eaton "to fulfill the promises by which I was seduced."

Eaton, in an accompanying note, made his case to Jefferson yet again. Unlike the vague threat of the previous letter, Eaton now tried to make a logical argument followed by an appeal to Jefferson's goodness.

On meeting with Hamet Bashaw . . . , I . . . pledged to him my life
and honor not to abandon him; and I did keep my faith—We marched
to the enemy's provinces and, though a modest member of Congress
[John Randolph] says, at the head of a handful of raggamuffins, our
host was sufficient to subdue the second garrisoned city in the
kingdom, vanquish an army, and revolutionize the country.

At a crisis, the enemy sued for peace—with no effort on the part of
the whole squadron to complete the conquest, so desirable to our
government and so fairly in view—And in direct disobedience of
positive instructions Mr. Lear paid money for our national disgrace
and ended our enterprise by an inglorious peace.

In order to induce Hamet Bashaw to evacuate the kingdom . . . ., he
stipulated in public treaty with the enemy that Hamet's family should
be restored to him—and assured me in an official letter that our
government would make suitable provisions for his future well

*being. . . . The baseness of [Lear's] duplicity, in its effect, stamps
dishonor on our whole nation, entails misery on a blameless friend; and
brings reflections to the soul of sensibility too painful for utterance.*

*I know it is enough, Sir, that you should be acquainted with all
these facts to engage the honorable interference of your influence and
feelings to relieve distress—and of your authority to punish the fraud
attempted to be passed on the public; nothing less that these can
retrieve, in my opinion, the sacrifice of our national dignity.*

Snows slowed the post coaches; Jefferson received the letter ten days
later in Washington City. Eaton, still at General Court in Boston, awaited
a reply. And he waited. He approached Senator Bradley for an appointment as general in the U.S. Army. He heard nothing from Bradley or Jefferson.

After the end of the state legislature session in Boston, Eaton found
himself called to Philadelphia to testify at a trial of one of Burr's alleged
accomplices. Sometime in late April of 1808, Eaton decided to quit
drinking. This dramatic resolution might yet save his reputation and his
life. He told a friend that he was now determined to quit "the cursed slow
poison," as he called it.

He avoided flask and decanter, and took nothing stronger than coffee or tea for four consecutive days. It was a start. He finished his trial
testimony and boarded a stage north, sober. He was delighted to discover
that the arch-Federalist Timothy Pickering would be his companion for
the entire journey to Brimfield. Since Pickering despised both Jefferson
and Lear and was an instigator of a secret New England secessionist
movement, he was Eaton's kindred spirit. The pair talked as the coach
bounced along the rutted roads. On day two of the journey and day five
of Eaton's sobriety, he and Pickering were pulled up Breakneck Hill into
picturesque Brimfield. A clear sky framed this lovely day in early May.

General Eaton convinced Pickering to alight from the stage for a
moment and come into Eaton's home for a brief visit. Eaton was eager to
show off his wife and daughters and young sons and teenage stepsons.
He was in a fine mood and asked stepson Timothy in a jaunty voice who
the district had just elected to represent it in Boston at the next state leg-

islature. Timothy replied: "Your old friend Stephen Pynchon is placed." According to an eyewitness, Eaton's countenance fell and revealed his deep disappointment at not being re-elected.

The mail coach waited for no one, not even a senator, and Pickering stayed only a few minutes. Eaton was deeply embarrassed. He wandered outside and looked in the stable and discovered that his carriage had been repossessed for debt.

He soon took a walk to the neighborhood tavern and topped off his glass again and again. From that disappointing day to his death three years later, Eaton's affairs headed steadily downhill; he would lose most everything but his anger.

"His domestic and financial concerns preyed upon his mind," wrote a friend. "His habits of intemperance became more constant and excessive; and excepting in moments of hilarity he appeared to view the world with gloom or indignation."

The general mood in Brimfield and the surrounding regions was somewhat grim as well. The ripple effect of Jefferson's Embargo Act was forcing bankruptcies. The records of the local justice of the peace show case after case of fellow townspeople going after each other over petty debts.

That summer, Eaton's beloved nineteen-year-old stepson, Eli E. Danielson, who had wandered in Egypt with him and had been on the *Argus* at Derne, died in a duel in Brooklyn, New York, on August 5, 1808. Eaton was profoundly disturbed by the news. "Brave, great and experienced men may sometimes find it necessary to . . . meet in personal contest; this may be justified when the fate of a nation is depending . . . but the trivial disputes which excite ardent young men to put life up at a game of hazard, cannot be reconciled to principles of morality, patriotism nor character."

Eaton settled down to an embittered life in Brimfield. Almost every month the sheriff came to the house to demand payment for some creditor or to execute some forfeiture of furniture or a horse or a piece of jewelry. During the Burr trial, Eaton had squandered thousands of dollars. Real estate records reveal him selling or mortgaging all his own and his wife's properties. He sold 5,000 acres in Maine at 50 cents an acre. He lost the other half to back taxes.

He continued drinking, and his old war wounds—his leg from the Revolutionary War and arm from Derne—began plaguing him more.

Around New Year's Day 1809, Eaton mustered one last effort to right the Hamet wrong. "Every sigh of Hamet Bashaw sinks deeply on my soul," he wrote to Senator Bradley, "and he breathes nothing but sighs!" Eaton launched yet another vague threat in the direction of Jefferson. "Unless I see liberal justice rendered towards Hamet Bashaw & merited punishment inflicted on the speculator Lear," he informed Bradley, "I shall feel myself justified in exposing some document to my country concerning Barbary affairs which shall stagger the devotion of the uninformed to the existing administration.—The man who will connive at fraud shall sit uneasy, even on a throne, where I am a subject."

Above all, Eaton wanted Lear crushed, and no newspaper had yet revealed the secret article. "Why seek to conceal his iniquity with secret injunction & closed doors? There must be a hidden reason for this carefulness to hide his compromise of our national honor. What has Tobias Lear done to entitle him to an exemption from responsibility? If the Executive have sound reasons for shielding him in duplicity amounting to fraud, I have a right to know those reasons—I shall demand them in a manner which will require an answer."

This was Eaton's last hurrah; it almost sounded as though in his agitated state, he was challenging Jefferson to a duel. That phrase, "which will require an answer," was then standard in affairs of honor.

Neither Bradley nor Jefferson ever replied.

In January of 1809, the president pushed through a measure to beef up the hated Embargo; he added the so-called Force Act, which allowed federal officials to seize any American vessel *on the suspicion* that it was headed to a foreign port.

Rumblings spread in New England to hold a convention to nullify the embargo, and to discuss possible secession from Jefferson's biased-against-New England America.

When the crisis *inside* the country began to loom larger than the threat from outside, Jefferson backed down. He ended his embargo experiment. Three days before the end of his term, he signed the repeal of the Embargo Act, enabling James Madison to enter office with less controversy. On March 4, 1809, Jefferson left Washington in mild disgrace and rode home on horseback through a snowstorm. He had squandered seven years of popularity over an economic theory, over a passionate but unconfessed pacifism. (Generations of historians would repair his briefly tarnished reputation.)

As Jefferson left office, Eaton's body—though he was only forty-five years old—was beginning to fail him. A half decade earlier, he had survived a desert trek, now he had trouble walking.

A family friend described his conduct toward his wife and family as "irregular and capricious, sometimes treating them with affability and gentleness and sometimes with harshness, severity and great rudeness." The friend, who was often a houseguest, added: "His commands were often foolish or absurd, [and were] obeyed from terror rather than respect or affection." Throughout it all, wife Eliza stayed with him. She showed "patience, good sense and singular fortitude . . . to correct his irregularities and promote his comfort."

Eaton was now a full-fledged drunk.

In December of 1809, a family friend, Charles Prentiss, tried to help Eaton resurrect himself. "I dwelt on the certainty of speedy ruin, without reformation, on the easy means of regaining health and reclaiming credit, peace, fortune and honor but more than all urged him how high his name still stood and how probable would be his advancement. He squeezed my hand, affected even to tears, applauded my frankness and repeatedly with much warmth . . . expressed his determination 'to be a man, to be Eaton again.'"

The next day early, Prentiss entered Eaton's drawing room, and Eaton greeted him: "Good morning—say what you please but no more lecturing—come take with me a glass of spirit and water."

Around Christmas, one of his Derne officers, eccentric Jean Eugene, came to Brimfield to visit. He and the general relived their adventures, and Eaton loaded him with letters of recommendation to hand out in Washington. (Jean Eugene, who now added the family name Leitensdorfer, eventually became a caretaker at the Capitol Building, living in a vacant chamber in the north wing, and Congress later awarded him with far more than it ever did Eaton; the Tyrolean native received 320 acres of land in Missouri, and back pay to 1805.)

Eaton was well aware of his own relentless downfall, though he found himself unable to slow its pace. "Fortune has reversed her tables," he wrote to Humbert, a French friend in Tunis. "I live, or rather stay in obscurity and uselessness. The wound I received on the coast of Tripoli and others more early, have deprived me of an arm's use and the use of a leg.—Want of economy, which I never learned, want of judgement in the speculative concerns of private life, which I never studied, and what is more, privation of the consideration of a government which I have served, have unmanned me."

He added, with a nice Barbary pirate touch: "Death has laid himself alongside and thrown his grappling hooks upon my quarter and forecastle but I keep him off midships yet."

He complained often and he knew where to pin the blame. "I am crippled in health & fortune," he wrote his brother Ebeneezer. "Ask you how? Burr and Jefferson."

He sought out other embittered souls. One J. Dunham wrote to him: "Our country is gone to the devil . . . You like others, have fought in vain."

By April 1811, his feet and ankles were so swollen he could barely climb out of bed. One day, in great pain, he struggled to a farm cart and visited his friend Colonel Morgan. A carpenter happened to come by and Eaton joked with him to be sure *not* to make his coffin out of pine because he hated the smell. He advised Colonel Morgan *not* to set him in the casket on his back. "For in that position, I am prone to nightmares."

As his health worsened, he decided that he wanted his children baptized. He made the request to the local minister, Mr. Fay, whom Eaton had helped select. Mr. Fay sent him a regretful note: "Your long absence from communication with the church and your immoral habits render it improper to perform such a service." Eaton was very un-Christian in his feelings toward the minister.

The night of May 31 his legs and stomach began to swell, and he became incoherent. At 8:40 P.M. on June 1, 1811, he died, at the age of forty-seven.

Four colonels carried the self-appointed general to his grave in Brimfield's cemetery, located down a dirt lane off Breakneck Hill with a view out over the valley.

The newspaper in Boston, *The Centinel,* which had devoted many column inches to his Tripoli exploits, now ran a succinct obituary. "Gen. EATON, the hero of Derne, and the victim of sensibility, was entombed at Brimfield, on Wednesday last."

The *Oxford English Dictionary* defines *sensibility,* as it was used during that era, as "a liability to feel offended or hurt by unkindness or lack of respect." No brief obituary was more apt. He festered at the ingratitude of his nation.

In 1876, Civil War veteran General Fitz Henry Warren came to Brimfield to give a centennial speech. He praised Eaton for having been "brave, impulsive and generous" but he also lamented the man's "hot chivalry," his "temper," his "imprudent speech." At the end of this frank assessment, General Warren gestured toward the cemetery and said: "William Eaton became a tenant in your dwelling of the dead where his humble headstone now reminds you of the vanity of human pursuits and the almost utter oblivion of a once widely known name."

Eaton had refused to bask in his abbreviated glory; instead he had dared to defy Thomas Jefferson, and no good can come of that.

Epilogue

Tobias Lear remained in the Mediterranean as consul general, and he continued to dote on his young wife, Fanny. During a rare separation in 1807, he wrote to her from aboard the USS *Constitution*, which had transported them on their honeymoon, "I am at last in our dear little cabin, which wants only yourself to make it an earthly paradise to me."

Lear also continued to coddle the Barbary powers, paying tribute and giving elaborate jeweled presents such as "a gold watch with diamonds, a diamond solitaire, etc." A congressional study later found that Lear had overseen spending more than $500,000 in four years, from 1805 to 1809. He never received an official reprimand for his handling of the treaty with Tripoli.

Finally, in 1812, not coincidentally *after* the death of Eaton, who had threatened him, Tobias decided to return to the United States. And the Dey of Algiers opted to extort one last $27,000 present out of him. Desperate to depart, Lear convinced the moneylenders Busnah & Bacri to advance him the sum; they charged 25 percent interest. In a couple of days, Lear had lost $33,750, close to the price of William Eaton's entire mission.

Lear, after run-ins with the British navy, finally reached home in 1813; he soon after asked a friend to deposit $4,900 for him; he also purchased a carriage and a pair of horses for $1,100. Lear apparently had done quite well—financially—as a diplomat to Barbary. He resumed his correspondence with Thomas Jefferson, who wrote back warmly and invited Colonel Lear, Fanny, and son Lincoln to come visit him at Monticello.

Though Lear hoped for a Cabinet-level appointment, President Madison offered him only the post of chief accountant in the War Department, which he reluctantly accepted. With Lear back in Washington City, fanatical Federalists such as Timothy Pickering renewed their harsh criticism of the consul general and his Tripoli treaty. They also revived the charge that Lear—seeking favors—had destroyed some of Washington's letters.

On October 11, 1816, with no hysterics and no warning, Tobias Lear committed suicide. His son discovered him bloodied, still holding the pistol. He left no note. The former secretary to George Washington was buried in Congressional Cemetery; he was joined forty years later by his beloved wife, Fanny, who never remarried.

* * *

Hamet Karamanli, impoverished exile, stayed on in Syracuse; his princely entourage dwindled down to a mere dozen; he survived on a $200-a-month dole from the U.S. Navy agent. Almost fourteen months after Congress approved it, Hamet did receive $2,400 in "temporary relief," with most of the money going to pay his debts.

The new U.S. consul to Tripoli, Dr. George Davis, as soon as he learned of Lear's secret article in May of 1807, informed Bashaw Yussef that the clandestine agreement had *not* been ratified by the U.S. Senate and therefore was *not* part of the agreed treaty. Yussef was furious and demanded a "consideration" to change it. Davis—in the hard diplomatic school of Eaton and Preble—held his ground and confronted Yussef during a session of the *divan*. "Our treaty is known to all the world and our public faith pledged in [Hamet's family's] behalf," said Davis. "Your brother cooperated with us and to deceive him in such a tender point would disgrace us as a nation."

Yussef caved and agreed to free the family. On October 13, 1807, at

10 P.M., Hamet's wife, three sons, and a daughter, with an entourage of nineteen servants and slaves, departed for Syracuse on an Italian vessel, chartered by the U.S. government. Reunion was sweet, but Hamet had no means to support his royal clan. "I do not see how he can provide bread," Davis soon wrote. Fleeing creditors, Hamet moved from Syracuse to Malta. He borrowed often and even pawned his wife's jewelry.

When the governor of Derne—Mustifa—died in late 1808, Davis lobbied Yussef to appoint his brother to rule there. The Bashaw surprisingly agreed, and in spring of 1809 Hamet and both his wives and all the children prepared to leave Malta. However, his landlord refused to let him go, and the United States, at the last minute, paid $2,360 in back rent to extricate him. Hamet and family moved into the palace at Derne, where by all accounts, he ruled wisely and fairly and was well liked by his people. Davis informed him that all U.S. responsibilities toward him had now officially ceased.

Two years later, Yussef tried to kill him. In 1811, Hamet fled to Alexandria, along that same desert route that he and Eaton had taken a half decade earlier. He died that year in unpleasant exile at the age of forty-seven. His son Mohammed tried to take over Tripoli in the 1830s but failed.

* * *

Bashaw **Yussef Karamanli** of Tripoli (1766–1838), despite being master of the smallest corsair fleet in Barbary, continued to extort a luxurious lifestyle out of the nations of Europe and the United States. The U.S. government, for one, sent a nice gift of $5,000, which included a diamond snuffbox. Yussef continued to enjoy the music of his Italian band and continued to prefer the company of his Negro wife to his Turkish one. Despite many coup attempts by his own sons, the Bashaw continued to rule and to thrive *for another twenty-seven years*, through 1832. During his waning days of power, however, with the French and British demanding payments, the sixty-eight-year-old ruler holed himself up in the castle, drinking brandy with his three favorite African concubines.

His desire to cover them in jewels had bankrupted the kingdom, claimed a French consul. Yussef's son then forced him from the throne, and the old man wound up living in a deserted part of the palace, half-naked in rags.

When Yussef died, unmourned, three years later, the Turkish government paid to have him buried near his ancestors in the Karamanli mosque in the heart of the city, not too far from where he had once let dogs feast on the remains of American sailors.

* * *

The Scottish pirate, **Murad Rais**—the former Peter Lyle, who had forsaken family and foreskin—led the corsair fleet out hunting in the wake of the American peace treaty. As usual, he stalked the weaker nations and, within weeks, had captured a Neapolitan ship with twenty slaves aboard, and then a merchant ship flying a Danish flag. Murad, married to Yussef's sister, rarely failed to reward his patron.

About a decade later, however, Murad's lush lifestyle suddenly came to an end, thanks to the anger of the United States. The American consul, Richard B. Jones, liked to shoot quail, sometimes venturing onto the edge of Murad's country estate. Murad ordered his slaves to attack him. One smashed him twice over the head with the thick shaft of a hoe. "My hat prevented the blow from being fatal," later wrote Jones.

The American demanded justice. So, Bashaw Yussef agreed to banish Murad until the United States would allow him to return. This Barbary pirate, whom Eaton had once called a "damned villain," boarded a British ship to Lampedusa with his eldest sons, the nephews of the Bashaw.

After three years, the United States allowed Murad to return to Tripoli, and he reclaimed his post as admiral. In 1832 he made the mistake of supporting *Hamet's son Mohammed* during a failed coup. Murad died that year when hit by a cannonball fired from the walls of Tripoli castle.

* * *

Dr. **Jonathan Cowdery** (1767–1852), the assistant surgeon of the USS *Philadelphia* who had served the Bashaw's family, returned to the United States in 1805, suffering from an eye disease prevalent on the Barbary Coast. In 1833, despite being blind in his left eye, he became chief surgeon of the U.S. Navy, a post that he held until his death.

* * *

Commodore **Samuel Barron** recovered from his liver ailment long enough to oversee building Jefferson's gunboats at Hampton, Virginia, and to father a son. He was never censured for shilly-shallying in the Mediterranean; this favorite of Jefferson died on October 29, 1810, long before the era of death benefits for widows. "In recognition of the service of his father," his son, **Samuel Barron III,** at the age of *two years and five weeks,* was appointed a midshipman, the youngest officer in the history of the U.S. Navy; he was immediately entitled to receive a portion of his salary. Late in life, Samuel III became a commodore during the Civil War . . . for the navy of the Confederate states.

* * *

After being feted for a while, **William Bainbridge** (1774–1833), the exonerated captain of the USS *Philadelphia,* took a furlough from the navy to earn money as a merchant captain. While climbing aboard a commercial vessel, he tripped and fell into the water. Unable to swim, he sank three times below the surface before a Negro servant dove in and rescued him.

During the War of 1812, Bainbridge finally had his moment of glory. He commanded the frigate USS *Constitution* against the British HMS *Java,* which had forty-nine cannon and 400 men. Early on, Bainbridge received a musket ball in the hip, then was sprayed with splinters when a British cannonball blew away the ship's wheel. He persevered on the quarterdeck and steered the *Constitution*—by ordering sailors to pull rudder cables belowdecks—to head directly at the *Java's* bow until their riggings became entwined. The Americans' superior gunnery then devastated the British ship.

Bainbridge thrived in the peacetime navy, establishing the first naval school in Boston harbor and overseeing various shipbuilding ports.

* * *

With the end of the War of 1812, **Stephen Decatur Jr.**, who had burned the *Philadelphia* in Tripoli harbor, was given the plum assignment of commanding a squadron heading to the Mediterranean to confront the Barbary nations. His mission was to deliver long overdue payback for decades of insolence.

Decatur captured the Algerian flagship *Mashuda* with 406 sailors aboard, and enjoyed the exquisite treat of dictating terms to Algiers—no tribute ever again, no American slaves ever again—and he demanded an immediate $10,000 payment for past wrongs.

Next stop was Tunis, where Decatur and his fleet again demanded an immediate payment, in this case of $46,000, to compensate for an American ship being looted the previous year. Decatur refused to be tricked ashore or delayed. The Bey paid.

Then Decatur continued east to Tripoli. He entered the port where 300 American sailors had toiled as slaves; he demanded that Bashaw Yussef immediately hand over $30,000 for violating the treaty between the United States and Tripoli. Yussef threatened to declare war and disparagingly offered a pittance on the dollar. Decatur was unmoved. Yussef, very quickly, paid $25,000 and freed ten Christian slaves.

Decatur returned home to the United States to extraordinary applause for being the first American officer successfully to defy the Barbary powers.

On March 22, 1820, the national hero fought a duel with Captain James Barron, younger brother of Commodore Samuel Barron. Captain James Barron, who had been disgraced during the *Chesapeake* incident with England, believed that Decatur had repeatedly slandered him and blocked his re-entry into the navy. Decatur chose Captain Bainbridge to negotiate the rules of the duel, and Bainbridge graciously allowed the severely nearsighted Barron to fire from the shortened distance of eight paces instead of the usual ten. Decatur died. For the rest of her life, Decatur's widow, Susan, called Bainbridge "one of my husband's murderers."

* * *

The days of the **Barbary corsair** were numbered. Decatur's regatta of defiance helped shame the European powers to end their centuries-old practice of placating the Barbary nations. Admiral Lord Exmouth led a combined English-Dutch fleet into **Algiers** in 1816, a year after Decatur. Heavy bombardment swayed the Dey to agree to renounce enslaving any Christians and to agree to a lasting peace without tribute. Within a few years, however, the Dey was back in the white slave trade and at war with France. In 1829, two armed French brigs ran aground in the harbor, and the enraged Dey offered a $100 reward for each severed French head brought to him. He paid for 109. France soon after attacked with massive force and in three weeks conquered Algiers, ending that nation's maritime crimes forever. France did not grant independence to Algeria until 1962.

Tunis struggled on as a second-rate pirate power, but the demise of Algiers spelled its own doom as a predator. France eventually controlled Tunis as well, from 1881 through 1956.

As for **Tripoli,** once Bashaw Yussef fell from power, his squabbling sons sent the nation into near constant civil war. The Ottoman Empire in 1835 sent a fleet and ended the Karamanli dynasty and officially stopped the piracies. Italy conquered the region in 1911 and held on until its own defeat in World War II. Libya was an Islamic monarchy in 1969 when Colonel Moammar Qaddafi staged a coup and took power. At first he preached anti-Westernism and a support for terrorism worldwide. However, many factors, including economic sanctions and a middle-of-night U.S. airstrike on his home in 1986, have led Qaddafi over the years to tone down that message.

* * *

Eaton's mission was the United States' **first overseas covert operation,** but certainly not the last. The CIA agenda for the latter half of the twentieth century was filled with agents seeking covert regime change—especially in Central and South America—to create governments sympathetic to U.S. interests. But dirty tricks often have strange results. In the 1980s, the United States' secret aid to the mujahideen "Freedom Fighters" in Afghanistan put American-made weapons in the hands of a fellow by the name of Osama bin Laden.

At this very moment, plans are afoot at CIA headquarters to prop up or topple regimes around the world. Many of these plans will remain secret for years, if not decades. Thomas Jefferson and James Madison had grave misgivings about taking this path, of trying to reshape the world through stealth, of unleashing kingmakers like William Eaton.

* * *

Congress never rewarded the marine privates who marched with Eaton on his forlorn mission across the desert. In fact, for almost a century after Tripoli the entire **United States Marine Corps** remained a lowly, underpaid, underrespected outfit, mostly assigned to guarding ships and navy yards, and to parading around on ceremonial occasions. The Marine Band played at presidential events.

The United States Marine Corps did not begin to evolve into one of the world's most elite fighting forces until its accomplishments in World War I—the Fourth Marine "Devil Dogs" of Belleau Wood, for one— followed by amphibious assaults and its heralded valor in World War II at Iwo Jima and elsewhere. The Corps successfully moved from its early "The Desperate, the Drunk" to its current "The Few, the Proud."

Lieutenant Presley O'Bannon (1776–1850), the fiddle-playing fearless marine who charged alongside Eaton, was the only U.S. Marine to receive a reward. The State of Virginia commissioned a fancy scimitar to be presented to him. Before he received it, though, disgusted over his lack of promotion, O'Bannon resigned from the marines on March 6, 1807, and spent two years in the U.S. Army. O'Bannon then moved back to Kentucky and started distilling whiskey with his brother-in-law under the brand "Old Pepper"; he was elected to the state legislature and amassed a small fortune in real estate. Years after his death, the Daughters of the American Revolution had his remains moved from obscure Russellville to Kentucky's premier cemetery in Frankfort. The tombstone reads: "As Captain [sic] of United States Marines he was the First to Plant the American Flag on Foreign Soil."

In 1826, Marine Commandant Archibald Henderson adopted a **curved Mameluke sword** for the U.S. Marines dress uniform. Marine tradition holds that Hamet Karamanli, in gratitude, had presented a similar scimitar to Lieutenant O'Bannon after the capture of Derne. Unfortunately, no evidence exists that Hamet, penniless as always, ever presented O'Bannon with a sword. (The legend first surfaced when an O'Bannon relative wrote it up as fact in the Louisville *Courier-Journal* in 1917.)

All that notwithstanding, the marines did carve out more than a little glory on that march with Eaton, and almost every day, someone somewhere loudly sings their praise: "From the halls of Montezuma **to the shores of Tripoli,** we will fight our country's battles on the land as on the sea. First to fight for right and freedom, And to keep our honor clean, We are proud to claim the title of United States Marine."

* * *

Slave girl **Anna Porcile** returned to Sardinia and slipped out of the history books. Her father, the chevalier, never repaid anyone for her ransom. Among the slaves captured alongside her during that Tunisian raid in 1798 was another appealing girl, Francesca Rosso, who was nine at the time. In 1810, Francesca married the Bey of Tunis, and their son Sidi Hamed, nicknamed "Il Sardo" (the Sardinian), later ruled Tunis for eighteen years.

To the present day, on the tiny island of San Pietro on November 15, the people celebrate their ancestors' liberation from Moslem slavery with a Catholic festival called The Madonna of the Slave. They exult in knowing they no longer have to fear that they might go to sleep free and wake up headed in chains to the coast of Barbary.

* * *

Thomas Jefferson (1743–1826) never apologized in any way to William Eaton; he never chastised Tobias Lear; he never publicly admitted regret over the Tripoli treaty. "Biologically, as well as psychologically, he was thin-skinned," wrote biographer Joseph Ellis in his award-winning *American Sphinx*. Jefferson spent his retirement working to found the University of Virginia, greeting an endless stream of visitors to Monticello, and answering more than a thousand letters a year.

And every so often in one of those letters, he would weigh in on a political topic. Though he rarely acknowledged his own contradictions, changes in his beliefs certainly did occur. Jefferson had always distrusted the idea of creating a strong permanent navy of massive warships. And yet, on June 19, 1813, he wrote to Tobias Lear: "I suppose we can do little with the Dey [of Algiers] till we have peace with England, *but then I would, at any expense, hunt him from the ocean, a navy equal to that object we should ever keep.*"

That is a strong statement from the Gunboat President.

Jefferson and Eaton always shared an abhorrence for the bullying of the Barbary pirates. In his later years, Jefferson inched closer to Eaton's view that the United States must spend money to create a military force large enough to compel respect. And, ultimately, a few years after Jefferson's death, it was military coercion and not diplomatic finesse that ended the three-century-long reign of terror of the Barbary pirates.

* * *

Eliza Danielson Eaton (1766–1833), William's patient, beautiful wife, was eventually forced to sell all her remaining Brimfield properties to pay off her husband's debts. After incurring lawyer bills fruitlessly searching for lost family lands in Ohio and Maine, she moved to upstate New York, where she lived frugally with support from her children. She watched her four sons join the military and saw three of them die young and be buried in their uniforms, including William Jr., at age twenty-three. Over the years, she rarely, if ever, complained about that lost soul she had married, whose combustible patriotism had led the U.S. Marines to the pirate coast of Tripoli.

Acknowledgments, Notes, Bibliography, and Credits

Acknowledgments

AFTER MY SEVENTH VIEWING of *Lawrence of Arabia*, I decided to study Arabic, and at age eighteen won a fellowship to Cairo. But my romanticized version of the Middle East quickly collided with the chaos and poverty of the Egyptian metropolis. I was appalled to see beggar women training their babies to sleep with a tiny hand thrust out, palm upward.

Impetuously, I dropped out of the Cairo language program to play blackjack in the casinos of the Mediterranean. The sum total of my knowledge of Arabic today is a handful of phrases from the Koran—which I can pronounce with precision—and that have on more than one occasion saved my life, or at least my shoulder bag.

But my fascination with the bygone Moslem world remained simmering somewhere, and I am thrilled to have traveled with General Eaton and hopefully taken the reader beyond the souks, into the slave quarters, the Bedouin camps, and onto the Barbary pirate ships.

This book required two years to research, one year to write. Eaton left more than three thousand pages of papers, almost all of which are carefully preserved at the magnificent Huntington Library and Gardens in San Marino, California.

I have never met Mieke van Leeuwen; I don't even know whether Mieke is a he or a she, but I do know that Mieke helped me immensely. As an afterthought, seduced by the ease of e-mail, I contacted the

National Archives in Holland, asking for any reports circa 1800 from Tripoli. I had never heard the name of Antoine Zuchet because this diplomat had never been quoted anywhere. Mieke van Leeuwen sent me more than a hundred pages of Zuchet's very candid letters, which reveal surprising details about Tripoli and about the lives of the three hundred Americans held hostage. Zuchet's words change our view of the Barbary war. Thomas Jefferson never knew the pitiful weakness of Tripoli at the moment Tobias Lear signed the treaty; American naval officers never knew the *Philadelphia* floated free a mere ten hours after Bainbridge beached it. From the bottom of my heart, I thank you, Mieke.

The story over at the Danish Archives played out dead opposite. A fellow by the name of Henrik Stissing Jensen e-mailed me that he had found a misfiled trove of material on Tripoli, and then Jensen tortured me for a full year by never sending it. I even brought in the Danish embassy in London, to no avail. Jensen, wherever you are, may your coffee always be a bit colder than you like it. My guess is that the Danish Archives was hoping to suppress Consul Nissen's double cross of the United States in 1805. (I found it out despite you, Jensen.)

The staff at Dartmouth Library Special Collections, especially Sarah Hartwell, was cheerful and refreshingly unpretentious.

I hired Nelly Malouf to translate Arabic, and she would be an asset to any research project in English, French, or Arabic. At a shop near my office in New York, Riad of Lebanon (who doesn't want his last name in the book) double-checked the Arabic treaty translations. You are a kind and gracious man.

At the eleventh hour, I tried to beef up the section on covert ops, and author Hank Schlesinger put me in touch with H. K. Melton, the scholar and collector extraordinaire. Thank you for your painstaking explanations. Thanks, too, to Jim Morris, Green Beret and author. You untangled the human aspect of Eaton, the arrogant outsider ready to do what three thousand sailors with all their cannons could not do. That insight helped frame him for me.

Gareth Thomas, you taught me about cutlass warfare. It will have to go in the next book. Every time I wrote some slash-and-pivot, duck-and-thrust, it sounded like pulp fiction; my fault, not yours.

The Naval Historical Center photo room needs a new photocopy machine. Is there some wealthy vet ready to donate one? Rob Hanshew was very helpful, as was Glenn Helm, a friendly, funny man who runs the Navy Department Library. Thanks for slipping me the ZB files. Over at the Marine Photo Department, a graceful bow to Lena Kaljot, and at the National Archives, to Katherine Vollen and Regina Davis. The gentlemen at the Manuscript Room at the Library of Congress were appropriately eccentric and helpful.

Once again, author Bill Prochnau read the manuscript and barked suggestions. He ordered me to amp up the verbs, avoid lazy phrases, shorten the quotations, and, above all, vivify the scenes without straying from documented details. We will all be fortunate if he writes another book.

Nick Cassavetes (*The Notebook*) bought the movie rights to my last book, *The Pirate Hunter*; that cash infusion helped tide me over. I'm rooting for you to make the film. So are my wife and my unborn grandchildren.

Thanks also go to my editor at Hyperion, Bill Strachan, gracious and supportive, and to Bob Miller, who has given me encouragement from the first day forward, and to Will Schwalbe and Judd Laghi and to fearless Esther Newberg.

As always, I want to thank my smart, perceptive mother, who now goes by the name of "Sister Gordon." My family tolerated all. Georgia, since you're sixteen, my absences probably didn't bother you much, but I missed you. Ziggy, pal, work on that jump shot, and Kris, you are more beautiful today than when I married you, and more clever, amusing, and perceptive. How is that possible?

Finally, I want to thank all readers of any of my books. You can reach me at rzacks@forbiddenknowledge.com.

—Richard Zacks, New York City

ABBREVIATIONS

WE-HL—William Eaton Papers. The Huntington Library. San Marino, Cal. Microfilm.

LIFE—*Life of the late General Eaton*, ed. Charles Prentiss (Brookfield, Mass., 1813).

ASP—*American State Papers Documents, legislative and executive, of the Congress of the United States . . . selected and edited under the authority of Congress*, 38 vols. (Washington, D.C., 1832–1861).

BW—*Naval Documents related to the United States Wars with the Barbary Powers* (Washington, D.C., 1939–1944), 6 vols.

RAY—*Horrors of Slavery, or The American Tars in Tripoli* by William Ray (Troy, N.Y., 1808, *Magazine of History* reprint, 1911).

AZ—Letters of Antoine Zuchet, consul in Tripoli for Batavian Republique (Holland) to Department of Foreign Affairs. Nationaal Archief. The Hague. Ministerie van Buitenlandse Zaken, 1796–1810. Access number 2.01.08. inv. nr. 356. Translation from French by Richard Zacks.

PM—*William Plumer's Memorandum of Proceedings in the United States Senate, 1803–1807* (N.Y., 1923).

PROLOGUE

2. "shame and villainies" *Appendice per gli anni dal 1773 al 1799 alla Storia di Sardegna del Barone Giuseppe Manno* (Capolago, 1847), p. 421. Translation: R. Zacks.

3. "*Six jeunes filles . . .*" Antoine Nyssen to Foreign Affairs Ministry of Republique Batave, January 21, 1799. National Archives. The Hague. inv. nr. 357A, 357, 5. Translation: R. Zacks.

3. "On these pillars, standing silent, sad, wings furled . . ." Dumas, Alexander. *Impressions de Voyage* (Paris, 1855), p. 222. Translation: R. Zacks.

4. "There was a huge crowd drunk with joy to see . . ." Antoine Nyssen to Foreign

Affairs Ministry of Republique Batave, January 21, 1799. National Archives. The Hague. inv. nr. 357A, 357, 5. Translation: R. Zacks.

5. "had fixed his desire on her" William Eaton (Tunis) to General Marshall, December 20, 1800, WE-HL, Reel 2. (This item is reproduced by permission of *The Huntington Library, San Marino, California,* as are all WE-HL items.)

7. "a fleet of Quaker meeting houses would have done . . ." William Eaton (Tunis) to James Cathcart, August 8, 1802, WE-HL, Reel 2.

7. "Here I am, under the mad rays of a vertical sun . . ." William Eaton (Tunis) to Stephen Pynchon, October 12, 1799, WE-HL, Reel 2.

7. "For my part, it grates me mortally when . . ." William Eaton (Tunis) to George Hough, September 15, 1799, LIFE, p. 170.

7. "Imagination better than language can paint . . ." William Eaton (Tunis) to General Marshall, December 20, 1800, WE-HL, Reel 2.

8. "I ransomed your daughter" William Eaton (Tunis) to Antonio Porcile, April 25, 1801. ASP. Class IX, p. 328.

8. "It was impossible to apprehend that the respect . . ." William Eaton (Tunis) to James Madison, March 5, 1803, LIFE, p. 239.

9. "thief," "violence and indignity" Ibid., p. 241.

9. "As security for the money paid by me . . ." Richard Morris to secretary of the navy, March 30, 1803, BW II, p. 384.

9. "[I hope] the hour is not too far distant . . ." William Eaton (Tunis) to Eliza Eaton, June 6, 1800, WE-HL, Reel 2.

9. "[Eaton] appeared to be a man of lively imagination . . ." Morris, Richard. "A Defense of the Conduct of Morris during His Command in the Mediterranean" (New York, 1804), p. 88.

CHAPTER I. TRIPOLI

11. "Would to God that the officers and crew of the *Philadelphia* . . ." Edward Preble (Syracuse) to secretary of the navy, BW III, p. 256.

13. "I believe there never was so depraved . . ." William Bainbridge (Tripoli) to Edward Preble, November 25, 1803, BW III, p. 176.

13. "maindeck of America" Rea, John. "A Letter to William Bainbridge Esq." (Philadelphia, 1802), p. 1.

14. "liberty, equality, peace and plenty" RAY, p. 63.

14. "How preposterous does it appear . . ." Rea, John. "A Letter to William Bainbridge Esq." (Philadelphia, 1802), p. 13.

15. "You tell an officer . . ." RAY, pp. 58–61.

16. "Every sail was set . . ." RAY, p. 80.

18. "fanfaronade" AZ, November 1, 1803.

18. "All sails were instantly set . . ." BW III, p. 190.

19. "barbarous negroes" Mather, Cotton. "The Glory of Goodness, . . . Barbarous Cruelties of Barbary" (Boston, 1703) as quoted in *White Slaves, African Masters* by Paul Baepler (Chicago, 1999), p. 62.

19. "[I] was forced to lie down in the street . . ." *The Algerine Captive* by Royall Tyler (New Haven, 1797), p. 125.

19. "The person is laid upon his face . . ." "A Journal of the Captivity and Sufferings of John Foss" as quoted in *White Slaves, African Masters* by Paul Baepler (Chicago, 1999), p. 82.

21. "I could not but notice the striking alteration . . ." RAY, p. 81.

24. "The Algerian Flag hoisted on the Main top . . ." Log of USS *George Washington*, BW I, p. 378.

25. "History shall tell that the United States . . ." Notes of William Eaton on a letter received from Consul Richard O'Brien, LIFE, p. 190.

25. "We all answer'd that all was done . . ." William Knight (Tripoli) to Thomas Bristoll, November 1, 1803, BW III, pp. 179–180.

26. "About four o'clock, the Eagle of America . . ." RAY, p. 82.

26. "strip of their clothes, or pillage . . ." "Rules and Regulations for the Government of the Navy." U.S. Congress, Sixth Congress, Session I. April 23, 1800.

27. "to behave with circumspection and propriety . . ." RAY, p. 83.

27. "We sent a boat and persuaded them that it was no . . ." Ibid., p. 82.

28. "most Barbary crewmen have no other means of . . ." Caronni, Felice. *Ragguaglio del viaggio in Barberia* (Milan, 1806/reprint 1993), p. 78. Trans.: R. Zacks.

28. "We are treated much better than I expected" William Knight (Tripoli) to Thomas Bristoll, November 1, 1803, BW III, pp. 179–180.

29. "At the beach stood a row of armed men . . ." RAY, pp. 86–87.

CHAPTER 2. WASHINGTON CITY

31. "If the Congress do not consent . . ." William Eaton (Tunis) to Richard O'Brien, June 2, 1799, WE-HL, Reel 2.

32. "It looks like a deserted city" PM, p. 642.

34. "tall, large-boned farmer" and "good natured . . ." Augustus Foster, secretary to the British Legation, as quoted in *History of the United States of America during the First Administration of Thomas Jefferson* by Henry Adams (New York, 1917/1986 reprint), p. 126.

34. "loose and rambling" etc. Senator Maclay. Ibid.

35. "I am an enemy to all these douceurs . . ." Thomas Jefferson to James Madison, as quoted in *American Sphinx* by Joseph Ellis, p. 241.

35. "Only the Legislature . . ." Thomas Jefferson (Washington City) to William Eaton (not sent) February 8, 1804. Thomas Jefferson Papers. Library of Congress.

36. Note to auditor. James Madison to Richard Harrison. February 11, 1804, WE-HL, Reel 2.

37. "needless expenses," "extravagances" Alexander Murray to secretary of the navy, May 7, 1802, BW II, p. 146.

38. "It may be asserted, without vanity or exaggeration . . ." and rest of speech. Petition of William Eaton to Committee of Claims, House of Representatives, February 16, 1804. ASP, Claims, vol. 1, pp. 299–307.

38. "looks very well in a veil" Journal of Henry Wadsworth, September 13, 1802, BW II, p. 273.

40. "well-founded claim for . . . service" John Cotton Smith, February 29, 1804, ASP Claims, vol. 1, p. 299.

41. "increase our force and enlarge . . ." Thomas Jefferson, *National Intelligencer* (Washington), March 21, 1804.

41. "Millions for Defense . . ." *National Intelligencer* (Washington), March 23, 1804.

41-42. "Mammoth Loaf" and "people of all classes & colors . . ." PM, pp. 179–180, and a grateful nod for all the cheese leads to Jeffrey L. Pasley of University of Missouri-Columbia.

42. "enterprise" and "The President and his Cabinet Council . . ." William Eaton (at sea) to Thomas Dwight, August 1804. Quoted in LIFE, p. 265.

42. "Although it does not accord with the general sentiments . . ." James Madison (Virginia) to William Eaton, August 22, 1802, BW II, p. 245. Same message to Cathcart.

44. "as much of a gentleman and soldier . . ." William Eaton (at sea) to Thomas Dwight, August 1804. Quoted in LIFE, p. 266.

44. "Navy Agent of the United States for the Several Barbary Regencies" William Eaton (Washington) to Eliza Danielson [undated], WE-HL, Reel 2.

CHAPTER 3. AMERICAN SLAVES IN TRIPOLI CITY

45. "I know not what will become of . . ." Edward Preble (Syracuse harbor) to his wife, December 12, 1803. Library of Congress. Manuscript Division.

46. "slight" and "indifferent morals," etc. Simon Lucas (Tripoli) to Henry Dundas, June 5, 1794. Public Record Office, Kew, England. FO161:10.

46. "Hang the d-mned villain if you catch him!" William Eaton (Tunis) to James Cathcart, December 30, 1802, in postscript, January 6, 1803, WE-HL, Reel 2.

47. "Do you think your captain is a coward or traitor?" RAY, p. 88.

47. "The sea wasn't choppy . . ." AZ, November 5, 1805.

49. "muffled up in blankets . . ." RAY, p. 96.

49. "walking stick . . . hard and very heavy" Ibid., p. 59.

51. "fresh bleeding" Ibid., p. 100.

51. "would caper, sing, jest, and look as cheerful . . ." Ibid., p. 95.

52. "enormous" Jonathan Cowdery, *American Captives in Tripoli* (Boston, 1806), November 8, 1804, p. 8.

52. "My Dear Susan, With feelings of distress . . ." William Bainbridge (Tripoli) to Susan Bainbridge, November 1, 1803, BW III, p. 178.

53. "mere scratch" RAY, p. 107.

54. "Thomas Prince was metamorphosed . . ." Ibid., p. 103.

55. "The boy was then brought forward . . ." Ali Bey, *Travels of Ali Bey in Morocco, Tripoli, etc., 1803–1807,* pp. 10–12.

55. "He . . . acted as a spy carrying . . ." RAY, p. 99.

56. "With the sacred promise of the divine . . ." AZ, December 3, 1803.

CHAPTER 4. HOME: NEW ENGLAND ROOTS

59. "[I hope] the hour is not far distant . . ." Eaton (Tunis) to Eliza, June 6, 1800, WE-HL, Reel 2.

60. Travel Diary, WE-HL, Reel 3.

60. "I love you and long to see you" Eaton (Tunis) undated, WE-HL, Reel 2.

60. "some Roman or Carthaginian Lady" Eaton (Tunis) October 13, 1799, WE-HL, Reel 2.

61. "intellectual vigor" LIFE, p. 10.

62. "FREEDOM—that sacred plant of paradise" *Connecticut Gazette* (New London), November 11, 1774.

62. "bake your baby into a pie" *A Historical Collection from Official Records, Files &c, of the Part Sustained by Connecticut during the War of Revolution* ed. Royal Hinman (Hartford, 1842), Appendix.

62. "try men's souls . . ." Thomas Paine, "The Crisis" (1776).

63. Alumnus sketch of Gen. Wm. Eaton. *New Hampshire Patriot & State Gazette* (Concord, N.H., September 21, 1835). Courtesy of Dartmouth College Library.

63. "no resource but industry" Eaton (Hanover, N.H.) to Dartmouth President John Wheelock, September 5, 1789. Courtesy of Dartmouth College Library.

64. "bell-igerant" Alumnus sketch of Gen. Wm. Eaton. *New Hampshire Patriot & State Gazette* (Concord, N.H., September 21, 1835). Courtesy of Dartmouth College Library.

64. "pull down the proud" Library of Congress, Manuscript Division. William Eaton papers. Masonic Lodge, mm 79005184.

65. "sycamore, elm" LIFE, p. 18.

65. "danger . . . in his element" LIFE, p. 20.

65. "slept more than a hundred nights in that same wilderness" Eaton (Tunis) to Eliza, June 6, 1800, WE-HL, Reel 2.

66. Butler. LIFE, pp. 15–17.

67. "monument in mud" LIFE, p. 21.

67. "debauched, unprincipled, old batchelor" LIFE, p. 51.

68. "this elevated brute" LIFE, p. 60.

CHAPTER 5. TRIPOLI: DECATUR'S RAID

71. "I shall hazard . . ." Edward Preble to secretary of the navy, December 10, 1803, BW III, p. 258.

71. "coldest season of the year" RAY, p. 109.

72. "as cruel to our men" RAY, p. 109.

73. "Altho' the fortune of War . . ." Preble, January 4, 1804, BW III, p. 312.

74. "About 11 o'clock . . ." RAY, p. 115.

76. "fine" black female slaves. Higgins to Preble, December 29, 1803. Malta, BW III, p. 302.

76. "The Turkish Officer alone . . ." Preble diary, December 24, 1803, BW III, p. 294.

76. "I am not without hope . . ." Thomas Jefferson to Secretary of the Navy Robert Smith, April 27, 1804. *The Works of Thomas Jefferson* ed. Paul L. Ford. (N.Y., 1904), vol. X, p. 77.

78. "The Captain and Crew having . . ." Preble to Tobias Lear, January 31, 1804, BW III, p. 378.

78. "the most bold and daring act of the age" Lord Horatio Nelson, as quoted in *Dawn Like Thunder* by Glenn Tucker, p. 283.

78. "On boarding the Frigate . . ." Preble to Decatur, January 31, 1804, BW III, p. 376.

79. "I am in hopes . . ." Ralph Izard Jr. to Mrs. Ralph Izard Sr., February 2, 1804, BW III, p. 381.

80. "The Tripolitans on board of her were dreadfully alarmed . . ." Ralph Izard Jr. to Mrs. Ralph Izard Sr., February 20, 1804, BW III, p. 416.

80. "the whooping and screaming of the enemy" Lewis Heerman, affidavit, April 26, 1828, BW III, p. 417.

80. "I immediately fired her . . ." Decatur to Preble, February 17, 1804, BW III, p. 414.

80. "were rushing from every side . . ." Lewis Heerman, affidavit, April 26, 1828, BW III, p. 417.

81. "The Americans have just partially erased . . ." AZ, February 28, 1804.

82. "Early in the morning . . ." RAY, p. 115.

83. "who to court favour" RAY, p. 116.

83. "Captain Bainbridge, however, bid us . . ." RAY, p. 116.

83. "massacred" Sidi Muhammed Dghies to William Bainbridge, March 5, 1804, BW III, p. 474.

CHAPTER 6. ALONE AT SEA

86. "finding his Brother's troops arrive . . ." Richard Farquhar (Malta) to Thomas Jefferson, November 15, 1803, BW III, p. 222.

86. "He has all the Arabs . . ." January 17, 1804. Preble (Malta harbor) to secretary of the navy, BW III, p. 339.

86. "On the first symptoms of a reverse . . ." Eaton (aboard *President*) July 1804 to Colonel Dwight, LIFE, p. 265.

86. "The auxillary supplies . . ." Ibid.

87. "What terms of peace with Tripoli . . ." Thomas Jefferson, "Anas," printed in *The Works of Thomas Jefferson* ed. Paul L. Ford. (N.Y., 1904), vol. 1, p. 382.

87. "Would it be believed . . ." *Jefferson Himself* ed. Bernard Mayo (Boston, 1932), p.104, citing "Diary Relative to Invasion of Virginia" 17:17–18.

88. "The arrangement of the presents is to form NO PART . . ." Secretary of State James Madison (Washington) to James Leander Cathcart, April 9, 1803, LIFE, p. 256; also in microfilm in Tobias Lear Papers, Clements Library and WE-HL.

89. "With respect to the ex-Bashaw . . ." Secretary of the Navy Robert Smith to Samuel Barron, June 6, 1804, BW IV, p. 152.

90. "multitudes of black skins and black coats" Eaton Travel Journal, June 7, 1804, in WE-HL.

90. "charming accomplished young lady . . ." Eaton Travel Journal, June 6, 1804, in WE-HL.

90. "He lodged in the same chamber with myself . . ." William Eaton, July 4, 1804 (aboard *President*), to Eliza Eaton, WE-HL.

90. "a million of dollars" secretary of state to U.S. consuls in Europe, June 2, 1804, BW IV, p. 142.

91. "UNHAPPY SLAVES . . . The horrid usage . . ." Anonymous to Samuel Barron, June 1804, BW IV, p. 203.

92. "to have his Head & Eye brows shaved . . ." John Rodgers to Samuel Barron, June 23, 1804, BW IV, p. 219.

93. ". . . evades the imputation of having embarked . . ." William Eaton (aboard *President*) to Colonel Dwight, July 1804, LIFE, p. 266.

94. "Though the adventure . . . be as forlorn . . ." Ibid., p. 267.

94. "We are now standing to sea before a beautiful breeze . . ." William Eaton to Eliza Eaton, July 4, 1804 (aboard *President*), WE-HL.

94. "Piristratides, going with some others . . ." William Eaton, Common Place Book, p. 27 in WE-HL.

97. "If this plan succeeds . . ." William Eaton, Common Place Book, August 21, 1804. p. 51 in WE-HL.

97. "The effect . . . on the ship's people . . ." Samuel Barron (Malta harbor) to Sir Alexander Ball (copied into Eaton's travel journal), WE-HL.

98. "The Commodore is not decided . . ." William Eaton (Malta harbor) to Secretary of the Navy Robert Smith, September 6, 1804, Eaton's Notebook, p. 11, WE-HL.

99. Betsy story. William Eaton (Tunis) to Jonathan Harris, April 12, 1799, WE-HL.

99. "The Lord give you many days and nights of . . ." William Eaton (Tunis) to Richard O'Brien, March 25, 1799, WE-HL.

100. "transport, not a frigate" William Eaton (Tunis) to Richard O'Brien, May 11, 1800, WE-HL.

101. "sentiments of perfect gratitude . . ." William Eaton, Common Place Book, pp. 68–78, WE-HL. Also: ASP, Class IX, p. 327.

102. "The foregoing letter, written in barbarous French . . ." William Eaton, Common Place Book, p. 78, WE-HL.

102. "Whatever may be Mr. Eaton's individual claims . . ." ASP, Class IX, p. 326.

102. "With this force, . . . it is conceived . . ." Secretary of the navy to Samuel Barron, June 6, 1804, BW IV, p. 153.

CHAPTER 7. YUSSEF

104. "If a Turk gets wounded or killed . . ." RAY, p. 130.

104. "The Commodore's ship when standing in . . ." John Darby, BW IV, pp. 475–476.

104. "The moment . . . the Americans started firing . . ." AZ, September 1, 1804.

105. "to one gunboat without bloodshed" RAY, p. 128.

105. "The Turks told us . . ." RAY, p. 128.

107. "that she prided herself . . ." *Narrative of a Ten Years' Residence in Tripoli in Africa* by Miss Tully (London, 1817), p. 232.

108. "Ah! Is this the last present . . ." Ibid., p. 233.

108. "His behaviour was mild, polite, and . . ." Ibid., p. 259.

109. "If a camel is necessary . . ." *Avventure e Osservazioni di Fillippo Pananti sopra le coste di Barberia* by Fillippo Pananti (Firenze, 1817), p. 224.

109. "The pacha usurper departed . . ." Consul Guys, as quoted in *Annales Tripolitaines* by L. Charles Feraud (Tunis, 1927), pp. 298–299.

110. "with expressions of joy as lively as sincere" Ibid., pp. 298–299.

110. "The Bashaw Sidy Hamed, having at best a weak understanding . . ." Simon Lucas to duke of Portland, June 30, 1795. Public Record Office, Kew, England, F.O. 76/5.

110. "very affable" "Relation envoyee au ministre de la marine, La Luzerne, par le consul de Frenace, Pellegrin" as quoted in *Histoire Abregée de Tripoly de Barbarie, 1794* by Anne-Charles Froment de Champlagarde (reprint: Paris, 2001), p. 72.

CHAPTER 8. THE MISSION: EATON UNLEASHED

113. "The written orders I here hand you . . ." "Secret Verbal Orders of Barron," September 15, 1804, WE-HL, copied into letterbook, pp. 21–22, at start of Reel 3.

114. "It seems you have wholly mistaken the intentions . . ." Eaton (Malta) to Don

Antonio Porcile, October [Sept. crossed out] 20, 1804, Eaton letterbook, WE-HL, Reel 2.

114. "I request you will be pleased to cause information to be forwarded . . ." Eaton (Malta) to Secretary of State Madison, September 18, 1804, letterbook, June 1804 to February 1805, p. 23, WE-HL, Reel 3.

115. "Commodore Barron declares he does not consider any construction . . ." Eaton (Malta) to secretary of the navy, September 18, 1804, BW V, p. 33.

115. "I hope to be organizing my saracen militia on the plains of Libya . . ." Eaton (Malta) to Colonel Dwight, September 20, 1804, BW V, p. 42.

116. "the torments sufferd from bugs & fleas" Edward Preble (Messina) to Samuel Barron, October 8, 1804, BW V, p. 79.

117. "He has had no calamities in his life" Robert Southey, quoted in *Perturbed Spirit: The Life and Personality of Samuel Taylor Coleridge* by Oswald Doughty (Rutherford, N.J., 1981).

117. "french grass-like streaks" *The Notebooks of Samuel Taylor Coleridge*, vol. 2 (London, 1957–1961), item: 2191.

117. "put up the musket to the ear . . ." Ibid., item: 2228.

117. "O Sorrow & Shame!" Ibid., item: 2237.

118. "that the largest ships of war . . ." Journal of purser John Darby, U.S. Navy, BW V, pp. 81–82.

118. "an affection of the liver" John Rodgers (USS *Constitution* in Syracuse harbor) to secretary of the navy, November 6, 1804, BW V, p. 124.

118. "The physician Doc Cutbush has been under serious apprehensions . . ." Eaton to secretary of the navy, postscript of October 27, 1804 (Malta), BW V, p. 35.

119. "Why not an answer!" Eaton, Common Place Book, "Note Oct. 29th 1804 at Malta," p. 92, WE-HL, Reel 3.

119. "I have sometimes seen a brave man dishonest . . ." Eaton, Common Place Book, p. 66, WE-HL, Reel 3.

119. "To secure himself in the secrecy of this disgraceful secession . . ." Eaton, WE-HL, Reel 3.

119. "Colonel Lear not to be leered at!!!" Eaton, Common Place Book, p. 67, WE-HL, Reel 3.

120. "I presume the co-operation of the Brother of the Bashaw . . ." Tobias Lear (Malta) to secretary of state, November 3, 1804, BW V, p. 116.

120. "I am so unwell to Day that I can scarcely write at all . . ." Samuel Barron (Syracuse) to John Rodgers, November 3, 1804, BW V, p. 117.

120. "If on your Arrival in Egypt it should be found necessary . . ." Samuel Barron (Syracuse) to Isaac Hull, November 10, 1804, BW V, p. 134.

121. "Commodore Barron being at present sick in . . ." Edward Preble (Syracuse) to Sir Alexander Ball, November 13, 1804, BW V, p. 140.

121. "On further consideration, I am of opinion that the supplies . . ." Eaton (Syracuse) to secretary of the navy, BW V, p. 140.

123. "I request that you will assist him and do everything . . ." Alexander Ball (Malta) to Samuel Briggs, November 16, 1804, BW V, p. 144.

123. "It was my intention to have taken along . . ." Eaton (Malta) to Samuel Barron, November 17, 1804, BW V, p. 146.

124. "It may have a good effect on his brother . . ." Samuel Barron (near Syracuse) to Tobias Lear, November 13, 1804, BW V, p. 139.

124. "I am not at all sanguine . . ." Tobias Lear (Malta) to Samuel Barron, November 20, 1804, BW V, p. 153.

CHAPTER 9. HUNTING HAMET IN EGYPT

127. "They make use of asses . . ." *Travels of Ali Bey in Morocco, Tripoli, Cyprus, Egypt, Arabia, Syria and Turkey between the years 1803 and 1807* by Ali Bey. Reprint Edition (Reading, UK, 1993), vol. I, p. 316.

129. "The battlegrounds there . . . we found still covered with human Skeletons" William Eaton (Rosetta) to Isaac Hull, December 2, 1804, BW V, p. 171.

130. "The billows are generally very strong" *Travels of Ali Bey in Morocco, Tripoli, Cyprus, Egypt, Arabia, Syria and Turkey between the years 1803 and 1807* by Ali Bey. Reprint Edition (Reading, UK, 1993), vol. II, p. 2.

130. "You will find in Major Missett all that can be comprized in the term of a Gentleman . . ." William Eaton (Rosetta) to Isaac Hull, December 2, 1804, BW V, p. 171.

131. "possessing dispositions congenial to the interests of the Bey's wife." William Eaton (Grand Cairo) to secretary of the navy, December 13, 1804, BW V, p. 186.

132. "The interior of this country being in a state of general revolt . . ." William Eaton (Alexandria) to secretary of the navy, November 28, 1804, BW V, p. 166.

132. "who restrained by no discipline ravage and murder" William Eaton (Grand Cairo) to secretary of the navy, December 13, 1804, BW V, p. 186.

133. "inhabitants oppressed and miserable" William Eaton, LIFE, p. 275. Also BW V, p. 174.

133. "In many of the villages are women for the convenience of strangers . . ." William George Browne, *Travels in Africa, Egypt and Syria from the year 1792 to 1798* (London, 1799), p. 34.

133. "astonished the inhabitants" William Eaton, LIFE, p. 275. Also BW V, p. 174.

134. "The Arab camp were within half a league . . ." William Eaton (Grand Cairo) to secretary of the navy, December 13, 1804, BW V, p. 187.

135. "We passed as American officers . . ." William Eaton (Grand Cairo) to secretary of the navy, December 13, 1804, BW V, p. 187.

136. "Hundreds and thousands of lights may be seen . . ." *Travels of Ali Bey in Morocco, Tripoli, Cyprus, Egypt, Arabia, Syria and Turkey between the years 1803 and 1807* by Ali Bey. Reprint Edition (Reading, UK, 1993), vol. II, p. 19.

136. "You are like the city ass . . ." William George Browne, *Travels in Africa, Egypt and Syria from the year 1792 to 1798* (London, 1799), p. 86.

136. "destitute of everything but resentment . . ." Eaton (Grand Cairo) to secretary of the navy, December 13, 1804, BW V, p. 187.

137. "magnificence" Eaton (Grand Cairo) to secretary of the navy, December 13, 1804, BW V, p. 188.

137. "embroidered purple and damask cushions" Ibid.

138. "The tobacco of Turkey is the best . . ." Charles Sonnini de Manoncourt, *Travels in Upper and Lower Egypt* (London, 1799), p. 158.

138. "was a man of much more frankness and liberality . . ." Eaton (Demanhour) to Edward Preble, January 25, 1805, BW V, p. 301.

139. "Both taught the existence and supremacy of *one* God . . . nor for spoil but to vindicate our rights." William Eaton (Grand Cairo) to secretary of the navy, December 13, 1804, BW V, p. 188.

139. "I found the means however . . ." William Eaton (Demanhour) to Edward Preble, January 25, 1805, BW V, p. 301.

140. "until the pleasure of the President shall be expressed . . ." William Eaton to Dr. Francisco Mendrici, December 13, 1804, BW V, p. 185.

140. "a letter of amnesty and permission . . ." William Eaton (Grand Cairo) to secretary of the navy, December 13, 1804, postscript. December 17, 1804, BW V, p. 189.

140. "God has ordained that you should see trouble . . ." William Eaton (Grand Cairo) to Hamet Karamanli, December 17, 1804, BW V, p. 197.

141. "I had been told that it was a delightful spot . . ." *Travels of Ali Bey in Morocco, Tripoli, Cyprus, Egypt, Arabia, Syria and Turkey between the years 1803 and 1807* by Ali Bey. Reprint Edition (Reading, UK, 1993), vol. II, p. 22.

141. "Ruined temples, pyramids, and catacombs, monuments of superstition . . ." William Eaton (Grand Cairo) to John Cotton Smith, December 26, 1804, LIFE, p. 285.

141. "If Government should reprove our arrangements, we will reimburse them from the spoils of Bengazi . . ." William Eaton (Grand Cairo) to Isaac Hull, December 19, 1804, BW V, pp. 202–203.

142. "We are more perplexed with contradictory reports, than were there free presses . . ." William Eaton (Grand Cairo) to Major Missett, December 19, 1804, BW V, p. 203.

142. "view all the ladies of the village . . ." William Eaton, LIFE, p. 277. Also BW V, p. 205.

142. "They are always attended by an old man . . ." William George Browne, *Travels in Africa, Egypt and Syria from the year 1792 to 1798* (London, 1799), p. 84.

143. "consist chiefly of very quick and truly astonishing movements of the loins . . ." Charles Sonnini de Manoncourt, *Travels in Upper and Lower Egypt* (London, 1799).

143. "At evening an exhibition at the English house of the *almee* . . ." William Eaton, LIFE, p. 277. Also BW V, p. 206.

143. "I have made arrangements for paying Mess.rs Briggs the Thousand Dollars . . ." Isaac Hull (U.S. Brig Argus, Alexandria harbor) to William Eaton, December 24, 1804, BW V, pp. 214–215.

CHAPTER 10. WHITE CHRISTMAS IN TRIPOLI

145. "The American sailors, it is a pity to see them . . ." AZ, September 15, 1804.

145. "They send us to work rain or shine . . ." Letter signed by "The *Philadelphia* Crew" (Tripoli Prison) to "Commander and Chief of the U.S. Forces up the Mediterranean." November 7, 1804. Manuscript Div., Library of Congress.

146. "*Tota Fora*" RAY, p. 151.

146. "The wardens whipped them until they were tired . . ." Jonathan Cowdery, *American Captives in Tripoli* (Boston, 1806), p. 25.

147. "I can't conceive that the least benefit could derive to the U.S. . . ." William Bainbridge (Tripoli) to Dr. George Davis, U.S. consul in Tunis, December 19, 1804, BW V, pp. 199–200.

148. "In helpless servitude, forlorn . . ." RAY, p. 154.

CHAPTER 11. REELING IN HAMET

151. "I confess I do not feel altogether at my ease . . ." Eaton (Cairo) to Hull, December 29, 1804, BW V, pp. 223–224.

151. "The undertaking will be hazardous . . ." Ibid., p. 224.

152. "break his bones" Ibid., p. 224.

152. "the most respectable Christian house in Grand Cairo" Eaton (Alexandria) to Hull, February 9, 1805, BW V, pp. 341–342.

152. "Her face is like a full moon . . ." Constantin-Francois Volney, *Travels through Syria and Egypt in the years 1783, 1784 and 1785* (London, 1787), p. 108.

152. "Choose a blond woman for your eyes . . ." Ibid., p. 108.

152. "what is somewhat more base . . ." Eaton (Cairo) to Hull, December 29, 1804, BW V, p. 224.

153. "Good God, when will our young men learn the weight of respect . . ." Ibid.

153. "conditionally" Eaton (Cairo) to Richard Farquhar, December 31, 1804, BW V, p. 229.

153. "approaching Cairo with imposing strides" Eaton (Cairo) to Hull, January 3, 1805, BW V, p. 252.

153. "At all events it is time to determine on something . . . in this letter." Hull (aboard USS *Argus* at Alexandria) to Eaton, January 5, 1805, BW V, p. 254.

154. "wild Arabs," "Arnaut Turks" . . . "If we fail . . . , you will do us the justice . . ." Eaton (Cairo) to Hull, January 8, 1805, BW V, p. 268.

154. "Not to give a dollar for peace . . ." Thomas Jefferson. "Anas." *The Works of Thomas Jefferson* ed. Paul L. Ford (N.Y., 1904), vol. I, p. 383.

155. "To our friend, the very good friend of our Highness, . . ." Hamet Karamanli (unspecified) to William Eaton, January 3, 1805, BW V, p. 252. Also: different translation in William Eaton letterbook (August 14, 1804, to February 11, 1805), WE-HL, Reel 3. Also: slightly different in French translation on microfilm, Reel 2.

155. "I cannot but congratulate you . . ." Eaton (Cairo) to Hull, January 8, 1805, BW V, p. 268.

155. "You're well aware that when we left Tunis . . ." Hamet Karamanli to Sheik Muhammed, son of Abdel Rahman. Italian translation enclosed in a letter from Muhammed, son of Abdel Rahman, to Dr. Francesco Mendrici, January 10, 1805, WE-HL.

156. "by drafts on Leghorn, Naples or Department of the Navy" Eaton (Cairo) to Hull, January 9, 1805, BW V, p. 270.

157. "The money that was given me by the general was very little . . ." Hamet Karamanli (Ohu'isa) to Mahmud, BW V, p. 280.

157. "We are in the desert . . ." Ibid.

159. "No Argument I could advance could at all modify . . ." Eaton (Demanhour) to Edward Preble, January 25, 1805, BW V, pp. 300–305.

160. "to prevent intruders" Ibid, p. 304.

161. "Nothing could be more amusing" Francois-Réné, comte de Chateaubriand, *Travels in Greece, Palestine, Egypt and Barbary, during the years 1806 and 1807* (N.Y., 1814), p. 409.

161. "British spies" William Eaton notes, BW V, p. 314.

161. "[Derne & Bengazi] will be . . . an easy conquest . . ." Eaton (Demanhour) to Hull, January 29, 1805, BW V, p. 319.

162. "to clear out from this" Eaton (Demanhour) to Hull, Sunday, February 4 [3], 1805, BW V, p. 330.

CHAPTER 12. PREPARING FOR WAR: FRESH ENEMIES AND MONEY, MONEY, MONEY

165. "I will do [the expedition] on the following conditions . . ." Richard Farquhar (Alexandria) to Isaac Hull, February 12, 1805, BW V, p. 344.

166. "beyond caprice" Eaton (Alexandria) to Samuel Barron, February 14, 1805, BW V, pp. 353–354.

167. "Convention between the United States of America . . ." BW V, pp. 367–369.

168. "Neither authorized, specified nor vouched . . ." Farquhar expense accounts, WE-HL, Reel 2.

168. "If the [messenger] has not the means of touching . . ." Eaton (Alexandria) to secretary of the navy, February 13, 1805, BW V, p. 350.

169. "principally old soldiers" Eaton (Alexandria) to Barron, February 14, 1805, BW V, p. 354.

169. "the cook," "the drummer" Richard Farquhar submitted to Eaton, February 25, 1805, WE-HL, Reel 2.

169. "I have endeavoured to perswead . . ." Richard Farquhar (Alexandria) to Eaton, February 18, 1805, BW V, p. 360.

169. "You will immediately make out your account . . ." Eaton (Alexandria) to Richard Farquhar, February 25, 1805, BW V, pp. 371–372.

170. "To our Friend and Son, Mister Fahr . . ." Hamet Karamanli (Marabout) to Richard Farquhar, February 28, 1805, BW V, p. 379.

171. "chiefly embezzled or misapplied" Eaton's travel journal, March 3, 1805, BW V, p. 388.

171. "Roc Maltais" "Extrait des Registrer de la chancellerie du Commissariat de l'Empire francais à Alexandrie d'Egypt, 10 Ventose, 13ème année [March 1, 1805]," WE-HL, Reel 2.

171. "I am persuaded that a regular report . . ." British consul Samuel Briggs (Alexandria) to Monsieur B. Drovetti, March 5, 1805, BW V, p. 390.

172. "My reports . . . [will] require your explanations . . ." Eaton (Alexandria) to Mr. B. Drovetti, March 3, 1805, BW V, p. 388.

172. "The firm and decided conduct of Mr. O'Bannon . . ." Eaton's travel journal, March 2, 1805, BW V, p. 384.

172. "We found . . . a supervisor of the revenue . . ." Ibid.

173. "be recognized as General, and Commander in Chief . . ." Convention between U.S. and Hamet Karamanli, BW V, p. 367–369.

173. "raised fresh demands for cash" Eaton's travel journal, March 5, 1805, BW V, p. 391.

174. "After marching near 40 miles . . ." Pascal Peck (Malta) to unnamed officer on the *Argus*, July 4, 1805. Reprinted in *National Intelligencer*, October 9, 1805, BW V, pp. 361–363.

CHAPTER 13. THE DESERT

178. "It was not safe to do it . . ." LIFE, p. 303.

178. "The Bashaw seemed irresolute and despondent . . ." Ibid.

178. "Money, more money was the only stimulus . . ." Ibid.

179. "[They] attempted to disarm . . ." Ibid., p. 304.

179. "barren rocky plain" . . . "upon the dividing ridge between Egypt and Tripoli . . ." Ibid.

180. "Arabs" . . . "We had heretofore experienced daily losses . . ." Ibid.

180. "Masrocah" . . . "very dear" Ibid., p. 305.

181. "I now learned, *for the first time,* that our caravan . . . no part of their pay" Ibid.

182. "perplexing and embarrassed" . . . "impossible to move without the caravan . . ." Ibid., p. 306.

182. "I thought this an argument that urged acceleration . . ." Ibid.

182. "runner" Ibid., p. 307.

182. "one of the most hypocritical fanatics" . . . "wretched victims . . ." Ibid.

183. "an elevated stony plain" Ibid.

184. "We were the first Christians ever seen by these wild people . . ." Ibid., p. 308.

184. "Cash, we find, is the only deity of Arabs . . ." Ibid.

184. "They examined it carefully . . ." Ibid.

185. "A woman offered her daughter . . ." Ibid., pp. 308–309.

185. "were a few days march from . . ." Ibid., p. 309.

185. "You have promised much and fulfilled nothing" Ibid., pp. 309–310.

187. "firmness" . . . "to render them more manageable" Ibid., p. 311.

187. "enchanting" Ibid.

187. "had discouraged and dissuaded them" Ibid.

187. "Curiosity brought every Arab" Ibid., pp. 313–314.

188. "To the inhabitants of the kingdom of Tripoli . . ." BW V, p. 467.

189–190. "At the uttermost limits of the West . . . in proof of our fidelity and our goodwill." Ibid., pp. 467–470.

191. "a savage independence of soul" LIFE, pp. 312–313.

191. "handful" Midshipman Pascal Peck (Malta) to unnamed recipient, July 4, 1805, BW V, p. 362.

191. "the cause of all our delays" LIFE, p. 315.

192. "Remember you are in a desert, and a country not your own" Ibid.

192. "I have found you at the head of every commotion . . ." Ibid., pp. 315–316.

193. "fine girls and young married women" "handsome" Ibid., pp. 316–317.

194. "The women had their places near the camels . . ." Ibid., pp. 318–320.

195. "[The older women] perform the office of examining . . ." William Eaton, travel journal, WE-HL, Reel 3.

196. "wild cat" "It was cooked . . ." LIFE, p. 320.

196. "remarkable ancient castle of hewn stone" Ibid., p. 320.

197. "fetid and saline" Ibid., p. 321.

198. "This was a precious repast to our thirsty pilgrims" Ibid., p. 322.

199. "If they prefer famine to fatigue . . ." Ibid., p. 323.

200. "manual exercize" . . . "The Christians are preparing to fire on us . . ." Ibid.

201. "W'allahi . . . In the name of Allah," Ibid.

202. "We find it almost impossible to inspire these wild bigots . . ." Ibid., p. 325.

203. "beautiful valley" Ibid., p. 325.

203. "Our situation is truly alarming" Ibid., p. 326.

204. "from pensive gloom to enthusiastic gladness" Ibid.

204. "spasms and vomiting" Ibid.

205. "Marched seven and a half miles . . ." Ibid., p. 327.

205. "No part of the animal capable of being gnawed by human tooth . . ." Frederick Horneman. *The Journal of Frederick Horneman's Travels from Cairo to Marzouk . . . 1797–1798* (London, 1802), p. 5.

205. "Marched fifteen miles . . ." LIFE, p. 327.

206. "Nothing could prevail on our Arabs to believe . . ." Ibid., p. 328.

206. "impracticable" Ibid.

207. "Language is too poor to paint the joy . . ." Ibid.

207. "When I think on our situation in the desert . . ." Pascal Peck (Malta) to unnamed officer on the *Argus,* July 4, 1805. Reprinted in *National Intelligencer,* October 9, 1805, BW V, pp. 361–363.

CHAPTER 14. TOBIAS LEAR: PEACE AT ANY COST

210. "We should not refuse to negotiate . . ." Tobias Lear (Malta) to Don Gerando Joseph de Souza, March 28, 1805, BW V, p. 463.

210. "I hope I have not acted incorrectly . . ." John Rodgers (USS *Constitution* off Tripoli) to Samuel Barron, April 16 or 18, 1805, BW V, p. 515.

210. "perfect inviolability" Nicholas Nissen (Tripoli) to Samuel Barron, March 18, 1805, BW V, pp. 421–423.

211. "A sincere & lasting peace . . ." Ibid.

211. "has great influence over the Bashaw" . . . "Permit me, my dear Barron . . ." William Bainbridge (Tripoli) to Samuel Barron, March 16, 1805, BW V, p. 417.

212. "I have no doubt that if a person . . ." William Bainbridge (Tripoli) to Samuel Barron, March 22, 1805, BW V, pp. 437–438.

212. "you will consider equal terms . . ." ". . . If the attack is made . . ." John Rodgers (aboard USS *Constitution* off Tripoli) to Tobias Lear, April 17, 1805, BW V, p. 518.

213. "I am only afraid that the Tripoline dogs . . ." John Rodgers (aboard USS *Congress* in Gibraltar Bay) to Minvera Denison, August 11, 1804, Rodgers Family Papers. Library of Congress. Manuscript Division.

214. "totally inadmissable" Tobias Lear (Malta) to John Rodgers, May 1, 1805, BW VI, p. 1.

214. "Now, it is a war over my personal . . ." William Bainbridge (Tripoli) to Samuel Barron, April 12, 1805, BW V, p. 505.

214. "The American prisoners—at the moment that Bashaw Yussef is forced to . . ." AZ, April 16, 1805.

215. "He will have his washing done . . ." George Washington to Benjamin Lincoln, January 4, 1786. Washington Papers. Library of Congress. Quoted in *The Checkered Career of Tobias Lear* (Portsmouth, N.H., 1985) by Ray Brighton, p. 33.

216. "Black Sam" "a number fine dishes" "long consultation" Tobias Lear (New

York) to Major Washington. William R. Perkins Library, Duke University, as quoted in *The Checkered Career of Tobias Lear* (Portsmouth, N.H., 1985) by Ray Brighton, p. 61.

217. "I must therefore request in explicit terms . . ." George Washington to Tobias Lear, Ibid., pp. 151–152.

217. "About ten o'clock, [Washington] made several attempts to speak to me . . ." Lear Diary, Ibid., p. 164.

218. "There are, as you well know, . . . among the several letters and papers . . ." Tobias Lear to Alexander Hamilton, Ibid., p. 171.

218. "Anglican monarchial & aristocratical" . . . "all timid men who . . ." Thomas Jefferson to Philip Mazzei, April 24, 1796, quoted by Dumas Malone, *The Ordeal of Liberty*, p. 257. Ibid., p. 170.

220. "hazard the goodwill of the French" Secretary of State James Madison (Washington) to Tobias Lear, January 17, 1803, Ibid., p. 192.

220. "full of lizards, spiders and many noxious insects" John Rodgers (Baltimore) to Secretary of State James Madison, June 1802, a copy in ZB file at Navy Department Library, Washington, D.C.

220. "highly patriotic" House of Representatives, Claims Committee report. February 18, 1803, as quoted in *The Checkered Career of Tobias Lear* (Portsmouth, N.H., 1985) by Ray Brighton, p. 194.

220. "I will fly on wings of love to your arms . . ." Tobias Lear (aboard USS *Constitution* in Gibraltar Bay) to Frances Lear, September 20, 1803. Tobias Lear Papers. University of Michigan. Clements Library. Microfilm.

CHAPTER 15. AN AMERICAN FLAG ON FOREIGN SOIL

223. "All was now rejoicing and mutual congratulation . . ." Pascal Paoli Peck (Malta), July 4, 1805, reprinted in *National Intelligencer*, October 9, 1805, BW V, pp. 361–363.

223. "He was a rough boisterous captain of the sea . . ." Edmund Quincy, as quoted in *Dictionary of American Biography*, vol. IX (N.Y., 1928), pp. 360–362.

224. "I cannot but applaud the energy and perseverance . . ." Samuel Barron (Malta) to Eaton, March 22, 1805, BW V, pp. 438–441.

225. "Besides the terror that Cannon impress . . ." several more quotations from the same letter. Eaton (Bomba) to Isaac Hull, April 21, 1805, BW V, pp. 527–528.

226. "unwilling to abandon an Expedition this far conducted" Presley O'Bannon (Bomba) to Isaac Hull, April 21, 1805, BW V, p. 528.

226. "I am actuated by . . . a wish to contribute generally by my . . ." Midshipman George W. Mann (on board *Argus*) April 21, 1805, BW V, p. 528.

226. "springing from the top of a mountain . . ." Eaton travel diary, April 23, 1805, LIFE, pp. 328–329.

227. "Marched fifteen miles over mountainous and broken ground . . ." Eaton travel diary, April 24, 1805, Ibid., p. 329.

227. "The night was passed in consultations . . ." Ibid.

228. "ten inch howitzer" . . . "could bring 800 men into battle, and he possessed all the batteries . . ." April 25, 1805, Ibid., pp. 329–330.

228. "Sir, I want no territory. With me is advancing . . ." Eaton (near Derne) to governor of Derne, April 26, 1805, Ibid., p. 337.

229. "My head or yours.—Mustifa" governor of Derne (Derne) to Eaton, April 26, 1805, Ibid. Also: BW V, p. 542.

229. "You will please send a large party down early . . ." Lieutenant John Dent (aboard USS *Nautilus*) to Eaton, April 26, 1805, BW V, p. 542.

232. "The fire of the enemy's Musketry became too warm . . ." Eaton (Derne) to Samuel Barron, April 29, 1805, BW V, pp. 553–555.

233. "At about a half past 3, we had the satisfaction to see . . ." Lieutenant Isaac Hull (aboard USS *Argus*) to Samuel Barron, April 28, 1805, BW V, pp. 547–548.

233. "They held safe positions to catch fugitives . . ." Eaton (Derne) to Samuel Barron, May 1, 1805, postscript to April 29, 1805, letter, BW V, pp. 550–553.

234. "musket ball through the left wrist" Lieutenant Isaac Hull (aboard USS *Argus*) to Samuel Barron, April 28, 1805, BW V, pp. 547–548.

234. "We are in possession of the most valuable province of Tripoli" Eaton (Derne) to Samuel Barron, April 29, 1805, BW V, p. 550.

235. "military talent and firmness" . . . "to be used solely as an instrument . . ." Eaton (Derne) to Samuel Barron, May 1, 1805, postscript to April 29, 1805, letter, BW V, pp. 550–553.

235. "At all events . . . I am deeply impressed . . ." Ibid.

236. "Used exertions to draw the Governor . . ." Eaton travel diary, May 2, 1805, LIFE, p. 330.

237. "The Christians no longer respect the customs of our fathers . . ." Ibid., p. 331.

237. "At ½ past 9 the parties met . . ." Lieutenant Isaac Hull (aboard USS *Argus*) to Samuel Barron, May 17, 1805, BW VI, p. 20.

238. "Very fortunately, a shot from one of our nine pounders killed . . ." Eaton (Derne) to Samuel Barron, May 15, 1805, BW VI, p. 14.

238. "The Enemy are shamefully flogged, we have collected . . ." Eaton (Derne) to Lieutenant Issac Hull, May 13, 1805, BW VI, p. 12.

239. "You would have yielded to the Christian General . . ." Eaton travel diary, LIFE, pp. 332–333.

240. "*Monsieur, Vu le desir et le courage* . . ." Officers (Derne) to Eaton, May 20, 1805, WE-HL, Reel 2. Also: BW VI, p. 28.

CHAPTER 16. MALTA: DISEASED LIVER AND COLD FEET

243. "I have never disguised from myself . . ." Samuel Barron (Malta) to John Rodgers, May 22, 1805, BW VI, p. 31.

244. "want of energy and military talents . . ." Samuel Barron (Malta) to Tobias Lear, May 18, 1805, BW VI, pp. 22–23.

245. "in a few days" . . . "Altho' I cannot, Sir, agree . . ." Tobias Lear (Malta) to Samuel Barron, May 19, 1805, BW VI, p. 24.

245. "The letter I have written to Mr. Eaton . . ." Samuel Barron (Malta) to Lieutenant Isaac Hull, May 19, 1805, BW VI, p. 24.

246. "would not discredit the character which our . . ." Samuel Barron (Malta) to Eaton, May 19, 1805, BW VI, pp. 25–26.

247. "Tuesday May 21, 1805—Employ'd as yesterday & in making visits to my acquaintances . . ." Tobias Lear diary, as copied for A. W. Whipple in the 1840s; manuscript formerly in Dudley Stoddard Collection in New York, as quoted in *The Checkered Career of Tobias Lear* by Ray Brighton (Portsmouth, N.H., 1985), p. 250.

248. "He has no respectability attached to his character . . ." February 3, 1804, BW III, p. 386.

249. "the importance of the Intelligence" Samuel Barron (Malta) to John Rodgers, May 26, 1805, BW VI, p. 49.

CHAPTER 17. TRIPOLI: FEAR

251. "Yesterday there arrived here from Derne . . ." AZ, May 23, 1805.

252. "It was apparent to the most indifferent observer that . . ." William Wormley (Washington) to Stephen Bradley, February 16, 1806, BW VI, pp. 373–374.

252. "They stopped through fatigue, and asked their driver . . ." Diary entry May 23, 1805. Jonathan Cowdery, *American Captives in Tripoli* (Boston, 1806), pp. 30–31.

252. "This is true but no more than what . . ." RAY, p. 159.

252. "The Bashaw was so much agitated at the news of the approach of his brother . . ." Diary entry May 24, 1805. Jonathan Cowdery, *American Captives in Tripoli* (Boston, 1806), p. 31.

CHAPTER 18. TRIPOLI HARBOR: LEAR TO THE RESCUE

253. "I shall, my dearest love, give you a detail of my situation . . ." Tobias Lear (aboard USS *Essex*) to Fanny Lear, May 25, 1805. Lear Papers. Clements Library at University of Michigan, Ann Arbor. Microfilm.

254. "At about 11 A.M., the smallest [frigate] came near in . . ." Jonathan Cowdery, *American Captives in Tripoli* (Boston, 1806), pp. 31–32.

255. "would put aside in toto" Tobias Lear (aboard USS *Constitution* in Syracuse harbor) to Secretary of State James Madison, July 5, 1805, BW VI, pp. 159–162.

256. "They returned at evening with the joyful news . . ." Jonathan Cowdery, *American Captives in Tripoli* (Boston, 1806), pp. 31–32.

256. "Both Turks and Christians were all anxiously . . ." Ibid., p. 32.

256. "The Turks began to think . . ." Ibid., p. 32.

257. "I told the Sp Consul, to prevent unnecessary delay . . ." Tobias Lear (aboard USS *Constitution* in Syracuse harbor) to Secretary of State James Madison, July 5, 1805, BW VI, pp. 159–162.

258. "Thus stands the business at present . . ." Tobias Lear (Tripoli harbor) to Fanny Lear, May 25–30, 1805. Lear Papers. Clements Library at University of Michigan, Ann Arbor. Microfilm.

258. "My dearest Fanny, I have not much time for my own amusement . . ." Ibid.

258. "I have declared that I will not recede one inch from it . . ." Ibid.

258. "How things will turn out is yet uncertain" John Rodgers (aboard USS *Constitution* off Tripoli) to Samuel Barron, May 30, 1805, BW VI, p. 64.

259. "I told him the business had already been protracted . . ." Tobias Lear (on board USS *Constitution* in Syracuse harbor) to Secretary of State James Madison, July 5, 1805, BW VI, pp. 159–162.

CHAPTER 19. DERNE: DEFIANCE

261. "Why don't he come and take it?" Eaton travel journal, LIFE, p. 334.

261. "We want nothing but cash to break up our enemy's camp . . ." Ibid.

262. "Five o'clock, P.M. Overwhelmed with the Scyroc . . ." Ibid.

263. "So piercing was the heat . . ." Ibid.

265. "They [perhaps feared] that we were an advanced party aiming to draw . . ." Eaton (Derne) to Samuel Barron, May 29, 1805, Ibid., p. 350.

265. "A Mirabout (saint) who has experienced some charities . . ." Eaton travel journal, Ibid., p. 335.

265. "He must be held as unworthy of further support . . ." Samuel Barron (Malta) to William Eaton, May 19, 1805, BW VI, p. 25.

266. "You would weep, Sir, . . . were you on the spot, to witness . . ." Eaton (Derne) to Samuel Barron, May 29, 1805, LIFE, pp. 349–361.

CHAPTER 20. TRIPOLI: PEACE? FREEDOM? HONOR?

270. "unreasonable" Report of Danish consul, Nicholas Nissen, June 10, 1805, BW VI, pp. 103–105.

271. "We stood in under the batteries . . ." Hezekiah Loomis, steward (aboard USS *Vixen* off Tripoli). Journal. June 1, 1805.

271. "it was more for the sake of peace than anything else . . ." Tobias Lear (aboard USS *Constitution* off Tripoli) to Fanny Lear, June 2, 1805. Lear Papers. Clements Library at University of Michigan, Ann Arbor. Microfilm.

272. "Christian dog" *Life and Services of Commodore Bainbridge* by Thomas Harris (Philadelphia, 1837), p. 122.

272. "I did not much desire this commission . . ." Report of Danish consul, Nicholas Nissen, June 10, 1805, BW VI, pp. 103–105.

273. "nothing has really been paid for peace" Ibid.

273. "who were so overjoyed that many of them shed tears" Jonathan Cowdery, *American Captives in Tripoli* (Boston, 1806), pp. 32–33.

274. "[Nissen] will be on board again this evening when I trust the business . . ." Tobias Lear (aboard USS *Constitution* off Tripoli) to Fanny Lear, June 2, 1805. Lear Papers. Clements Library at University of Michigan, Ann Arbor. Microfilm.

274. "This demand seemed severe to the Pacha . . ." Report of Danish consul, Nicholas Nissen, June 10, 1805, BW VI, pp. 103–105.

274. "Our business is so far finished . . ." John Rodgers (USS *Constitution* off Tripoli) to Samuel Barron, June 3, 1805 (Rodgers almost always uses a nautical time frame, that is, June 3 begins at noon on what landlubbers are calling June 2), BW VI, p. 78.

275. "quite honorable but not corresponding to my own ideas" John Rodgers (aboard USS *Constitution* in Tunis Bay) to Minerva Denison, August 21, 1805. Rodgers Family Papers. Manuscript Division. Library of Congress.

275. "If the Bashaw would consent to deliver up our Countrymen . . ." Ibid.

275. "We had a glance at them as they passed our prison . . ." RAY, p. 162.

275. "[Nissen] said the Bashaw would never agree to the article . . ." Tobias Lear (aboard USS *Constitution* off Tripoli) to Fanny Lear, June 5, 1805. Lear Papers. Clements Library at University of Michigan, Ann Arbor. Microfilm.

276. "It is peace" *Life and Services of Commodore Bainbridge* by Thomas Harris (Philadelphia, 1837), p. 123.

276. "He came onb.d again with the article signed by the Bashaw" Tobias Lear (aboard USS *Constitution* off Tripoli) to Fanny Lear, June 5, 1805. Lear Papers. Clements Library at University of Michigan, Ann Arbor. Microfilm.

277. "I was met by thousands of people . . ." Ibid.

277. "I found [him] a sensible, liberal and well-informed man" Tobias Lear (aboard USS *Constitution* in Syracuse harbor) to Secretary of State James Madison, July 5, 1805, BW VI, pp. 159–162.

278. "The intoxication of Liberty & Liquor . . ." Tobias Lear (Tripoli) to John Rodgers, June 4, 1805, BW VI, p. 82.

278. "He paid me many compliments . . ." Tobias Lear (aboard USS *Constitution* in Syracuse harbor) to Secretary of State James Madison, July 5, 1805, BW VI, pp. 159–162.

279. "The sailors who go off sh.d not be permitted to come on shore . . ." Tobias Lear (Tripoli) to John Rodgers, June 4, 1805, BW VI, p. 83.

279. "The manner in which [peace] has been made . . ." Tobias Lear (aboard USS *Constitution* off Tripoli) to Fanny Lear, June 5, 1805. Lear Papers. Clements Library at University of Michigan, Ann Arbor. Microfilm.

280. "I will not evacuate Derne until I receive an answer . . ." John Rodgers (quoting Dent) (aboard USS *Constitution* off Tripoli) to Tobias Lear, BW VI, p. 83.

281. "[I] have to desire that no farther hostilities by the forces . . ." John Rodgers (aboard USS *Constitution* off Tripoli) to William Eaton, June 6, 1805, BW VI, p. 91.

281. "I found the heroic bravery of our few countrymen at Derne . . ." Tobias Lear (Tripoli) to William Eaton, June 6, 1805, BW VI, p. 92.

CHAPTER 21. FROM A KINGDOM TO BEGGARY?

283. "to chastise a perfidious foe rather than . . ." William Eaton (Derne) to Samuel Barron, May 29, 1805, ongoing, LIFE, p. 352.

284. "During the alarm, a detachment from the garrison . . ." Ibid., p. 357.

284. "I have . . . to inform you that the *Argus* & *Hornet* . . ." Isaac Hull (aboard *Argus* off Derne) to William Eaton, June 4, 1805, BW VI, p. 84.

285. *even if he had to sell his wardrobe.* William Eaton (Derne) to Samuel Barron, May 29, 1805, ongoing, LIFE, p. 357 (slight rewording, since this was a translation of an Arabic report).

285. "who would devour his family and lands" William Eaton (Derne) to Samuel Barron, May 29, 1805, LIFE, p. 358.

286. "Be assured, Sir, we only want cash and a few marines . . ." Ibid., p. 358.

286. "Had some conversation with [Eaton] . . . first good opportunity" Isaac Hull, logbook of the USS *Argus,* June 9, 1805, BW VI, p. 103.

287. "energy & talent" "means & resources" Samuel Barron (Malta) to Eaton, May 19, 1805, BW VI, p. 25.

287. "He answers that, even with supplies it would be fruitless for him to attempt . . ." William Eaton (Derne) to Samuel Barron, May 29, 1805, ongoing, LIFE, p. 361.

288–289. "about half a gunshot" . . . "springs" . . . "warmly" . . . "keeping up a brisqu fire" Isaac Hull, logbook for USS *Argus,* June 9, 10, 1805, BW VI, pp. 101, 107.

289. "though frequently charged, the Bashaw lost not . . ." William Eaton (Derne) to Samuel Barron, May 29, 1805, ongoing, LIFE, p. 360.

290. "very heavy sea" Isaac Hull, logbook for USS *Argus,* June 10, 1805, BW VI, p. 107.

290. "I was under very great apprehension for her safety . . ." Ibid., BW VI, p. 108.

292. "[I] have to desire that no farther hostilities by the forces . . ." John Rodgers (aboard USS *Constitution* off Tripoli) to Eaton, June 6, 1805, BW VI, p. 91.

292. "The Americans will use all means . . ." Article 3 of treaty, BW VI, p. 81.

292. "Aunt Lear" William Eaton (Springfield, Mass.) to Edward Preble, February 3, 1806, BW VI, p. 360.

292. "Could this not have been exchanged for 200 . . ." and subsequent Eaton quotes on that and the following page. Eaton (aboard *Franklin* in Mediterranean) to secretary of the navy, August 9, 1805, BW VI, pp. 213–219.

293. "requiring of you to withdraw the American forces from Derne . . ." Hugh Campbell (aboard USS *Constellation* off Derne) to Eaton, June 12, 1805, BW VI, p. 111.

294. "I doubt the propriety of showing . . ." Eaton (Derne) to Hugh Campbell, June 12, 1805, BW VI, p. 111.

295. "astonishment" Eaton (aboard USS *Constellation* off Derne) to John Rodgers, June 13, 1805, BW VI, pp. 116–117.

296. "My name shall be written in blood on the walls of Tripoli . . ." John Rodgers's remark, heard by Eaton in May 1804, BW VI, p. 145.

296. "In a few minutes more, we shall loose sight . . ." and the rest of Eaton quotes. Eaton (aboard USS *Constellation* off Derne) to John Rodgers, June 13, 1805, BW VI, pp. 116–117.

CHAPTER 22. TRIPOLI: LEAR PAYS

299. "Finding that the translation of two copies of the Treaty into Arabic . . ." Tobias Lear (Tripoli) to Fanny Lear, June 6, 1805. Tobias Lear Papers. William Clements Library, University of Michigan, Ann Arbor. Microfilm.

299. "Within twenty four hours after I landed . . ." Tobias Lear (Tripoli) to William Higgins, naval agent at Malta, June 6, 1805, BW VI, p. 95.

300. "What misery has this Bashaw caused by his behavior!" AZ, June 8, 1805.

301. "No pretence of any periodical tribute or further payment of any denomination . . ." James Cathcart (Leghorn) to secretary of state, May 5, 1803. Consular Letters, Tripoli. National Archives. Microfilm M466, Roll 2.

302. "No Consular present is mentioned in the Treaty . . ." Tobias Lear (aboard USS *Constitution* in Syracuse harbor) to secretary of state, July 5, 1805, BW VI, pp. 159–162.

303. "In case of future war . . . , captives on each side . . ." Convention between United States and Hamet Caramanly, February 23, 1805. "Treaties and other International Acts of the United States of America," ed. by Hunter Miller, p. 553.

303. "The Prisoners captured by either party shall not be made *slaves*" Treaty of Peace and Amity. Ibid., pp. 543, 546.

303. "On my arrival here [Farfara] like a pusillanimous scoundrel . . ." James L. Cathcart (Tripoli) to William Eaton, August 12, 1799. *Tripoli: First War with the United States, Inner History* by James Cathcart (LaPorte, Ind., 1901), p. 63.

304. "Whereas his Excellency the Bashaw of Tripoli has well grounded . . ." Secret article, BW VI, p. 82.

305. "Although this matter might seem of very little importance . . ." Nicholas Nissen (Tripoli) Official Report. June 10, 1805, BW VI, pp. 103–105.

306. "They carried a present . . ." AZ June 24, 1805.

306. "Mr. Lear never opposed a single demand; never evaded a . . ." "Correspondence and documents relative to the attempt to negotiate for the release of the American captives at Algiers" (Washington, 1816) by Mordecai Noah, p. 96.

306. "I was therefore obliged to make it appear . . ." Tobias Lear (aboard the USS *Constitution* in Syracuse harbor) to secretary of state, July 5, 1805, BW VI, pp. 159–162.

307. "to be divided among marine captains, first and second . . ." ASP, Class X, vol. 2, p. 26.

307. "dark features of the subject . . ." John Rodgers (aboard USS *Constitution* off Tripoli) to chargé d'affaires, Beaussier, June 20, 1805, BW VI, p. 128.

308. "I have finished all our affairs . . . much to my satisfaction . . ." Tobias Lear (aboard USS *Constitution* in Malta harbor) to Fanny Lear, June 24, 1805. Tobias Lear Papers. William Clements Library, University of Michigan, Ann Arbor. Microfilm.

CHAPTER 23. WOUNDED AND RESTLESS

309. "detestable" Ralph Izard Jr. (Syracuse) to Mrs. Ralph Izard Sr., February 2, 1804, BW III, p. 382.

310. "Had you any boats . . ." Court Enquiring into the Loss of the U.S. Frigate *Philadelphia*, BW III, pp. 189–194.

311. "I cannot forbear expressing . . ." Hamet Karamanli (Syracuse) to William Eaton, June 29, 1805, BW VI, p. 144.

311. "hold [himself] responsible" Eaton (Syracuse) to John Rodgers, July 3, 1805, BW VI, p. 153.

312. "a pay roll, with a statement . . ." John Rodgers (aboard USS *Constitution* in Syracuse harbor) to William Eaton, July 3, 1805, BW VI, pp. 154–155.

312. "that Singular expedition" John Rodgers (aboard USS *Constitution* in Syracuse harbor) to secretary of the navy, July 6, 1805, BW VI, p. 165.

313. "If it was double the Sum . . ." John Rodgers (USS *Constitution* in Syracuse harbor) to secretary of the navy, July 6, 1805, BW VI, p. 167.

313. "agreeable to the treaty . . . I urged the measure . . ." William Eaton (Washington) to Senator Stephen Bradley, February 16, 1806, BW VI, p. 371.

314. "Recently, the Bashaw tired himself to the point of exhaustion . . ." AZ, June 24, 1805.

314. "for which aspersion he would call on him . . ." William Bainbridge (aboard USS *President* off Malta) to Lieutenant David Porter, July 10, 1805, BW VI, p. 174.

315. "Tell him if I do not hear from him . . ." Ibid.

315. "call for mercy on bended knees" Rodgers to secretary of the navy. Report of July 7 to September 1, 1805, BW VI, p. 261.

315. "appropriations to foreign intercourse" James Madison as quoted in *Dawn Like Thunder* by Glenn Tucker (Indianapolis/NY, 1963), p. 430.

CHAPTER 24. HOMECOMING

317. "I am yet at sea but a pilot boat . . ." William Eaton (off coast) to Sarah E. Danielson, November 1805, WE-HL, Reel 3.

319. "With heartfelt joy, I announce . . ." *Salem Register*, August 29, 1805, reprinted in *National Intelligencer*, September 4, 1805.

319. "by the intrepid spirit of our countryman . . ." *Boston Gazette*, August 29, 1805.

319. "This event [the peace treaty] is said to have been accelerated by the success . . ." *New Hampshire Gazette,* September 3, 1805.

319. "The Public are anxious to learn . . ." *Poulson's Daily Advertiser* (Philadelphia), September 6, 1805.

320. "Our servants, Tom, Bob, Jim, Albert . . ." *Washington Federalist,* September 11, 1805.

321. "Cambyses and Alexander traversed . . ." *National Intelligencer* (Washington), September 25, 1805.

321. "Madam, I love you much but I love glory more" *Richmond Enquirer,* October 4, 1805.

321. "a distinguished officer and patriot" *National Intelligencer,* November 20, 1805.

321. "General Eaton—May each American when required . . ." *Richmond Enquirer,* November 19, 1805.

321. "a bare-faced prodigality of praise" Charles Prentiss, LIFE, p. 441.

321. "GENERAL WILLIAM EATON. This brave and meritorious . . ." *Richmond Enquirer,* November 15, 1805.

323. "The United States—Tho' peace is its policy . . ." *National Intelligencer,* December 5, 1805.

323. "I believe it will be no difficult task . . ." William Eaton (Washington City) to James Madison, November 27, 1805, ASP, Class IX: Claims, p. 325.

324. "The people of the United States . . ." *Richmond Enquirer,* December 10, 1805.

324. "The FEDERAL UNION . . ." Ibid.

324. "The President was in an undress . . ." PM, p. 333.

325. "energetic & warlike" PM, p. 339.

325. "I congratulate you . . ." "Draft of the Fifth Annual Message" in *Works of Thomas Jefferson* ed. Paul L. Ford, vol. X, pp. 192–193.

326. "His company was gratifying . . ." PM, p. 339.

327. "It is impossible for me to undertake . . ." William Eaton to secretary of the navy, December 5, 1805, BW VI, p. 315.

328. "mean pusillanimous selfish conduct of Lear" PM, p. 350.

328. "a man of little mind—jealous—cowardly . . ." Ibid.

329. "I am arrested here and put under . . ." William Eaton (Philadelphia) to Edward Preble, December 30, 1805, BW VI, p. 328.

329. "The cooperation of the exile was to cost no more than 20,000 dollars . . ." Thomas Jefferson's note, December 30, 1805. Thomas Jefferson Papers, Library of Congress.

CHAPTER 25. JEFFERSON VS. EATON

331. "The result of my investigation . . ." PM, pp. 453–455.

332. "concerted operations by those who have a common enemy" and following quotes from same speech. ASP Class I, vol. 2, p. 695.

333. "The [documents] clearly show the imprudence & folly of Lear . . ." PM, p. 372.

334. "justice which you have so richly merited . . ." BW VI, p. 349.

334. "In the bonds of wedlock, you have . . ." William Eaton (Leghorn) to Eliza Eaton, February 13, 1802, WE-HL, Microfilm, Reel 2.

335. "with a view of helping Aunt Lear . . ." William Eaton (Springfield) to Edward Preble, February 3, 1806, BW VI, p. 360.

335. "If government do you the justice . . ." Edward Preble (Portland) to Eaton, February 8, 1806, BW VI, p. 364.

335. "undaunted courage and brilliant services so . . ." *Richmond Enquirer,* March 18, 1806.

335. "I moreover believe that general Eaton could have marched . . ." Lieutenant William Wormley testimony for Bradley Committee, February 19, 1806, BW VI, p. 374.

336. "We have a bold and enterprising sergeant-at-arms . . ." John Randolph in House of Representatives, January 7, 1806, as quoted in PM, p. 368.

336. "Nothing will satisfy that man but the throne of God" Rufus King, as quoted in PM, p. 539.

337. "Perhaps no man's language was ever so apparently . . ." PM, p. 518.

337. "I listened to the exposition . . ." LIFE, p. 399.

337. "integrity and the attachment to the Union" Thomas Jefferson, as quoted by William Eaton, during his Burr deposition, January 26, 1807, LIFE, p. 401.

337. "I never have done a single act or been concerned . . ." Thomas Jefferson, April 15, 1806, in "Anas," *The Works of Thomas Jefferson,* vol. 1, p. 392.

338. "dictated every measure, paralyzed every military operation by land . . ." Bradley Report. Annals of Congress, 9th Congress, 1st Session, pp. 185–188, BW VI, p. 391.

339. "The sense of honor, justice and indignation against baseness . . ." William Eaton (Washington City) to Edward Preble, March 21, 1806, BW VI, p. 398.

339. "report was circulating with much industry . . ." PM, pp. 465–471.

341. "uncandid" Ibid., p. 473.

342. "to the first Monday in December next" Senate Journal, April 9, 1806.

342. "There is too many—We have too much noise" PM, p. 458.

342. "William Eaton Esq (alias the Arab Genl)" Ibid., p. 479.

343. "to submit to the drudgery" Ibid., pp. 448–449.

343. "After 4 O'Clock . . ." Ibid., pp. 482–483.

344. "temporary relief" Senate Journal, April 21, 1806.

344. "The money paid for the redemption of an Italian girl . . ." PM, pp. 494–495.

345. "Congress has just closed a long and uneasy session . . ." Thomas Jefferson (Washington City) to John Tyler, April 26, 1806, Thomas Jefferson Papers at Library of Congress.

CHAPTER 26. BURR, BOTTLE, AND SIX FEET UNDER

347. "I am Eaton no more" Eaton (Brimfield) to Humbert, January 15, 1810, quoted in LIFE, p. 425.

347. "You will not take it unkind . . ." Darius Munger (South Brimfield) to Eaton, May 28, 1806, WE-HL, Reel 2.

347. "Tea parties, turkey suppers, apple bees, husking bees, . . ." Quoted in "Historical Celebration of the Town of Brimfield" by Reverend Charles Hyde (Springfield, 1879).

348. "The Great I" as in "A Reply to the Address Written by the Great I" Ibid.

348. "I have already refused . . ." Eaton (Brimfield) to Joseph Williams, October 16, 1806, WE-HL, Reel 2.

349. "the first formal intelligence received by the Executive . . ." Eaton deposition, Washington City, January 26, 1807. Quoted in LIFE, p. 402.

349. "to have him strictly watched and on committing any overt act . . ." Thomas Jefferson, "Anas" in *The Works of Thomas Jefferson*, vol. 1, p. 401.

349. "Wm Eaton . . . was . . ." PM, p. 550.

349. "the deranged state . . ." William Eaton (Brimfield) to General Stephen Bradley, November 17, 1806. Eaton Papers at Rauner Special Collections. Courtesy of Dartmouth College Library in Hanover, NH.

350. "hurricane," "the strongest wind . . ." PM, p. 603.

350. "You cannot bring back to me nine years of active life . . ." William Eaton (Washington) to Committee of Claims, February 9, 1807, quoted in LIFE, p. 406.

352. "Acco.t of the Chev. Porcilla for the redemption . . ." Treasury Roll no. 19140. "Statement of the Acc.t of William Eaton" National Archives. Microfilm M235. Roll 58.

353. "The once redoubted Eaton has dwindled down . . ." Harman Blennerhassett from his "Papers" (p. 315) as quoted in *History of the United States of America during the Administrations of Thomas Jefferson* by Henry Adams (N.Y., 1986 reprint), p. 921.

354–357. "Concerning any fact which may go to prove . . ." Trial testimony taken from ASP, Class X Misc., vol. 1, pp. 493–496.

359. "In the depth of my miseries . . ." Hamet Karamanli (Syracuse) to "Their Most Serene Highnesses," February 18, 1807, ASP, House of Representatives, 10th Congress, 1st Session, Foreign Relations: Vol. 3, pp. 26–29.

359. "The danger of the American prisoners in Tripoli?" Eaton (Washington), November 9, 1807, WE-HL, Reel 2.

360. "Have we then an Emperor . . ." Eaton (Washington) November 18, 1807. Notebook. Ibid.

361. "How it has happened that . . ." Thomas Jefferson. Confidential Message. ASP. Senate, Foreign Relations: vol. 2, no. 192, pp. 695–724, Tripoli.

362. "his influence and resources . . . were so small . . ." Tripoli—Hamet Caramalli,

December 18, 1807, ASP, House of Representatives, 10th Congress, 1st Session, Foreign Relations: vol. 3, pp. 26–29.

363. "govern his glass" and "at such times, his wit was out" LIFE, p. 409.

363. "His Excellency Thomas Jefferson . . ." William Eaton (Boston) to Thomas Jefferson, January 26, 1808. Thomas Jefferson Papers. Library of Congress.

364. "Having lost the hope of the restitution of my family . . ." Hamet (Syracuse) to General Eaton, September 30, 1807, contained in William Eaton (Boston) to Thomas Jefferson, February 12, 1808. Thomas Jefferson Papers. Library of Congress.

364. "On meeting with Hamet Bashaw . . ." Ibid.

365. "the cursed slow poison" LIFE, p. 436.

366. "His domestic and financial concerns preyed upon his mind . . ." LIFE, pp. 409–410.

366. "Brave, great and experienced men may sometimes find it necessary to . . ." William Eaton to Lieutenant Fitz Babbit, August 14, 1808, LIFE, p. 410.

367. "Every sigh of Hamet Bashaw sinks deeply . . ." Eaton to General Bradley, undated, placed in late 1808. WE-HL, Reel 2.

368. "irregular and capricious, sometimes treating them with affability . . ." LIFE, pp. 445–446.

368. "I dwelt on the certainty of speedy ruin . . ." Ibid., p. 443.

369. "Fortune has reversed her tables . . ." Eaton (Brimfield) to Humbert, January 15, 1810, LIFE, p. 425.

369. "I am crippled in health & fortune . . ." Eaton (Brimfield) to Ebeneezer Eaton, January 2, 1809, WE-HL, Reel 2.

369. "Our country is gone to the devil . . ." J. Dunham to Eaton, March 15, 1811, WE-HL, Reel 2.

369. "For in that position, I am prone . . ." LIFE, p. 426.

369. "Your long absence from communication with the . . ." Ibid., p. 440.

370. "Gen. EATON, the hero of Derne, and the victim of sensibility . . ." *Boston Centinel,* June 12, 1811.

370. "brave, impulsive and generous" . . . "hot chivalry" . . . "widely known name" Quoted in "Historical Celebration of the Town of Brimfield" by Reverend Charles Hyde (Springfield, 1879).

EPILOGUE

371. "I am at last in our dear little cabin . . ." Tobias Lear (aboard USS *Constitution*) to Fanny Lear, March 6, 1807. Lear Papers. William R. Clements Library. University of Michigan, Ann Arbor. Microfilm.

371. "a gold watch with diamonds, a diamond solitaire, etc." "Expenses of Intercourse with the Barbary Powers," ASP, "Miscellaneous," vol. 2, p. 32.

372. "Our treaty is known to all the world and our public faith pledged . . ."

Dr. George Davis (Tripoli) to secretary of state, June 2, 1807. Consular Letters, Tripoli, Microfilm no. 466, Roll 2. All quotes from this section on Hamet from Davis's series of letters, 1807–1809.

374. "My hat prevented the blow . . ." Richard B. Jones (Tripoli) Journal Entries submitted to secretary of state. Consular Letters, Tripoli. National Archives. Microfilm no. 466, Roll 2.

375. "In recognition of the service of his father" From *Dictionary of American Biography*, as quoted in ZB File of "Samuel Barron" in U.S. Navy Library, from letter, April 5, 1936.

380. "Biologically, as well as psychologically, he was thin-skinned" *American Sphinx: The Character of Thomas Jefferson* by Joseph Ellis (N.Y., 1996), p. 274.

380. "I suppose we can do little with the Dey . . ." Thomas Jefferson (Monticello) to Tobias Lear, June 19, 1813. Thomas Jefferson Papers. Library of Congress.

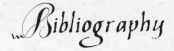

Bibliography

MANUSCRIPT SOURCES

Dartmouth College Library. Rauner Special Collections Library. Hanover, N.H. Some Eaton letters, some choice articles from his college days.

Huntington Library. San Marino, California. William Eaton papers. Paradise: several thousand manuscript pages available on three reels of microfilm.

Library of Congress. Manuscript Division. Papers of William Eaton, Tobias Lear, Edward Preble, John Rodgers, Samuel Barron, and others.

Library of Congress online: Thomas Jefferson Papers.

Nationaal Archief. The Hague, Netherlands. Archief van het departement van Buitenlandse Zaken, 1796-1810. Access number 2.01.08. Inv. nr. 356. Weekly reports from inside Tripoli, written in French by Dutch diplomat. Very frank. Never quoted before in English.

National Archives. College Park, Maryland. Consular Letters for Tripoli (M466: roll 1–3), Tunis, Algiers (M23, rolls 7–10); Treasury Reports (M235, roll 58)

Public Record Office, Kew, England. Consular reports from Tripoli. FO161:10

University of Michigan. William R. Clements Library. Ann Arbor, Michigan. Tobias Lear Papers.

PRINTED SOURCES

Adams, Henry. *History of the United States during the Administrations of Thomas Jefferson* (1921, reprint 1986).

———. *History of the United States during the Administrations of James Madison* (1921, reprint, 1986).

Ali Bey. *Travels of Ali Bey in Morocco, Tripoli, Cyprus, Egypt, Arabia, Syria and Turkey, between the years 1803 and 1807* (Philadelphia, 1816).

Allen, Gardner. *Our Navy and the Barbary Corsairs* (Hamden, Conn., 1965).

Allison, Robert J. *The Crescent Obscured: The United States & the Muslim World, 1776–1815* (N.Y./Oxford, 1995).

"American State Papers" *Documents, legislative and executive, of the Congress of the United States . . . selected and edited under the authority of Congress,* 38 vols. (Washington, D.C., 1832–1861).

Baepler, Paul. *White Slaves, African Masters: An Anthology of American Barbary Captivity Narratives* (Chicago, 1999).

Barnby, H. G. *The Prisoners of Algiers: An Account of the Forgotten American-Algerian War, 1785–1797* (London, 1966).

Blydon, Stephen. *History of the War between the United States and Tripoli* (Salem, Mass., 1806).

Bonnel, Ulane. *La France, les États-Unis et la guerre de course, 1797–1815* (Paris, 1961). The French perspective on Bainbridge's surrender.

Bono, Salvatore. *I Corsari barbareschi* (Torino, 1964).

Braun, Ethel. *The New Tripoli, and What I Saw in the Hinterland* (London, 1914).

Brighton, Ray. *The Checkered Career of Tobias Lear* (Portsmouth, N.H., 1985).

Browne, William G. *Travels in Africa, Egypt and Syria from the year 1792 to 1798* (London, 1799).

Caronni, Felice. *Ragguaglio del viaggio in Barberia* (Milan, 1806/reprint 1993).

Cathcart, James. *Tripoli: First War with the United States. Inner History* (LaPorte, Ind., 1901). A collection of letters.

Champlagarde, Anne-Charles Froment de. *Histoire Abregée de Tripoly de Barbarie, 1794* (reprint: Paris, 2001). American consul James Cathcart lifted huge sections to pad his own report on Tripoli.

Chateaubriand, Francois-Réné. *Travels in Greece, Palestine, Egypt and Barbary during the Years 1806 and 1807* (New York, 1814).

Chidsey, Donald. *Wars in Barbary: Arab Piracy and the Birth of the United States Navy* (N.Y., 1971).

Chinard, Gilbert. *Volney et l'Amérique d'après des documents inedits et sa correspondence avec Jefferson* (Baltimore/Paris, 1923).

Clissold, Stephen. *The Barbary Slaves* (London, 1977).

Coleridge, Samuel T. *The Notebooks of Samuel Taylor Coleridge,* ed. by Kathleen Coburn (London, 1957–1961).

Cooper, James Fenimore. *History of the Navy of the United States of America* (N.Y., 1856).

Cowdery, Jonathan. *American Captives in Tripoli* (Boston, 1806). Officer memoir.

Dearden, Seton. *A Nest of Corsairs: The Fighting Karamanlis of the Barbary Coast* (London, 1976).

Doughty, Oswald. *Perturbed Spirit: The Life and Personality of Samuel Taylor Coleridge* (Rutherford, N.J., 1981).

Dupuy, E. *Américains et Barbaresques, 1776–1824* (Paris, 1910).

Earle, Peter. *Corsairs of Barbary and Malta* (London, 1970).

Eaton, William. *Life of the Late General Eaton,* ed. by Charles Prentiss. (Brookfield,

Mass., 1813). A fine collection of documents, assembled by a family friend.

————. *Interesting Detail on the Operations of the American Fleet in the Mediterranean* (Springfield, Mass., [1804]).

Edwards, Samuel (Noel Gerson). *Barbary General: The Life of William H. Eaton* (Englewood Cliffs, N.J., 1968). A font of colorful misinformation that unfortunately has been used in many subsequent books.

Ellis, Joseph. *American Sphinx: The Character of Thomas Jefferson* (N.Y., 1996).

Feraud, L. Charles. *Annales Tripolitaines* (Tunis, 1927).

Fisher, Godfrey. *Barbary Legend: War, Trade and Piracy in North Africa, 1415–1830* (Oxford, 1957).

Folayan, Kola. *Tripoli during the Reign of Yusuf Pasha Qaramanli* (Ile-Ife, Nigeria, 1979). That rare book pro-Tripoli in English.

Forester, C. S. *The Barbary Pirates* (N.Y., 1953). Landmark Book no. 31. A pleasure.

Fowler, William. *Jack Tars & Commodores, The American Navy, 1783–1815* (Boston, 1984).

Furnas, J. C. *A Social History of the United States, 1587–1914* (N.Y., 1969).

Green, Constance. *Washington: Village and Capitol, 1800–1876* (Princeton, N.J., 1962).

Harris, Thomas. *Life and Services of Commodore Bainbridge* (Philadelphia, 1837). A friend's biography.

Hinman, Royal. *A Historical Collection from Official Records, Files &c, of the Part Sustained by Connecticut during the War of Revolution* (Hartford, 1842).

Horneman, Frederick. *The Journal of Frederick Horneman's Travels from Cairo to Marzouk . . . 1797–1798* (London, 1802).

Hyde, Reverend Charles. *Historical Celebration of the Town of Brimfield* (Springfield, Mass., 1879).

Irwin, Ray. *Diplomatic Relations of the United States with the Barbary Powers, 1776–1816* (Chapel Hill, 1931).

Jefferson, Thomas. *Jefferson Himself*, ed. by Bernard Mayo (Cambridge, 1942).

————. *The Works of Thomas Jefferson*, ed. by Paul L. Ford (N.Y., 1904).

Kitzen, Michael. *Tripoli and the United States at War: A History of American Relations with the Barbary States, 1785–1805* (Jefferson, N.C., 1993).

Knox, Dudley, ed. *Naval documents related to the United States wars with the Barbary Powers* . . . Prepared by the Office of Naval Records and Library, Navy Department. 6 vols. (Washington, U.S. Govt. Print., 1939–44). Spectacular resource of primary source documents.

————. *A History of the United States Navy* (N.Y., 1936).

Leiner, Frederick. *Millions for Defense: The Subscription Warships of 1798* (Annapolis, 2000).

Long, David F. *Ready to Hazard: A Biography of Commodore Bainbridge, 1774–1833* (Hanover, N.H., 1981). Superb research and writing by underpraised author.

————. *Nothing Too Daring: A Biography of Commodore David Porter, 1780–1843* (Annapolis, 1970).

Loomis, Hezekiah. *Journal of Hezekiah Loomis* (Salem, Mass., 1928).

Manno, Giuseppe. *Storia di Sardegna* (Capolago, 1847).

Martini, Pietro. *Storia delle Invasioni degli Arabi, delle piraterie, dei barbareschi in Sardinia* (Cagliari, 1861).

Miller, David Hunter. *Treaties and Other International Acts of the United States of America* (Washington, D.C., U.S. Government Printing Office, 1931).

Millett, Allan. *Semper Fidelis: The History of the United States Marine Corps* (N.Y., 1991).

Morris, Richard. *A Defense of the Conduct of Morris during His Command in the Mediterranean* (N.Y., 1804).

Nash, Howard. *Forgotten Wars: The Role of the U.S. Navy in the Quasi War with France and the Barbary Wars 1798–1805* (South Brunswick, N.J., 1968).

Noah, Mordecai. *Correspondence and Documents Relative to the Attempt to Negotiate for the Release of the American Captives at Algiers* (Washington, 1816).

————. *Travels in England, France, Spain and the Barbary States in the years, 1813, 1814 and 1815* (N.Y., 1819).

O'Toole, George. *Honourable Treachery: A History of U.S. Intelligence, Espionage and Covert Action from the American Revolution to the CIA* (N.Y., 1991).

Pananti, Fillippo. *Avventure e Osservazioni di Fillippo Pananti sopra le coste di Barberia* (Firenze, 1817).

Pennell, R. "Tripoli, A Guidebook to the City, 1767," printed in *Revue d'histoire maghrebine*, vol. 25–26, June 1982, pp. 91–123.

Perkins, Roger, and Captain K. J. Douglas-Morris. *Gunfire in Barbary* (Homewell, 1982).

Plumer, William. *William Plumer's Memorandum of Proceedings in the United States Senate, 1803–1807* (N.Y., 1923).

Ray, William. *Horrors of Slavery, or The American Tars in Tripoli* (Troy, N.Y., 1808, *Magazine of History* reprint, 1911). Schoolteacher-turned-sailor memoir of captivity.

Rea, John. "A Letter to William Bainbridge Esq. . . ." (Philadelphia, 1802).

Rodd, Francis Rennell. *General William Eaton: The Failure of an Idea* (N.Y., 1932).

Smyth, W. H. *Sailor's Word-Book: An Alphabetical Digest of Nautical Terms* (London, 1867).

Sonnini de Manoncourt, Charles. *Travels in Upper and Lower Egypt* (London, 1799).

Sumner, Charles. *White Slavery in the Barbary States* (Boston, 1853).

Todd, Mabel Loomis. *Tripoli: The Mysterious* (London, 1912).

Tucker, Glenn. *Dawn Like Thunder: The Barbary Wars and the Birth of the U.S. Navy* (Indianapolis/NY, 1963). A fine account of the U.S. Navy vs. Tripoli.

————. *Mad Anthony Wayne and the New Nation* (Harrisburg, Penn., 1973).

Tully, (Miss). *Narrative of a Ten Years' Residence at Tripoli in Africa* (London, 1817). Fascinating memoir by the sister of British consul Richard Tully.

Tyler, Royall. *The Algerine Captive* (New Haven, 1797).

Volney, Constantin-Francois. *Travels through Syria and Egypt in the years 1783, 1784 and 1785* (London, 1787).

Wafi, Muhammed abd al-Karim. *Yusuf Basha al-Qaramanli wa-al-hamlah al-Faransiyah alá Misr* (Tripoli, 1984).

Waldo, S. Putnam. *Life and Character of Stephen Decatur* (Hartford, Conn., 1821).

Ward, Philip. *Tripoli: Portrait of a City* (Stoughton, Wis., 1969).

Wheelan, Joseph. *Jefferson's War: America's First War on Terror, 1801–1805* (N.Y., 2003).

Whipple, A. B. C. *To the Shores of Tripoli: The Birth of the U.S. Navy and Marines* (N.Y., 1991).

White, Arthur Silva. *From Sphinx to Oracle: Through the Libyan Desert to the Oasis of Jupiter Ammon* (London, 1899).

Wright, Louis, and Julia Macleod. *First Americans in North Africa: William Eaton's Struggle for a Vigorous Policy against the Barbary Pirates, 1789–1805* (Princeton, 1945).

Credits

Pages xii-xiii. "Map of the Regencies of Tripoly and Tunis," reproduced from *Narrative of a Ten Years' Residence at Tripoli in Africa* by Miss Tully (London, 1817).

Page 20. *Historie van Barbaryen* by Pierre Dan (Amsterdam, 1684).

Page 32. Courtesy of the Library of Congress.

Page 39. *Historie van Barbaryen* by Pierre Dan (Amsterdam, 1684).

Page 54. Tobias Lear Papers at William R. Clements Library at the University of Michigan, Ann Arbor.

Page 190. *Pictorial Field-Book of the War of 1812* by Benson J. Lossing (New York, 1869).

Page 255. *Tripoli the Mysterious* by Mabel Todd (Boston, 1912).

RICHARD ZACKS SPECIALIZES IN OFFBEAT HISTORY. He is the author of *The Pirate Hunter: The True Story of Captain Kidd,* chosen by *Time* as one of the five best nonfiction books of the year; the bestselling *History Laid Bare;* and the perennial book club favorite *An Underground Education.*

Visit www.piratecoast.com

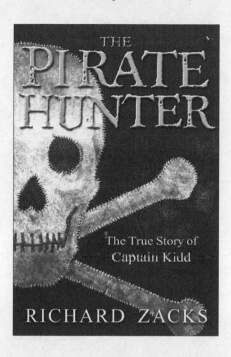